The Arts
in the
MIDDLE AGES
and the
Renaissance

The Arts
in the
MIDDLE AGES
and the
Renaissance

Paul Lacroix

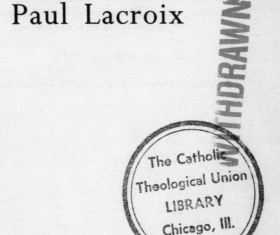

BRACKEN BOOKS
LONDON

The Arts in the Middle Ages and the Renaissance

First published in 1870 as
The Arts in the Middle Ages and at the Period of the Renaissance
by Chapman & Hall, London

This paperback edition first published in 1996 by Bracken Books,
an imprint of Random House UK Ltd, Random House,
20 Vauxhall Bridge Road, London SW1V 2SA

ISBN 1 85170 531 7

Printed and bound in Guernsey by The Guernsey Press Co. Ltd

PREFACE OF THE EDITOR.

THE aim and scope of this work are so explicitly set forth in the appended Preface by its Author as to require for the book no further introduction. The position held by M. LACROIX in the Imperial Library of the Arsenal, Paris, is a sufficient guarantee of his qualifications for undertaking a publication of this nature. How far his labours were appreciated in France is evident from the fact that, when the first edition made its appearance, it was exhausted within a few days.

It may fairly be presumed that THE ARTS IN THE MIDDLE AGES will find equal favour in England, where so much attention has of late years been given to the subject in all its various ramifications; and where,— in our National Museum, Kensington, especially,—we are accumulating so extensive and valuable a collection of objects associated with the epochs referred to by M. LACROIX.

In preparing these sheets for the press, my task has been little more than to put an excellent and conscientious *literal* translation of the French text into language somewhat in harmony with the construction of our own. In so doing, however, it has been my object to retain, as far as practicable, the peculiar—sometimes the quaint—phraseology of the original writing. A few notes are added when they appeared necessary by way of explaining terms, &c., or to render them more intelligible to the general reader. But some words are used by the Author for which no English equivalent can be found : these have been allowed to stand without note or comment.

JAMES DAFFORNE.

Brixton, *February*, 1870.

PREFACE TO THE SECOND FRENCH EDITION.

ORE than twenty years ago we published, with the aid of our friend Ferdinand Séré, whose loss we regret, and with the co-operation of other learned men and of the most eminent writers and artists, an important work, entitled "The Middle Ages and the Renaissance." That work, which consists of no less than five large quarto volumes, treated in detail the manners and customs, the sciences, literature, and the arts of those two great epochs, a subject as vast as it is interesting and instructive. Thanks to the learning it displays, to its literary merit and its admirable execution, it had the rare good fortune to attract immediately the attention of the public, and even now it maintains the interest which marked its first appearance. It has taken its place in the library of the amateur, not only in France but also among foreigners; it has become celebrated.

This exceptional result, especially as regards a publication of such extent, induces us to believe that our work, thus known and appreciated by the learned, may and ought henceforth to have still greater success by addressing itself to a yet larger number of readers.

With this conviction we now present to the public one of the principal portions of that important work, and perhaps the most interesting, in a

form more simple, easier, and more pleasing; within the reach of youth
who desire to learn without weariness or irksomeness, of females interested
in grave authors, of the family that loves to assemble round a book
altogether instructive and attractive. We would speak of the "ARTS IN
THE MIDDLE AGES, AND AT THE PERIOD OF THE RENAISSANCE." After
having reunited the scattered materials on this subject, we have ranged
them each in its own rank, taking care to discard all crudity of learning,
and to preserve in our work the brilliant colouring in which it was first
clothed.

All the Arts are interesting in themselves. Their productions awaken
attention and excite curiosity. But here it is not one Art only that is
treated of. We pass in review all the Arts, starting from the fourth
century to the second half of the sixteenth—Architecture raising churches
and abbeys, palaces and public memorials, strong fortresses and the
ramparts of cities; Sculpture adorning and perfecting other Arts by its
works in stone, marble, bronze, wood, and ivory; Painting, commencing
with mosaic and enamels, contributing to the decoration of buildings
jointly with stained glass and frescoes, embellishing and illuminating
manuscripts before it arrived at its highest point of perfection, with the
Art of Giotto and Raphael, of Hemling and Albert Dürer; Engraving
on wood and metal, with which is associated the work of the medallist
and the goldsmith; and after attempting to touch upon Playing-cards and
Niello-work, we suddenly evoke that sublime invention destined to change
the face of the world—Printing. Such are, in brief, some of the principal
features of this splendid picture. One can imagine what an infinity, what
variety and richness, of details it should contain.

Our subject presents, at the same time, another kind of interest more
elevated and not less alluring. Here each Art appears in its different
phases and in its diversified progress. It is a history, not alone of the
Arts, but of the epoch itself in which they were developed; for the Arts,
regarded in their generality, are the truest expression of society. They
speak to us of tastes, of ideas, of character: they exhibit us in their works.
Of all an age can leave to the future concerning itself, that which repre-

sents it most vividly is Art: the Arts of an epoch revivify it, and bring it back before our eyes.

It is this which forms our book. Yet, we must remark, here its interest is redoubled, for we retrace not only a single era, but two eras very distinct from each other. In the first, that of the Middle Ages, which followed the invasion of the Northmen, society was in a great measure formed of new and barbarous elements, which Christianity laboured to break up and fashion. In the second epoch, on the contrary, society was organised and firmly established; it enjoyed peace, and reaped its fruits. The Arts followed the same phases. At first rude and informal, they rose slowly and by degrees, like society, out of chaos. At length they flourished in perfect freedom, and progressed with all the energy of which the human mind is capable. Hence the successive advances whose history presents a marvellous interest.

During the Middle Ages, Art generally followed the inspirations of that Christian spirit which presided at the formation of this new world. It arose to reproduce in an admirable manner the religious ideal. Only towards the end of that period it searched out for beauty of form, and began to find it when the Renaissance made its appearance: the Renaissance, that is, the intellectual revolution which, in the fifteenth and sixteenth centuries, restored among modern nations the sceptre to Literature and the Arts of antiquity. Then, with the Renaissance, the Arts changed their direction, and especially the principal Arts, those by which the genius of man expresses most forcibly his ideas and his feelings. Thus, in the Middle Ages, a new style of architecture is created that rapidly attained the highest degree of perfection, the *ogival* (later Gothic or flamboyant), of which we see the *chefs-d'œuvre* in our cathedrals: at the Renaissance, this was replaced by architecture derived from that of the Greeks and Romans, which also produced admirable works, but almost always less in harmony with the dignity and splendour of worship. In the Middle Ages, Painting chiefly applied itself to represent the *beau idéal* of the religious mind reflecting itself in the countenance; at the Renaissance, it is the beauty of the physical form, so perfectly expressed by the ancients. Sculpture, which comes nearer to Painting, followed at the same time all similar phases, drawing the art of Engraving with it. Do not the diversified changes through which the Arts passed, as retraced in this book during two epochs, present to the intelligent reader a succession of facts of the highest interest and a history most instructive?

Our work is the only existing one on this great and magnificent subject, of which the materials are scattered through a multitude of volumes. Thus for the success of this undertaking it became necessary to unite with us in our task men most distinguished by their learning and talents: we are permitted to cite the names of MM. Ernest Breton, Aimé Champollion, Champollion-Figeac, Pierre Dubois, Duchesne, Ferdinand Denis, Jacquemart, Arch. Juvinal, Jules Labarte, Lassus, Louandre, Prosper Mérimée, Alfred Michiels, Gabriel Peignot, Riocreux, De Saulcy, Jean Designeur, le Marquis de Varennes. After such a list we record our own name only to acknowledge that we have gone over and recast these various works, and presented them in a form which gives them more unity, but owes to them all the interest and all the charm it may offer.

The numerous illustrations that adorn the work will engage the eye, while the text will speak to the intelligence. The designs in chromolithography are executed by M. Kellerhoven, who for several years has made the art one of a high order, worthy to shine among the finest works of our greatest painters, as is proved by his "Chefs-d'œuvre of the Great Masters," "Lives of the Saints," and "Legend of St. Ursula."

No one is ignorant of the attention given in these days to archæology. Information about objects of antiquity is necessary to every instructed person. It ought to be studied so far as to enable us to appreciate, or at least to recognise, the examples of olden time in Architecture, Painting, &c., that present themselves to our notice. Thus it has become for the young of each sex indispensable to good education. The perusal of this book will be for such an attractive introduction to that knowledge which for too long a time was the exclusive domain of the learned.

PAUL LACROIX
(Bibliophile Jacob).

TABLE OF CONTENTS.

THE ARTS IN THE MIDDLE AGES,

AND AT THE PERIOD OF

THE RENAISSANCE.

———•———

FURNITURE:

ORDINARY HOUSEHOLD, AND APPERTAINING TO ECCLESIASTICAL PURPOSES.

Simplicity of Furniture among the Gauls and Franks.—Introduction of costly taste in articles of Furniture of the Seventh Century.—Arm-chair of Dagobert.—Round Table of King Artus.—Influence of the Crusades.—Regal Banquet in the time of Charles V.—Benches.—Sideboards.—Dinner Services.—Goblets.—Brassware.—Casks.—Lighting.—Beds.—Carved-wood Furniture.—Locksmith's Work.—Glass and Mirrors.—Room of a Feudal Seigneur.—Costliness of Furniture used for Ecclesiastical Purposes.—Altars.—Censers.—Shrines and Reliquaries.—Gratings and Iron-mountings.

E shall be readily believed when we assert that the furniture used by our remote ancestors, the Gauls, was of the most rude simplicity. A people essentially addicted to war and hunting,—at the best, agriculturists,—having for their temples the forests, for their dwellings huts formed out of turf and thatched with straw and branches, would naturally be indifferent to the form and description of their furniture.

Then succeeded the Roman Conquest. Originally, and long subsequent to the formation of their warlike republic, the Romans had also lived in contempt of display, and even in ignorance of the conveniences of life. But when they had subjugated Gaul, and had carried their victorious arms to the confines of the world, they by degrees appropriated whatever the manners and habits of the conquered nations disclosed to them of refined luxury, material progress, and ingenious devices for comfort. Thus, the Romans brought with them into Gaul what they elsewhere had acquired.

Again, when, in their turn, the semi-barbarous hordes of Germany and of the Northern steppes invaded the Roman empire, these new conquerors did not fail to accommodate themselves instinctively to the social condition of the vanquished.

This, briefly stated, is an explanation—we admit, rather concise—of the transition connecting the characteristics of the society of olden days with those of modern society.

Society in the Middle Ages—that social epoch which may be compared to the state of a decrepit and worn-out old man, who, after a long, dull torpor awakes to new life, like an active and vigorous child—society in the Middle Ages inherited much from preceding times, though, to a certain extent, they were disconnected. It transformed, perhaps; and it perfected, rather than invented; but it displayed in its works a genius so peculiar that we generally recognise in it a real creation.

Proposing rapidly to pursue our archæological and literary course through a twofold period of birth and revival, we cannot indulge the belief that we shall succeed in exhibiting our sketches in a light the best adapted to their effect. However, we will make the attempt, and, the frame being given, will do our best to fill in the picture.

If we visit any royal or princely abode of the Merovingian period, we observe that the display of wealth consists much less in the elegance or in the originality of the forms devised for articles of furniture, than in the profusion of precious materials employed in their fabrication and embellishment. The time had gone by when the earliest tribes of Gauls and of Northmen, who came to occupy the West, had for their seats and beds only trusses of straw, rush mats, and bundles of branches; and for their tables slabs of stone or piles of turf. From the fifth century of the Christian era, we already find the Franks and the Goths resting their muscular forms on the long soft seat which the Romans had adopted from the East, and which have become our sofas or our couches; changing only their names. In front of them were arranged low horse-shoe tables, at which the centre seat was reserved for the most dignified or illustrious of the guests. Couches at the table, suited only to the effeminacy induced by warm climates, were soon abandoned by the Gauls; benches and stools were adopted by these most active and vigorous men; meals were no longer eaten reclining, but sitting: while the thrones of kings, and the chairs of state for nobles, were of the richest sumptuousness. Thus, for instance, we find St. Eloi, the celebrated worker in metals, manufacturing and embellishing two state-chairs of gold for Clotaire, and a throne of gold for Dagobert. The chair ascribed to St. Eloi, and known as the Fauteuil de Dagobert (Fig. 1), is an antique consular chair, which originally was only a folding one; the Abbé Suger, in the twelfth century, added to it the back and arms. Artistic display was equally lavished on the

Fig. 1.—The Curule Chair called the "Fauteuil de Dagobert," in gilt bronze, now in the Musée des Souverains.

manufacture of tables. Historians tell us that St. Remy, a contemporary of Clovis, had a silver table decorated all over with sacred subjects. The poet Fortunat, Bishop of Poitiers, describes a table of the same metal, which had a border representing a vine with bunches of grapes.

Coming to the reign of Charlemagne, we find, in a passage in the writings of Eginhard, his minister and historian, that, in addition to a golden table which this great monarch possessed, he had three others of chased silver;

one decorated with designs representing the city of Rome, another Constantinople, and the third "all countries of the universe."

The chairs or seats of the Romanesque period (Fig. 2) exhibit an attempt to revive in the interior of the buildings, where they were used, the architectural style of contemporary monuments. They were large and massive, and were raised on clusters of columns expanding at the back in three semicircular rows. The anonymous monk of Saint-Gall, in his chronicle written in the ninth century, alludes to a grand banquet, at which the host was seated on cushions of feathers. Legrand d'Aussy tells us, in his "Histoire de la Vie Privée des Français," that at a later date—referring to the reign of Louis

Fig. 2.—Chair of the Ninth or Tenth Century, taken from a Miniature of that period (MS. de la Bibl. Imp. de Paris).

le Gros, in the beginning of the twelfth century—the guests were seated, at ordinary family repasts, on simple stools; but if the party was more of a ceremonious than intimate character, the table was surrounded with benches, or *bancs*, whence the term banquet is derived. The form of table was commonly long and straight, but on occasions of state it was semicircular, or like a horse-shoe in form, recalling the Romanesque round table of King Artus of Brittany (Fig. 3).

The Crusades, bringing together men of all the countries of Europe with the people of the East, made those of the West acquainted with luxuries and customs which, on returning from their chivalrous expeditions, they did not fail to imitate. We find feasts at which they ate sitting cross-legged

Fig. 3.—Round Table of King Artus of Brittany, from a Miniature of the Fourteenth Century (MS. de la Bibl. Imp. de Paris).

on the ground, or stretched out on carpets in the Oriental fashion, as represented and described in miniatures contained in the manuscripts of that period. The Sire de Joinville, the friend and historian of Louis IX., informs us that this saintly king was in the habit of sitting on a carpet, surrounded by his barons, and in that manner he dispensed justice; but at

the same time the practice of using large *chaires*, or arm-chairs, continued,
for there still is to be seen a throne in massive wood belonging to that period,
and called *le banc de Monseigneur St. Louis*, embellished with carvings representing fanciful and legendary birds and animals. It is unnecessary to add
that the lower orders did not aspire to so much refinement. In their abodes
the seats in use were settles, chests, or at best benches, the supports of which
were, to a slight extent, carved.

This was the period when the practice commenced of covering seats with
woollen stuffs, or with silk figured on frames, or embroidered by hand,
displaying ciphers, emblems, or armorial bearings. From the East was
introduced the custom of hangings for rooms, composed of glazed leather,
stamped and gilt. These skins of the goat or sheep were called *or basané*,
because plain gilt; or embossed leather, in gold colour, was made from
them. *Or basané* was also used to conceal the bare look of arm-chairs.
Towards the fourteenth century, tables of precious metals disappeared, in
consequence of fashion ruling in favour of the stuffs which covered them;
tapestry, tissues of gold, and velvets, thenceforth formed the table-cloths. On
great occasions, the place of the principal guests was distinguished by a
canopy, more or less rich, erected above their seats, as represented in the
account of the sumptuous feast given by King Charles V. to the Emperor
Charles of Luxemburg, in the great hall of the palace. M. Fréguier thus
describes the banquet from contemporary documents in the "Histoire de
l'Administration de la Police de Paris:"—

"The dinner was served on a marble table. The Archbishop of Rheims,
who had officiated that day, first took his place at table. The Emperor then
sat down, then the King of France, and the King of Bohemia, the son of the
Emperor. Above the seat of each of the three princes was a separate
canopy of gold cloth, embroidered all over with fleurs-de-lis. These three
canopies were surmounted by a larger one, also of cloth of gold, which
covered the whole extent of the table, and was suspended behind the guests.
After the King of Bohemia, three bishops took their seats, but far removed
from him, and near the end of the table. Under the nearest canopy the
Dauphin was seated, at a separate table, with several princes or nobles of
the Court of France, or of the Emperor. The hall was adorned with three
buffets, or dressers, covered with gold and silver plate; these three dressers,
as well as the two large canopies, were protected by a railing, to prevent the

intrusion of the crowds of people who had been permitted to witness the magnificence of the display. Finally, there were to be seen five other canopies, under which were assembled princes and barons round private tables; also numerous other tables."

It is noteworthy that from the time of St. Louis these same chairs and seats, carved, covered with the richest stuffs, inlaid with precious stones, and engraved with the armorial bearings of great houses, issued for the most part from the workshops of Parisian artisans. Those artisans, carpenters, manufacturers of coffers and carved chests, and furniture-makers, were so celebrated for works of this description, that in inventories and appraisements of furniture great care was taken to specify that such and such articles among them were of Parisian manufacture; *ex operagio Parisiensi* (Fig. 4).

Fig. 4.—Louis IX. represented in his Regal Chair, tapestried in fleurs-de-lis, from a Miniature of the Fourteenth Century. (MS. de la Bibl. Imp. de Paris.)

The following extract, from an invoice of Etienne La Fontaine, the royal silversmith, affords, in terms which require no comment, an idea of the costliness lavished on the manufacture of an arm-chair, then called *faudesteuil*, intended for the King of France, in 1352 :—

"For making a fauteuil of silver and of crystal decorated with precious stones, delivered to the said seigneur, of which the said seigneur ordered the said goldsmith to make the framework, who ornamented it with several crystals, illuminated pieces, many designs, pearls, and other stones . . . . vii° lxxiiii^{lt} (774 louis).

" For illuminated pieces placed under the crystals of the said fauteuil, of which there are 40 of the armorial bearings of France, 61 of the prophets holding scrolls, 112 half-length figures of animals on gold ground, and 4 large representations of the judgments of Solomon . . . . vi^{xx ^{lt}} (620 louis).

" For twelve crystals for the said fauteuil, of which five are hollow, to hold the bâtons, six flat, and one round," &c.

It was only towards the commencement of the fifteenth century that chairs stuffed with straw or rushes first appeared ; they folded in the form of the letter X (Fig. 5) ; the seats and arms being stuffed. In the sixteenth

Fig. 5.—Seats from Miniatures of the Fourteenth and Fifteenth Centuries.

century chairs with backs (*chaires* or *chayeres à dorseret*), in carved oak or chestnut, painted and gilt, fell into disuse, even in the royal castles, as being too heavy and inconvenient, and on account of their enormous size (Figs. 6 and 7).

The dresser, which has just been described as used at the grand feast of Charles V., and which moreover has been retained, altered to a sideboard with shelves, almost to our time, was an article manufactured much less for use than for show. It was upon this dresser,—the introduction of which does not appear to go further back than the twelfth century, and the name whereof sufficiently describes its purpose,—that there was displayed, in the vast halls of manorial residences, not only all the valuable plate required for the table, but many other objects of goldsmith's work which played no part in the banquet—vases of all sorts, statuettes, figures in high relief, jewels, and even reliquaries. In palaces and mansions, the dressers were of gold, silver, or copper gilt; as were previously the tables. Persons of inferior rank had only wooden tables, but they were scrupulous in covering them with tapestry, embroidered cloth, and fine table-cloths. At one time the display

Fig. 6.—Christine de Pizan, contemporary with Charles V. and Charles VI., seated on a Chair in carved wood with back and canopy, and tapestry of worsted or figured silk. The box or chest which formed the writing-table contained books. (Miniature from a MS. in the Bibl. of Burgundy-Bruxelles, Fifteenth Century.)

of wealth on the dressers in ecclesiastical establishments attained to such a point, that we are reminded, among other censures levelled against that fashionable exhibition of vanity, of the expostulations of Martial d'Auvergne, author of the historical poem, "Les Vigiles de Charles VII.," addressed to the bishops on the subject. One item significant enough is mentioned in ancient documents; it is the tribute of half-a-dozen small bouquets, which the

inhabitants of Chaillot were bound to tender annually to the Abbey of
Saint-German des Prés, to decorate the dressers of Messire the Abbot.

Fig. 7.—Louise de Savoie, Duchess or Angoulême, mother of Francis I., seated in a high-backed Chair of carved
wood. (Miniature from a MS. in the Imp. Bibl. of Paris.)

More plain, but also more useful, were the *abace* and the *crédence*, other
kinds of sideboards which generally stood at a little distance from the table;

on one of these were placed the dishes and plates for removes, on the other the goblets, glasses, and cups. It may be added that the *crédence*, before it was introduced in the dining-halls, had from very remote times been used in churches, where it was placed near the altar to receive the sacred vessels during the sacrifice of mass.

Posidonius, the Stoic philosopher, who wrote about a hundred years before the Christian era, tells us that, at the feasts of the Gauls, a slave used to bring to table an earthenware, or a silver, jug filled with wine, from which every guest quaffed in turn, and allayed his thirst. We thus see the practice of using goblets of silver, as well as of earthenware, established among the Gauls at a period we consider primitive. In truth, those vessels of silver were probably not the productions of local industry, but the spoil which those martial tribes had acquired in their wars against more civilised nations. With regard to the vases of baked clay, the majority of those frequently exhumed from burial-grounds prove how coarse they were, though they seem to have been made with the help of the potter's wheel, as among the Romans. However that may be, we think it best to omit the consideration of the question in this place, and to resume it in the chapter on the Ceramic Art. But we must not forget to notice the custom which prevailed among the earliest inhabitants of our country, of offering to those most renowned for their valour beverages in a horn of the *urus*, which was either gilt or ornamented with bands of gold or silver. The *urus* was a species of ox, now extinct, that existed in a wild state in the forests with which Gaul was then partly covered. This horn goblet long continued to be the emblem of the highest warlike dignity among the nations who succeeded the Gauls. William of Poitiers relates, in his "Histoire de Guillaume le Conquérant," that towards the end of the eleventh century, this Duke of Normandy still drank out of the horn of a bull, when he held his full court at Fécamp.

Our ancient kings, whose tables were made of the most precious metals, failed not also to display rare magnificence in the plate that stood on those superb tables. Chroniclers relate, for example, that Chilperic, "on the pretext of doing honour to the people whom he governed, had a dish made of solid gold, ornamented all over with precious stones, and weighing fifty pounds;" and again, that Lothaire one day distributed among his soldiers the fragments of an enormous silver basin, on which was designed "the world, with the courses of the stars and the planets." In the absence of any authentic documents, it must be presumed that, in contrast to this regal style, or rather far removed therefrom, the rest of the nation scarcely used any other utensils but those of earthenware, or wood; or else of iron or copper.

Advancing in the course of centuries, and till the period when the progress of the ceramic art enabled its productions at length to rank among articles of luxury, we find gold and silver always preferred for dinner services; but marble, rock crystal, and glass appeared in turn, artistically worked in a thousand elegant or singular forms, as cups, ewers, large tumblers, goblets, &c. (Fig. 8.)

Fig. 8.—A State Banquet in the Fifteenth Century, with the service of dishes brought in and handed round to the sound of musical instruments. (Miniature from a MS. in the Imp. Lib. in Paris.)

To the goblet, especially, seem to belong all honorary privileges in the etiquette of the table; for the goblet, a sort of large chalice on a thin stem, was more particularly regarded as an object of distinction by the guests, on account of the supposed antiquity of its origin. Thus we see represented among the presents given to the Abbey of St. Denis by the Emperor Charles the Bald, a goblet which is alleged to have belonged to Solomon, "which goblet was so marvellously wrought, that never (*oncques*) was there in all the kingdoms of the world a work so delicate (*subtile*)."

The goldsmiths, sculptors, and workers in copper had recourse to all the devices of art and imagination to embellish goblets, ewers, and salt-cellars. We find allusions, in the recitals of chroniclers, the romances of chivalry, and especially in old invoices and inventories, to ewers representing men, roses, and dolphins; to goblets covered with flowers and animals; to salt-cellars in the form of dragons, &c.

Several large pieces of gold plate, discontinued at a later period, glittered then at grand banquets. Especially may be noted the portable fountains, raised in the middle of the table, and from which, during the repast, flowed several sorts of beverages. Philip the Good, Duke of Burgundy, had one in the form of a fortress with towers, from the summit of which the figure of a woman poured out hippocras (spiced wine) from her bosom, and that of a child, which sprinkled perfumed water.

There were also plate-holders, well described by Du Cange as large dishes made to contain vessels, cups, knives; comfit-boxes, which have been replaced by our modern *bonbonnières*, and which formerly were valuable caskets chased and damaskeened; and lastly, alms-boxes, a description of metal-urns, richly chased; these were placed before the guests in order that, according to an ancient custom, each might place therein some portions of meat, to be subsequently distributed to the poor.

If we glance at the other minor objects which completed the table-service—knives, spoons, forks, bottle-stands, plate-mats, &c.—we shall see that they no less indicate refinement and luxury. Forks, that now seem to us so indispensable, are mentioned for the first time in 1379, in an inventory of Charles V. They had only two prongs, or rather two long sharp points. As for knives, which, with spoons, had to supply the place of forks for the guests to eat with, their antiquity is undoubted. Posidonius, whom we have already quoted, says, when speaking of the Celts: —" They eat in a very slovenly manner, and seize with their hands, like lions with their claws, whole quarters of meat, which they tear in pieces with their teeth. If they find a tough morsel, they cut it with a small knife which they always carry in a sheath at their side." Of what were these knives made? Our author does not tell us; but we may assume that they were of flint or of polished stone, like the hatchets and arrow-heads so frequently found where these ancient people dwelt, and which bear testimony to their industry.

In the thirteenth century mention is made of knives, under the name of *mensaculæ* and *artavi*, which a little later were known by the word *kenivet*, from which evidently is derived *canif*. To complete this connection, we may remark that it is to be gathered, from a passage by the same author, that the blades of some knives of that period were made to slide into the handle by means of a spring, like our pocket-knives.

Spoons, which necessarily were used by all nations as soon as dishes more or less liquid were introduced, are described from the date of almost our earliest history. Accordingly, we see, in the "Life of St. Radegonde," that that princess, who was constantly engaged in charitable acts, used a spoon for feeding the blind and the helpless whom she took under her care.

At a very remote period we find in use *turquoises*, or nut-crackers. Cruet-stands were, excepting in form, very similar to stands for two bottles; for they are thus described:—"A kind of double-necked bottle in divisions, in which to place two sorts of liquors without mixing them." The plate-mats were our *dessous de plat*, made of wicker, wood, tin, or other metal.

The manufacture of the greater number of these articles, if intended for persons of rank, did not fail to engage the industry of artisans and the talent of artists. Spoons, forks, nut-crackers, cruet-stands, sauce-boats, &c., furnished inexhaustible subjects for embellishment and chasing; knife-handles, made of ivory, cedar-wood, gold, or silver, were also fashioned in the most varied forms. Until ceramic art introduced plates more or less costly, they naturally enough followed the shape of dishes, which in fact they are, on a small scale. But if the dishes were of enormous size, the plates were always very small.

If from the dining-room we pass to the kitchen, so as to form some idea of culinary utensils, we must admit that, anterior to the thirteenth century, the most circumstantial documents are all but silent on the subject. Nevertheless, some of the ancient poets and early romancers allude to those huge mechanical spits on which, at one and the same time, large joints of different kinds, entire sheep, or long rows of poultry and game, could be roasted. Moreover, we know that in palaces, and in the mansions of the nobility, copper cooking-utensils possessed real importance, because the care and maintenance of the copper-ware was entrusted to a person who bore the title of *maignen*, a name still given to the itinerant tinker. We also find that from the twelfth century there existed the corporation of braziers (*dinans*), who executed historical designs, in relievo, by the use of the hammer in beating out and embossing copper,—designs that would bear comparison with the most elaborate works produced by the goldsmith's art. Some of these artisans obtained such reputation that their names have descended to us. Jean d'Outremeuse, Jean Delamare, Gautier de Coux, Lambert Patras, were among those who conferred honour on the art of brazier's work (*dinanderie*).

From the kitchen to the cellar the distance is usually but short. Our forefathers, who were large consumers, and in their way had a delicate appreciation, of the juice of the vine, understood how to store the barrels which contained their wines in deep and spacious vaults. The cooper's art, when almost unknown in Italy and Spain, had existed for a long time in France, as is attested by a passage taken from the "Mémoires de l'Académie des Inscriptions:"—"We see by the text of the Salic law that, when an estate changed hands, the new proprietor gave, in the first place, a feast, and the guests were bound to eat, in the presence of witnesses, a plate of boiled minced meat. It is remarked in the 'Glossaire de Du Cange' that, among the Saxons and Flemings, the word *boden* means a round table; because the peasantry used the bottom of a barrel as a table. Tacitus says that for the first meal of the day the Germans had each their own table; that is to say, apparently a full or empty barrel placed on end."

A statute of Charlemagne alludes to *boñs barils* (*bonos barridos*). These barrels were made by skilled coopers (Fig. 9), who gave all their care to form of staves, hooped either with wood or iron, the casks destined to hold the produce of the vintage. According to an old custom, still in vogue in the south of France, the inside of the wine-skin used to be painted with tar, in order to give a flavour to the wine; to us this would perhaps be nauseous, but at that time it was held in high favour. In alluding to wine-skins, or sewn skins coated with pitch, we may remark that they date from the earliest historic times. They are still employed in countries where wine is carried on pack-animals, and they were much used for journeys. If a traveller was going into a country where he expected to find nothing to drink, he would fasten a wine-skin on the crupper of his horse's saddle, or, at least, would sling a small leather wine-skin across his shoulder. Etymologists even maintain that from the name of these light wine-skins, *outres légères*, was derived the old French word *bouteille;* that, first having been designated *bouchiaux*, and *boutiaux*, they finally were named *bouties* and *boutilles.* When, in the thirteenth century, the Bishop of Amiens was setting out for the wars, the tanners of his episcopal town were bound to supply him with two leathern *bouchiaux*—one holding a hogshead, the other twenty-four *setiers.*

Some archæologists maintain that, when there had been a very abundant vintage, the wine was stored in brick-built cisterns, such as are still made in Normandy for cider; or that they were cut out of the solid rock, as we see them sometimes in the south of France; but it is more pro-

Fig. 9.—A Cooper's Workshop, drawn and engraved, in the Sixteenth Century, by J. Amman.

bable that these ancient cisterns, which are perhaps of an earlier date than the Middle Ages, were more especially intended for the process of fermentation—that is to say, for making wine, and not for storing it; which, indeed, under such unfavourable circumstances, would have been next to impossible.

What light did our ancestors use? History tells us that at first they used lamps with stands, and hanging lamps, in imitation of the Romans; which, however, must not lead us to the conclusion that, even in the remotest times of our annals, the use of fat and wax for such purposes was absolutely unknown. This fact is the less doubtful because, from the time when trade corporations were formed, we find the makers of candles and wax-chandlers of Paris governed by certain statutes. As for the lamps, which, as in ancient times, were on stands placed for this purpose in the houses, or were suspended by light chains (Figs. 10 and 11), they were made in accordance with the means of those for whom they were intended, and were of baked earth, iron, brass, and gold or silver, all more or less ornamented. Lamps and candlesticks are not unfrequently mentioned in the inventories of the Middle Ages. In the fifteenth and sixteenth centuries, German artisans made torch-holders, flambeaux, and chandeliers in copper, wrought and embellished with representations of all kinds of natural or fantastic objects ;

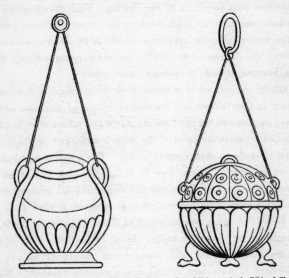

Figs. 10 and 11.—Hanging Lamps of the Ninth Century, from Miniatures in the Bible of Charles the Bald (Bibl. Imp. de Paris).

and in those days these works of art were much in request. The use of lamps was all but general in the early days of the monarchy ; but as the somewhat dim and smoky flame which they furnished did not give sufficient brilliancy to the entertainments and solemn assemblies held in the evening, it became an established custom to add to these lamps the light of resinous torches, which serfs held in their hands. The tragic episode of the Ballet des Ardents, as told by Froissart—which we shall hereafter relate in the chapter on Playing Cards—shows that this custom, which we already see alluded to in Grégoire de Tours, our earliest historian, was in fashion until the reign of Charles VI.

In subjugating the East, the Romans assumed and brought back with them extreme notions of luxury and indolence. Previously their bedsteads were of planks, covered with straw, moss, or dried leaves. They borrowed from Asia those large carved bedsteads, gilt and plated with ivory, whereon were piled cushions of wool and feathers, with counterpanes of the most beautiful furs and of the richest materials.

These customs, like many others, were handed down from the Romans to the Gauls, and from the Gauls to the Franks. With the exception of bed-linen, which came into use much later, we find, from the time of our earliest kings, the various sleeping appliances nearly as they are now—the pillow (*auriculare*), the foot-coverlet (*lorale*), the counterpane (*culcita*), &c. No mention, however, is made of curtains (or *courtines*).

At a later period, while still retaining their primitive furniture, bed-steads vary in their shapes and dimensions: those of the poor and of the monks are narrow and homely; among kings and nobles they, in process of time, became veritable examples of the joiner's work, and only to be reached by the aid of stools, or even steps (Fig. 12). The guest at a château could not receive any greater honour than to occupy the same bed as the lord of the manor; and the dogs by whom the seigneurs—all great sportsmen—were constantly surrounded had the privilege of reposing where their masters slept. Hence we recognise the object of these gigantic bedsteads, which were sometimes twelve feet in width. If we are to believe the chronicles, the pillows were perfumed with essences and odoriferous waters; this we can understand to have been by no means a useless precaution. We see, in the sixteenth century, Francis I. testifying his great regard for Admiral Bonnivet by occasionally admitting him to share his bed.

Having completed our review of furniture, properly so called, we have now to treat of that which may be termed highly artistic articles of furni-ture—that is, those on which the workers in wood exercised their highest talents—elevated seats of honour, chairs and arm-chairs, benches and trestles; all of which were frequently ornamented with figures in relief, very elaborately sculptured with a knife (*canivet*); the *bahuts*, a kind of chest with either a flat or convex top, resting on feet, and opening on the upper side, whereon were placed stuffed leather cushions (Fig. 13); tubs, buffets, presses, coffers both large and small, chess-boards, dice-tables, comb-boxes, which have been superseded by our dressing-cases, &c. Many specimens of these various kinds of furniture have descended to our time; and they prove to what a degree of perfection and of elaborate finish the art of

Fig. 12.—Bed furnished with Canopy and Curtains, from a Miniature at the end of the Fourteenth Century. (MS. de la Bibl. Imp. de Paris.)

cabinet-making and of inlaying had attained in the Middle Ages. Elegance and originality of design in inlaid metals, jasper, mother-of-pearl, ivory; carving, various kinds of veneering, and of stained woods, are all found combined in this description of furniture; some of which was ornamented

with extreme delicacy of taste (Plate I.), and still remains inimitable, if not
in all the details of execution, at least in rich and harmonious effect.

At the time of the Renaissance, cabinets
with numerous drawers and in several compartments were introduced: these were known in
Germany by the name of artistic cabinets
(*armoires artistiques*) : the sole object of the
maker was to combine in one piece of furniture,
under the pretext of utility, all the fascination
and gorgeous caprices of decorative art.

To the Germans must be awarded the merit
of having been the first to distinguish themselves in the manufacture of these magnificent
cabinets, or presses ; but they soon found rivals
in both the French (Fig. 14) and Italians
(Fig. 15), who
proved them-
selves equally
skilful and in-
genious in the
execution of
this kind of
manufacture.

The art of
working in
iron, which
can legiti-
mately rank
as one of the
most notable
industries of
the Middle
Ages, soon

Fig. 13.—Chest shaped like a Bed, standing in front of a Fireplace, and a Chair
with cushions, in carved wood, from Miniatures of the Fifteenth Century. (Bibl.
Roy. de Bruxelles.)

came to lend its aid to that of cabinet-making, both in embellishing and
giving solidity to its *chefs-d'œuvre*. The ornamentation of cabinets and coffers
was remarkable for the good taste and the high finish displayed in them.

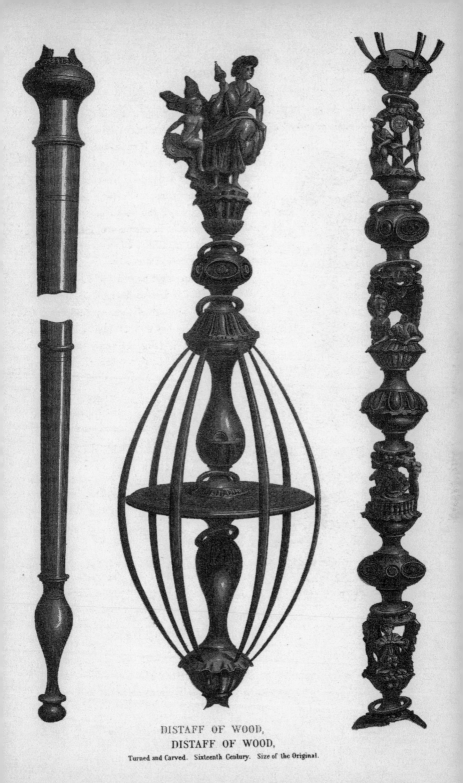

DISTAFF OF WOOD,
DISTAFF OF WOOD,
Turned and Carved. Sixteenth Century. Size of the Original.

In the hands of skilful artisans, of unknown artists dating from the twelfth to the sixteenth century, iron seemed to assume great ductility—indeed, we might say unprecedented submission. Observe, in the gratings of court-yards, in the iron-work of gates, how those lines are interlaced, how attractive are those designs, how those wrought stems are delicately lengthened

Fig. 14.—Small Cabinet for Jewels, in carved wood, after the style of Jean Goujon, from the Château d'Ecouen, and which formerly belonged to the Montmorency family. (In the Collection of M. Double.)

out, at once strong but light, and finally how they expand with natural grace into leaves, fruits, and symbolic figures.

Moreover, the workers in metal did not confine themselves to the application of iron on articles already prepared and manufactured by other artisans; they had also to originate and execute, to ornament caskets and reliquaries: but their special art was to manufacture bolts (Fig. 16), locks, and keys;

examples of this kind of ancient work will always be admired. "Locks,"
says M. Jules Labarte, "were at that time carried to such a degree of
perfection that they were considered as veritable objects of art; they were
carried from place to place, as would have been done with any other valuable
article of furniture. Nothing could be more artistic than the figures in
high relief, the armorial bearings, the letterings, the ornaments and the
engravings which embellished that portion of the key which the fingers
grasp (Fig. 17), and for which we have substituted a common ring."

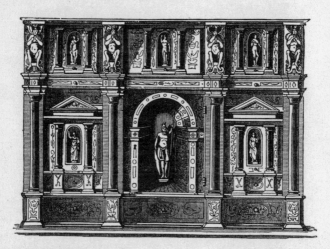

Fig. 15.—Cabinet in Damaskeened Iron, inlaid with gold and silver. An Italian work of the Sixteenth Century.

Glass and glazing claim particular notice. It may be said that glass was
known in the remotest ages, for Phœnicia and ancient Egypt were, in the
time of Moses, renowned for their innumerable productions in vitrified sand.
In Rome they cast, cut, and engraved glass—they even worked it with the
hammer, if we are to believe Suetonius, who relates that a certain artist had
discovered the secret of making glass malleable. This industrial art, which
extended and improved under the emperors, found its way to Byzantium,
where it flourished during several centuries; until Venice, claiming as she
then did a prominent position in the history of the arts, imported the process
of the Byzantine method of making glass, and in her turn excelled in this
manufacture. Although articles in glass and crystal, painted, enamelled,

and engraved, are frequently alluded to in historical and poetical narratives, and also in the inventories of the Middle Ages, we know they were all the result of Greek or Venetian manufacture. In this art France especially seems to have been somewhat late in taking her first artistic step; such

Fig. 16.—Bolt of the Sixteenth Century,
with Initial of Henry II.
(In the Castle of Chenonceaux.)

Fig. 17.—Key of the Thirteenth Century, with
two Figures of Chimeras, back to back.
(Soltykoff Collection.)

objects as were manufactured for the use of the rich never passed beyond the limits of the rudest art. We should, however, observe that France must have long been acquainted with the art of glazing, for in the middle of the seventh century we find St. Benoît—called Biscop, who built so many churches and convents in England—coming to France in search of workmen for the purpose of glazing the church and the cloisters of his abbey at Canterbury. And it is also mentioned in the chronicles of the Venerable Bede, that the French taught their art to the English glaziers.

Towards the fourteenth century the windows of even the commonest houses were generally glazed; at that date glass manufactories were found in operation everywhere; and although they may not have rivalled in a remarkable degree their predecessors of the Merovingian period, they nevertheless made in large quantities all kinds of articles ordinarily in use, as we can judge by the terms of a charter, dated 1338, by which one Guionnet, in order to have the privilege of establishing a glass factory in the forest of Chambarant, was bound to furnish as an annual due to his seigneur, Humbert, Dauphin of Viennois, one hundred dozen glasses in the shape of a bell, twelve dozen small shallow glasses, twenty dozen goblets, twelve dozen amphoræ, twenty dozen lamps, six dozen candlesticks, one dozen large cups, one large stand (or *nef*), six dozen dishes without borders, twelve dozen jars, &c.

We have alluded to Venice and the celebrity she attained in the art of working glass. It was especially for the manufacture of mirrors and looking-glasses that this large and industrious city made herself renowned over all the world. If we are to believe Pliny, the Romans purchased their glass mirrors at Sidon, in Phœnicia, where, in the remotest ages, they had been invented. At this time were these mirrors silvered? We must believe that they were, for a plate of glass, without quicksilvering, could never be anything than glass more or less transparent, and would permit of the light passing through, without reflecting objects. But Pliny asserts nothing of the kind; and, moreover, as the practice of using mirrors of polished metal, which was taken from the Romans, was for a long time maintained among modern nations, we may conclude either that the invention of glass mirrors was not a great success, or that the secret of making them was lost. In the thirteenth century an English monk wrote a treatise on optics, in which allusion is made to mirrors lined with lead. Nevertheless, mirrors of silver continued in use among the rich, and of iron and polished steel by the poorer classes, till the time when glass became less expensive, and Venetian looking-glasses were introduced, or cleverly imitated, in all European countries; metal mirrors, which easily became dim, and did not give the natural colour to reflected objects, were then discontinued. At the same time, the elegant shape of the ancient hand-mirrors was retained, the workers in gold and silver still continuing to encircle them with most graceful designs; the only difference being that the surface of polished steel or silver was replaced by a thick and bright piece of Venetian glass, sometimes ornamented with reflected designs produced in the coating of quicksilver (Fig. 18).

Fig. 18.—Hand or Pocket Mirror in gold or chased silver, from an Engraving by Etienne Delaulne. a celebrated French goldsmith and engraver (Sixteenth Century).

From all these details, the reader will have the gratification of ascertaining at a glance the general effect of furniture in use for domestic purposes; and thus, after the analysis, he will have its opposite. Fig. 19, a reproduction, taken from the "Dictionnaire du Mobilier Français," by M. Viollet-le-Duc,

Fig. 19.—Dwelling-room of a Seigneur of the Fourteenth Century.

represents a dwelling-room of a rich nobleman in the fourteenth century. What we now designate as a bedroom, and which then was called simply *cambre* or *chambre*, contained, besides the bed—which was very large—a variety of other furniture in use for the ordinary requirements of daily life ; for the time that was not given to business, to out-door amusements, to state receptions, and to meals, was passed, both by nobles and citizens, in this room. In the fourteenth century requirements for comfort had developed themselves in a remarkable degree in France. To be convinced of this, we have only to glance at the inventories, to read the romances and narratives of the day, and to study with some little care the mansions and houses erected in the reign of Charles V. A huge chimney admitted many persons to the fireside. Near the hearth was placed the *chaire* (seat of honour) of the master or of the mistress. The bed, which usually stood in a corner, surrounded by thick curtains, was effectually screened, and formed what was then called a *clotet ;* that is, a sort of small room enclosed by tapestry. Near the windows were *bancals*, or benches with backs covered with drapery, on which persons could sit and talk, read, or work, while enjoying the view. A dresser was ranged along one side of the room, and on its shelves were placed pieces of valuable plate, dishes for comfits, and flower-vases. Small stools, arm-chairs, and, especially, numerous cushions, were placed here and there in the room. Flemish carpets, and those which were called *sarrasinois*, covered the floor ; this was composed of enamelled tiles ; or, in the northern provinces, of thick squares of polished oak. These large, lofty, wainscoted rooms always communicated with private staircases, through dressing-rooms and wardrobes in which were located the domestics in immediate attendance.

Let us now pass from domestic furniture to that used for ecclesiastical purposes. We now leave the palaces of kings, the mansions of nobles, and the dwellings of the rich, and enter the buildings consecrated to worship.

We know that in the early ages of Christianity religious ceremonies were characterised by the greatest simplicity, and that the buildings in which the faithful were wont to assemble were for the most part devoid of any kind of decoration. By degrees, however, rich display entered into churches, and pomp accompanied the exercise of religious worship, especially at the period when Constantine the Great put an end to the era

of persecutions and proclaimed himself the protector of the new faith. It
is related that among the rich presents which this emperor distributed
throughout the Christian temples in Rome, were a golden cross weighing two hundred pounds, patens of the same metal, lamps representing animals, &c.   At a later period, in the seventh century, St. Eloi,
who was a celebrated goldsmith before he became Bishop of Noyon, gave
his whole mind and talents to the manufacture of church ornaments.   He
enlisted from among the monks of the various monasteries that were
subject to his episcopal authority, all those whom he fancied had an aptitude
for these works of art; he instructed and directed them himself, and made
them excellent artists; he transformed entire monasteries into gold and
silver-smiths' workshops; and numerous remarkable works increased the
splendour of the Merovingian basilicas; such, for example, were the shrine
of St. Martin of Tours, and the tomb of St. Denis, the marble roof of which
was profusely ornamented with gold and precious stones.   "The bounty of
Charlemagne," says M. Charles Louandre, "added new riches to the immense
wealth already accumulated in the churches.   Mosaics, sculpture, the rarest
kinds of marble, were lavished on those basilicas for which the emperor
evinced partiality; but all these treasures were dispersed by the Norman
invasions.   From the ninth to the eleventh centuries it would seem that,
with the exception of a few shrines and crosses, objects employed for ecclesiastical purposes were not enriched by the addition of anything note-worthy;
at any rate, the works of that period and those of anterior date have not
been handed down to us, if we except some rare fragments.   The reason is,
that, independently of the constant causes of destruction, the furniture of
churches was renewed towards the end of the eleventh century, when the
edifices themselves were rebuilt; and it is only from the date of this
mystical Renaissance that we begin to find in the texts precise indications,
and in museums or temples perfectly preserved monuments."

Ecclesiastical appendages include altars, altar-screens, the pulpit, monstrances, chalices, incense-burners, candlesticks or lamps, shrines, reliquaries,
basins for containing holy water, and some other objects of lesser relative
importance, as crosses, bells, and banner-poles.   To these we may add votive
offerings, which were generally either of gold or silver.

In the infancy of religious worship the altar took two distinct shapes;
sometimes the form of a table, with a top of stone, wood, or metal,

supported by legs or by columns; sometimes it resembled an ancient tomb, or a long coffer, narrowed at the base, and surmounted by a similar covering, which invariably formed the upper portion, or the table, of the altar.

In addition to altars, more or less monumental, which were fixtures in the churches, and which, from the earliest period, were placed under *ciboria* (a kind of dais or canopy supported by columns), small portable altars were employed, in order to meet the requirements of the service. They were intended to accompany the bishops, or the ordinary clergy, who had to preach the faith in countries where no churches existed. These altars, which were alluded to when the Christian religion had made but slight progress, were no longer seen after it became general; but we again find them at the time of the Crusades, when pious pilgrims, who journeyed from place to place preaching the Gospel, were obliged to say mass in fields and public places, where the faithful assembled to hear them, and to "take up the cross." M. Jules Labarte gives the following summary description of a portable altar of the twelfth century:—"It consists of a slab of lumachella marble, set in a box of gilt copper, 36 centimètres in height by 27 in width, and 3 in thickness. The top of the box is cut in such a manner as to leave uncovered the stone on which the chalice was placed during the celebration of mass."

Throughout all the periods of the Middle Ages, the ardent faith of which seemed to consider sufficient honour could never be rendered to the real presence of God in the holy sacrifice, the ornamentation of the altar was everywhere looked upon as an object of the most extraordinary pomp and of the most elevated artistic taste. Among the marvels of this kind we must name, as occupying a leading place, the gold altar of St. Ambrose, in Milan, which dates from 835, and those of the cathedrals of Basle and Pistoia, which belong to the eleventh and twelfth centuries. These gold altars, wrought with the hammer, were chased and sometimes enamelled, and in addition to remarkably well executed designs in carved work, taken from religious books, they usually also had on them portraits of the donors.

The altars and tabernacles were executed with an equal amount of art and costliness; and from the earliest period of the fabrication or the importation of carpets, embroideries, and gold and silver fabrics, we see them employed for the purpose of covering, adorning, and of rendering more striking and imposing the altar and its accessories, to which the name of chancel was given (Fig. 20).

The chalice and the altar-vessels, which date from the very cradle of Christian worship, since without these sacred vases the fundamental services of the religion of Jesus Christ could not have been performed, perhaps owe it to this exceptional fact that they are not spoken of before the eleventh century (Fig 21). In truth, nowhere do we find an indication of their ordinary shape, nor of the mode of their manufacture in early times; but it is reasonable to suppose that the chalice originally was identical, as it was in times approaching nearer to our own, with the goblet of the ancients: or

Fig. 20.—An Altar-cloth, embroidered in silver on a black ground, representing the procession of a friar of the Abbey of St. Victor. Fifteenth Century (copied from the original belonging to N. Achille Jubinal).

perhaps, to define it more particularly, was the well-known *hanap* (drinking-cup), the earliest type of which tradition endeavours to trace to so early a date. At a later period, and until the time when the artists of the Renaissance period were called upon to remodel sacred ornaments, and they transformed them into marvels of art on which were lavished all the resources of casting, chasing, and glyptic, we observe that chalices continued to be manufactured with the greatest care, adorned with exquisite elegance, and enriched with all the brilliancy that art can give them.

All that can be said regarding the chalice applies equally to the monstrances and the pyxes employed to contain and to exhibit the conse-

crated wafers; as also to the censers, which originated in the Jewish form of
worship, and which, in accordance with the successive epochs of Christianity,
affected different mystical and symbolic shapes (Fig. 22). Of these M. Didron
gives the following description :—"They were first formed of two openwork
spheroids, in cast and chased copper, ornamented with figures of animals and
inscriptions." Originally they were suspended by three chains, which, according to tradition, signified "the union of the body, the soul, and the divinity
in Christ." At another period the censers represented, in miniature,
churches and chapels with pointed arches. Again, at the Renaissance, they
took the form of that now in use.

Fig. 21.—An Altar-Tray and Chalice, in enamelled gold, supposed to be of the Fourth or Fifth Century, found
at Gourdon, near Chalon-sur-Saône, in 1846. (Cabinet des Antiques, Bibl. Imp. de Paris.)

From the first, the lighting of churches was, to a certain extent, carried
out on much the same principle as that employed in princely abodes and
important mansions. Fixed or movable lamps were used; also wax candles
in chandeliers, for the ornamentation of which pious donors and pious
artisans, the former paying the latter, vied with each other in skill and
liberality. We may here observe that even in the early days of Christianity, numerous candlesticks were generally employed both by day and by
night. The candlesticks on the altar represented the apostles surrounding
Christ; thus their number ought to be twelve. Placed around the dead, they

signified that the Christian finds light beyond the grave. To the faithful
they typified the day which shines brightly in celestial Jerusalem.

The worship of relics, established in the early days of the Church,
subsequently led to the introduction of shrines and reliquaries, a kind of
portable tomb which the disciples of the Gospel devoted to the memory, and
in honour, of martyrs and confessors of the faith. Thus from the first,
in collecting these holy relics, to which the faithful attached every kind
of miraculous powers, they dedicated what, according to ecclesiastical
writers, had been the temple of the living God, a gorgeous sanctuary, worthy

Fig. 22.—Censer of the Eleventh Century, recalling the shape of the Temple of Jerusalem, in copper
repoussé.   (Formerly in Metz Cathedral, now at Trèves.)

of so many virtues and miracles. Hence the introduction of shrines into
churches, and reliquaries into private houses.

Owing to the care bestowed on some of these by St. Eloi, from the seventh
century they had become real marvels of intrinsic richness and artistic
finish. Nevertheless, we are unacquainted with the shape which, in accordance with the Christian liturgy, was originally given to the shrines and
reliquaries, although the Latin word *capsa*, from which the word *châsse*
(shrine) is derived, conveys the idea of a kind of box or coffer. Indeed this
shape was retained for a long time by the whole of Christendom; but the

majority of shrines in gold and silver-work which do not date further back
than the eleventh or twelfth century represent tombs, chapels, and even
cathedrals. This symbolic shape continued in use to the time of the
Renaissance, but with successive modifications suggested by the architectural
style of each period. We thus see there was no precious material or
delicate workmanship which was not employed to contribute in making the
shrines and reliquaries more magnificent. Gold, silver, rare marbles, precious

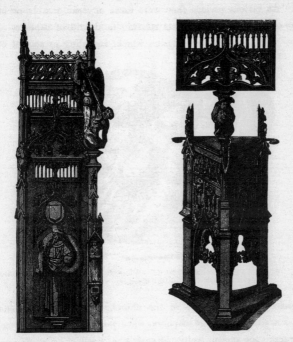

Figs. 23 and 24.—Stall and Reading-desk in carved wood, from the Church of Aosta (Fifteenth Century).

stones, were lavished on their construction; the chaser and enameller embellished with figures and emblems, with incidents taken from Holy Writ and
from the lives of saints, the shrines in which are deposited their remains.

We know that in the early days of Christianity the rite of baptism was
performed by immersion in rivers or in fountains, but at a period nearer to
our own time, basins or vessels of various dimensions were placed in a small
detached edifice, by the side of the church; into these the neophytes were

plunged when receiving the first sacrament. These baptistries disappeared as soon as the practice of sprinkling holy water on the forehead of the catechumen was definitively substituted for that of immersion. Baptismal fonts then became what they now are, that is, a kind of small erection above the level of the floor—piscinas, shells (*vasques*), or basins, recalling to our minds, though on a reduced scale, the primitive baptistries. They were placed inside the church, either near the entrance, or in one of the side-chapels. At various periods they were made of stone, marble, or bronze; and were ornamented with subjects relating to the rite of baptism. It was the same with the holy-water basins, which, according to ancient custom,

Fig. 25.—Bas-relief in carved wood, representing a Domestic Scene, from the Stalls called "Misericordes," in the Choir of the Cathedral of Rouen (Fifteenth Century).

were placed at the entrance to the church, and generally assumed the form of a shell, or of a large amphora, when not made simply of a hollowed stone to recall the ancient baptismal vessels.

We must not overlook the altar and procession-crosses, which, as being typical of the divine emblem of the Christian faith, could not fail to become real objects of art even from the time of the catacombs. It would be needless repetition to enumerate here the different materials used in the manufacture of crosses, the various shapes that were given to them, according to the purpose for which they were intended, and the subjects and figures they represented. The sculptor, the modeller, the chaser, the enameller, and even the painter, were associated with the goldsmith in producing most exquisite works of this kind. The art of the wood-carver and that of the worker in iron, which we have seen executing such marvels for household furniture, could not fail to find scope in the manufacture of objects used for religious purposes. It was especially in making pulpits, ornamental screens, wainscoting, and stalls, that the art of the wood-carver became renowned; he was no longer simply an artisan, but became an artist of the highest order. In the ornamentation of railings of choirs and tombs, the iron-work on doors, of bolts, locks, and keys, the remarkable talent of the locksmiths of the Middle Ages was displayed. Let us here remark, that in the early days of worship the pulpit was simply a kind of stool on which the preacher stood in order that his congregation might see him. By degrees the pulpit was raised on supports or columns; and later again, but only towards the end of the fifteenth century, we find it fixed at a great height against one of the central pillars of the church, and usually magnificently carved, as was also the dais, and the sounding-board by which it was surmounted.

To form an idea of the degree of perfection attained in wood-carving from the thirteenth to the fourteenth century, we ought to inspect the stalls of St. Justine, at Padua, those of the cathedrals of Milan and Ulm, the Church of Aosta (Figs. 23 and 24), &c., and the stalls of the churches of Rodez, Albi, Amiens, Toulouse, and Rouen (Fig. 25). And if we would examine a very ancient example of the art attained by workers in iron, we have but to notice the hinges, dating from the thirteenth century, which stretch, in arabesque designs, over the panels of the western door of Notre-Dame, Paris.

Fig. 26.—Design on the Stalls in the Church of St. Benoît-sur-Loire.

TAPESTRY.

F there is an art which bears brilliant testimony to the
industry and ingenuity of mankind in the remotest ages,
undoubtedly it is that of weaving, or of embroidering
tapestry; for, however far back we trace the annals of
nations, we find this art flourishing and producing marvels
of workmanship.

Let us first open the Bible, the oldest of all historical
documents; we read therein of woven fabrics, not only
worked on the loom, but also made by hand, that is,
richly embroidered in needlework on linen or canvas.
These magnificent fabrics, which were laboriously and
minutely executed, represented all kinds of designs in
relief and in colours; they were used as decorations for the holy temple,
and as ornamental garments for the priests who performed the religious
ceremonies. Indubitable proof of this is the description, in the book
of Exodus, of the curtains surrounding the tabernacle. Some of these
embroideries, in the manufacture of which gold and silver thread, combined
with dyed wools and silk, was used, were named *opus plumarii* (work in
imitation of bird's plumage) ; others—such, for example, as the veil of the
Holy of Holies, which represented cherubim in the act of adoration—were
called *opus artificis* (work of the artisan), because they were made by the
weaver on the loom; and, with the aid of numerous shuttles, the woof of
wools and silks of various hues was introduced.

In the traditions of the magnificent city of Babylon we also find figured tapestry delineating the mysteries of religion, and handing down to us the recollection of historical incidents. "The palace of the kings of Babylon," says Philostratus, in the "Life of Apollonius of Tyana," "was ornamented with tapestries in gold and silver tissues, which recorded the Grecian fables of Andromeda, of Orpheus, &c." The Greek poet Apollonius of Rhodes, who wrote a century before our era, relates in his poem of "The Argonauts" that the women of Babylon excelled in the execution of these gorgeous textures. The famous tapestries which were sold in the time of Metellus Scipio for 800,000 sesterces (about 165,000 francs), and a hundred years later were purchased for the exorbitant sum of two million sesterces (about 412,000 francs) by Nero, to place on his festive couches, were of Babylonian workmanship.

Ancient Egypt, which would seem to have been the early cradle of an advanced civilisation, was also renowned for this marvellous art, the invention of which the Greeks attributed to Minerva, and to which allusion is frequently made in their mythology. Penelope's web, whereon were delineated the exploits of Ulysses, has remained the most celebrated among them all. It was on a similar web that Philomela, in her prison, illustrated in embroidery the narrative of her misfortunes, after Tereus had cut out her tongue, to prevent her telling her sister Progne the outrage she had suffered at his hands.

Throughout the poems of Homer we find embroidery of this kind either mentioned, or described as made with the needle or loom, and intended for decorative drapery, or as garments for men and women. During the siege of Troy, Helen embroidered, upon a fine tissue, the sanguinary combats of the heroes who were destroying each other for her sake. The cloak of Ulysses represents a dog pulling down a fawn, &c.

The custom of embroidering such scenes as combats and hunting-incidents seems to have lasted during a long time. According to Herodotus, certain races bordering on the Caspian Sea were accustomed to have figures of animals, flowers, and landscapes delineated on their garments. This custom is mentioned among the pagans by Philostratus, and among Christians by Clement of Alexandria. Pliny, the naturalist, who lived in the first century of our era, also alludes to it on several occasions in his works. Three hundred years later, Amasius, Bishop of Amasia, deplores the folly which "set a great value on this art of weaving, a vain and useless art, which by the combination of the warp and woof imitates painting." "When persons thus dressed appear in the street," adds the pious bishop, "the passers-by look at them as walking pictures, and the children point at them with their finger. We see lions, panthers, bears, rocks, woods, hunters; the religiously inclined have Christ, his disciples, and his miracles figured on their garments. Here we see the wedding of Cana, and the pitchers of water turned into wine; there we have the paralytic carrying his bed, or the sinner at the feet of Jesus, or Lazarus being raised from the dead."

We have only to look into the works of the writers of the time of Augustus to learn that the halls in the houses of the wealthy were always hung with tapestry; and that the tables, or rather the beds, upon which the guests were seated, were covered with carpets.

The Attalian carpets, which were thus named because they came from the inheritance bequeathed to the Roman people by Attalus, King of Pergamos, were indescribably magnificent. Cicero, who was a connoisseur in such matters, speaks of them with enthusiasm in his works.

Under Theodosius I., that is to say, at the time of the decline of the great empire which was soon to break up and be separated, and at last to merge into new nationalities, a contemporaneous historian shows us "the youth of Rome engaged in making tapestry-work."

In the early period of French history, this ingenious and delicate work would seem to have been mainly carried on by women, and especially by those of the highest rank. At any rate it is a fact that rich tapestries were in common use, both in private houses and for ecclesiastical purposes, as early as the sixth century; for Gregory of Tours does not fail to tell us of the embroidered hangings, and also of the tapestry, in most of the ceremonies which he describes. When King Clovis renounced paganism and asked to be baptised, "this intelligence was the greatest joy to the bishop; he orders the sacred fonts to be prepared; the streets overhung with painted cloths; the churches ornamented with hangings." When the abbey-church of St. Denis had to be consecrated, "its walls are covered with tapestry embroidered in gold and ornamented with pearls." These tapestries were for a long time preserved in the abbey-treasury. Subsequently, this same treasury received, as a present from Queen Adelaide, the wife of Hugh Capet, "a chasuble, a valance, as also some hangings, worked by her own hand;" and Doublet, the historian of this ancient abbey, states that Queen Bertha (the same whom the old French proverb makes an indefatigable worker with her needle) embroidered on canvas a series of historical subjects, depicting the glorious deeds of the family.

Nevertheless, there is no written authority for asserting that in France the manufacture of tapestries and hangings worked on the loom can be traced beyond the ninth century; but at this period, and a little later, we find some documents which are as precise as they are curious—proving that this industry, the principal object of which, at that period, was the ornamentation of churches, had to a certain extent obtained a footing, and was flourishing in religious establishments. The ancient chronicles of Auxerre relate that St. Anthelm, the bishop of that city, who died in 828, caused to be made, under his own directions, numerous rich carpets for the choir of his church.

One hundred years later we find a regular manufactory established at the monastery of St. Florent, at Saumur. "In the time of the abbot Robert III.," says the historian of this monastery, "the vestry (*fabrique*) of the cloister was further enriched by magnificent paintings and pieces of sculpture, accompanied by legends in verse. The above-mentioned abbot, who was passionately devoted to similar works, sought for and purchased a considerable quantity of magnificent ornaments, such as large *dorserets** in wool, curtains, canopies, hangings, bench-covers, and other ornaments, embroidered with various devices. Among other objects, he caused to be made two pieces of tapestry of large size and of admirable quality, representing elephants; and these two pieces were joined together with a rare kind of silk, by hired workers in tapestry. He also ordered two *dorserets* in wool to be manufactured. It happened that, during the time one of these was being completed, the above-mentioned abbot went to France. The ecclesiastic left in charge took advantage of his absence to forbid the artisans to work the woof according to the customary method. 'Well,' said they, 'in the absence of our good abbot we will not discontinue our employment; but as you thwart us we shall make quite a different kind of fabric.' And this now admits of proof. They made several square carpets, representing silver lions upon a field of *gules* (red), with a white border covered with scarlet animals and birds. This unique piece of workmanship was looked upon as a perfect specimen of this kind of fabric, until the time of the abbot William, when

---

* *Dorserets*, covers to backs of chairs, beds, &c.

it was considered the most remarkable piece of tapestry belonging to the monastery. In fact, on the occasions of great solemnities the abbot had the elephant tapestry displayed, and one of the priors showed that on which were the lions."

From the ninth or tenth century there was also a manufactory at Poitiers; and its fabrics, on which figured kings, emperors, and saints, were of European celebrity, as appears to be attested, among other documents, by a remarkable correspondence which took place, in 1025, between an Italian bishop named Léon, and William IV., Count of Poitou. To understand rightly this correspondence, it must be borne in mind that at the time Poitou was as famous for its mules as for tapestry. In one of his letters, the bishop begs the count to send him a mule and a piece of tapestry, both equally marvellous (*mirabiles*), and for which he has been asking six years. He promises to pay whatever they may cost. The count, who must have had a facetious disposition, replied, " I cannot, at present, send you what you ask, because for a mule to merit the epithet of marvellous, he would require to have horns, and three tails, or five legs—and this I should not be able to find in our country. I shall therefore content myself with sending you one of the best I can procure. As to the tapestry, I have forgotten the dimensions you desire. Let me have these particulars again, and it will then soon be sent to you."

But this costly industry was not limited to the French provinces. In the "Chronique des Ducs de Normandie," written by Dudon, in the eleventh century, it is stated that the English were clever workers in this art; and when designating some magnificent embroidery, or rich tapestry, it was described as of English work (*opus Anglicanum*). Moreover, the same chronicle relates that the wife of Richard I.,* the Duchess Gonnor, assisted by her embroiderers, made hangings of linen and of silk, embellished with images and figures representing the Virgin Mary and the Saints, to decorate the church of Notre Dame, Rouen.

The East, also, which from the earliest times had been renowned for the art of producing beautiful embroidered fabrics, became still more famous during the Middle Ages for those of wool and silk, embroidered with silver and gold. It was from the East were brought the rich stuffs covered all

* Richard I., surnamed *Sans-peur*, third Duke of Normandy, was natural son of William I., and grandson of Rollo. He died in 996.—[ED.]

over with emblazonments, and with figures of animals, and probably also
embroidered in open-work: these fabrics were called *étoffes sculptées, ou pleines
d'yeux.*

The librarian Anastasius, in his book the "Lives of the Popes," which
undoubtedly was written before the eleventh century, gives, when describing
church decorations, some curious and circumstantial details regarding the
subject we are now discussing. According to him, as early as the time of
Charlemagne (eighth century), Pope Leo III. "had a veil made of purple
worked in gold, on which was the history of the Nativity and of Simon,
having in the centre the Annunciation of the Virgin." This was to ornament
the principal altar of the Holy Mother of God, at Rome. He also ordered
for the altar of the church of St. Laurence, "a veil of silk worked in gold,
having on it the histories of the Passion of our Saviour and of the Resurrection." He placed on the altar of St. Peter's "a veil of purple, of a remarkable size, worked in gold, and ornamented with precious stones; on one side
was seen our Saviour giving St. Peter the power to bind and to loose, on the
other the Passion of St. Peter and St. Paul." In the same book, several
other pieces of tapestry are described in such terms that it seems difficult
to realise the richness and the beauty of finish of these artistically-worked
fabrics, which for the most part came from Asia or Egypt. It was only
in the twelfth century, after the return from the first crusades had
enabled Western nations to admire and to appropriate to themselves luxuries
quite new to them, that the custom of using tapestry, while becoming
far more general in churches, found its way also into private dwellings.
If, in the cloisters, the monks, in order to find employment, lavished their
utmost care on the weaving of wool and of silk, there was the more reason
why this occupation should prove pleasing to the noble *châtelaines* who were
confined to their feudal castles. It was then, when surrounded by their tire-
women, as in earlier times were the Roman matrons by their slaves, that these
fair dames, while listening to the reading of tales of chivalry which deeply
interested them, or inspired by a profound faith, gave themselves to the
task of reproducing with the needle either the pious legends of the saints
or the glorious exploits of warriors. The bare walls, when thus draped with
touching incidents or warlike memorials, assumed a peculiar eloquence which
doubtless inspired the mind with grand visions, and aroused noble sentiments
in the heart.

Among the finest specimens of this kind is one which, owing to its really exquisite character, has escaped what would have seemed inevitable destruction. We allude to the famous Bayeux tapestry called "*de la Reine Mathilde*" (of the wife of William the Conqueror). This work represents the conquest of England by the Normans. If we are to accept the ancient traditions to which it owes its name, it must date from the last half of the eleventh century.

In these days we may be permitted to doubt, in consequence of the many discussions that have taken place among the learned, if this embroidery is as ancient as was at one time supposed. And although we first find it alluded to in an inventory (prepared in 1476) of the treasury of Bayeux Cathedral, we may venture, with a certain degree of confidence, to believe that it was made in the twelfth century by Englishwomen, who at that time were particularly famous for their needlework; an opinion confirmed by more than one author contemporaneous with William and Matilda.

This tapestry, which is 19 inches in height, by nearly 212 feet in length, is a piece of brown linen, on which are embroidered with the needle, in wool of different colours (and these seem to have lost none of their early freshness), a series of seventy-two groups or subjects, with legends in Latin interspersed with Saxon, embracing the whole history of the Conquest, as related by the chroniclers of the period (Figs. 27 and 28).

At the first glance, this embroidery may seem to be but a rudely executed grouping of figures and animals; nevertheless there is character throughout, and the original outline, discoverable beneath the intersections of the wool, is not wanting in a certain accuracy that brings to our mind the vigorous simplicity of the Byzantine style. The decoration of the double border, between which is delineated a drama wherein 530 figures are introduced, is the same as those of the paintings in manuscripts of the Middle Ages. And, in short, failing any exact proof, if we are determined not to deprive this immense work of its traditional antiquity, it might, with much probability, be attributed to a female embroiderer of Queen Matilda, named Leviet, whose skill has rescued her name from oblivion. It may also be well to observe, that at the time it is first alluded to in history, this tapestry is found belonging to the very church in which Matilda desired to be buried.

We have already seen (in the chapter on Furniture) that towards the twelfth and thirteenth centuries, under the influence of Eastern habits and

customs, the practice of sitting on carpets was established at the court of our
kings.   From this date rich tapestries were frequently used for making tents

Fig. 27.—A piece of the Bayeux Tapestry, representing the construction of Boats for William (with Border).

for campaigning or for hunting.   They were displayed on festive occasions;
as, for instance, when princes were entering a town, the object being to hide
the bare walls.   The dining-halls were hung with magnificent tapestries,

giving additional splendour to the interludes (*entremets,* ou *intermèdes*) performed during the repast. The champions in the lists saw glittering around them, suspended from the galleries, fabrics on which heroic deeds were embroidered. Lastly, the caparison of the charger (the war-horse's garb of honour) displayed its brilliant emblazonings to the eyes of admiring crowds.

It was moreover the custom that the tapestries made for noblemen

Fig. 28.—A portion of the Bayeux Tapestry, representing two mounted men of Duke William's army armed from head to foot, and in the act of fighting.

should bear their respective armorial devices, the object being, no doubt, that it might be known to whom they belonged when used on the occasion of the entry of royal, and other distinguished, personages in solemn processions; and also at jousts and tournaments.

In the fourteenth century the manufactories of Flanders, which were of considerable reputation even about the twelfth century, made great advance, and the success of the Arras tapestries became so general that the most handsome hangings were called Arras tapestry, although the greater part of them did not come from that city. It may here be noticed that the term *Arrazi* is, in Italy, still synonymous with valuable tapestry (Fig. 29).

These fabrics were generally worked in wool, and sometimes in flax and linen; but at the same period Florence and Venice, which had imported this industry from the East, wove tapestries wherein gold and silk were blended.

Fig. 29.—Marriage of Louis XII. and Anne of Brittany. Tapestry in wool and silk, with a mixture of gold and silver thread. Made in Flanders the end of the Fifteenth Century. (Lent by M. Achille Jubinal.)

An inventory, dated 21st January, 1379, contained in a manuscript now in the "Bibliothèque Impériale,"—in which are enumerated "all the jewels in gold and silver, all the rooms with embroidery and tapestries belonging to Charles V.,"—gives us an idea not only of the multiplicity of hangings and tapestries that appertained to the personal property of royalty, especially at the Hôtel Saint-Pol, but it also shows us the variety

THE ADORATION OF THE MAGI.
Tapestry of Berne of the fifteenth Century
(Communicated by M. Achille Jubinal.)

of subjects therein represented. A few of these pieces of tapestry are still preserved, but among some which have been destroyed or lost we may mention those representing the Passion of our Saviour, the Life of St. Denis, the Life of St. Theseus, and that entitled Goodness and Beauty—all these were of large dimensions. Then again, the tapestry of the Seven Mortal Sins, two pieces of the Nine Bold Knights, that of the ladies hunting and flying (*qui volent*), in other words, hawking; that of the Wild Men; two of Godfrey de Bouillon; a white tapestry for a chapel, in the centre of which was seen "a compass with a rose," emblazoned with the arms of France and of Dauphiny, this was three yards square; one large handsome piece of tapestry, "the king has bought, which is worked with gold, representing the Seven Sciences and St. Augustin;" the tapestry of Judith (the queen who subsequently appears on playing-cards); a large piece of Arras cloth, representing the Battles of Judas Maccabæus and Antiochus; another of "the Battle of the Duke of Aquitaine and of Florence;" a piece of tapestry "whereon are worked the twelve months of the year;" another of "the Fountain of Jouvent" (Jouvence), a large piece of tapestry "covered with azure fleurs-de-lys, which said fleurs-de-lys are mingled with other small yellow fleurs-de-lys," having in the centre a lion, and, at the four corners, beasts holding banners, &c.—in fact, the list is endless. We must still, however, add to these figured tapestries those with armorial bearings, made for the most part with "Arras thread," and bearing the arms of France and Behaigne (the latter being those of the queen, daughter of the King of Bohemia). There was also a piece of tapestry "worked with towers, fallow bucks and does, to put over the king's boat." The tapestry called *velus*, or velvet, which now we call *moquettes*, was as commonly seen as any other kind. There were also to be noticed the *Salles d'Angleterre*, or the tapestries from that country, which, as we have said, had previously acquired a great celebrity in that art. Among these one was "*ynde* (blue), with trees and wild men, with wild animals, and castles;" others were vermilion, embroidered with azure, having vignette borders, and in the centre lions, eagles, and leopards.

In addition to these, Charles V. possessed at his castle of Melun many "silken fabrics and tapestries." At the Louvre one could but admire, among other magnificent pieces of tapestry, "a very lovely green room, ornamented with silk covered with leaves; and representing in the centre a lion, which two queens were in the act of crowning, and a fountain wherein swans were disporting themselves."

Yet we must not be led away with the idea that it was only the royal palaces which presented such sumptuousness; for it would be easy to enumerate many instances similar to those we have given, by looking over the inventories of the personal property of nobles, or those of the treasuries of certain churches and abbeys. In one place the tapestries represent religious subjects taken from the Bible, the Gospels, or the legends of the saints; in another the subjects are either historical or relating to chivalry, more especially battles or hunting scenes (Fig. 30).

We are thus justified in asserting that the luxury of tapestry was general among the higher classes. An expensive taste it was; because not only does an examination of these marvellous works show us that they could have been purchased only at a very high price, but in old documents we find more than one certain confirmation of this fact. For example, Amaury de Goire, a worker in tapestry, received in 1348, from the Duke of Normandy and Guienne, 492 livres, 3 sous, 9 deniers, for "a woollen cloth," on which were represented scenes from the Old and New Testaments. In 1368, Huchon Barthélmy, money-changer, received 900 golden francs for a piece of "worked tapestry," representing La Quête de St. Graal (the search for the blood of Christ); and in 1391, the tapestry exhibiting the history of Theseus, to which we have already alluded, was purchased by Charles V. for 1,200 livres; all these sums, considering the period, were really exorbitant.

The sixteenth century, remarkable for the progress and the excellence to which the arts of every kind had attained, gave a renewed impulse to that of tapestry. A manufactory was established by Francis I., at Fontainebleau, where the tapestry was woven in one entire piece, instead of being made up, as had been the practice, of separate pieces matched and sewn together. In this new fabric gold and silver threads were mixed with silk and wool.

When Francis sent for the Primate from Italy, he commissioned him to procure designs for several pieces of tapestry, to be made in the workshops of Fontainebleau. But, while liberally rewarding the Italian or Flemish artists and artisans collected in the dependencies of his château, the king still continued to employ Parisian tapestry-workers; proof of which is to be found in a receipt of the sieurs Miolard and Pasquier, who give an

Fig. 30.—Tapestry representing a Hunting Scene, from the Château d'Effiat.
(In the possession of M. Achille Jubinal.)

acknowledgement of having been paid 410 *livres tournois,* " to begin the purchase of materials and other requisites for a piece of silk tapestry, which the said seigneur had ordered them to make for his coronation, according to the patterns which the said seigneur has had prepared for this purpose, and on which must be represented a Leda, with certain nymphs, satyrs, &c."

Henry II. did even more than maintain the establishment at Fontaine-bleau ; in addition he instituted, in compliance with the request of the guardians of the Hôpital de la Trinité, a manufactory of tapestry in Paris,

Fig. 31.—The Weaver. Drawn and Engraved by J. Amman.

in which the children belonging to the hospital were employed in dyeing wool and silk, and in weaving them in the loom with a high and low warp.

The new manufactory, whether on account of the excellence of its productions, or from influential patronage, obtained so many privileges that the public peace was on several occasions seriously disturbed by the jealousy of the guild of tapestry-workers ; an ancient and numerous corporation still possessing great authority and influence.

The manufactory of the Hôpital de la Trinité continued to flourish during the reign of Henry III. ; and Sauval, in his " Histoire des Antiquités de

PLAN OF PARIS IN THE FIFTEENTH CENTURY.

Beauvais Tapestry (Communicated by M. Achille Jubinal.)

PLAN OF PARIS IN THE FIFTEENTH CENTURY,

WITH THIS LEGEND :

Mil cinq cents ans quarante et neuf passez
Du déluge : Paris le noble roy
Dix-huitième : fonda en grand arroy
Ville et cité de Paris belle assez
Devant que Rome eust des gens amassez
Six cent cinquante et huit ans comme croy.

TRANSLATION.

One thousand five hundred and forty-nine years after the Deluge, the noble King Paris, the eighteenth of his name, founded with great pomp the fine town and city of Paris, anterior to the foundation of Rome, which took place, as I think, 658 (?) years before Jesus Christ.

Paris," informs us that in the following reign it reached its highest point of prosperity. In 1594, Dubourg made in these workshops, from the designs of Lerembert, the beautiful tapestries which, to a date very near our own, decorated the Church of Saint-Merry. Henry IV., says Sauval, hearing this work much spoken of, desired to see it, and was so pleased therewith that he resolved to restore the manufactories in Paris, "which the disorder of preceding reigns had abolished." He therefore established Laurent, a celebrated tapestry-worker, in the *maison professe* of the Jesuits, which had remained closed since the trial of Jean Chastel. He allowed one crown a day, and one hundred francs a year, as wages to this skilful artist; his apprentices receiving ten sous a day, and his fellow workmen twenty-five, thirty, and even forty sous, according to their skill. At a later period Dubourg and

Fig. 32.— Banner of the Tapestry Workers of Lyons.

Laurent, who had entered into partnership, were both installed in the galleries of the Louvre. Henry IV., following the example of Francis I., brought from Italy skilled workers in gold and in silk. These he lodged in the Hôtel de la Maque, Rue de la Tisseranderie: the special works they made were hangings in fine cloth of gold and silver (*frisé*).

Subsequently to the sixteenth century, the tapestries fabricated at the manufactories of the Savonnerie, the Gobelins, and at Beauvais, &c., although more perfect as regards the weaving, and therefore presenting greater regularity of design and a better comprehension of colour and perspective, unfortunately lost the original simplicity which characterized them in olden times. Approaching the reign of Louis XIV., under the influence of the school of Le Brun,* they affected an imitation of Greek and Roman forms, which seem out of place in France. Handsome countenances are the result, but accompanied by meaningless figures; the frankness of truth gives place to staid coldness, the ideal usurps the place of nature, conventionality that of spontaneity. We find them ingenious, pretty, and even beautiful productions, but wanting character, the real soul of works of art.

* Charles le Brun, a distinguished painter of the French school, flourished during the seventeenth century. The son of a sculptor, who placed him under Simon Vouet, the young artist made such progress that at the age of fifteen he painted a remarkable picture, "Hercules Destroying the Horses of Diomede," which brought him at once into public notice. Le Brun's patron, the Chancellor Seguier, sent him to Italy, with an introduction to Nicholas Poussin, whose pure and correct taste, however, seems to have had little influence on the French artist, who, though possessing an inventive and somewhat elevated genius, often showed himself a mannerist.—[ED.]

CERAMIC ART.

 E can assuredly say, with M. Jacquemart, that "the history of the ceramic art of the Middle Ages is shrouded by a veil which probably will always remain impenetrable. Notwithstanding the constant investigations of local societies, and the numerous documents that have been brought to light, nothing has transpired to remove the doubts of the archæologist regarding the places where the manufacture of pottery had its birth among us."

Nevertheless, it is certain that at the Gallo-Romano period—that is to say, when the Romans, having made themselves masters of that country, had introduced their customs and their industry—Gaul possessed numerous and considerable pottery workshops, which produced vessels and vases of all kinds. Maintaining the ancient forms and processes of manufacture, these factories continued to furnish, till about the sixth century, amphoræ, basins, cups on stems, dishes, plates, and bottles. They were made, with the aid of the potter's wheel, of grey, yellow, or brown clay. Some of the finest quality were covered with a brilliant varnish, resembling red sealing-wax both in colour and appearance; and these articles were often ornamented with much care and delicacy. We find vases surrounded with garlands of leaves, cups embellished with figures of men and animals: these are so many proofs that this was a manufacture to which the influence of art was by no means unknown.

Yet it is also evident that this industry—one of a sufficiently elevated kind—nearly disappeared about the period of the invasions and wars amidst the tumult of which French monarchy had its birth; and there remained but the simple art that provided for ordinary requirements an assemblage of articles rude and devoid of character.

It must be remembered, however, that the ceramic art which had flourished in the West merely migrated, instead of becoming extinct; and it found, like so many other arts, a new country in that Byzantium destined to be the sanctuary of ancient magnificence. Whatever may be the reason, ceramic art disappeared from the soil of France during a long period; and it is still a question what was the real origin of its revival. Did it revive of itself, or was it under the influence of example? Did it owe its

Fig. 33.—Vases of ancient shape represented in the decorative sculpture of the Church of St. Benoît, Paris. (Twelfth Century.)

resuscitation to any immigration of artisans, or to the importation of some process of manufacture? These questions still remain unanswered.

The ceramic art, which perhaps we somewhat wrongly style modern, is characterised by the use of enamel, or overlaying articles with a glaze having a metallic basis; this the fire of the oven vitrifies; it is a process of which the ancients were entirely ignorant.

But, in searching the tombs that belonged to the ancient abbey of Jumièges (in Normandy), and which date from the year 1120, there have been found fragments of pottery of a fine but porous clay, covered with a glazing somewhat similar to that now used.

Moreover, we read in a chronicle of the ancient province of Alsace, that in the year 1283 "died a potter of Schelestadt, who was the first to cover earthen vessels with glass."

But we also know that at the time when these isolated attempts were being carried out in France, the Persians and Armenians had long before discovered the art of making magnificent enamelled ware for covering the exterior of their monuments; and that the Arabs settled in Spain produced wonderful examples of painted and enamelled earthenware, with which they decorated and furnished those palaces whose grand ruins are still to us like the fairy visions of a dream or of enchantment. The vases of the Alhambra, types of an art as original as it was singularly ingenious, claim, and doubtless will always claim, the admiration of minds that can appreciate the beautiful in whatever form it may present itself.

Fig. 34.—Vases of ancient form, represented in the decorative sculptures of the Church of St. Benoît, Paris (Twelfth Century).

And now, are we to suppose that the intercourse between nations and the transactions of commerce must necessarily have made western Europe acquainted with the enamelled dishes of Asia, or the *chefs-d'œuvre* of the African race in Spain? Or, on the other hand, shall we say that it was by a spontaneous effort of invention that our forefathers opened up the road to a new domain of art? In the one case we have the opinion, deservedly respected, of Scaliger, who affirms the fact, apparently very significant, that during the Middle Ages there existed in the Balearic Islands manufactories of pottery of Arab origin; our learned author even adds, that in accordance with the most probable etymology, the name of *Majolica*, which was first given to Italian ware (the earliest in the European revival of the ceramic art), was derived from *Majorca*, the largest, as we know, of the Balearic

Islands, in which locality the principal manufactory of these pottery wares was situated. But, on the other hand, a comparative examination of Arab and Italian wares excludes all idea not only of affiliation, but even of imitation or reminiscence between them.

In the face of such contradictory coincidence, if we may say so, it would be as difficult as it would be rash to pronounce an opinion; we consider it better, while disregarding problematical indications, to boldly face a train of facts now determined by historical proof.

"At the commencement of the fifteenth century"—we cannot do better than borrow from M. Jacquemart a passage which he himself took from the Italian work by Passeri, on Majolica (Pesaro, 1838, in 8vo.)—"Luca della Robbia, the son of Simone di Marro, apprenticed himself to a Florentine goldsmith, Leonardo, the son of Giovanni; but disliking the confinement of a laboratory, he soon became a pupil of the sculptor Lorenzo Ghiberti, who made the gates of the Baptistry at Florence. His rapid progress under so able a master placed him in a position, when he could not have been more than fifteen years old, to undertake the task of ornamenting a chapel for Sigismond Malatesta, at Rimini. Two years later, Pietro di Medici, who was having an organ erected in Santa-Maria dei Fiori, at Florence, directed Luca to execute some marble sculptures in that church. The fame which he gained by these works drew everybody's attention to the young sculptor. Orders reached him in such numbers that he clearly saw the impossibility of executing them in marble or in bronze; added to this, he bore with impatience the restraint imposed by working with such rigid materials, of which the laborious handling trammelled the flights of his imagination. Soft and plastic clay was a material far better suited to his readiness of conception. At the same time, Luca dreamt of the future, and of glory; and thus having in view the object of executing works which, though less perishable, might be rapidly executed, he devoted all his efforts to discover a coating which would give to clay the polish and the hardness of marble. After many trials, a varnish made of tin (*étain*), which was white, opaque, and of a resisting nature, furnished him with the result he hoped for. The art of producing fine earthenware was discovered, which first received the name of vitrified clay (*terra invetriata*).

"Luca's enamel was a most perfect white; he first used it alone for figures, in semi-relief, which were raised on a blue background. At a later period he ventured to colour his figures, and Pietro di Medici was one of the first who encouraged this kind of work for the decoration of palaces. The fame of this novel art spread with rapidity; all the churches were anxious to possess some specimen of the master, so that Luca was soon compelled to associate with himself his two brothers Ottaviano and Agostino, in order

Fig. 35.—Enamelled Terra-cotta, by Luca della Robbia.

to keep pace with the requirements of the public. He endeavoured, nevertheless, to extend the application of his discovery by painting flowers and groups of figures on a smooth surface; but in the year 1430 death cut short his remarkable career, and stayed, in the hands of the inventor, the progress of *enamelled pottery* (Fig. 35).

"The family of Luca, however, made public the secret of his discovery.

His two nephews, Luca and Andrea, produced some figures and designs of singular merit in terra-cotta. Luca ornamented the floor of the Loggia of Raphael. Girolamo, a relative of Luca, came to France, where he decorated the château of Madrid, in the neighbourhood of Paris. Two females, Lisabetta and Speranza, added to the renown of the family Della Robbia."

Such is the history of the revival, or rather of the creation, of ceramic art in Italy, as briefly recorded by a man thoroughly acquainted with the subject. An ancient author, and, moreover, a competent writer, instances some monuments of an earlier date; among others, a tomb at Bologna, in which were tiles covered with a green and yellow varnish, and vessels (*écuelles*) of the same kind inserted in the façades or porticoes of the churches of Pesaro and the abbey of Pomposa. But to the honour of Luca della Robbia it may be remarked, that these specimens of an earlier industry differed essentially from his productions; because the glazing that covered them, the basis of which was lead, was so transparent, that through it could be seen either the clay or the colours underneath; whereas the enamel discovered by Luca, the basis of which was tin, had, on the contrary, for its essential character, an opacity which may be termed intense. Let us observe, moreover, that in order to embellish his productions with paintings, Luca was accustomed to apply colours to the first and general coating, which became fixed by a subsequent process of baking.

It is by recognising the distinction we have just laid down between these two processes, that the productions of Italian ceramic art are ordinarily classified: the *demi-majolica*, with transparent glaze, somewhat like the Spanish-Arabian pottery, and also, perhaps, like Asiatic tiles; then the *majolica*, by which we understand fine earthenware, where the clay is covered with a coating of opaque varnish, distinguishing the invention due to Luca della Robbia.

Having given priority of invention to Luca della Robbia, it is as well, nevertheless, here to state, that from the eleventh and twelfth centuries there existed in France a kind of ceramic art employed especially in the manufacture of varnished pottery-tiles. Many, of baked clay, have been found with drawings and designs in black or brown on a white or yellow ground (Plate IV.). At a later period these tiles, of which we see such brilliant specimens in the small pictures in manuscripts, especially in those

PAVING TILES OF THE FOURTEENTH AND FIFTEENTH CENTURIES.

of the fourteenth and fifteenth centuries, were embellished with designs, emblems, armorial bearings, and scrolls. As already stated, in the passage from the author whom we have taken as our guide, the impulse which Luca della Robbia gave to ceramic art extended itself with rapidity in every direction ; and if any other reason were wanting, beyond the intrinsic value of this art, to account for its development, we should say that the circumstances in the midst of which Luca made his discovery were eminently favourable to its advancement.

Luxurious display was, at that time, prominent among the classes who aspired to ostentation. When writing of furniture, we saw to what a pitch of splendid profusion kings, princes, and nobles carried the mania for displaying their wealth. We particularly pointed out sideboards in the dining-rooms, covered with plate and all kinds of objects, which were only placed there to dazzle the eyes. The custom of these displays having been introduced, it could nevertheless be only indulged in by those in possession of considerable fortunes, and therefore it will be readily understood how quickly fashion affected the productions of ceramic art; which, in addition to being recognised as works of art, were singularly well suited, both in character and by their comparative cheapness, to the spirit of ostentation which had taken possession of people of inferior rank. It was sufficient that some piece of majolica should have found a place on the sideboard of a prince amidst the gold and the silver which hitherto had alone enjoyed this privilege, for the lower ranks of the *bourgeoisie* and the *tiers-état* to adopt the fashion, in their dining-rooms, of decorating them either with majolica alone, or associated with plate.

And admitting this fact, that the productions of ceramic art were thus allowed to find admittance, and, as it were, in some measure an equally distinguished position, amidst plate and objects of precious metals, it resulted that this new industry, supported by the best artists, soon became remarkable for works which were at the same time most beautiful and original.

As something new in history, we find simple pieces of pottery—to give them their generic name—passing as valuable offerings among the great, and employed on very many occasions to denote ardent admiration in the world of courtly gallantry. It is thus we have handed down to us, principally on cups by renowned masters, portraits of the beauties who in those times adorned the ranks of the nobility : the Dianas, the Francescas, the

Lucias, the Proserpines, whom their admirers caused to be portrayed in order to offer them their own likenesses.

It was at Florence, about the year 1410, that Luca della Robbia first introduced his invention; but as soon as the process became known, the greater part of the towns of Italy, especially those of Tuscany, established manufactories, among which a remarkable rivalry soon arose: Pesaro, Gubbio, Urbino, Faenza, Rimini, Bologna, Ravenna, Ferrara, Citta Castellana, Bassano, Venice, emulated each other, and almost all succeeded in giving, as it were, an individual character to their productions.

Pesaro—the place where the earliest workshops of ornamental pottery in Italy were seated, and the processes of which (derived from Luca della Robbia) seem to have blended with the ancient Spanish, or *Majorquaises*—presents to us a design of a rather harsh and stiff character. "The outlines of figures," adds M. Jacquemart, "are drawn in manganese black, the flesh is the colour of the enamel, and the drapery alone is of uniform tint."

It was at Pesaro that the celebrated Lanfranco flourished. The ceramic museum of Sèvres has two of his pieces: it was he who invented the method of applying gold to earthenware, at a time when the early processes of ornamenting this manufacture had ceased to be employed, and had given place to delicate paintings, which, although no longer executed by the most renowned artists of Italy, were nevertheless the work of intelligent pupils who had received the benefit of their teaching and example.

The manufactory at Gubbio had for its founder Giorgio Andreoli, who, both as a sculptor and an artist in majolica, executed works as remarkable in form as in effect. "The palette of mineral colours adopted by Andreoli was the most perfect of the period; and coppery yellows, ruby reds, are frequently used in his works." There are still extant some works signed by this *master* (a title officially conferred on him by a patent of nobility); one is a slab in the Sèvres collection, and another a tablet representing the Holy Family.

Urbino—of which the dukes, especially Guidobaldo II., signalized themselves as the most zealous patrons of ceramic art—became famous through the works of Francesco Xanto, who executed historical subjects on enamelled clay. Xanto had as a successor Orazio Fontana, who has been named "the Raphael of Majolica," and who produced, among other magnificent objects, some vases which, when subsequently seen by Christina of Sweden, so impressed her by their beauty that she offered to exchange for them silver vases of equal size.

It was at the manufactory of Deruta that imaginative subjects on majolica were first introduced; Bassano was famous for its landscapes with ruins; Venice became celebrated for delicate ware with *repoussé* reliefs; Faenza is still proud of her Guido Salvaggio; Florence of her Flaminio Fontana, &c.

Majolica attained to its highest point of brilliancy under the Duke of Urbino whom we have already named, Guidobaldo II., who was ever ready to make any sacrifice in order that this art might be introduced into the manufactories under his patronage. He even obtained from Raphael and Giulio Romano some original drawings to serve as examples; and this feeling having once been inculcated, we soon find artists of renown, such as Batista Franco and Raphael del Colle, tendering their services for the ornamentation of majolica. Thus the productions of this period are distinguishable among all others for harmony of composition and accurate drawing, qualities which render them specially noteworthy (Fig. 36). Then, almost immediately, followed the decline of this art. While flourishing more and more until the middle of the sixteenth century, the art of making majolica had fallen, at the termination of that epoch, into a kind of degenerate industry, swayed by the caprice of fashion, and thereby reduced to mannerism.

Nearly at the commencement of the renovation of ceramic art, Italian artisans had established themselves in various places, which then became so many artistic centres. Eastern Europe had for its earliest instructors three brothers, Giovanni, Tiseo, and Lazio, who settled at Corfu. Flanders was indebted for the knowledge of these processes to Guido of Savino, who took up his abode at Antwerp. And about the year 1520 we find a manufactory at Nuremberg, of which the ware, though materially differing in character from Italian majolica, may still very probably have been derived from Italy.

We may add that letters of the King of France mention that from 1456 there were certain revenues derivable from the " Beauvais Potteries; " and in the twenty-seventh chapter of the first book of " Pantagruel," published in 1535, Rabelais places among the various articles composing the trophy of Panurge, "a saucer, a salt-cellar of clay, and a Beauvais goblet;" which proves, as M. de Sommerard remarks, "that as early as this date, there were manufactured in this city vessels of clay sufficiently good in quality to be placed on the table with silver and pewter utensils;" but it does not naturally follow that France had not long to wait for the man of genius who would soon leave her nothing to covet from Italy.

About the year 1510, in a small village in Périgord, a child was born who, after receiving the rudiments of education, was obliged while still quite young to try to gain a livelihood by his own industry. This child's name was Bernard Palissy. He first learnt the trade of a glazier, or rather of a

Fig. 36.—Cup, Italian Ware. In the Collection of Baron Alph. Rothschild. Taken from MM. Carle Delange and C. Borneman's work.

glass-fitter and painter. This trade, while it initiated him into the principles of drawing, and gave him a certain insight into chemical manipulations, at the same time aroused in him a taste for art and the study of natural sciences. While "painting figures in order to gain his daily bread," as he himself tells us in one of the works he has left behind him, and which gives us the highest opinion of his simple yet energetic nature, he applied himself to the study of the true principles of art in the works of the great Italian painters—the only artists then in repute. Owing to various circumstances the trade of glazier proving unprofitable, he at once began the study of geometry, and soon obtained credit, in the part of the country wherein he dwelt, as "a clever draughtsman of plans." Such comparatively mechanical labour as this could not long suffice for the active vigour of a mind thirsting after progress and discovery. Moreover, Palissy, while employed on his calling as a land-surveyor, had never ceased to give close observation to the structure and composition of geological strata. With the purpose of dispelling the doubts in his mind, and also with the object of obtaining substantial confirmation regarding the system he had already originated, he began to travel. The result of his journeyings was the inauguration of a theory which, after having long been contemptuously

Fig. 37.—A figured Border of an Enamelled Dish, by Bernard Palissy.

rejected by the learned, was nevertheless destined to form the foundation of principles which are now considered as the basis of modern geological science.

But if the certain knowledge which Palissy thought he had acquired as to the early convulsions of the globe had succeeded in satisfying his own mind, the glazier-surveyor (who was now a married man with a family) still remained in straitened circumstances, and was obliged to find some means of avoiding actual want. We must refer to what he himself says more than a quarter of a century later, and when success had completely crowned his efforts, to learn what were his recollections of his early and hazardous experiments in a new channel. "Know," says he, in his expressive language, "that it is twenty-five years since an earthen vessel was shown to me; it was turned, enamelled, and of such exquisite beauty, that from that very moment I began to argue with myself, while remembering observations made derisively to me by some persons when I was painting figures. And seeing that they were beginning to give up the use of these objects in the country where I lived, and that glazing also was not in great demand, I set myself to think that had I but discovered the art of making enamel, I might make earthen vessels and other articles of beautiful appearance; for God had given me the capacity to understand a little about ceramic painting, and from that instant, without in the least regarding my utter ignorance of siliceous substances, I set myself to discover enamels like a man groping in the dark."

It has been much disputed, but we may as well say at once to no purpose, how to assign with certainty a particular locality whence came this object which inspired Palissy; but whatever may have been its origin, it seems to us to be a question of little moment, because at the time when Palissy must have seen it, the Italian manufactories, and even those which were afterwards established in various localities, had succeeded in disseminating their wares far and wide; and, besides this, the works of Palissy, which we still see, bear testimony to a style that was peculiarly his own, and in some measure original.

However this may have been, here we have him seeking out and grinding all kinds of substances, mixing them, and coating with them pieces of ware which he first subjected to the action of an ordinary potter's oven, afterwards to the more powerful heat employed by glass-makers. Then we see him building an oven in his own house—taking into his service a working potter, to whom, on one occasion, when he has no money for the payment of wages, he is obliged to give his own clothes; again we find him turning, single-handed, a mill for grinding his materials which ordinarily required "two powerful men" to work it; then again, wounding his hands in repairing the oven that the fire cracked, and the bricks and mortar of which had become "liquified and vitrified;" so that he is obliged for several days "to eat his soup with his fingers tied up in rags;" pushing the conscientiousness and zeal of an experimentalist so far as to fall down in a state of insensibility on finding that the whole contents of an oven, on which he had been relying, proved to have numerous defects. In despite

BIBERON OF HENRI II WARE.

Or Oiron fayence. (Pourtales' Collection.) Now in the possession of J. Malcolm, Esq.

of his poverty we see him destroying pieces of work that he considered were not quite perfect, though a fair price was offered him for them, merely because "they might bring discredit on him and loss of reputation;" and finally, we see him breaking up and putting into the fire, for want of other fuel, the flooring of his house and the furniture of his humble abode.

The magnificent discovery, brought about by the single initiative of an individual who had said that he would succeed, and who heroically endured all kinds of misery, privations, and humiliations, in order to attain his object, was the labour of not less than fifteen years.

"To console me," relates Palissy, "even those from whom I had a right to expect help laughed at me" (he here alludes to his family—his wife, and children—who had not the same unbounded faith as himself in the ultimate success of his labours); "they paraded the town exclaiming that I was burning the woodwork of my house; thus was my credit injured, and I was looked upon as a fool. Others said I was attempting to make base coin. I went about quite humiliated, ashamed of myself. I owed money in several quarters, and generally had two children out at nurse, and not able to pay the cost. All ridiculed me, saying: 'He deserves to starve because he has given up his trade.'

"Struggling on in this way, at the end of ten years I became so thin that my legs and arms had no roundness of shape left about them; my legs were all of a size (*toutes d'une venue*); so that as soon as I began to walk, the garters with which I fastened my stockings used at once to slip down, stockings and all, on to my heels. . . . For many years, having nothing wherewith to cover my ovens, I was exposed all night long to the winds and the rains, without receiving any help or consolation, except from the screech-owls hooting on one side and the dogs howling on the other. . . . Sometimes I found myself, with all my garments wet through from the rain, going to bed at midnight, or at dawn of day; and when proceeding in this condition to bed, I went reeling along without a light, and stumbling from side to side like a man drunk with wine; I was overcome by previous sorrow, the more so because after long-continued work I saw my labour lost. And on entering my chamber I found a fresh persecution awaiting me—the complaints of my wife—worse than the first, and which now makes me wonder how it was I did not die of grief. . . . I have been in such anguish that many and many a time I fancied I was at death's door."

At last, despite all these obstacles, disappointments, physical and mental suffering, the determined experimentalist succeeded in his anticipations, and gave to the world those works he called *rustics*, and which were so original and so beautiful that they had but to be seen in order to invite attention, and to gain for him all the praise, as well as the profit, he received.

We have just intimated it was at Saintes that Palissy, when in search of immortal fame, underwent his rude apprenticeship. A short time after he had attained these definite results, religious questions having caused some disturbances in Saintonge, the Constable de Montmorency, who had been sent to suppress the Huguenot rising, had an opportunity of seeing Palissy's works: he requested that he should be presented to him, and at once declared himself his friendly protector. And we must take this word protector in its widest sense, for the potter, who had zealously embraced the doctrines of the Reformation, and who subsequently preferred to be imprisoned for life rather than abjure his faith (if he did not die in the Bastille, at least he was imprisoned there at the time of the Massacre of St. Bartholemew), indeed required protection, as much for the exercise of liberty of conscience as for carrying on his artistic labours. After Montmorency had commissioned him to execute some considerable works, which also gained him the patronage of several important personages, he obtained for him the favour of royalty. Palissy was summoned to Paris, and received the title of "inventeur des rustiques figulines du roi et de la reine-mère"—Henri II. and Catherine de Médicis. He was lodged in the Tuileries; and was not long there before he became renowned, not only for his ceramic productions, but also for his scientific knowledge.

In the recent building operations at the Tuileries, on digging a trench in the garden, the workshop of Bernard Palissy was discovered; being recognised by fragments and various pieces of enamelled pottery with figures in relievo. Among these was found a large fragment of the dish of Palissy, known under the name of the Baptismal Dish, on account of the subject represented thereon. In July, 1865, while excavating in the part of the palace where the "Salle des Etats" has been built, the workmen discovered, below the level of the surface soil, two ovens for baking pottery, in a tolerably good state of preservation. One contained pieces of those muffles (*gazettes*) Palissy is said to have invented, and which were employed in baking delicate pieces of work—imprints of various kinds of ornaments and figures in alto-relievo : two of these are described by Palissy himself in the " Devis d'une grotte pour la royne, mère du roy " ("device of a grotto for the queen, the king's mother "), and which he thus indicates in the following sentence :— " I should wish to make certain figures from nature, following her so closely, even to the small hair in the beard and eyebrows, as to make them the natural size." These peculiarities are to be seen in the fragments of the moulds which have been discovered. In the same page Palissy says, " Also there would be another, composed completely of sea-shells of different kinds ; that is to say, the two eyes of two shells, the nose, mouth, and chin, forehead and cheeks, all made out of sea-shells, as well as even the remainder of the

Fig. 38.—Ornamentation on Pottery by Bernard Palissy.

body." This was found in fragments, as also a hand moulded from nature, and holding a sword of ancient make (Fig. 39). Among the fragments moulded from the naked and the draped form, is the one which we give (Fig. 40); it is thus described by Palissy :—"Also for the sake of astonishing mankind, I wished to make three or four (figures) draped, and with their hair dressed in quaint ways, whose dresses and head-dresses shall be of divers linen, cloths, or striped materials so natural that no man would think but it was the object itself which the workman had wished to imitate."*

We thus see how Palissy, called "Maître Bernard des Thuilleries," deserved the esteem of the sovereigns who desired he should be near them.

* "Historical Topography of Ancient Paris in the district of the Louvre and Tuileries." By Berty and Legrand.

M. Jacquemart says of Palissy ware :—"It is remarkable in more ways than one—for its white paste with a shade of yellowish grey, for its hardness, and its infusibility, equalling that of fine earthenware or pipe-clay. These give it a special character, that distinguishes it from Italian productions, the clay of which is of a dirty and dusky red. The enamel has great brilliancy; it is hard, and is not unfrequently wavy (*tresaille*). The colours vary a little, but they are bright—pure yellow, yellow ochre, indigo blue, grey blue, emerald green produced from copper, yellow green, violet brown, and

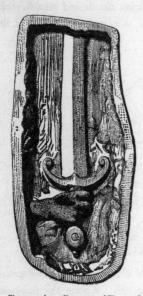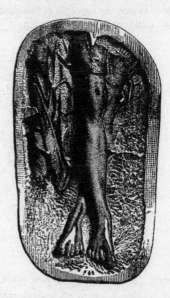

Figs. 39 and 40.—Fragments of Figures of which the Moulds have been found in one of Palissy's Ovens, at the Tuileries.

manganese violet. As for the white, it is somewhat dull, and cannot be compared with Luca della Robbia ware; wherefore the most persevering researches of Palissy, who invented all the processes which he employed in his work, aimed at the attainment of greater brilliancy. The under part of Palissy ware is never of a uniform tone of colour; it is spotted or tinted with blue, yellow, and violet brown.

"It would be exceedingly difficult, not to say impossible, to enumerate the various shapes he was able to give to his enamelled ware. Combining in

himself all the artistic talent of his day, he was at the same time a skilful
designer and an intelligent modeller; and thus he discovered a thousand
resources for the display of elegance and richness; sometimes in the multiplicity of relievos and in the outline of his vases, sometimes in the mere
application of colour. . . . In many of his productions, particularly dishes

Fig. 41.—Goblet, by Bernard Palissy. (Museum of the Louvre.)

and bowls, are seen natural objects represented with astonishing truthfulness
as to form and colour; nearly all these are modelled from nature, and
grouped with perfect taste; from the lower surface, rippled by streams of
water in which fish of the river Seine are swimming, coiled reptiles rise

gracefully from among fossil shells (we must remember that Palissy was a geologist), found in the tertiary strata of Paris; on the *marli* (the sloping edge of the dish), amidst delicate ferns arranged in masses, lizards, crayfish, and large-bodied frogs, climb and jump (Fig. 42). The accuracy of their movements, the truth of tones produced by a limited variety of colours—all indicate a close observer. We must not, however, form our opinion of Palissy from these *rustic* works alone, but also from his vases, where he introduced all the ornamental richness of those times, and on which he took a pleasure in developing all his fertility of composition and his knowledge as a designer. . . . On this point Palissy followed the same law to which all artists of the sixteenth century were subject—he was a worker in precious metals. By their graceful originality, their fringed (*frangeés*) borders, their figured accessories, these vases put us in mind of metal. How could it have been otherwise? Was not Benvenuto Cellini at that time, we will not say the object of all imitations, for this would be an insult to the skilful artists of that period, but at all events the ideal towards which the inspirations of others were directed? As regards the human figure, Palissy's constant endeavour was to approach the Italian type; and as doubtless the school of Fontainebleau furnished him with most of his models, in the greater part of his figures we trace that graceful *elongation* of form, that elegant simplicity, which, in the works of Jean Goujon, fall into mannerism (Figs. 43 and 44).

"Palissy did not limit himself to the production of small and moderate-sized vases for ornamenting sideboards, buffets, tables, and brackets; he raised pottery to the most gigantic proportions in his *rustiques figulines*, intended as ornaments for gardens, grottoes, fountains, and the halls of stately mansions. The castles of Nesle and of Chaulnes, of Reux and of Ecouen, and the garden of the Tuileries, contained some remarkable specimens. All have perished with the devastation of the buildings in which they stood; a single fragment of a capital, preserved in the Museum of Sèvres, proves the truthfulness of the writers of the sixteenth century regarding the monumental creations of the potter of Saintes.

"After the death of Palissy, in 1589, the art which he had created insensibly declined, until soon it almost completely disappeared in France."

This latter remark has reference to the style which was peculiarly of Palissy's own invention, and not to the production of ceramic works generally; though the art failed not to give evidence of a certain vitality, it employed as guides or models the fanciful examples of Italian ware, in preference to the really masterly specimens of the French artist. Among

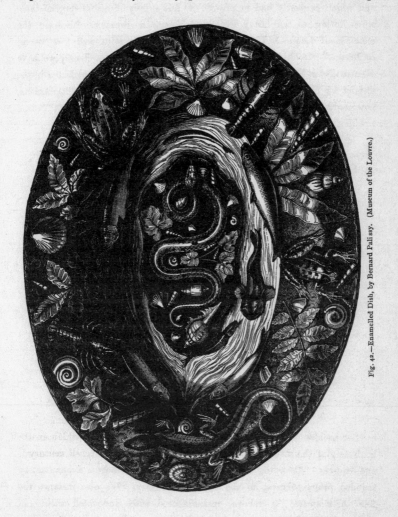

Fig. 42.—Enamelled Dish, by Bernard Palissy. (Museum of the Louvre.)

the different centres of manufacture which, at that period, were deserving of notoriety, we must specially name Nevers, whence came numerous examples characterised by subjects taken from biblical narratives, as well as from

Roman and contemporaneous times; Rouen, where the manufacture probably
was not of an earlier date than the beginning of the seventeenth century,
and which evidently had to provide its full supply of dishes for the table
when, owing to the heavy expenses of war, the courtiers, following the
example of Louis XIV., sent their plate to the mint and "*se mirent
en faïence,*" "took to earthenware," as Saint-Simon says. Lastly we have
Montreuil-sur-Mer, which, if we are to credit the specimens collected in the
district by M. Boucher de Perthes, one of our most learned antiquarians,
possessed a manufactory that produced some remarkable "open-work" vases.

Fig. 43—Four-handled Water-jug.
German ware
of the Sixteenth Century.

Fig. 44.—Egg-shaped Coffee-pot.
German ware
of the Sixteenth Century.

Let us also mention the Dutch pottery, called *Delft ware,* which, in the
beginning of the seventeenth century, began to find a place on all sideboards
and dressers. According to M. Brongniart, these came from a manufactory
founded prior, perhaps, to the sixteenth century. We also instance the
fine earthenware, in relievo, manufactured with undoubted ability in
Germany, especially in the town of Nuremberg. In the Louvre and in
the Cluny Museums may be seen magnificent specimens of enamelled slabs
and vases of architectural forms, ornamented with figures. Majolica was

equally esteemed on the banks of the Rhine. Many specimens are found, dating from the latest years of the sixteenth century, in which identity of form or similarity of *sigles* (earths or clays) to primitive works had led to their being, at first, classified among Italian majolica. However, the majority of these examples, ornamented with escutcheons and arabesques, combined generally with Latin or German inscriptions, bear on the reverse a cipher in Gothic letters, leaving no doubt as to the artist's country.

Now a word on a question we ought not to pass in silence, though it yet remains unanswered, and doubtless will never be explained.

Why is this name of *faïence* commonly given in France, almost from the revival of the ceramic art, to the productions of the new industry? Some say, "because Faenza was the first among Italian manufactories that introduced, generally, painted and ornamented potteries into France, where it acquired great reputation." Others discover in France itself, a small town called Faïence, near Fréjus, in Provence, "where the manufacture of enamelled clays was in full activity before there was any evidence of it elsewhere;" and thus it gave its name to the pottery called *majolica* by the Italians : this would be nothing less than to deprive Luca della Robbia of the merit, if not of the invention, at least of priority. Unfortunately for this last opinion, those who state it cannot bring in support of their assertion any certain details of the nature of the productions ascribed to that locality, and which by their very celebrity ought to have been safe from destruction. Thus it is evident there is here a point of dispute regarding which it is difficult to form a decisive opinion.

Though, in a certain measure, lying out of the province to which our observations have hitherto been limited, we have still to notice a small group of productions which are known by connoisseurs under the title of *faïences fines d'Henri II.;* of these there are not more than forty authenticated specimens. The locality of this manufacture, which seems, so to speak, to have been isolated—for the ware is unlike any contemporaneous productions—is quite unknown. "We only know," says M. Jacquemart, "that most of the examples came from the south-west of France, from Saumur, from Tours, and especially from Thouars. As to the date, it is indelibly inscribed on the vases, some having the salamander of Francis I., others the arms of France with three crescents interlaced, the emblem adopted by Henri II. They consist of cups, ewers, drinking-vases, oval sugar-basins, salt-cellars, and candlesticks. The form is ornate and pure, and is relieved by elegant mouldings. On the clay—a yellowish white, and covered with a crystallized varnish, the basis of which is lead, and consequently is transparent—wind bands of yellow ochre bordered with dark brown, and interlaced with all the inventive richness which characterised the period; small designs in green, violet, black, and occasionally in red, enhance this decoration."

Much search has been made, but, as yet, without any reliable result, for the name of the artist to whom might be attributed the creation of these works, and of the individual style they denote.

However this may be, if England claims the first application of pipe-clay to fine earthenware, the French can, by showing her the *faïence d'Henri II.*, prove that, two hundred years before, an unknown artist in France was setting an example in that art in which England now prides herself.

Fig. 45.—Ornament of a Dish, Italian ware. (Collection of M. le Baron Alph. de Rothschild.).

ARMS AND ARMOUR.

Arms of the Time of Charlemagne.—Arms of the Normans at the Time of the Conquest of England.—Progress of Armoury under the Influence of the Crusades.—The Coat of Mail.—The Crossbow.—The Hauberk and the Hoqueton.—The Helmet, the Hat of Iron, the Cervelière, the Greaves, and the Gauntlet; the Breastplate and the Cuish.—The Casque with Vizor.—Plain Armour and Ribbed Armour.—The Salade Helmet.—Costliness of Armour.—Invention of Gunpowder.—Bombards.—Hand-Cannons.—The Culverin, the Falconet.—The Arquebus with Metal-holder, with Match, and with Wheel.—The Gun and the Pistol.

HE most ancient and authentic document that presents to us a just and almost perfect idea of the arms in use towards the end of the eleventh century, is the celebrated tapestry of Bayeux, of which we have already spoken.

It is sufficient to examine with some attention that complex and illustrated narrative of the conquest of England in 1066, to learn what was the general aspect of war at that period. But any one who has at all studied the ancient historians and the annals of our earliest career as a people, will not fail to recognise, as so many constituent parts combining to form the equipment of war, most of those weapons that were adopted among various races, the contests and the union of which was to give birth to modern nations.

If we can rely on the testimony of some miniatures in manuscripts of the time of Charlemagne, Roman customs are constantly recalled in the costume and arms of the warriors of the eighth and ninth centuries (Fig. 46), "but with the modifications necessarily resulting from contemporaneous corrupt taste," as observed by M. de Saulcy, whom, it may be remarked, we follow step by step, as it were, in the labours which he has conscientiously devoted to the history of warlike arms; "for at that time the helmets, the bucklers, and the swords had assumed forms very unlike the models whereof they were supposed to be an imitation. One can readily imagine that costume had become subjected to the same sort of change as language, corrupted as this was by the admixture of German manners with those of the nations subjected to Rome."

In the middle of the ninth century the Normans disembarking, possessed themselves of Neustria, and introduced among the French nation, with which they at first contended, and at length concluded a peace, an entire series of defensive arms entirely novel in form, if not in their nature. It is then, according to certain learned men, that warriors are seen, in illustrated manuscripts, attired in dresses furnished with small rings or iron scales,

Fig. 46.—Gallo-Romano Soldiers. Fac-simile of Miniatures in the MS. of Prudentius. (Imp. Library of Paris.)

wearing pointed helmets, and using shields cut horizontally above, and terminating at the base in a point more or less sharp.

In the Bayeux tapestry we see the army of William that fought the battle of Hastings composed of three different bodies of troops: the archers, light infantry, armed with arrows and darts; foot-soldiers, or heavy infantry, using weightier arms, and clad in iron mail; and cavalry, in the midst of which figures the Duke William (Fig. 47).

The costume exhibits little variety; only two sorts of accoutrements are observable: one very plain, worn by men who have no helmet, is evidently that of an inferior soldier; the other, covered with iron rings, not interlaced, extends from the shoulders to the knees, and belongs only to warriors whose head-dress is a narrow, conical helmet, more or less sharply pointed, extending behind (*en couvre nuque*) to cover the nape of the neck (Fig. 48), and in front provided with a metal protector for the face, called the *nasal*.

Among the horsemen thus encased in iron, are some who have boots and stirrups, others are without them, and even wear no spurs. Their shields are convex, secured to the arm by a leather strap, generally circular at

Fig. 47.—King William, as represented on   Fig. 48.—Lancer of William's Army.
his seal preserved in England.

top, and terminating in a point below. Some, however, are polygonal and convex, and in the centre show a rather long point.

Offensive arms consist of swords, axes, lances, javelins, and arrows. The swords are long, of uniform width nearly to the extremity which comes abruptly to a point, and have heavy, strong hilts. The axes exhibit no remarkable peculiarity. The spears terminate in an iron point, probably sharpened, and equal in length to one-sixth of the handle. We see also clubs, maces, and, finally, pronged staves (*bâtons fourchus*), doubtless the earliest form of the weapon; these last were subsequently called *bisaguë*, and, with maces and clubs, were ordinarily used by serfs and peasants; the sword and the spear being reserved for freemen.

The sling is not to be found in the hands of any warrior; but it is remarkable that, in the border of the Bayeux tapestry, it is used by a peasant aiming at a bird; from which it may be inferred that the sling had become a mere weapon for field-sport. Moreover, this was also the case with the bow among the French; which was again held in honour after the advent of the Normans, especially since the latter could ascribe to it their success at the battle of Hastings, where Harold, the opponent of William, was killed by an arrow. Nevertheless, the statutes of the Conqueror, who himself excelled with the bow, did not include that weapon among those of the nobility.

From the conquest of the Normans to the Crusades, we scarcely find anything worth notice, except the adoption of a very murderous implement of war, which acquired the name of the flail, or armed whip (*fleau*, or *fouet d'armes*); it was formed of iron balls studded with points, and was attached to the end of a strong staff by small chains. But we come to a period when the events which occurred in Asia had a considerable influence on the arms and the military costume of Europe. The first and principal of the importations due to those distant expeditions was that of the coat of mail, then in common use among the Arabs, and which has since been discovered in the sculptures of the period of the Sassanidæ, a royal race that ruled over Persia from the third to the seventh century.

It is not affirmed that prior to the first crusade we had no knowledge of iron chain-work, of which the Orientals made defensive helmets; but we imitated it only in a heavy and clumsy manner. This armour, which was of ponderous weight, and besides, was far from rendering invulnerable those who were burdened with it, had not displaced the *haubergeons*, the *jacques de fer*, the *brigandines*, the *armures à macles* (Fig. 49), (such were the names given to the cuirasses of leather and of cloth covered with metal plates); but when such defensive armour came to be better known, with all its original good qualities; and when we had learned to make it according to the Oriental method, there was no further delay in adopting that network of iron (*tricot*) at once flexible, light, and, in some degree, impenetrable. However, since the manufacture of ancient armour was more simple, and consequently less costly, it was not altogether abandoned. It is only so late as the time of Philip Augustus and Louis IX. (the thirteenth century) that the use of coats of mail became general; to this some knights attached mail hose, to protect the thighs, legs, and feet (Fig. 50).

In the reign of Louis le Gros (twelfth century) we see the first attempt at a movable vizor adapted to the conical helmet of the Normans; and to the same period must be referred the invention of the crossbow: or, it may rather be said that a stock, or *arbrier*, was added to the bow, which afforded greater facility for stretching the string, and also aided in directing the

Fig. 49.—Norman Archer.

Fig 50.—Jean Sansterre, as represented on his Seal. Reproduced by Meyrick

arrow. This new weapon, after being exclusively used in the chase, appeared in warfare; but, in 1139, Pope Innocent II., confirming the decisions of the Council of Lateran, which had condemned it as too destructive, prohibited its use. The crossbow was not restored to military equipments until the third crusade, under Richard Cœur de Lion, who, having permitted his men to resume the weapon, was subsequently assumed to have invented it.

During the first crusade, barons and knights wore a hauberk of links of iron or steel. Every warrior had a helmet—silver-plated for royalty, of steel for nobles, and of iron for the private soldiers. The crusaders used the lance, the sword, a kind of dagger called *miséricorde*, the club and the battle-axe, the sling and the bow.

In the windows which Suger, minister of Louis VII., caused to be painted for the church of the abbey of Saint-Denis, and which represented the principal events of the second crusade, we see the chiefs of the crusaders still clothed in hauberks of links, or *macles* (plates of iron); the helmet is conical and without the nose-piece (*nasal*); and, lastly, the buckler, formed like a scutcheon, covers the breast, generally suspended from the neck by a leather thong.

Towards the middle of the twelfth century, the iron breastplate is said to have been introduced; it was placed over the chest to support the hauberk, the direct pressure of which being found detrimental to health. But no description of it is to be met with in the romances of chivalry, that furnish the best documentary evidence regarding the armour of the twelfth and thirteenth centuries.

Under Philip Augustus, who, as we know, was one of the leaders of the

Fig. 51.—Helmet of Don Jaime el Conquistador (Armeria Real, Madrid).

third crusade, the conical helmet assumed a cylindrical form; to this was occasionally added a vizor called *ventail*, intended to protect the face. Richard I., King of England, is represented on his seal with this kind of helmet; level with the eyes and also at the height of the mouth are two horizontal slits, which admit of seeing and breathing. Still the use of the conical helmet without vizor or nose-piece was retained even to the thirteenth century in Spain, as is proved by that worn by Jaime I., King of Aragon (Fig. 51), which is preserved in the Armeria Real, Madrid. It is of polished steel, is surmounted by a dragon's head, and portions of it are richly ornamented.

Thus in the third crusade the use of the "coat-of-arms" became general, —a sort of overcoat, if we may so term it, of cloth or of silk stuff, and the purpose of which, at first, was only to mitigate the insupportable effect of the

Fig. 52.—Knight in his Hauberk (after Meyrick).

rays of an Eastern sun on metal armour. This new garment soon served moreover, when made of various colours, to distinguish different nations marching under the standard of the Cross (Fig. 52). It became really a dress of military splendour, was made of the richest stuffs, and embroidered in gold or silver with excessive refinement.

The slingers, who had never been otherwise recruited than from the

lower orders, disappeared from the French armies after the reign of St. Louis.
As for the archers, those of England wore at that time, over the hauberk,
a leather jacket, adopted subsequently by the French archers, and called
jacque d'Anglois.   An old author, in fact, thus mentions it:—

> " C'étoit un pourpoint de chamois ;
> Farci de bourre sus et sous ;
> Un grand vilain jacque d'Anglois,
> Qui lui pendoit jusqu'aux genoux."

The *jacque* having become the fashion in France was soon recognised in
every kind of material more or less costly ; it continued in use until the
end of the fourteenth century ; Charles VI. wore one of black velvet during
a journey he made in Brittany.

The casque, or helmet, from that time enclosing the head entirely,

Fig. 53.—Helmet of Hughes, Vidame of Chalons.
(End of Thirteenth Century.)

Fig. 54.—Tournament Helmet, screwed on the
Breastplate.   (End of Fifteenth Century.)

assumed, under St. Louis, the form of two truncated cones " réunis par leurs
grandes bases."   In addition to the helmet there was also worn at that time
the *chapel de fer,* which at first was only a simple cap underneath the hood
of the hauberk ; but when, curtailing the hood, a brim was added to the cap,
it thus became a hat almost of the form of the felts now in use.   To
protect the neck there was also attached to the rim of the hat a tippet of
mail, falling on the shoulders, and called *camail.**   The iron cap then took

* Probably an abbreviation, or corruption, of cap-mail.—[ED.]

CASQUE, MORION, AND HELMETS,
With and without vizors, from the Armeria Real at Madrid.

the name of *coiffre* or *cervelière*, and later it became a kind of reversed pot, concealing the entire head, and kept in position by its weight only (Fig. 53).

Again; there had for some time been manifested a movement which gradually caused the knights to be entirely cased in iron. A king of Scotland, contemporary with Philip Augustus, is represented on his seal with a plate of armour intended to protect the elbow. The knee-cap followed.

Fig. 55.—Plain Armour of the Fifteenth Century, about 1460. (Museum of Artillery, Paris.)

Under Philip the Bold, successor of St. Louis, the iron *grévières* (greaves), or half leg-pieces, protecting the front of the legs, were adopted. In the reign of Philip the Fair we have the first example of an iron gauntlet with its fingers separate and jointed: previously it was merely an inflexible piece covering the back of the hand. About the same time the *cervelière*, either flat or spherical, became pointed at the top, and took the name of *bassinet;* but this bassinet was unlike the casque which, in the following century, retained that name and was made completely closed. The exact period of the transition from mailed armour to that of plain iron or steel, called also plate-armour, dates from the first thirty years of the fifteenth century (Fig. 55).

The annals of Florence contain a statute of 1315, requiring every

Fig. 56.—Convex Armour of the Fifteenth Century, said to be that of Maximilian. (Museum of Artillery, Paris.)

horseman serving in a campaign to have a helmet, a breastplate, gauntlets, cuishes, and leg-pieces, all of iron; but in France and England the whole of these pieces were not adopted until somewhat later. In the reigns of Philip V. and Charles IV. we see the ventail of the helmet with a grating, and the vizor opening with a hinge. The bassinet, lighter than the helmet, was at first worn by the knight when no hostile encounter was anticipated; but subsequently, and at an early date, the vizor was added to the bassinet, as well as to the casque; and then it became as much used as the helmet, which, towards the end of the fourteenth century, was abandoned.

About the same period some portions of iron horse-armour began to make their appearance. We find entered in the inventory of the

Fig. 57.—Crossbow Men protected by Shield-bearers. Fifteenth Century. After a Miniature from the Chronicles of Froissart. (MS. Bibl. Imp. de Paris.)

armour of Louis X., a *chanfrein* (a plate of iron fastened on the horse's forehead).

The crossbow, for some time prohibited by ecclesiastical authority, was the weapon most in use at the period spoken of; as having the double advantage of being drawn with more power than the ordinary bow, and of throwing its arrows to a longer distance with greater precision. Historians say that at Crécy, in 1346, there were fifteen thousand crossbow men in the French army. The Genoese were considered the most skilful in Europe; and next,

those of Paris. A manuscript in the British Museum shows them wearing
iron helmets, *brassières*,* and leg-pieces ; and for body-covering, jackets with
long, hanging sleeves. While the bowmen had both hands occupied in
discharging their arrows, shield-bearers were employed to protect them by
means of large bucklers (Fig. 57).

In the year 1338 the use of firearms is for the first time noted in France.
But we think it right to reserve all we have to say of these modern
offensive weapons until our history of the ancient system of armour is
finished. Considering the early imperfections of firearms, the old system
must have long continued, especially among combatants of noble degree—
for they affected contempt for the new warlike equipments, by means of
which personal valour became in a manner useless and could no longer
ensure victory in battle.

Under John the Good, that is, in the middle of the fourteenth century,
plain armour was generally adopted; the long coat of mail, heavier and
less convenient, was entirely abandoned; but chain-armour still covered
certain parts of the body not yet protected by iron plates. The *bassinet*,
then very pointed, was furnished with mail, covering the neck and a portion
of the shoulders. The upper part of the arm was protected by a half-armlet,
called the *épaulette*, but the lower part was provided with mail.

Ornaments began to be introduced in armour in the reign of Charles V.;
until that time it had a simple and plain appearance. For instance ;
the *camail* of the *bassinet* is embroidered on the shoulders with gold and
silver, and the point surmounting it is decorated with an imitation of foliage
—an ornament which, according to the " Chronicle of Du Gueslin," had the
disadvantage of presenting a kind of handle to an opponent. The cuirass, to
which it was then deemed sufficient to impart a bright polish, or to paint in
ordinary colours, sometimes bright, sometimes dark, began to be engraved
and chased towards the end of the following reign.

In the time of Charles VI. there was introduced, for the first time, four
or five flexible plates, called *faldes*, which protected the lower part of the
stomach without impeding the movements of the body. A little later
tassettes were added; they were attached to the top of the thigh to guard
the hips and the groin. It appears that at this period the artisans of Milan

---

* Or *brassarts*—pieces to protect the upper part of the arms.—[Ed.]

were especially renowned for the manufacture of armour; for Froissart relates that Henry IV., King of England, when Earl of Derby,* and preparing to enter the lists with the Duke of Norfolk, requested armour from Galeas, Duke of Milan, who sent it with four Milanese armourers. The swords and spears made at Toulouse and at Bordeaux were also held in great repute; so also were the double-handed swords in use from the middle of the thirteenth century, and manufactured at Lubeck, in Germany. The steel helmets of Montauban were also much in request.

Towards the commencement of the fifteenth century, engines of war, distinct from those in which powder was used, had attained a remarkable degree of perfection. When John the Fearless, Duke of Burgundy, marched upon Paris in 1411, there was with his army a considerable number of machines called *ribaudequins*, a species of gigantic crossbow drawn by a horse, and which with enormous strength threw javelins to a great distance.

Under Charles VII., the breastplate of the cuirass was composed of two parts: one covered the breast; the other, reaching to the hips, protected the stomach, and was attached to the former by clasps and leather straps. Generally the breastplate was convex.

Taught by the disastrous defeat of Agincourt,—where ten thousand men, of whom eight thousand were of the nobility, had fallen, owing to the precision and the celerity of the fire of the English archers,—Charles VII. instituted in France the *franc archer* (Fig. 58), who wore the *salade* and the jacket or *brigandine*, and carried the dagger, the sword, the bow, the quiver or crossbow *garnie*. These archers were exempt from all taxes or imposts; their equipments were declared not distrainable for debts, and during war they received pay at the rate of four livres a month.

The *salade*, a part of armour which has remained particularly celebrated, and the name of which has been applied subsequently to helmets of divers forms, is pre-eminently the helmet of the epoch of Charles VII. At first it was a head-dress for war, composed of a simple cap (*timbre*), that covered the top of the head, with a pendent piece of metal of greater or less length at the back, which sometimes was made for protecting the neck, and

---

* This title is not chronologically correct. Henry of Bolingbroke had been created Duke of Hereford nearly a year before his intended combat with Norfolk at Coventry, in 1398; when the king, Richard II., interfered, and banished both nobles from the kingdom.—[ED.]

sometimes to guard a portion of the shoulders. Towards the end of the fifteenth century there was added to the salade a small vizor, that was gradually lengthened downwards to near the upper lip, and in which a

Fig. 58.—Franc Archers (Fifteenth Century), from the Painted Hangings of the Town of Rheims.

narrow opening was then made for the sight. In the reign of Louis XII. the salade received a chin-piece, the lower part of which was a *gorget*, that surrounded and protected the neck. The top of the cuirass had a cord, to which was attached the salade; and this helmet, so different to the primitive salade, continued to bear the same name (Fig. 59).

The *brigandine*, recalling the early armour abandoned for the coat of mail, was composed of small plates of steel or iron arranged on a strong piece of leather, and stitched or fixed with wire, in the form of the scales of a fish. A decree of Peter II., Duke of Brittany, issued in 1450, ordered the nobles to equip themselves as archers, or in brigandine, if they knew how to use arrows; but otherwise, to be provided with *guisarmes*, with good salades, and leg-armour; each noble was to be attended by one *coustillier*,

Fig. 59.—Knights in complete Armour, with the *Salade*. (End of Fifteenth Century.) A Single Combat, taken from "The Triumph of Maximilian," by Burgmayer, after a drawing by Albert Dürer.

and to have two good horses. The *guisarme* was a sort of two-edged and pointed javelin. The *coustillier* was a foot-soldier, or a horseman, whose duty it was to act as servant to the nobleman, and to carry the *coustille*, a long, slender sword, triangular or square, apparently resembling the foil in our fencing-rooms.

About this period French noblemen displayed much magnificence in the adornment of the *chanfrein* of their horses. For instance, we know that at the siege of Harfleur, in 1449, the charger of the Count de Saint-Pol had on its head a massive gold chanfrein, of the most delicate work, valued at not

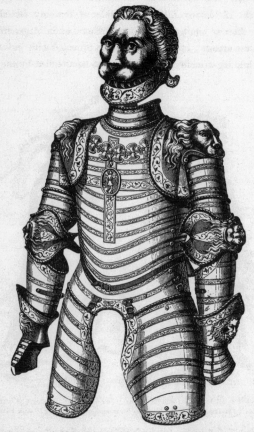

Fig. 60.—Armour ornamented with Lions, supposed to be that of Louis XII. (Museum of Artillery, Paris.)

less than twenty thousand crowns. In the same year, at the siege of Bayonne, the Count de Foix entered the conquered city mounted on a horse whose chanfrein of polished steel was enriched with gold and precious stones to the value of fifteen thousand gold crowns.

Half a century later—that is, in the reign of Charles VIII. and that of Louis XII.—chargers wore, besides the chanfrein, the *manefaire*, protecting the neck, the *poitrail*, the *croupière*, the *flancois*, which respectively covered the chest, the back, and the flanks of the horse; and to these was added another piece of armour placed under the tail.

Of the date of Louis XII., we still see embossed suits of armour ornamented with fluting, sometimes blended with beautiful engraved work executed in the metal by the use of aquafortis, or subjects in relievo produced by embossing: ornamentation of this nature elevated the equipments of the warrior to real works of art (Fig. 60).

Louis XII. was the first to admit Greek mercenaries into his army. These were named *stradiots ;* they tendered their military services equally to both Turks and Christians. The armour of these troops consisted of a cuirass with sleeves and gauntlets in mail, and over this a jacket; on their head a vizorless helmet was worn. The stradiots were armed with a large sword, called a *braquemart*, much resembling the Turkish sword, but with a cross-handle; the sword and its scabbard were ornamented with Grecian devices. They carried in addition several small arms at the saddle-bow, and also a *zagaye*, a very long lance tipped at both extremities with iron.

At this period also was introduced the *pertuisane*,* the blade of which, wider than that of the lance, formed a crescent immediately above the handle.

There were at that time two kinds of crossbows—one for discharging bolts, the other for bullets. The bow was slung by means of a *moulinet*, a kind of hand-winch.

Embossed and fluted armour was not the only kind used in France and in Italy at the end of the fifteenth and the commencement of the following century. The monuments in the former country of the time of Louis XII., and on the other side of the Alps, show how prevalent was a peculiar description of plain armour, whereof the cuirass, which was longer than that of the embossed armour, had a rib or raised line in the middle. This rib, which completely altered the character of the cuirass, in that it served to turn aside the thrust of the lance, became increasingly distinctive as the seventeenth century drew near.

In the reign of Francis I. embossed and ribbed armour were equally

* *Anglice,* partisan—a kind of pike or lance.—[ED.]

used (Fig. 61). In the Museum of Artillery, in Paris, is preserved the armour which that king wore at the battle of Pavia. The body is longer

Fig. 61.—Damaskeened Armour of the end of the Sixteenth Century. (Portrait of François, Duc d'Alençon, from Montfaucon's "La Monarchie Françoise.")

than in the cuirass of the preceding century, the rib in the centre is more raised, the gusset of the shoulder-piece is made of several movable plates, and of large size. The *casque*, a generic name given since those times to all descriptions of head-armour, assumed a comfortable and elegant shape, which was maintained as long as the use of armour continued.

Another cuirass of the same date, still longer in the body, was made to turn up towards the lower extremity, and then took an inward bend to fit the hip. It was made with movable plates overlapping from below; this allowed the wearer to stoop, which it was almost impossible to do when the breast-piece and the back-piece were in one. Sometimes these plates were only three or four in number over the stomach, and the others over the breast were only represented, not genuine plates.

The armour called *à éclises*, or *à écrevisse*, worn at a certain period by the halberdiers, must not be passed over; it received this name because the cuirass was made of horizontal plates (*éclisses*), three or four inches in width, which, though they covered the entire body, did not in any way impede its movements.

We must, however, refer to a peculiarity in this armour which prevented its general adoption; it was that as the movement or "play" of the *éclisses* made it convenient to wear, so from this flexibility it was found that the plates frequently became disconnected, and thus left a part of the body defenceless. In making the *éclisses* to overlap from below, regard was had to the usual direction of a sword-cut or dagger-thrust, which usually came from below; but there was all the more danger from blows of the *martel**
and battle-axe, the stroke of which weapons was directed downwards.

Bronzed armour came in about the middle of the sixteenth century, and was somewhat commonly worn in 1558; it was introduced on account of its being far more easily kept clean than polished steel. For the same reason black armour was tried, but the engravings and chasings, the gildings and damaskeenings were more effective on the greenish ground; consequently black varnish was given up in favour of bronze. At the end of the sixteenth century, and during the long civil wars which desolated France, armour took a variety of shapes, and as regards ornamentation at least, there was generally to be seen a strange medley of the style of the previous century

---

* *Martel-de-fer*—a weapon combining a hammer and pick; used by cavalry in the Middle Ages, to damage and destroy armour. It was generally hung at the saddle-bow.—[ED.]

with that of the period (Fig. 61). However, the decline of the use of armour, which became in a measure inevitable, was at hand.

De la Noue, an eminent Huguenot officer of the time of Charles IX., says, in his "Discours Militaires"—" The penetrating power of pikes and arquebuses has very naturally led to the adoption of armour stronger and more capable of great resistance than formerly. It is now so heavy that one is laden with anvils rather than protected by armour. Our men-at-arms and light cavalry in Henry II.'s time presented a much finer appearance, with their helmets, their brassarts, tassets,* and the morion,† carrying the lance with a flag; their armour was not so heavy but that a strong man was able to support its weight for twenty-four hours; but those of the present day are so ponderous that a young knight of thirty has his shoulders quite crippled."

Thus, in endeavouring to make the resistance of armour keep pace with the improvement in new warlike engines, they rendered it useless; because the weight was intolerable, especially in warm weather, during long marches, or in lengthened combats. Having vainly tried to make suits of armour invulnerable, men began to leave off wearing such portions as were of minor importance, which by degrees were entirely discontinued. Under Louis XIII. we see armour undergoing further modifications, but of fashion rather than of utility: finally, there is every reason to think that the magnificent armour presented by the Republic of Venice to Louis XIV., in 1668, and which is now to be seen in the Museum of Artillery in Paris, was one of the latest sets made in Europe.

Let us now retrace our steps to examine a series of arms, the gradual adoption of which was destined to completely change the art of warfare.

It is now the almost universal opinion that the invention of gunpowder, —assumed to have been discovered in 1256, or at all events its application to artillery, which first dates from 1280,—is due to Berthold Schwartz, an Augustin friar, born at Fribourg. Some writers, however, make these dates a century later, and affirm that powder and cannons were first known from 1330 to 1380. Nevertheless, the employment of artillery only became general during the wars of Charles-Quint and of Francis I., that is, towards 1530, or two centuries after its invention.

---

* *Tassets*—parts of the cuirass.

† *Morion*—a kind of helmet, usually worn by foot-soldiers.—[ED.]

But perhaps in place of giving, as we have done, the unconditional acceptation to the word *artillery* which it now has, we ought perhaps to have said artillery used with gunpowder; for long before the invention of gunpowder the word *artillery* was employed when speaking of all machines or engines of war (Fig. 62). Thus in the middle of the thirteenth century we find among the *personnel* of the *artillery* a grand master of the crossbow men, masters of the engines, of the cannoniers (the word *cannon* was even then applied to the tube forming one of the principal portions of an engine

Fig. 62.—Engine for hurling Stones; taken from a Miniature of the Chevalier au Cygne. (Bibl. Imp. de Paris, No. 340, S. F.)

for hurling projectiles), and in 1291 we see Philip the Fair appointing a grand master of the artillery of the Louvre.

In order to follow methodically the progress of the manufacture of arms such as we shall call novel, we will, in the first place, treat separately of the engines of large calibre which were first employed, and then of portable arms.

The earliest allusion to cannons in France is found in 1338, in an account of the treasurer of war, wherein we read:—" To Henri de Vaumechon, for buying powder and other necessaries for cannons," which had been used at the siege of Puy-Guilhem, in Périgord.

In Froissart, we next find that, in 1340, the inhabitants of Quesnoy, when repelling the attack of the French, made use of bombards and cannon which hurled huge bolts at the besiegers. But the statement of Villani, that the English were indebted to the employment of artillery for the victory of Crécy, in 1346, must be treated as a pure invention, because it is certain that the firearms which may have been in use at that time were in no way suited to field warfare ; and that they were only employed with the older engines in the attack and defence of fortresses. Not only did their cumbrous weight and the rude construction of their carriages render them extremely

Fig. 63.—Bombards on fixed and rolling carriages. (From the MSS. 851 and 852, Bibl. Imp. de Paris.)

difficult of transport, but, intended as they were to be employed as catapults, they were generally constructed for hurling heavy projectiles, by causing these to describe a curved line, like modern shells ; and their shape is, in fact, much more like that of our mortars than of cannon (Fig. 63).

" It would seem," says M. de Saulcy, " that, in loading them, hollow cylinders (manchons), or movable chambers, were used ; in which the charge was previously laid, and these fitted, by means of a wedge, into the body of the piece. Sometimes these cylinders were at the side, and formed a right angle with the axis of the piece, but usually they fitted into the breech, of which they formed a prolongation."

The name *bombards,* which we have just used, and which is derived, as we may conclude, from the Greek *bombos* (noise), was the first employed for designating cannon; but these engines were so imperfect in principle, and so feeble in power, that catapults, which had played so signal a part in sieges during the Middle Ages, were used in preference when very heavy projectiles had to be hurled (Fig. 64).

Originally the piece rested, as it were, fixedly on a massive support; but soon the means of sighting had to be considered: thus we see depicted in early manuscripts pieces that could be moved up and down by means of

Fig. 64.—Mangonneau; an Engine of War of the Fifteenth Century. (Miniature in the MS. 7,239, Bibl. Imp. of Paris.)

trunnions; or which were elevated or depressed for firing by a sort of tail, or long projection behind the tube; at other times the muzzle of the cannon is sustained by a fork more or less buried in the ground. This bombard, attached to a platform on wheels, received the denomination of *cerbotana ambulatoria;* this last word conveying the idea of the movability of the engine.

We have seen that projectiles were of stone, but there is no doubt

that from the fourteenth century they were also made of metal; that was
nothing new, for ancient engines of war, including the sling, threw leaden
balls and masses of red-hot iron. No doubt it was with the object of giving
the largest size possible to projectiles of artillery by means of powder, that
stone was used; which, in the state of the art at that time, was much
better adapted than metal for large balls.

Christine of Pisa, who wrote in the time of Charles VI. the " Livre
des Faits d'Armes et de Chevalrie," has left us a collection of very interesting
details of the condition of artillery used with powder, which, as early as the
fifteenth century, had become much more extended than would be easily
believed; moreover, in the descriptions this author gives of armaments, or
of narratives of battles, we almost always still see catapults, the large crossbows, &c., appearing by the side of cannon; a certain proof that the use
of powder found its equivalent in more than one instance in the ancient
means of the propulsion of projectiles.

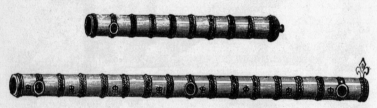

Fig. 65.—Earliest Models of Cannon. In the Tower of London.

Valturio, an Italian writer, whose treatise on military art was first
printed in 1472, has described and drawn all the engines of war then in use.
Cannons are not forgotten. We observe that the greater number of
these pieces have no longer any box forming a movable chamber; this
implies an important advance in the art of making them; but, on the other
hand, these cannons, bound with cords to a block of wood, or resting on
platforms, must have been very difficult to move.

At this period pieces of the largest calibre, which projected enormous
balls of stone, were more commonly called *bombards;* mortars, the very short
cannons throwing heated projectiles; cannons, pieces of medium calibre
carrying iron projectiles (Fig. 65); culverins, the long pieces loaded with
leaden balls, which, as well as the powder, were rammed in with an iron rod;

hand-cannons, or *bâtons à feu* (Fig. 66), were in a manner portable, for if they were handled by one man, it was never without his having recourse to another for firing them.

This last-named term, *bâtons à feu*, like that of *cannon*, existed before the invention of gunpowder. As swords and lances had often been designated under the generic name of *bâtons*, it followed that the name which implied arms in general should also be applied to the earliest portable firearms. In

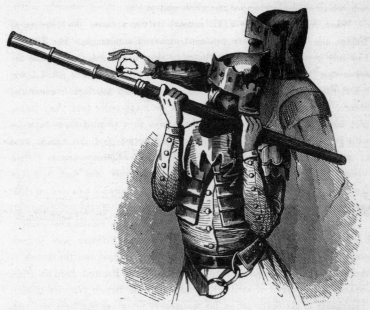

Fig. 66.—Hand Cannon (or *Bâton à feu*), taken from a piece of Tapestry belonging to the Church of Notre Dame de Nantilly, Saumur.

ancient royal ordinances we even see the term *gros bâtons* used to designate large pieces of artillery.

According to M. de Saulcy, the most important improvement ever made in artillery is certainly that which consisted in placing a gun with trunnions on a carriage *à flasques*—upright beams of wood, between which the gun can oscillate, and united by cross-pieces; this carriage was mounted on wheels, and admitted of the gun being inclined by the simple use of a

wedge of wood placed under the breech. But, strangely enough, it is most
difficult to state precisely the date of this improvement. Nevertheless,
circumstances tend to the belief that it was between 1476 and 1494—that
is, during the reigns of Louis XI. and of Charles VIII.—that they succeeded
in making pieces of all calibres carrying iron shot, and also in solidly fixing
the trunnions, which not only supported the weight, but also resisted the
recoil of the cannon. The carriages for these guns were mounted on wheels.
From this period the art of fortifying towns underwent a complete revolution, which suddenly changed the whole system.

When, in 1494, Charles VIII. entered Italy to conquer the kingdom of
Naples, the French artillery produced universal admiration. The Italians
had only iron guns, drawn by bullocks in rear of the army, and more for
appearance than for use. After the first discharge it was some hours
before the gun was ready for a second. The French had lighter cannon of
bronze, drawn by horses, and moved with so much order that their transport hardly delayed the march of the army; they planted their batteries
with incredible promptitude, considering the period, and the rounds were
as quickly delivered as they were well aimed. Cotemporaneous Italian
writers say that the French used almost exclusively iron shot, and that
the guns, both of large and small calibre, were admirably balanced on their
carriages.

Yet no single specimen, or even a drawing, of this remarkable artillery
has been handed down to us. The Museum of Artillery does, indeed,
possess one small piece, on which, between the trunnions and the breech, is
this inscription :—" Presented by Charles VIII. to Bartemi, Lord of Pins,
captain of the bands of artillery, in 1490." This cannon presents nothing
remarkable in its construction, for we already recognise the form, one that
has scarcely varied since then, and which, it seems, was definitely adopted
under Louis XII. and Francis I. Of this period we still have two magnificent bronze cannons. They were found at Algiers in 1830; the porcupine,
the salamander, and the fleur-de-lys that ornament them, made their
origin known.

Artillery, which in the reign of Charles VIII. had become an important
arm, and had, besides, the prestige of success in Italy, became a subject to
which particular attention was given in succeeding reigns. But, we again
say, the true principles of manufacture and mounting were already well

ascertained, and only improvements in matters of detail remained to be discovered.

The Armoury Real of Madrid contains a curious *dragonneau*,* cast at Liège in 1503, which figured in the siege of Santander in 1511 (Fig. 67). The carriage, consisting of a single piece of carved oak, is by its delicacy and finish worthy of sustaining this masterpiece of bronze-work, which presents a double interest, first as regards art, and then on account of the rapid advance already made in firearms; for this *dragonneau* has a double barrel, and is loaded at the breech.

Fig. 67.—Double-barreled Dragonneau. Armoury Real of Madrid.

Having arrived at this point, let us again retrace our steps, in order to note, and rapidly follow from its origin, the progress of firearms.

The earliest of these used in the middle of the fourteenth century were called hand-cannon, and were merely formed of an iron tube pierced with a vent, without stock or lock.

A manuscript of that period represents a warrior who, standing on one of those little movable towers then forming part of the siege *matériel*, is shooting a stone with a gun of this description. The piece is resting on the parapet. By the side a sling is placed with its stone—a circumstance which

* So called, it may be presumed, from its form and make.—[ED.]

indicates the relative power of the hand-cannon, as no doubt each engine was to be used alternately. In another place is a horseman holding a small gun with a prolongation; the muzzle is supported by a prong fixed on the pommel of the saddle. Thus it was impossible for him to take aim, and he applied the fire with his hand.

A little later, to prevent the effect of the recoil, there was added below the barrel, a little short of the centre, a sort of hook, intended to serve the purpose of checking the piece. When fired, it was supported on a fork or on a wall; hence the name of *arquebuse à croc*, which took the place of that of *canon à main*.

Fig. 68.—Arquebusier. Drawn and Engraved by J. Amman.

The *arquebuse à croc* sometimes weighed from fifty to sixty pounds, measured from five to six feet in length, and in principle was chiefly adapted for firing from a wall; it was lightened a little that it might be used by foot-soldiers, who, however, never fired it without a fixed or a movable rest.

The inconvenience of applying fire with the hand, which, moreover, prevented the right direction of the missile, was soon partially superseded by adapting to the barrel a stock to fire from the shoulder, and a lock for a match, called a *serpentin*, which had only to be let down to ignite the powder at the touch-hole. This was the matchlock arquebus still used by certain Eastern nations in our time, and which secured victory to the Spaniards at the battle of Pavia.

Although the matchlock arquebus, which was made lighter, and was then called *mousquet*, continued to be the usual arm of infantry until the time of Louis XIII., many serious objections to the use of the *serpentin* continued. It compelled the soldier always to have a lighted match, or some means of striking a light. Besides, for nearly each shot it was necessary so to regulate the match that the end of it, which was placed in the head of the *serpentin* (lock), should come exactly into the priming-pan;

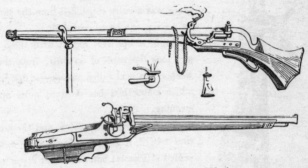

Fig. 69.--Arquebus with Wheel and Match.

then the priming-pan had to be opened; these operations were, so to speak, impossible for mounted men, who at the same time had to manage their horses.

About 1517 the Germans invented the screw-plate called *à rouet*,—wheel-lock (Fig. 69).

To the Spaniards is due the merit of the improvement that followed, the type of which is still in a measure perpetuated in our percussion guns; which, in their turn, have just been replaced by the needle-gun. The Spanish screw-plate, often called the *miquelet* screw-plate, had on the outside a spring, which pressed, at the extremity of its movable limb, on one of the catches of the hammer; when the gun was cocked the other catch pressed against a pin which projected from the inside and traversed the screw-plate; this pin could be removed, and then the spring acted on the hammer,

Fig. 70.—Battle-axe and Pistol of the 16th Century. (Museum of Artillery, Paris.)

which was no longer held back; the flint (for at that time a flint was fitted to the gun) struck upon a ribbed plate of steel forming part of the cover of the priming-pan, the action of the flint on the plate produced the fire.

Among the arms in use during the sixteenth century was one called *petrinal* or *poitrinal* (petronel), on account of the bent stock, which rested on the chest. This short and heavy arquebus, which could only throw balls, but of a very large size, to a short distance, was usually suspended from the shoulder by a strap or a broad cross-belt.

Light troops were armed with these guns, and took the name of *carabins*; from this the weapon was next called *carabine*—a designation which since then has received quite another meaning.

Then followed the *pistoles* and the *pistolets*, thus named, it is said, because they were invented at Pistoia; but, with other etymologists, we can also believe that they owed the name to the fact of their bore being of equal diameter with that of the *pistole*, a coin of the time. The earliest pistols were made with wheels (*à rouet*), and the barrel did not measure more than a foot in length. Subsequently they varied in shape and in use; some were made which fired several shots in succession, and in other cases they attempted to combine a pistol with the dagger or the battle-axe (Fig. 70, &c.). This is a notably fine specimen.

We must not forget to note, in what may be called *les armes de luxe*, the joint application of the match-holder and the wheel to highly-finished arms, this combination being available.

The screw-plate *à miquelet*, improved by French experiments, led to the mechanism called flint-lock (*fusil*). There were also then pistols and arquebuses with flint-locks, as formerly there had been pistols and arquebuses with wheels. Subsequently the explanatory became the absolute term, and the entire weapon was known as *fusil*.

Fig. 71.—Banner of the Sword-cutlers of Angers.

CARRIAGES AND SADDLERY.

THE horse has been described by Buffon as "the noblest conquest made by man." Historians, both sacred and profane, inform us that the conquest dates from the most remote ages. In the Book of Job we have this magnificent description:—"Then the Lord said, Hast thou given the horse strength? hast thou clothed his neck with thunder? Canst thou make him afraid as a grasshopper? the glory of his nostrils is terrible. He paweth in the valley, and rejoiceth in his strength: he goeth on to meet the armed men. He mocketh at fear, and is not affrighted; neither turneth he back from the sword. The quiver rattleth against him, the glittering spear and the shield. He swalloweth the ground with fierceness and rage: neither believeth he that it is the sound of the trumpet. He saith among the trumpets, Ha, ha; and he smelleth the battle afar off." The sacred writer is here referring expressly to the fiery animal trained for war, and obedient to the master who has tamed him.

Xenophon, in his "Treatise on Horsemanship" and his "Instructor of Cavalry," and Diodorus in his "Histories," are among the Greeks who adduce the most numerous testimonies to the honour in which equestrian exercises were held. Among the Latins, Virgil, in reference to the funereal games celebrated by Acestes in honour of Anchises, tells us that the Roman youth were taught equestrian art as practised by the Trojans. The horse and

chariot races, which took place at the solemn games in Greece, have always
been justly celebrated; as were those which continued in Rome and in all
the great cities of the Roman world until the fifth or sixth century.

We are disposed to believe that the use of the saddle-horse and the

Fig. 72.—The Carruca or Pleasure-Carriage, drawn by a pair of Horses, dating from the Fifth to the Tenth Century. (Taken from a MS. of the Ninth Century, in the Royal Library at Brussels.)

carriage-horse was introduced about the same time. But it seems that
chariots were rarely mounted by any but chiefs, who fought from that
ambulatory elevation while squires managed the horses.

To Cyrus the Great is ascribed the first idea of arming chariots with

scythes, which cut to pieces in every direction those who opposed the progress of the vehicle, or who were thrown down by the violence of the shock.
The same war-carriages were found among the Gauls; for a king named
Bituitus, having been taken prisoner by the Romans, appeared in his chariot
armed with scythes in the triumphal procession of the general who had
conquered him.

Riding on horseback was not only practised, but was carried to the
highest degree of perfection, among the nations of antiquity; and the use of
chariots was, in former times, almost general in war and on certain state

Fig. 73.—Cart drawn by Oxen, end of the Fifteenth Century. (Taken from the "Chroniques de Hainault,"
MS. in the Royal Library at Brussels.)

occasions. The Romans, and in imitation of them the Gauls who prided
themselves on being skilful carriage-builders, had several sorts of wheeled
vehicles. Those adopted by the Romans and the Gauls, but discountenanced
by the Franks, who preferred to ride on horseback, were the *carruca*, or
carruque, with two wheels and a pair of horses (Fig. 72), richly ornamented with gold, silver, and ivory; the *pilentum*, a four-wheel carriage
with a cloth canopy; the *petoritum*, an open carriage suitable for rapid
travelling; the *cisium*, a basket-carriage drawn by mules, and used for long
journeys; and finally, various carts—the *plaustrum*, the *serracum*, the *benne*,

the *camuli* (trucks), &c. These last, which were chiefly employed as field-carts, continued in use even after pleasure-carriages had entirely disappeared. There remained, however, independent of mule-litters, the *basterna* and *carpentum*, state-carriages of the Merovingian period; but only queens and ladies of high rank, who were unequal to long journeys on horseback, indulged in such means of locomotion, while men—even kings and high personages—would have blushed to be conveyed like "holy relics," as picturesquely expressed by one of Charlemagne's courtiers; but certainly not at the period of the "lazy kings," when, as Boileau has well said,—

> "In Paris, four oxen, in pace soft and slow,
> Drew the indolent monarch, when airing he'd go."

"Chivalry," wrote M. le Marquis de Varenne, "the exercises of which were the image of war, rendered horsemanship a new art always indispensable in the education of the nobility; and *chevalier* soon became synonymous with a man of good birth." "The Book of Facts," by the "Bon Chevalier Messire Jean le Maingre, called *Baucicaut*, Marshal of France," written in the beginning of the fifteenth century, enumerates the exercises which a youth aspiring to the title of a gentleman had to undergo:—"They endeavoured to leap (*sailler*) upon a charger, fully armed; *item*, leaped, without placing the foot in the stirrup, on a charger in all its armour; *item*, leaped from the ground a-straddle on to the shoulders of a tall man on a large horse, seizing the man by the sleeve with one hand, without other assistance; *item*, placing one hand on the saddle-bow of a large charger, and the other near the ears, taking him by the mane, and from the level ground jumping to the other side (*côté*) of the charger."

The Chevalier Bayard, while yet page to the Duke of Savoy, and only seventeen years of age, performed, as his historian relates, wonders in the meadows of Ainay, at Lyons, before King Charles VIII., "in leaping on his charger," and by his management of it creating a favourable impression of his merits. This will suffice to show the estimation in which horsemanship was held. No one was regarded as a valiant knight until he had proved his prowess in jousts and tournaments (Fig. 74) in the rank of squire. Although his functions were essentially those of serving, a squire, who ranked higher than a page, was to the knight rather an auxiliary and a companion than a servant. It was his duty to carry the arms of the knight, to take charge of his table, his house, and his horses. On the field of battle he remained in his rear, ready to defend him, to lift him up if he were overthrown, and to provide him, when necessary, with another horse or other arms. He guarded the prisoners captured by the knight, and occasionally fought for him at his side.

The principal sign distinguishing knights from squires consisted in the material of which their spurs were made—of gold for the former, of silver for the latter. It is well known that, at the disastrous battle of Courtray,

Fig. 74.—A Knight entering the Lists. (From a Miniature in the "Tournois du Roi René.")

the Flemings collected after the action, from the slain, four thousand pairs of gold spurs; consequently, four thousand knights of the army of Philip the Fair had fallen.

In order to *win his spurs* (of gold)—an expression become proverbial—it was indispensable that one who aspired to the honour should perform some valiant deed, proving him worthy of being "dubbed," or armed as a knight. The ceremony of admission commenced by presenting the spurs; and whosoever conferred the order of chivalry, were he king or prince, condescended to put on and fasten the spurs for the recipient. In pursuance of the same principle, when a knight, having committed a fault or any cowardly act, had incurred blame or correction, it was by deprivation of, or by changing his spurs, that his degradation commenced. For a slight offence a herald substituted silver spurs for those of gold, which lowered a knight to the grade of squire. But in a case of "forfeiture," as it was termed, an executioner or a cook cut off the straps of his spurs, or they were struck off on a dunghill with an axe: infamy was the future portion of him who had been subjected to that public disgrace.

The privilege of wearing spurs was regarded as a mark of independence and authority; so that when a noble tendered faith and homage to his sovereign he was obliged to take off his spurs in token of vassalage. In 816, ere chivalry had been instituted, an assembly of lords and bishops prohibited ecclesiastics from adopting the profane fashion of wearing spurs then prevailing among the higher classes of the clergy.

The use of the spur appears to date from the most ancient times. The origin of the word has been much disputed. From the time of Louis le Débonnaire it was called *spuors*, which has become *sporen* in Germany, *sperane* in Italian, *spur* in English, *éperon* in French. The Latins called it *calcar* (which originally signified cock's spur), doubtless from the form first given to the spur. That form has strangely varied during centuries. The oldest known shape is that of the spur found in the tomb of Queen Brunehaut, who died in 613, and which is simply like a skewer. This seems to have long continued to be the form; but, from the commencement of the thirteenth to the end of the sixteenth century, the spur is seen in the form of a rose, or of a star with a turning rowel, and was mostly fashioned in a very rich and delicate manner. At the period when horses were clad in steel or leather, the spurs were necessarily very long, in order to reach the animal's flanks (Figs. 75 and 76). The spurs of Godfrey of Bouillon, which have been preserved (their authenticity is more or less questionable), are in that style. In the reign of Charles VII. the young nobles wore, rather for show than for use, spurs the rowel of which was as large as the hand, and fixed at the end of a metal stem half a foot long.

If, therefore, from time immemorial every mounted horse "felt the spur," there was at least a period when every sort of spur could not be indiscriminately applied to the flanks of each individual of the equine race. "There are," says Brunetto Latini, a writer of the thirteenth century, in his "Treasury of all Things"—a sort of encyclopædia of the age—"there are horses of several kinds: chargers, or tall horses, for the combat, whence the expression, 'mounting the high horse;' others, for gentle exercise, use palfreys, which were also called amblers and hackneys; others employ pack-horses, *courtants* (cropped horses), to carry a load (*somme*)." *Somme* here signifies a burden, and this, which we now call baggage, con-

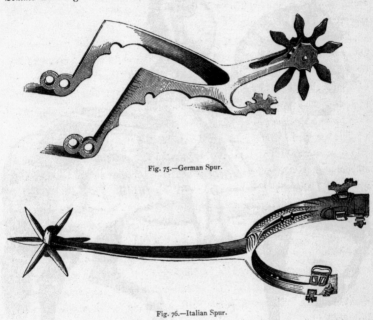

Fig. 75.—German Spur.

Fig. 76.—Italian Spur.

sisted of spare arms and hauberk, which a knight was careful to take with him when he went to the wars. Mares and *bât*-horses (horses carrying the *bât*, or load) were reserved for agriculture and other field-purposes; and it was clearly on that account that a knight was not allowed to ride them. To make a knight ride upon a mare was, like the loss of his spurs, one of the most degrading punishments that could be inflicted on him, and thenceforth "any one who regarded his own honour would no more have touched that disgraced knight than a shaven idiot (leper)."

The horses of French knights were without ears or mane; those of the Germans without tails. According to Carrion-Nisas, the armour of the horse, and the style in which it was caparisoned, were the cause of

Fig. 77.—A Knight armed and mounted for War. (Museum of Artillery, Paris.)

these mutilations. We have elsewhere remarked that if the men were cased in steel their horses were not less heavily cuirassed (Fig. 77). The entire armour and appointments of a horse were called the harness;

the plates of steel or leather (for leather also was often used) were called *bardes*. We find enumerated, not only the articles of which the harness consisted—*chanfrein, nasal, flancois,* &c.—but examples are cited to denote the sumptuousness of this equipment of the horse. We need not, however, dwell longer here on this subject, that refers more properly to the manufacture of arms; but a few words must be said regarding the saddle, which is, if we may use the expression, an implement of horsemanship, and not a part of the armour.

The use of saddles seems to have been unknown in early times, and never to have been introduced among certain nations which, by the way, were most famous in the art of training the horse and making him serviceable. The Thessalonians and the Numidians rode on the bare back, without saddle or stirrups; seated firmly on the horse simply by the pressure of the knees and the calf of the legs; a position which is still that of the boldest riders in the East and in Africa. Hippocrates has ascribed the common and severe diseases of the hips and legs which afflicted the Scythians to the rider's want of support on horseback. Galen makes the same remark regarding the Roman legions, who only introduced the use of a saddle about the year 340 of the Christian era. The Gauls and Franks used neither saddles nor stirrups; but when steel armour was adopted, it would have been impossible for knights to preserve an equilibrium without the aid of a saddle, or to sustain the slightest shock to which they were exposed, as armour rendered them in a manner rigid, or with little flexibility on their large horses.

They therefore had recourse to a high, or rather a deep, saddle, closely adhering to the thighs and loins, with large stirrups serving as supports to the feet. The several parts of the armour being splendidly ornamented, it followed that the saddles, which also were exposed to view, were no more neglected than other ornaments of the animal. Engraved and chased, they were also gilt and painted, and thus, with the shield, helped to distinguish, by the "devices" they bore, the armed warrior completely cased in his steel covering (Figs. 78 to 81).

As to stirrups, of which there certainly is no trace among the Greeks or the Romans, it may be said they were coeval with the invention of saddles. They made their appearance in the earliest days of the Merovingian dynasty; and if we accept the German etymology which the learned have offered (*streben*, to support one's self), the name and the object was introduced by the Franks into Gaul. However that may be, they were no longer dispensed with, especially in war, and when the weight of armour rendered their use necessary. They were of course very large, very massive, and very clumsy in the days of chivalry. When they diminished in size and weight

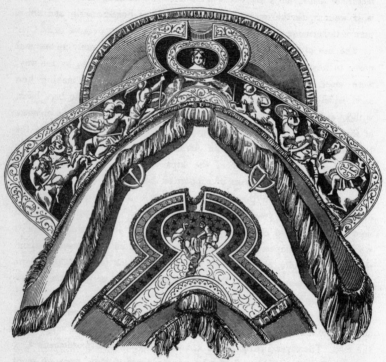

Figs. 78 and 79.—Tournament Saddles, ornamented with Paintings, taken from the Armoury Real, Madrid.
Sixteenth Century. (Communicated by M. Ach. Jubinal.)

they were wrought with more care, and became objects of art, charged with ingenious ornaments, and embellished with engraving, chasing, and gilding.

In accordance with the opinion held by M. de la Varenne, we have already ascribed the disuse of private carriages to the contempt with which the Franks regarded a mode of conveyance deemed by them to be effeminate. But, following the same author, we must observe that a reason might also be discovered in the wretched condition into which, after the decline of the Romans, those magnificent roads formed by them in all their conquered provinces had fallen. In towns, moreover, the streets, narrow, crooked, and with no regular direction, were very frequently so many holes and quagmires. Philip Augustus I. had some of the streets of Paris paved in that *lutèce* * which already, at the time of the Roman conquest, had deserved the significant epithet of *miry*. The princes and the nobles who, as Molière humorously makes Mascarilla say, feared "to leave the impression of their shoes in mud," and could not without difficulty drive about the towns in

Fig. 80.—The Caparison of the Horse of Isabel the Catholic. (Communicated by M. Ach. Jubinal.

carriages, consequently had recourse to the horse or the mule. The ladies made use of them also; but very frequently, if not carried in litters, they rode on a pillion behind the horseman.

In the thirteenth century chariots reappeared; but the fashion did not long prevail, for Philip the Fair discouraged them, in one of the clauses of his sumptuary ordinance of 1294, by declaring that "no citizen may have a chariot."

The litter continued to be held in repute for processions; but queens frequently rode on horseback. Isabel of Bavaria rode on a beautiful

* Latin, *Luteus*—muddy.—[ED.]

palfrey, with her ladies and her maids also on horseback, on the occasion of her entering Paris to espouse Charles VI. And when Mary of England, who went to be married to Louis XII., made her entry into Abbeville, she also, as Robert de la Marck relates, was mounted on a palfrey, as were most of her ladies, " and the remainder in chariots; and the king, riding a large, prancing bay horse, came to receive his bride, with all the gentlemen of his household and of his guard on horseback." The meeting of Henry VIII. and Francis I. in the camp of the Field of the

Fig. 81.—Saddle-cloth.   Sixteenth Century.

Cloth of Gold, presented the most beautiful display that had ever been seen of caparisoned horses, decorated and furnished with unprecedented richness (Fig. 82).

Charles V., in consequence of frequent attacks of gout, was soon compelled to renounce riding. When he went into the country, or on a journey, he was generally followed by a litter and a chair. Mules bore the litter, in which he could recline, while bearers carried the chair, which was

ENTRANCE OF THE QUEEN ISABEAU OF BAVARIA INTO PARIS.

provided with a movable back; its four uprights could be fitted with a sort of canopy of canvas or leather.

In 1457 the ambassadors of Ladislaus V., King of Hungary, presented to Marie of Anjou, Queen of France, a chariot which excited the admiration of the whole court and the inhabitants of Paris, "because," as the historian of the times says, "it was *branlant* (suspended), and very rich."

It is difficult to reconcile the inference to be drawn from the ordinance of Philip the Fair with the assertion of many historians, that coaches

Fig. 82.—Henry VIII. in the Camp of the Field of the Cloth of Gold (1520). From the Bas-reliefs of the Hôtel of the Bourg Herolde at Rouen.

first appeared in France only in the time of Francis I. The point is still doubtful. Nevertheless, one may suppose historians to mean that coaches, instead of being the only vehicles employed in Paris in the time of Francis I., were but chariots of a grander and more gorgeous description than any seen before that time. But we know for certain that, during the Middle Ages, the horse and the mule were generally ridden by everybody, by citizens and by nobles, by women and by men. The horse-blocks fixed in the streets—too narrow evidently, if not for one carriage, at least for two to pass each other—and the rings fastened on doors sufficiently denote that it was so. The mule was especially ridden by sedate men, such as magistrates and doctors, who had to "amble" through the towns. "To take care of the mule," a proverbial expression signifying to wait impatiently, is derived from the custom of lawyers' servants remaining in the court of the Palace to take charge of the riding-horses or mules belonging to their masters.

According to Sauval, the two first coaches seen in Paris, and which called forth the wonder of the people, belonged, one to Queen Claude, the first wife of Francis I.; and the other to Diana of Poitiers, his mistress.

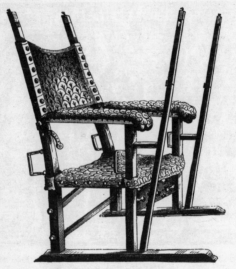

Fig. 83.—Sedan-chair of Charles V.　(Armoury Real, Madrid.)

The fashion was soon followed; so much so, that even where the sumptuary laws were still regarded as efficient, we find parliament entreating Charles IX. to prohibit the circulation of coaches (*coches*) through the town. The magistrates continued, until the commencement of the seventeenth century, to attend at the courts of justice on their mules. Christopher of Thou, father of the celebrated historian, and first President of Parliament, was the first who came thither in his carriage; but only because he suffered from gout, for his wife continued to ride on horseback, seated pillion-fashion behind a servant.

Henry IV. had only one carriage. "I shall be unable to go and see you," he one day wrote to Sully, "for my wife uses my coach (*coche*)." These coaches were neither elegant nor convenient. For doors they were provided with leathern aprons, which were drawn or opened for entrance or exit, with similar curtains to protect against the rain or the sun.

Marshal Bassompierre, in the time of Louis XIII., had a glass coach made for him, which was regarded as a real marvel: it originated the impulse which has led to the productive era of modern coach-building.

Formerly there were in Paris, as appears from numerous documents, several corporations representing the saddler's trade. First came the *seilliers-bourreliers*, and the *selliers-lormiers-carrossiers*. The privileges of the first secured to them specially the manufacture of saddles and harness (collars and other articles for draught). The second made also carriages, bridles, reins, &c. Another very ancient corporation was that of the *lormiers-éperonniers*—"artisans," says the Glossary of Jean de Garlande, "whom the military nobles greatly patronised, because they manufactured silvered and gilt spurs, metal breastplates for their horses, and well-executed bits." There were also *chapuissiers*, who made saddle-bows and pack-frames for the beasts of burden, which were mostly manufactured of alder-wood.

The *blazenniers* and *cuireurs* then covered with leather the packs and the saddles prepared by the *chapuissiers;* and, finally, saddle-painters were employed to ornament them, either in compliance with fashion, which has always been omnipotent in France, or according to the laws of heraldry, when intended for men of rank for purposes of state or war.

Fig. 84.—Banner of the Corporation of the Saddlers of Tonnerre.

GOLD AND SILVER WORK.

IN the remarks upon furniture, we were compelled to trespass
on the domain which we now again approach; for, having to
trace the history of secular and religious luxury, we cannot but
frequently encounter the goldsmiths and their splendid works.
It will thus happen more than once that we shall have to indicate briefly certain important facts already described, in some
details, in preceding chapters.

It is known that in old times, even the most remote, the
goldsmith's art flourished. There is scarcely any ancient narrative
which does not allude to jewels; and every day the discovery of
precious objects, found in ruins and in tombs, still attests the
high state of perfection the art of gold and silver work had attained among
races long since extinct.

The Gauls, when under Roman dominion, applied themselves successfully to the business of the gold-worker. We may again say that the
triumph of the Christian religion, under Constantine the Great, while encou-
raging the interior decoration of places of worship, added a fresh impulse
to the development of this beautiful art.

The popes succeeding St. Sylvester (who had stimulated the liberality
of Constantine) continued to accumulate, in the churches at Rome, the
most costly and massive articles of gold-work. Symmachus (498 to 514)
alone, according to a calculation made by Seroux d'Agincourt, enriched
the treasures of the basilicas to the amount of 130 pounds weight of gold,
and 1,700 of silver, forming the material of objects most finely wrought.

It was from the very court of the Greek emperors that the examples of this magnificence were derived; for we hear St. John Chrysostom exclaiming, "All our admiration is at present reserved for the goldsmiths and the weavers;" and it is well known that in consequence of his bold indiscretion in rebuking the extravagance of the Empress Eudoxia, this eloquent Father of the Church expiated in exile and persecutions his ardent zeal and his sincerity.

The brilliant specimens of the gold-work of the Visigoths, which, in 1858, were exhumed in the field of Guarrazar, near Toledo, and which have been obtained for the Cluny Museum, throw a new light on the monuments of that period. Far from indicating any original style, they afford further proof that the barbarians who came from the North became subjected, in the

Fig. 85.—Gallic Bracelet, from a Cabinet of Antiquities. (Imp. Library, Paris.)

arts, to Byzantine influence. The most remarkable, not only in its dimensions and extreme richness, but in the peculiarity of its ornaments, is a votive crown, intended to be hung, according to the custom of those times, in a sacred place—that of Recesvinthe, who reigned over the Goths of Spain from 653 to 672. It is composed of a large fillet, jointed, and formed of a double plate of the finest gold. Thirty uncut sapphires, and as many pearls, regularly alternating, arranged in three rows and in quincunxes,* are seen on its exterior circle. Chased ornaments occupy the spaces between the stones. The votive crown of King Suintila, which we here reproduce (Fig. 86), is fully as rich, and about thirty years older.

---

* Quincunx order is a method of arranging five objects, or pieces, in the form of a square; one being in the centre, and one at each corner.—[Ed.]

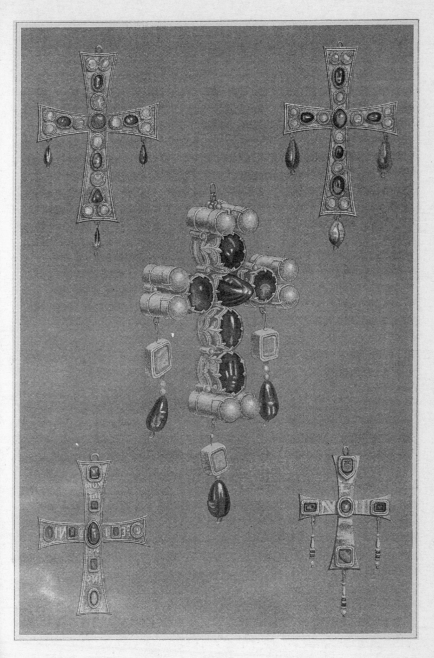

GOLD CROSSES OF A KING OF THE GOTHS.

Found at Guarrazar. Seventh Century. (Museum of the Hotel Cluny)

(Taken from the work of M. Ferdinand de Lasteyrie)

It is of massive gold, ornamented with sapphires and pearls arranged in rose-pattern, and set off by two borders similarly set with delicate stones. But the originality of this precious gem consists in the letters hanging as pendants from its lower border. These letters, open-worked, are filled with small pieces of red glass, set in gold; their combination presents the following inscription:— "*Suintilanus Rex offeret*" (offering of the King Suintila). Each of them is suspended from the fillet by a chain with double links, sustaining a pendant of violet sapphire, pear-shaped. Finally, the crown is suspended by four chains attached to a circular top of rock-crystal.

"Five of the crowns so fortunately discovered at Guarrazar," says M. de Lasteyrie, "have crosses. These, attached by a chain to the same circular top, were evidently intended to remain suspended across the circle of the crown." The cross belonging to the crown of Recesvinthe is by far the richest; eight large pearls and six sapphires, all mounted in open-work, adorn the front. The four other crosses are of the form which in heraldry is called *croix patée;* but they differ in size and in the ornaments with which they are enriched.

We have already stated that the kings and grandees of the Merovingian period displayed in their plate and in some of their state-furniture a richness

Fig. 86.—Votive Crown of Suintila, King of the Visigoths from 621 to 631. (Armoury Real, Madrid.)

of gold-work the profuseness of which was ordinarily opposed to good taste. We have seen at his work the celebrated Saint Eloi, bishop-goldsmith; and we have mentioned not only his remarkable productions, but also the enduring influence he exercised over a whole historical period of art. Finally, we have observed that Charlemagne—whose object seems to have been not only to imitate Constantine, but to surpass him —endowed the churches magnificently with works of art, without prejudice to the numberless splendours which his palaces contained.

Fig. 87.—The Sword of Charlemagne.   Preserved in the Imperial Treasury at Vienna.

According to a tradition, the loss of most of the beautiful objects of gold-work belonging to that monarch may have been owing to the circumstance that they were disposed around him in the sepulchral chamber where the body was deposited after death; and the emperors of Germany, his successors, may not have scrupled to appropriate those riches, of which some rare specimens, particularly his diadem and sword, are still preserved in the Museum of Vienna (Figs. 87 and 88).

Ecclesiastical display, notably extinct during the period of trouble and suffering through which the Church passed in the seventh and eighth centuries, and to which the power of Charlemagne was to put an end, manifested itself in an extraordinary degree from that time. For example,

Fig. 88.—Diadem ot Charlemagne.   Preserved in the Imperial Treasury at Vienna.

it was calculated that under Leo III., who occupied the pontifical chair from 795 to 816, the weight of the plate which the Pope gave to enrich the churches, amounted to not less than 1,075 pounds of gold and 24,744 pounds of silver !

To that period belongs the famous gold altar of the basilica of St. Ambrose of Milan, executed in 835, by order of Archbishop Angilbert, by Volvinius; and which, notwithstanding its immense intrinsic value, has come down to our time. "The four sides of this monument," says M.

Labarte, " are of extreme richness. The front, entirely of gold, is divided into three panels by a border of enamel. The centre panel represents a cross of four equal projections, formed by fillets of ornaments in enamel, alternating with precious stones uncut but polished. Christ is seated in the centre of the cross. The symbols of the Evangelists occupy its branches. Three of the Apostles are placed in each angle. All these figures are in relief. The right and left panels contain each six bas-reliefs, the subjects of which are taken from the life of Christ; they are encircled by borders of enamels and precious stones alternately disposed. The two sides, in silver relieved with gold, exhibit very rich crosses, treated in the same style as the borders. The back, which is also of silver relieved with gold, is likewise divided in three large panels; that in the centre contains four medallions, and each of the others six bas-reliefs, of which the life of St. Ambrose supplied the subjects. In one of the medallions of the centre panel is seen St. Ambrose receiving the gold altar from the hands of Archbishop Angilbert; in the other, St. Ambrose is giving his benediction to Volvinius, the master goldsmith (*magister faber*), as he is designated in the inscription transmitting to us the name of the author of this work, of which no description can give an exact idea."

It was not Italy alone which possessed skilful goldsmiths, and encouraged them. We have in particular, among other enlightened and active supporters of ecclesiastical gold-work, a succession of the bishops of Auxerre, to whom must be added Hincmar, bishop of Rheims, who caused a splendid shrine to be made for the relics of the illustrious patron of his church. It was cased in plates of silver, and statues of twelve bishops adorned its borders.

But, notwithstanding all its artistic magnificence, the jewellery of the West could only appear to be the reflex of the wonders produced at the same epoch by the goldsmiths of the East, or the Byzantines, to adopt a term generally sanctioned.

One of the most curious specimens of Byzantine art, preserved in Russia, is a gold reliquary lined with a plate of silver, in the centre of which is an embossed representation of the Crucifixion. Above the head, on a gilt nimbus, is an inscription in Greek, "Jesus Christ, King of Glory." This treasure, remarkable for its extreme finish, is covered with a mosaic of precious stones of different colours, in partitions of gold; the cross being quartered

in enamel, with silver filigree. At the back the names of the archiman-
drite Nicolos are engraved. It is a work of the tenth century, and was
found in the Iberian monastery on Mount Athos.

If rare specimens only of jewellery have come down to us of a date prior
to the eleventh century, this may be accounted for not merely by their

Fig. 89.—Byzantine Reliquary, in Enamel, brought from Mount Athos. Tenth Century.
(Collection of M. Sebastianof.)

intrinsic value having indicated them to the uncivilised as fit objects of
plunder during the invasions which took place after the reign of Charlemagne, but also, as we have elsewhere remarked, by the re-introduction of
church furniture, which was in some measure a necessary result of renovated
architecture. It was right to adapt the style of plate to that of the edifice

it was to adorn. The forms which were then employed for various objects of church-service showed the influence of the severe style derived from the original Byzantine type; the latter, moreover, explained itself by the repute, especially in metallurgy, enjoyed by the city of Constantine, to which the East generally had recourse when taking in hand any work of importance.

The *German* school particularly would acquire a Byzantine character, owing to the marriage of the Emperor Otho II. with the Greek princess Theophania (972)—an alliance which naturally bound the two empires in closer ties, and attracted a considerable number of artists and artisans to

Fig. 90.—Altar of Gold, presented to the ancient Cathedral of Basle by the Emperor Henry II., now in the Cluny Museum.

Germany from the East. Of the works of that period still in existence, one of the most remarkable is the rich gold cover of the book of the Gospels, now in the Royal Library, Munich; on which are executed, in the embossed style, various bas-reliefs of great delicacy, and designed with the purity at that time distinguishing the Greek school.

The emperor Henry II. was therefore welcomed (*bien-venu*), and, if one may say so, well served by the condition of art in Germany, when, elevated to the throne in 1002, and inspired by ardent piety, he sought, by princely liberality to the churches, to surpass even Constantine and

Charlemagne. It is to Henry that the Cathedral of Basle owes the decorations of the altar, to which none can be compared for richness, except
that of Milan; yet without recalling it by its style, which has lost every
trace of the antique, and is a clearly-pronounced type of the art which the
Middle Ages were to create as their own. It is right to mention also the
crown of the sainted emperor, and that of his wife, now preserved in the

Fig. 91.—Enamelled Shrine, in Limoges Work of the Twelfth Century. (Museum of Cluny.)

Treasury of the King of Bavaria; both are in six jointed parts, making a
circle; the former bears figures of winged angels; the other, stalks with
four leaves designed with correctness and grace, and executed in a manner
which evinces the greatest dexterity. "Moreover," says M. Labarte, "the
taste for jewellery was then generally diffused throughout Germany; and
many prelates followed the example set by the emperor. Willigis, the
first Archbishop of Mayence, may be cited; he endowed his church with

a crucifix weighing 600 pounds, the several parts of which were adjusted with such art that each could be detached at the joints; and Bernward, bishop of Hildesheim, who, like St. Eloi, was himself a celebrated goldsmith, and to whom is ascribed a crucifix enriched with precious stones and filigrees, and two magnificent candelabra, which still constitute a portion of the treasures of the church whereof he was the pastor."

About the same period—that is, in the early days of the eleventh century—a monk of Dreux, named Odorain, who had made himself famous in France by his works in precious metals, executed a large number of objects for King Robert, intended for the churches the monarch had founded.

Fig. 92.—Shrine in Copper Gilt. (End of the Twelfth Century.)

It has been remarked in the preceding chapter, that the Crusades gave a great impulse to the goldsmith's art in Europe, in consequence of the great demand for shrines and reliquaries intended for the reception of the venerated remains of saints which the soldiers of the faith brought back from their distant expeditions (Figs. 91 and 92). The offerings of consecrated vessels and of altar-fronts were also multiplied. The Holy Scriptures received cases and coverings which were so many splendid works entrusted to the goldsmiths. To speak truly, had it not been for the essentially religious direction which, at that period, certain departments of luxury acquired by the Crusaders in the East had taken, we might perhaps have seen the arts, that only in the West recommenced a real existence, become extinguished, and in a manner perish in the first burst of their revival.

It is chiefly to the minister of Louis le Gros, Suger, Abbot of Saint-Denis, who died in 1152, that the honour of this consecration of arts is due, for he distinctively proclaimed himself their protector; he endeavoured to render legitimate their position in the State, by opposing their pious aims to the too exclusive censures of St. Bernard and his disciples.

Conjointly with the powerful abbot, there is deserving of special mention a simple monk, Theophilus, an eminent artist who wrote in Latin a description of the Industrial Arts of his time (*Diversarum Artium Schedula*), and devoted seventy-nine chapters of his book to that of the goldsmith. This valuable treatise shows us, in the most unmistakable manner, that the goldsmiths of the twelfth century must have possessed a comprehensiveness of knowledge and manipulation, the mere enumeration of which surprises us the more now that we see industry everywhere tending to an almost infinite division of labour. At that time the goldsmith was required to be at once modeller, sculptor, smelter, enameller, jewel-mounter, and inlay-worker. He had to cast his own models in wax, as well as to labour with his hammer or embellish with his graver: he had to make the chalice, the vases, and the pyx, for the metropolitan churches, on which were lavished all the resources of art; and to produce, by the ordinary process of punching, the open-work or the designs of copper intended to ornament the books of the poor (*libri pauperum*), &c.

The treasury of the Abbey of Saint-Denis still possessed, at the time of the Revolution, several *chefs-d'œuvre* produced by the artists whose processes are described by Theophilus; especially the rich mounting of a cup of Oriental agate, bearing the name of Suger, which it is believed he used for the service of mass; and the mounting of an ancient sardonyx vase, known as the cup of the Ptolemies, which Charles the Simple had given to the abbey. Having been deposited, in 1793, in the Cabinet of Medals, Paris, the mounting of the cup of the Ptolemies and the chalice of Suger remained there until they were stolen in 1804.

Among the examples of that period still existing, and which, conditionally, every one is permitted to inspect, we may distinguish, with M. Labarte,—in addition to "the great crown of lights" suspended under the cupola in the cathedral of Aix-la-Chapelle, and the magnificent shrine in

which Frederick I. collected the bones of Charlemagne,—in the Museum of
the Louvre, a vase of rock-crystal mounted in gold and embellished with
gems, presented to Louis VII. by his wife Eleanora; in the Cluny Museum,
several candelabra; in the Imperial Library in Paris, the covering of a Latin
manuscript, numbered 622; a cup of agate onyx (Fig. 93), bordered with
a belt of precious stones raised on a groundwork of filigree; and the beautiful gold chalice of St. Remy (Fig. 94), which, after having appeared in
the Cabinet of Antiquities, was restored in 1861 to the treasury of the church
of Notre-Dame, Rheims.

Severe forms and an elevated style were the characteristics of the jewelled
works of the eleventh and twelfth centuries; and, for the principal elements

Fig. 93.—A Drinking Cup, called Gondole, of Agate; from the Treasury of the Abbey of Saint-Denis.
(Cabinet of Antiquities, Imp. Library, Paris.)

of accessory embellishment, we most frequently see pearls, precious stones,
with enamelled divisions which, according to the minute description of
Theophilus, are only delicate mosaics whose various coloured segments are
separated by plates of gold.

In the days of St. Louis, a period of active and generous piety, there was
(an assertion which may appear hazardous after what we have said of the
zeal of preceding centuries) a remarkable accession to the number and the
splendour of the gifts and offerings of jewellery to the churches. For
instance, it was then that Bonnard, Parisian goldsmith, assisted by the
ablest artisans, devoted two years to the manufacture of the shrine of

St. Geneviève, on which he expended one hundred and ninety-three marks of silver and seven and a half marks of gold; the mark weighing eight ounces. The shrine, consecrated in 1212, was in the form of a little church, with statuettes and bas-reliefs enriched with precious stones. It

Fig. 94.—Chalice, said to be of St. Remy. (Treasury of the Cathedral of Rheims.)

was deposited in the French mint in 1793; but the spoil realised only twenty-three thousand eight hundred and thirty livres. Half a century earlier, the most celebrated German goldsmiths were engaged during seventeen years upon the famous reliquary in silver gilt, called the "Great Relics," which the cathedral at Aix-la-Chapelle still possesses; it was fabricated from the gifts

deposited in that space of time by the faithful in the poors'-box of the
porch; an edict of the Emperor Barbarossa having appropriated all the
offerings to that object, " so long as it remained unfinished."

Moreover, that period, which may be regarded as denoting the zenith
of the goldsmith's art for sacred purposes, is also that wherein occurred
the important transition which was to introduce into domestic life the same
lavishness so long devoted only to objects applicable to ecclesiastical use.
But, before entering upon that new phase, we ought to mention, not
without much commendation, the enamelled gold-work of Limoges, which
was greatly celebrated for several centuries. From the Gallo-Romano
period Limoges had acquired a reputation for the works of its goldsmiths.
St. Eloi, the great goldsmith in the time of the Merovingian kings
(Fig. 95), was originally from that country, and he was working under
Alban, a goldsmith, and master of the mint at Limoges, when his reputation
led to his being called to the court of Clotaire II. The ancient Roman
colony had retained its industrial speciality, and during the Middle Ages
was remarkable for the production of works of a peculiar character, which
are supposed to have been fabricated there prior to the third century, if we
may judge from a passage in Philostratus, a Greek writer of that period.

This work consisted of a mixed style, inasmuch as the material forming
the ground of the work is copper; and, moreover, the principal effects are
due not less to the skill of the enameller than to the talent of the worker
in metal. The process of fabrication is very simple—that is, in the way of
description—yet the execution must have been extremely protracted and
minute.

" After having prepared and polished a plate of copper," says M. Labarte,
whose account we transfer to our own pages, " the artist marked on it all
the parts which were to rise to the surface of the metal, in order to produce
the outlines of the drawing or of the figure he wanted to represent;
then, with gravers and scrapers, he dug deeply in the copper all the space
which the various metals were to cover. In the hollows thus *champlevés*
(a word sometimes used to signify the mode of producing this kind of
work), he placed the material to be vitrified, which was afterwards melted in
a furnace. When the enamelled piece was cold, he polished it by various
means, so as to bring to the surface of the enamel all the lines of the drawing produced by the copper. Gilding was afterwards applied to the parts

of the metal thus preserved. Until the twelfth century, only the outlines
of the drawing ordinarily rose to the surface of the enamel, and the tints of

Fig. 95.—Cross of an Altar, ascribed to St. Eloi.

the flesh, as well as the dresses, were produced by coloured enamel; in the
thirteenth century enamel was no longer used but to colour the ground-

work. The figures were entirely preserved on the plate of copper, and the outlines of the drawing were then shown by a delicate engraving on the metal."

Between the enamels partitioned (*cloisonnés*) and the enamels *champlevés* the difference, as we can see, is only the first arrangement of the divisions to receive the several vitrifiable compositions. Making allowances for

Fig. 96.—An Abbot's Enamelled Crozier, made at Limoges. (Thirteenth Century.)

Fig. 97.—A Bishop's Crozier, which appears to be of Italian manufacture. (Fourteenth Century. Cathedral of Metz.)

the influence of fashion, these two styles of analogous works were held in almost equal estimation. Nevertheless, it seems that the preference ought to be assigned to the goldsmith's art in Limoges, which, at a time when there was manifested a demand for private reliquaries and collective offerings to the churches, had this advantage over the other, that it was much less costly, and consequently more accessible to all classes (Fig. 96) In the present day there is scarcely a museum, or even a private collection, that does not contain some specimen of the ancient Limousine* industry.

With the fourteenth century the splendour of the goldsmith's art ceases to display, as its exclusive object, ecclesiastical decoration and embellishment ; but it suddenly became so developed among the laity that King John (of France) desiring, or pretending to desire, to restore it to the exclusive line it had till then retained, prohibited by an ordinance, in 1356, the goldsmiths from "*working* (fabricating) gold or silver plate, vases, or silver jewellery, of more than one mark of gold or silver, excepting for the churches."

But it is possible to issue ordinances in order to show the advantage of evading them, and to benefit exclusively by the exception. This is what appears to have then occurred ; for, in the inventory of the treasury of Charles V., son and successor of the king who signed the sumptuary edict of 1356, the value of the various objects of the goldsmith's art is estimated at not less than nineteen millions. This document, in which the greater number of the articles are described to the minutest detail, would suffice in itself to exhibit a truthful historical view of the art at that period ; and, at all events, it affords a striking idea of the artistic progress made in that direction, and of the extravagance to which the trade was subservient.

When considering the subject of furniture in domestic life, we indicated the names and the uses of several articles which were displayed on the tables or sideboards — plateholders, ewers, urns, goblets, &c. ; we also adverted to the numerous and capricious forms they assumed—flowers, animals, grotesque images ; we need not, therefore, recur to the matter ; but we ought not to overlook the jewellery, of all sorts—insignia, or ornaments of the head-dress, gems, clasps, chains and necklaces, antique cameos (Fig. 98), which appear in the treasury of the King of France.

In treating of ecclesiastical furniture we, moreover, observed that the goldsmith's art, although devoting itself to secular ornaments, nevertheless

---

* *Limousine*—a term applied to enamelling, and derived, as some writers assume, from Leonard Limousin, a famous artist in this kind of work, resident at Limoges. It is, however, more probable it came from the province Limousin, or Limosin, of which Limoges was the capital ; and that Leonard acquired the surname of Limousin from his place of birth or residence ; just as many of the old painters are best known by theirs.—[ED.]

continued to work marvels in the production of objects for ecclesiastical use ; it would be mere repetition to support this assertion by other examples.

But, dismissing those two questions, let a contemporary poet raise a third, which deserves a place here.   Eustache Deschamps, who died in 1422, equerry and usher-at-arms to Charles V. and Charles VI., enumerates the

Fig. 98.—An ancient Cameo-setting of the time of Charles V.   (Cab. of Ant., Bibl. Imp., Paris.)

jewels and gems which the female nobility of the time aspired to possess. " It was indispensable," he says—

> " Aux matrones,
> Nobles palais et riches trônes;
> Et à celles qui se marient
> Qui moult tôt (bientôt) leurs pensers varient,
> Elles veulent tenir d'usaige . .

Vestements d'or, de draps de soye,
Couronne, chapel et courroye
De fin or, espingle d'argent . . .
Puis couvrechiefs à or batus,
A pierres et perles dessus . . .
Encor vois-je que leurs maris,
Quand ils reviennent de Paris,
De Reims, de Rouen et de Troyes,
Leur rapportent gants et courroyes . . .
Tasses d'argent ou gobelets . . .
Bourse de pierreries,
Coulteaux à imagineries,
Espingliers (étuis) taillés à émaux."

They desired, moreover, and said that they ought to have given to them—

" Pigne (peigne) et miroir d'ivoire . . .
Et l'estui qui soit noble et gent (riche et beau),
Pendu à chaines d'argent;
Heures (livres de piété) me fault de Notre-Dame,
Qui soient de soutil (delicat) ouvraige,
D'or et d'azur, riches et cointes (jolies),
Bien ordonnés et bien pointes (peintes),
De fin drap d'or très-bien couvertes,
Et quand elles seront ouvertes,
Deux fermaux (agrafes) d'or qui fermeront."

We thus see that, according to the above programme, the jewel-box of a princess, or of a lady of rank, must have been really splendid. Unfortunately for us, the specimens of these female ornaments of the fourteenth and fifteenth centuries are still more rare in collections than objects of massive plate; and one is almost left to imagine their appearance and their richness from the entries in inventories, that chief source of information regarding the times of which the memorials have disappeared.

It is there we see the costliness of the *fermails*, or clasps of cloaks and copes, called also *pectoraux*, because they fastened the garments across the breast; girdles, chaplets (head-dresses), portable reliquaries, and other "little jewels (Fig. 99) *pendants et à pendre*," the fashion of which we have restored under the name of *breloques*, and which represent every variety of object more or less whimsical. We see, for instance, gold clasps representing a peacock, a fleur-de-lis, two hands "clasped." This one is embellished with six sapphires, sixty pearls, and other large gems; that one with eighteen rubies, and four emeralds. From a girdle of Charles V., which is made "of scarlet silk adorned with eight gold mountings," are suspended "a knife, scissors, and a pen-knife," ornamented in gold; the trinkets (pendants) represent "a man on horseback, a cock holding a mirror in the form of a trefoil," or "a stag of pearls with enamelled horns;" or, again, a man mounted on a double-headed serpent, "playing on a Saracenic horn" (of Saracen origin).   Finally, we remark that in reliquaries a fashion

Fig. 99.—Scent-box in Chased Gold.   (A French Work of the Fifteenth Century.)

long established was maintained, which consisted of forming them of a statuette representing a saint (Fig. 100), or of a subject that comprised his image, and to which were attached, by a small chain, relics inlaid in a little tabernacle of gold or silver, preciously wrought.

But now the fifteenth century opens out, and with it a period of tumult. France suddenly beheld that impulse to industry paralyzed, which, to prosper, requires a condition of affairs very different from sanguinary civil dissensions and foreign invasion.   Not only were the workshops closed, but princes and nobles were more than once constrained to appropriate the gorgeous decorations of their tables and their collections of gems, to pay and arm warriors under their command, or even to redeem themselves from captivity.

At that time the goldsmith's art flourished in the neighbouring country of Flanders, then quietly submissive to the powerful house of Burgundy, which, with equal taste and liberality, encouraged the art, which had installed itself in the principal cities.   This was also an epoch of magnificent productions in that country, but not more than one or two examples remain;

Fig. 100.—Reliquary, Silver-gilt, surmounted by a Statuette of the Virgin with the Infant Jesus, representing Jeanne d'Evreux, Queen of France. (Museum of Sovereigns, in the Louvre.)

these are attributed to Corneille de Bonte, who worked at Ghent, and was generally considered the most skilful goldsmith of his time (Figs. 101 and 102). However that may be, the style of the goldsmith's art of the fifteenth century continued, as in the two or three preceding centuries, conformable to the contemporaneous style of architecture. For instance, the shrine of Saint-Germain-des-Près, which was of that period, had the form of a small ogivale* church; and some specimens still existing in Berlin are of the Gothic character, the prevailing style of the edifices of those times. But an

Fig. 101.—The Ensign of the Collar of the Goldsmiths of Ghent. (Fifteenth Century.)

influence was making itself felt that was not long in entirely modifying the general aspect of the productions of the trade we are considering. That transformation must have been promoted by Italy; in the midst of which, in spite of intestine troubles and serious contentions with other nations, a luxury and opulence prevailed. Genoa, Venice, Florence, Rome, had long been so many centres where the Fine Arts struggled for pre-eminence and inspiration. Among the majority of the wealthy merchants who had

* *Ogivale*—a term used by French architects to denote the Gothic vault, with its ribs and cross-springers, &c. It is also employed to denote the pointed arch.—Gwilt's *Encyclopædia of Architecture.*—[Ed]

become patricians of those gorgeous republics were found so many Mæcenases, under whose patronage flourished great artists whom popes and princes emulously countenanced. "From the moment," says M. Labarte, "when

Fig. 102.—Escutcheon in Silver-gilt, executed by Corneille de Bonte, in the Fifteenth Century.
(Museum of the Hôtel de Ville, Ghent.)

the Nicolases, the Jeans of Pisa, and the Giottos, throwing off the Byzantine yoke, caused Art to emerge from languor and supineness, that of the gold-

smith could no longer find favour in Italy but by maintaining itself on a
level with the progress of sculpture, whose daughter it was.* When we
know that the great Donatello,—Philip Brunelleschi, the bold architect of
the dome of Florence,—Ghiberti, the author of the marvellous doors of the
Baptistery, had goldsmiths for their earliest masters, we may judge what
artists the Italian goldsmiths of that period must have been." The first in
date is the celebrated Jean of Pisa, son of Nicolas, who, brought from Arezzo
in 1286, to sculpture the marble table of the high-altar, and a group of the
Virgin between St. Gregory and St. Donato, desired to pay tribute to the
taste of the time by ornamenting the altar with those fine chasings on
silver coloured with enamels to which we give the name of translucid enamels
in relief; and also by designing a clasp or jewel with which he decorated
the breast of the Virgin. Both chasings and clasp are now lost.

To Jean (Giovanni) of Pisa succeeded his pupils Agostino and Agnolo
of Siena.

In 1316 Andrea of Ognibene executed, for the Cathedral of Pistoia, an
altar-front, which has come down to us, and must have been followed by
more important works. Then come Pietro and Paulo of Arezzo, Ugolino of
Siena, and finally Master Cione,† the author of the two silver bas-reliefs
still to be seen on the altar of the Baptistery of Florence. Master Cione,
whose school was numerous, had for his principal pupils Forzane of Arezzo
and Leonardo of Florence, who worked on the two most noted monuments of
the goldsmith's art which time and depredations have respected—the altar
of Saint-Jacques at Pistoia, and that same altar of the Baptistery to which
the bas-reliefs of Cione were afterwards adapted. During more than a
hundred and fifty years the ornamentation of these two altars, of which no
description can give an idea, was, if we may so say, the arena wherein all
the most famous goldsmiths met.

At the end of the fourteenth century Luca della Robbia, who, as we have
seen, distinguished himself in ceramic art, and afterwards Brunelleschi, no
less great as an architect than as a sculptor, came forth from the studio

---

* This is a literal rendering of the text of M. Labarte ; but the artists to whom allusion is
made were only two, Niccola and Giovanni, sculptors and architects of Pisa. According to Vasari,
Niccola, father of Giovanni, (Jean or John), first worked under certain Greek sculptors who were
executing the figures and other sculptural ornaments of the Duomo of Pisa and the Chapel of
San Giovanni.—[ED.]

† Andrea di Cione Orcagna.—[ED.]

of a goldsmith. At the same period shone Baccioforte and Mazzano of Placentia, Arditi the Florentine, and Bartoluccio, master of the famous sculptor Ghiberti, to whom we owe those doors of the Baptistery, which Michael Angelo pronounced worthy of being placed at the entrance to Paradise.

It is well known that the execution of these doors was, in 1400, submitted to competition; and it may be said, in honour of the goldsmith's art, that Ghiberti, vying with the most celebrated competitors—for among them were Donatello and Brunelleschi—owed his triumph, perhaps, to the simple fact that he had treated, as it

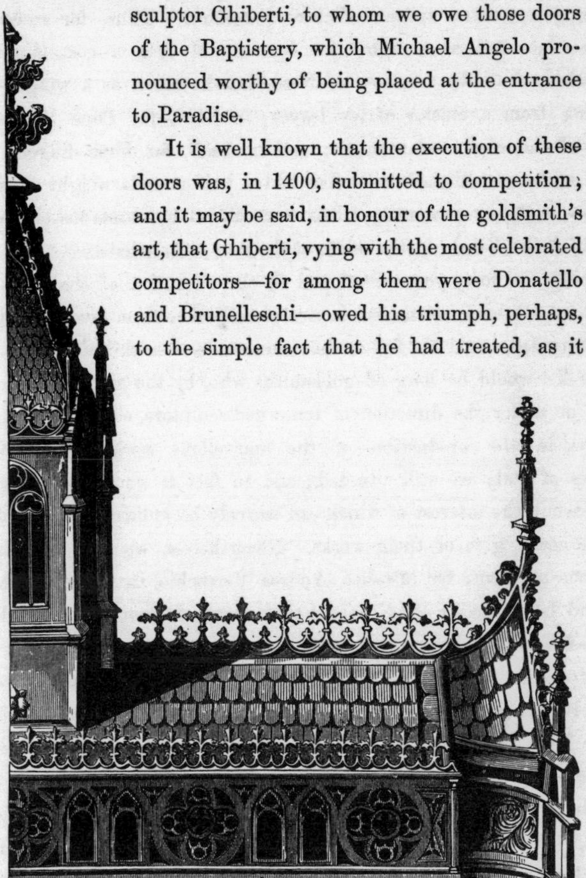

Fig. 103.—Shrine of the Fifteenth Century. (Collection of Prince Soltykoff.)

were by habit, his model with all the delicacy of the goldsmith's art. And it must be added, and to the praise of the great artist, that although in great reputation for sculptured works of the highest importance, he adhered faithfully all his life to his first profession, and considered it not derogatory even to manufacture jewellery. Thus, for example, in 1428 he mounted as a signet for Jean de Medicis, a cornelian said to have belonged to the treasury of Nero, and he set it as a winged-dragon emerging from a cluster of ivy leaves; in 1429, for Pope Martin V., a button of the cope, and a mitre; and in 1439, for Pope Eugene IV., a golden mitre, embellished with five and a half pounds weight of precious stones,—its front representing Christ surrounded by numerous cherubs, and at the back the Virgin in the midst of the four Evangelists.

During the forty years employed in the execution of the doors of the Baptistery, Ghiberti continued to derive assistance from several goldsmiths, who, so guided, could not fail in their turn to become skilful masters.

The list would be long of goldsmiths who, by the single force of their talents, or under the direction of renowned sculptors, competed during two centuries in the production of the marvellous works with which the churches of Italy are still crowded; and in fact it would be only a monotonous detail, the interest of which can scarcely be enhanced by any description we could give of their works. Nevertheless, we may cite the most illustrious of them: for instance, Andrea Verrochio, in whose studio Perugino and Leonardo da Vinci passed their time; Domenichino Ghirlandajo, so called because when a goldsmith he had invented an ornament in the form of garlands, of which the ladies of Florence were passionately fond; he afterwards relinquished the hammer and the graver for the painter's pencil; Maso Finiguerra, who, reputed to be the cleverest niello-worker of his time, engraved a *pax*, or paten, still preserved in the cabinet of bronzes in Florence; it is acknowledged to be the plate of the first engraving printed,—the Imperial Library of Paris possesses the only early proof of it.

In 1500 was born Benvenuto Cellini, who was to be the embodiment of the genius of the goldsmith's art, and who raised it to the zenith of its power. "Cellini, a Florentine citizen, now a sculptor," as his contemporary Vasari relates, "had no equal in the goldsmith's art when devoting himself to it in his youth, and was perhaps for many years without a rival, as well as in the execution of small figures in full relief and in bas-relief, and all works of that nature. He mounted precious stones so skilfully, and decked them in such marvellous settings, with small figures so perfect, and sometimes so original and with such fanciful taste, that one could not imagine anything better; nor can we adequately praise the medals which, when he was young, he engraved with incredible care in gold and silver. At Rome he executed, for Pope Clement VII., a fastening for the cope, in which he represented with admirable workmanship the Eternal Father. He also mounted with rare talent a diamond, cut to a point, and surrounded by several young children carved in gold. Clement VII. having ordered a gold chalice with its cup supported by the theological attributes, Benvenuto executed the work in a surprising manner. Of all the artists who, in his own time, tried their hands at engraving medals of the Pope, no one succeeded better, as those well know who possess them or have seen them. Also to him was entrusted the execution of the coins of Rome; and finer pieces were never struck. After the death of Clement VII., Benvenuto returned to Florence, where he engraved the head of Duke Alexander on the coins, which are so beautiful that to this day several specimens are preserved as precious antique medals; and rightly so, for in them Benvenuto surpassed himself. At length he devoted himself to sculpture and to the art of casting statues. He executed in France, where he was in the service of Francis I., many works in bronze, silver, and in gold. Returning to his native country, he was employed by the Duke Cosmo de Medicis, who at once required of him several works in jewellery, and afterwards some sculptures."

Thus, Benvenuto is at the same time goldsmith (Fig. 104), engraver in medals, and sculptor, and he excels in these three branches of the art, as the productions which have survived him attest. Nevertheless, unfortunately, the greater part of his works in the goldsmith's art have been destroyed, or are now confounded with those of his contemporaries, upon whom Italian taste, combined with his original genius, had exercised a powerful influence. In France there remains of his works only a magnificent salt-cellar, which he executed for Francis I.; in Florence is preserved the mounting of a cup in lapis-lazuli, representing three anchors in gold enamelled, heightened by diamonds; also the cover, in gold enamelled, of another cup of rock-crystal. But, besides the bronze bust of Cosmo I., we may still admire, with the group of Perseus and Medusa, which ranks among grand sculptures, the reduced form, or rather the model of that group, which in size approaches goldsmith's work; and the bronze pedestal, decorated with statuettes, on which Perseus is placed; works that enable us to see of what Cellini was capable as a goldsmith. And, let us repeat, the influence which he exercised over his contemporaries was immense, as well in Florence as in Rome, as well in France as in Germany; and, had his work been thought utterly worthless, he would remain not less justly celebrated for giving an impulse to his time by imprinting on the art which he professed a movement as fertile as it was bold.

Fig. 104.—A Pendant, after a Design by Benvenuto Cellini. Sixteenth Century.
(Cabinet of Antiquities, Bibl. Imp., Paris.)

Moreover, in imitation of the monk Theophilus, his predecessor of the twelfth century, Benvenuto Cellini, after having given practical example, desired that the theories he had found prevailing, and those which were due to his faculty for originating, should be preserved for posterity. A treatise ("Trattato intorno alle otto principali Arti dell' Orificeria"), in which he describes and teaches all the best processes of working in gold, remains one of the most valuable works on the subject; and even in our days goldsmiths who wish to refer back to the true sources of their art do not neglect to consult it.

The artistic style of the celebrated Florentine goldsmith is that of a period when, by an earnest return to antiquity, the mythological element was introduced everywhere, even in the Christian sanctuaries. The character, which we may call autochthone,* of the pious and severe Middle Ages, ceased to influence the production of plastic works, when the models were taken from the glorious remains of idolatrous Greece and Rome. The art which the religion of Christ had awakened and upheld suddenly became again Pagan, and Cellini proved himself one of the enthusiasts of the ancient temples raised in honour of the gods and goddesses of Paganism; that is to say, under the impulse given by him, and in imitation of him, the phalanx of artists, of which he is in a manner the chief, could not fail to go far on the new road by which he had travelled among the first.

When Cellini came to France he found, as he himself says in his book, that the work consisted "more than elsewhere in *grosserie*" (the *grosserie* comprised the church plate, vessels, and silver images), "and that the works there executed with the hammer had attained a degree of perfection nowhere else to be met with."

The inventory of the plate and jewels of Henry II., among which were many by Benvenuto Cellini—the inventory prepared at Fontainebleau in 1560—shows us that, after the departure of the Florentine artist, the French goldsmiths continued to deserve that eulogium; and to comprehend of what they were capable in the time of Charles IX., it is sufficient to recall the description, preserved in the archives of Paris, of a piece of plate which the city had caused to be made to offer as a present to the king on the occasion of his entry into his capital in 1571.

"It was," says that document, "a large pedestal, supported on four dolphins, and having seated on it Cybele, mother of the gods, representing the mother of the king, accompanied by the gods Neptune and Pluto, and the goddess Juno, as Messeigneurs the brothers, and Madame the sister, of the

---

* *Autochthone*—relating to the aboriginal inhabitants of a country: the use of the word here is not very intelligible.—[ED.]

king. This Cybele was contemplating Jupiter, who represented our king, and was raised on two columns, the one of gold, the other of silver, having his device inscribed—'Pietate et Justitia.' Upon this was a large imperial crown, on one side held in the beak of an eagle perched on the croup of a horse on which Jupiter was mounted ; and on the other side supported by the sceptre he held—thus being, as it were, deified. At the four corners of the pedestal were the figures of four kings, his predecessors, all of the same name —that is, Charles the Great, Charles V., Charles VII., and Charles VIII., who in their time fulfilled their missions, and their reigns were happy, as we hope will be that of our king. In the frieze of that pedestal were the battles and the victories, of all kinds, in which he was engaged; the whole made

Fig. 105.—Cup of Lapis-lazuli, mounted in Gold enriched with Rubies, and a Figure in Gold enamelled. (Italian Work of the 16th Century.)

Fig. 106.—Vase of Rock-crystal, mounted in Silver-gilt and enamelled. (Italian Work of the 16th Century.)

of fine silver, gilt with ducat gold, chased, engraved, and in workmanship so executed that the style surpassed the material."

That rare piece was the work of Jean Regnard, a Parisian goldsmith ; and the period when such works were produced was precisely that during which religious wars were about to cause the annihilation of a great number of the *chefs-d'œuvre*, ancient and modern, of the goldsmith's art. The new iconoclasts, the Huguenots, shattered and melted down, wherever they triumphed, the sacred vessels, the shrines, the reliquaries. Then were lost the most precious gold-wrought memorials of the times of St. Eloi, of Charlemagne, of Suger, and of St. Louis.

At the same period Germany, where the influence of the Italian school had made itself felt less directly, but which could not escape from its impulse, possessed also, especially at Nuremburg and Augsburg, goldsmiths' workshops of high character; these furnished the empire, and even foreign countries, with remarkable works. A new career opened to the German goldsmiths when the cabinet-makers of their country had invented those *cabinets*, whereof we have already said something (*vide* FURNITURE), and in the intricate decoration of which appear statuettes, silver bas-reliefs, and inlay-work of gold and precious stones.

The *treasuries* and the museums of Germany have succeeded in preserving many rich objects of that period; but one of the most rare collections of the kind is that in Berlin, where, in substitution for the originals in silver which have been melted down, are gathered a great number of beautiful bas-reliefs in lead, and several vases in tin,—copies of pieces of plate supposed to be of the sixteenth and seventeenth centuries. And on this point it may be remarked that the high price of the material, together with the sumptuary laws not always admitting of the possession of gold or silver vases by the citizens, it sometimes happened that the goldsmiths manufactured a table-service of tin, on which they bestowed so much pains that these articles were transferred from the sideboards of citizens to those of princes. The inventory of the Count d'Angoulême, father of Francis I., alludes to a considerable table-service of tin. Indeed, several goldsmiths devoted themselves exclusively to this description of work; and, to this day, the tins of François Briot, who flourished in the time of Henry II., are regarded as the most perfect specimens of plate of the sixteenth century.

However that may be, after Cellini, and until the reign of Louis XIV., the goldsmith's art did but follow faithfully in the footsteps of the Italian master. Elevated by the impulse of the Renaissance, the art succeeded in maintaining itself in that high position without, however, any striking individuality discovering itself, until, in a century not less illustrious than the sixteenth, new masters appeared and imparted to it additional lustre and magnificence. These are named Ballin, Delaunay, Julien Defontaine, Labarre, Vincent Petit, Roussel, goldsmiths and jewellers of Louis XIV., who retained them in his pay, and lodged them in the Louvre. It was for that prince they produced an imposing collection of admirable works, for which Le Brun often furnished the designs, and under an inspiration altogether French, abandoned the graceful, though rather *fluette* forms of the Renaissance, and gave to them a character more diffuse and grand. Then, for a short time, every article of royal furniture proceeded from the hands of the goldsmith. But, alas! once more the majority of these marvels must disappear, as happened to so many others. Even the monarch who had ordered them despatched his acquisitions to the crucibles of the mint, when, the war having exhausted the public treasury, he found himself compelled, at least for example's sake, to sacrifice his silver plate and to deck his table with earthenware.

Having finished this sketch of the goldsmith's art in general, it may not be inappropriate to add a brief notice of the more special history of the French goldsmiths, of which the wealthy corporation may be considered not only as the most ancient, but as the model of all those that were formed among us in the Middle Ages. But first, since we have already referred to the exceptional part taken by the goldsmiths of Limoges in the industrial movement of that period, we cannot proceed further without noting another description of works, which, although derived from the oldest examples, nevertheless gave, and with justice, a kind of new lustre to the ancient city where the first goldsmiths of France had distinguished themselves.

"Towards the end of the fourteenth century," says M. Labarte, "the taste for gold and silver articles having led to the disuse of plate of enamelled copper, the Limousine enamellers endeavoured to discover a new mode of applying enamel to the reproduction of graphic subjects. Their researches led them to dispense with the chaser for delineating the outlines of designs; the metal was entirely concealed under the enamel, which, spread by the brush, formed altogether both the drawing and the colouring. The first attempts at this novel painting on copper were necessarily very imperfect; but the processes gradually improved, until at length, in 1540, they attained perfection. Prior to that period, the enamels of Limoges were almost exclusively devoted to the reproduction of sacred subjects, of which the German school furnished the designs. But the arrival of Italian artists at the court of Francis I., and the publication of engravings of the works of Raphael and other great masters of Italy, gave a new direction to the school of Limoges, which adopted the style of that of Italy. Il Rosso and Primaticcio painted cartoons for the Limousine enamellers; and then

DRAGEOIR, OR TABLE ORNAMENT

Of Enamelled and Gilt Copper. German, latter part of Sixteenth Century.

they who had previously worked only on plates intended to be set in diptychs, on caskets, created a new species of goldsmith's art. Basins, ewers, cups, salt-cellars, vases, and utensils of all sorts, manufactured with thin sheet-copper in the most elegant forms were decorated with their rich and brilliant paintings."

In the highest rank of artists who have rendered this attractive work illustrious we must place Léonard (Limousin), painter to Francis I., who was the first director of the royal manufacture of enamels founded by that king at Limoges. Then followed Pierre Raymond (Figs. 107 to 110), whose works date from 1534 to 1578, the Penicauds, Courteys, Martial Raymond, Mercier, and Jean Limousin, enameller to Anne of Austria.

Figs. 107 and 108.—Faces of an Hexagonal Enamelled Salt-cellar, representing the Labours of Hercules. Executed at Limoges, for Francis I., by Pierre Raymond.

With the remark that, at the end of the sixteenth century, Venice, doubtless imitating Limoges, also manufactured pieces of plate in enamelled copper, we return to our national goldsmiths.

This celebrated corporation could, without much trouble, be traced back in Gaul to the epoch of the Roman occupation ; but it is unnecessary to search for its origin beyond St. Eloi, who is still its patron, after having been its founder and protector. Eloi, become prime-minister to Dagobert I. —thanks in some measure to his merits as a goldsmith, which distinguished him above all, and gained him the honour of royal friendship—continued to work no less at his forge as a simple artisan. " He made for the king," says the chronicle, "a great number of gold vases enriched with precious stones, and he worked incessantly, seated with his servant Thillon, a Saxon by birth, at his side, who followed the lessons of his master."

This extract seems to indicate that already the goldsmith's art was organised as a corporation, and that it comprised three ranks of artisans— the masters, the journeymen, and the apprentices. Besides, it is clear that St. Eloi founded two distinct corporations of goldsmiths—one for secular, the other for religious works, in order that the objects sacred to worship should

Fig. 109.—Interior base of a Salt-cellar, executed at Limoges; with a Portrait of Francis I.

not be manufactured by the same hands that executed those designed for profane uses or worldly state. The seat of the former in Paris was first the Cité, near the very abode of St. Eloi long known as the *maison au fèvre*, and surrounding the monastery of St. Martial. Within the jurisdiction of that monastery was the space comprised between the streets of La Barillerie, of La Calandre, Aux Fèves, and of La Vieille Draperie, under the denomination of "St. Eloi's Enclosure." A raging fire destroyed the entire quarter inhabited by the goldsmiths, excepting the monastery; and the lay goldsmiths went forth and established themselves as a colony, still under the auspices of their patron saint, in the shadow of the Church of St. Paul des Champs, which he had caused to be constructed on the right bank of the Seine. The assemblage of forges and shops of these artisans soon formed a sort of suburb, which was called *Clôture*, or *Culture St. Eloi*. Subsequently some of the goldsmiths returned to the Cité; but they remained on the Grand-Pont, and returned no more to the streets, where the cobblers had established themselves. Moreover, the monastery of St. Martial had become, under the administration of its first abbess, St. Anne, a branch of the goldsmith's school which the "Seigneur Eloi" had established in 631 in the Abbey of Solignac, in the environs of Limoges. That abbey, whose

Fig. 110.—Ewer in Enamel, of Limoges, by Pierre Raymond.

first abbot, Thillon or Théau—a pupil, or, as the chronicle expresses it, a servant of St. Eloi—was also a skilful goldsmith, preserved during several centuries the traditions of its founder, and furnished not only models, but also skilful workmen, to all the monastic ateliers of Christendom which exclusively manufactured for the churches jewelled and enamelled plate.

However, the goldsmiths of Paris engaged in secular works continued to maintain themselves as a corporation; and their privileges, which they ascribed to the special regard of Dagobert for St. Eloi, were recognised, it is said, in 768 by a royal charter, and confirmed in 846 in a capitulary of Charles the Bald. These goldsmiths worked in gold and silver only for kings and nobles, whom the strictness of the sumptuary laws did not reach.

The Dictionary of Jean de Garlande informs us that, in the eleventh century, there were in Paris four classes of workmen in the goldsmith's trade—those who coined money (*nummularii*), the clasp-makers (*firmacularii*), the manufacturers of drinking-goblets (*cipharii*), and the goldsmiths, properly so called (*aurifabri*). The ateliers and the shop-windows of these last were on the Pont-au-Change (Fig. 111), in competition with the money-changers, who for the most part were Lombards or Italians. From that epoch a

Fig. 111.—Interior of the Atelier of Etienne Delaulne, a celebrated goldsmith of Paris, in the Sixteenth Century. Designed and Engraved by himself.

rivalry commenced between these two trade guilds, which only ceased on the complete downfall of the money-changers.

When Etienne Boileau, Provost of Paris in the reign of Louis IX., wrote in obedience to the legislative designs of the king, his famous "Livre des Métiers," to establish the existence of guilds on permanent foundations, he had scarcely more to do than to transcribe the statutes of the goldsmiths almost the same as those instituted by St. Eloi, with the modifications consequent on the new order of things. By the terms of the ordinances drawn up by Louis, the goldsmiths of Paris were exempt from the watch, and from all other feudal services ; they elected, every three years, two or three *anciens*

(seniors) "for the protection of the trade," and these *anciens* exercised permanent vigilance over the works of their colleagues, and over the quality of
the gold and silver material used by them. An apprentice was not admitted
as a master until after ten years' apprenticeship; and no master could have
more than one apprentice, in addition to those belonging to his own family.
The corporation, so far as concerned the fraternity with respect to works for
charitable and devotional purposes, had a seal (Fig. 116) which placed it
under the patronage of St. Eloi; but, with regard to its industrial association, it imprinted on manufactured articles a *seing*, or stamp, which
guaranteed the value of the metal. The corporation soon obtained, from
Philip of Valois, a coat-of-arms, which conferred on it a sort of professional
nobility; and acquired, owing to the distinguished protection extended to

Fig. 112.—Stamp of Lyons.   Fig. 113.—Stamp of Chartres.

Fig. 114.—Stamp of Melun.   Fig. 116.—Ancient Corporate Seal of the   Fig. 115.—Stamp of Orléans.
Goldsmiths of Paris.

it by that king, a position which nevertheless it did not succeed in preserving in the united constitution of the six mercantile bodies; for, although
it laid claim to the first rank on account of its antiquity, it was forced,
notwithstanding the undeniable superiority of its works, to be contented
with the second, and even to descend to the third rank.

The goldsmiths, at the time of the compilation of the code of professions
by Etienne Boileau, were already separated, voluntarily or otherwise, from
several trades which had long appeared in their train: the *cristalliers*, or
lapidaries; the gold and silver beaters; the embroiderers in *orfroi* (gold-
fringe); the *patenôtriers* (bead-stringers) in precious stones lived under their
own regulations; the *monétaires* (bullion-dealers) remained under the control
of the king and his mint; the *hanapiers* (drinking-cup makers), the *fermailleurs*

(makers of clasps), the pewterers, boxmakers, inferior artisans and others who worked in common metals, had no longer any connection with the goldsmiths of Paris. But in the provinces, in towns where the masters of a trade were insufficient to constitute a community or fraternity having its chiefs and its own administration, it was indispensable to reunite under the same banner the trades between which there was the most agreement, or rather the least contrariety. Thus, in certain localities in France and the Low Countries, the goldsmiths, proud as they might be of the nobility of their origin, sometimes found themselves united as equals with the

Fig. 117.—Arms of the Corporation of Goldsmiths of Paris, with this device:
" Vases Sacrés et Couronnes, voilà notre Œuvre."

pewterers, the mercers, the braziers, and even the grocers; and thus it came to pass that they combined on their banners of fleurs-de-lis the proper arms of each of these several trades. Thus, for instance, we see the banner of the goldsmiths of Castellane (Fig. 118) united with the retail mercers and tailors—it shows a pair of scissors, scales, and an ell measure; at Chauny (Fig. 119), a ladder, a hammer, and a vase, indicate that the goldsmiths had for compeers the pewterers and the slaters; at Guise (Fig. 120), the association of farriers, coppersmiths, and locksmiths, is allied with the goldsmiths by a horse-shoe, a mallet, and a key; the brewers of Harfleur

(Fig. 121) quartered in their arms four barrels between the bars of the cross *gules* charged with a goblet of gold, which was the emblem of their associates the goldsmiths; at Maringues (Fig. 122), the gold cup on a field *gules* surmounts the grocer's candles.

These banners were displayed only on great public ceremonies, in solemn processions, receptions, marriages, the obsequies of kings, queens, princes, and princesses. Exempted from military service, the goldsmiths, unlike other trade corporations, had not the opportunity of distinguishing themselves in the militia of the communes. They, nevertheless, occupied the first place in the state processions of trades, and frequently filled posts of honour.

Fig. 118.   Fig. 119.   Fig. 120.

Fig. 121.   Fig. 122.

Thus in Paris they had the custody of the gold and silver plate when the good city entertained some illustrious guest at a banquet; they carried the canopy above the head of the king on his joyful accession; or, crowned with roses, walked bearing on their shoulders the venerated shrine of St. Geneviève (Fig. 123).

In the wealthy cities of Belgium, where the corporations were queens (*reines*), the goldsmiths, by virtue of their privileges, dictated the law and swayed the people. No doubt in France they were far from enjoying the same political influence; nevertheless, one of them was that provost of merchants, Etienne Marcel, who, from 1356 to 1358, played so bold a part during the regency of the Dauphin Charles. But it was especially in periods of peace and prosperity that the goldsmith's art in Paris shone in all its splendour; then its banners incessantly waved in the breeze for the festivals and processions of its numerous and wealthy brotherhoods to the churches of Notre-Dame, St. Martial, St. Paul, and St. Denis of Montmartre.

In 1337 the number of the wardens of the goldsmith's guild in Paris had increased from three to six. They had their names engraved and their

Fig. 123.—The Corporation of the Goldsmiths of Paris carrying the Shrine of St. Geneviève.
(From an engraving of the Seventeenth Century.)

marks stamped on tablets of copper, which were preserved as archives in the town-hall. Every French goldsmith, admitted a master after the production of his principal work, left the impression of his sign manual, or private mark, on similar tablets of copper deposited in the office of the guild; while the stamp of the community itself was required to be engraved at the mint to authorise its being used. Every corporation thus had its mark, which the wardens set on the articles after having assayed and weighed the metal. These marks, at least in the later centuries, represented in general the special arms or emblems of the cities: for Lyons, it is a lion; for Melun, an eel; for Chartres, a partridge; for Orléans, the head of Joan of Arc, &c. (Figs. 112 to 115).

The goldsmiths of France manifested, and with reason, a jealousy of their privileges, it being more indispensable for them than for any other artisans to inspire that confidence without which the trade would have been lost; for their works were required to bear as authentic and legal a value as that of money. Therefore, it may be understood that they exercised keen vigilance over all gold or silver objects which were in any way under their

Fig. 124.—Gold Cross, chased. (A French Work of the Seventeenth Century.)

warranty; hence the frequent visits of the sworn masters to the ateliers and shops of the goldsmiths; hence the perpetual lawsuits against all instances of negligence or fraud; hence those quarrels with other trades which arrogated to themselves the right of working in precious metals without having qualified for it. Confiscation of goods, the whip, the pillory, were penalties inflicted on goldsmiths in contraband trade who altered the standard, concealed copper beneath the gold, or substituted false for precious stones.

It, indeed, seems remarkable that while for the most part other trades were subject to the control of the goldsmiths, the latter were responsible only to themselves for the aggressions which they constantly

committed within the domain of rival industries. Whenever the object to
be manufactured was of gold, it belonged to the goldsmith's trade. The
goldsmith made, by turns, spurs as the spur-maker; armour and arms, as
the armourer; girdles and clasps, as the belt-maker and the clasp-maker.
However, there is reason to believe that in the fabrication of these various
objects, the goldsmith had recourse to the assistance of special artisans, who
could scarcely fail to derive all possible advantage from such fortuitous
association. Thus, when the gold-wrought sword which Dunois carried
when Charles VII. entered Lyons in 1449, mounted in diamonds and
rubies, and valued at more than fifteen thousand crowns, was to be made,
the work of the goldsmiths probably consisted only of the fashioning and

Fig. 125.—Pendant, adorned with Diamonds and Precious Stones.　(Seventeenth Century.)

chasing the hilt, while the sword-cutler had to forge and temper the blade.
In the same manner, when it was required to work a jewelled robe such as
Marie de Medicis wore at the baptism of her son in 1606, the robe being
covered with thirty-two thousand precious stones and three thousand
diamonds, the goldsmith had only to mount the stones and furnish the design
for fixing them on the gold or silk tissue.

Long before Benvenuto and other skilful Italian goldsmiths were
summoned by Francis I. to his court, the French goldsmiths had proved
that they needed only a little encouragement to range themselves on a level
with foreign artists. But that patronage having failed them, they left the
country and established themselves elsewhere; thus at the court of Flanders,

Antoine of Bordeaux, Margerie of Avignon, and Jean of Rouen, distinguished themselves. It is true that in the reign of Louis XII., whose exchequer had been exhausted in the Italian expeditions, gold and silver had become so scarce in France, that the king was obliged to prohibit the manufacture of all sorts of large plate (*grosserie*). But the discovery of America having brought with it an abundance of the precious metals, Louis XII.

Figs. 126 to 131.—Chains.

recalled his ordinance in 1510; and thenceforth the corporations of goldsmiths were seen to increase and prosper as luxuriousness, diffused by the example of the great, descended to the lower ranks of society. Silver plate soon displaced that of tin; and before long personal display had attained such a height, "that the wife of a merchant wore on her person more jewels than were seen on the image of the Virgin." The number of gold-

Figs. 132 to 136.—Rings.

smiths then became so great that in the city of Rouen alone there were in 1563 *two hundred and sixty-five* masters having the right of stamp!

To sum up this chapter. Until the middle of the fourteenth century it is the religious art which prevails: the goldsmiths are engaged only in executing shrines, reliquaries, and church ornaments. At the end of that century, and during the one following, they manufactured gold and silver plate, enriching with their works the treasuries of kings and nobles, and imparting brilliant display to the adornment of dress. In the sixteenth and seventeenth centuries the goldsmiths applied themselves more to chasing, enamelling, and inlay-work. Everywhere are to be seen marvellous trinkets —necklaces, rings, buckles, chains, seals (Figs. 124 to 142). The weight of metal is no longer the principal merit; the skill of the workman is especially appreciated, and the goldsmith executes in gold, in silver, and in precious stones, the beautiful productions of painters and engravers. Nevertheless, the demand for delicate objects had the disadvantage of requiring much solder and alloy, which deteriorated the standard of metal. Then a desperate struggle commenced between the goldsmiths and the mint—a struggle which was prosecuted through a maze of legal proceedings, petitions, and ordinances, until the middle of the reign of Louis XV. At the same time, the Italian and German goldsmiths, making an irruption into

Figs. 137 to 141.—Scals.

France, and introducing materials of a low standard, the old professional integrity became suspected and was soon disregarded. At the end of the sixteenth century very little plate was ornamented: there is a return to massive plate, the weight and standard of which could be easily verified. Gold is scarcely any longer employed, except for jewels; and silver in a thousand forms creeps into the manufacture of furniture. After *cabinets,* covered and ornamented with carving in silver, came the articles of silver furniture invented by Claude Ballin. But the mass of precious metal withdrawn from circulation was soon returned to it, and the fashion passed away. The goldsmiths found themselves reduced to manufacture only objects of small size; and for the most part they limited themselves to works of jewellery, which subjected them to less annoyance from the mint. Besides, the art of the lapidary had almost changed its character, as well as the trade in precious stones. Pierre de Montarsy, jeweller to the king, effected a kind of revolution in his art, which the travels of Chardin, of Bernier, and of Tavernier, in the East had, so to say, enlarged. The cutting and mounting of precious stones has not since been excelled. It may be said that Montarsy was the first jeweller, as Ballin was the last goldsmith.

Fig. 142.—Chased and Enamelled Brooch, embellished with Pearls and Diamonds. (Seventeenth Century.)

HOROLOGY.

MONG the ancients there were three instruments for measuring time—the *gnomon,* or sun-dial, which is only, as we know, a table whereon lines are so arranged as successively to meet the shadow cast by a gnomon,* thus indicating the hour of the day according to the height or inclination of the sun ; the water-clock (*clepsydra*), which had for its principle the measured percolation of a certain quantity of water ; and the hour-glass, wherein the liquid is exchanged for sand. It would be difficult to determine which of these three chronometric modes can lay claim to priority. There is this to be said that, according to the Bible, in the eighth century before Christ, Ahaz, King of Judah, caused a sun-dial to be constructed at Jerusalem ; again, Herodotus says Anaximander introduced the sun-dial into Greece, whence it passed on to the other parts of the then civilised world ; and that, in the year 293 before our era, the celebrated Papirius Cursor, to the astonishment of his fellow-citizens, had a sun-dial traced near the temple of Jupiter Quirinus.

According to the description given by Athena (Athenæus ?), the water-clock was formed of an earthenware or metal vessel filled with water, and then suspended over a reservoir whereon lines were marked indicating

---

* *Gnomon*—literally the upright piece of wood or metal which projects the shadow on the plane of the dial.—[ED.]

the hours, as the water which escaped drop by drop from the upper vessel came to the level. We find this instrument employed by most ancient nations, and in many countries it remained in use until the tenth century of the Christian era.

In one of his dialogues Plato declares that the philosophers are far more fortunate than the orators—"these being the slaves of a miserable water-clock; whereas the others are at liberty to make their discourse as long as they please." To explain this passage, we must remember that it was the practice in the Athenian courts of justice, as subsequently in those of Rome,

Fig. 143.—The Clockmaker.   Designed and Engraved by J. Amman.

to measure the time allowed to the advocates for pleading by means of a water-clock. Three equal portions of water were put into it—one for the prosecutor, one for the defendant, and the third for the judge. A man was charged with the special duty of giving timely notice to each of the three speakers that his portion was nearly run out. If, on some unusual occasion, the time for one or other of the parties was doubled, it was called "adding water-clock to water-clock;" and when witnesses were giving evidence, or the text of some law was being read out, the percolation of the water was stopped: this was called *aquam sustinere* (to retain the water).

The hour-glass, which is still in use to a considerable extent for measuring short intervals of time, had great analogy with the water-clock, but was never susceptible of such regularity. In fact, at different periods important improvements were applied to the water-clock. Vitruvius tells us that, about one hundred years before our era, Ctesibius, a mechanician of Alexandria, added several cogged-wheels to the water-clock, one of which moved a hand, showing the hour on a dial. This must have been, so far as historical documents admit of proof, the first step towards purely mechanical horology.

In order, then, to find an authentic date in the history of horology, we must go to the eighth century, when water-clocks, still further improved, were either made or imported into France; among others, one which Pope Paul I. sent to Pepin le Bref. We must, however, believe that these instruments can have attracted but little attention, or that they were speedily forgotten; for, one hundred years later, there appeared a water-clock at the court of Charlemagne, a present from the famous caliph Aroun-al-Raschid, regarded, indeed almost celebrated, as a notable event. Of this Eginhard has left us an elaborate description. It was, he says, in brass, damaskeened with gold, and marked the hours on a dial. At the end of each hour an equal number of small iron balls fell on a bell, and made it sound as many times as the hour indicated by the needle. Twelve windows immediately opened, out of which were seen to proceed the same number of horsemen armed *cap-à-pie*, who, after performing divers evolutions, withdrew into the interior of the mechanism, and then the windows closed.

Shortly afterwards Pacificus, Archbishop of Verona, constructed one far superior to all that had preceded it; for, besides giving the hours, it indicated the date of the month, the days of the week, the phases of the moon, &c. But still it was only an improved water-clock. Before horology could really assume an historical date, it was necessary that for motive power weights should be substituted for water, and that the escapement should be invented; yet it was only in the beginning of the tenth century that these important discoveries were made.

"In the reign of Hugh Capet," says M. Dubois, "there lived in France a man of great talent and reputation named Gerbert. He was born in the mountains of Auvergne, and had passed his childhood in tending flocks near Aurillac. One day some monks of the order of St. Benedict met him in the fields : they conversed with him, and finding him precociously intelligent, took him into their convent of St. Gérauld. There Gerbert soon acquired a taste for monastic life. Eager for knowledge, and devoting all his spare moments to study, he became the most learned of the community. After he had taken vows, a desire to add to his scientific attainments led him to set out for Spain. During several years he assiduously frequented the universities of the Iberian peninsula. He soon found himself too learned for Spain; for, in spite of his truly sincere piety, ignorant fanatics accused him of sorcery. As that accusation might have involved him in deplorable consequences, he preferred not to await the result; and hastily quitting the town of Salamanca, which was his ordinary residence, he came to Paris, where he very soon made himself powerful friends and protectors. At length, after having successively been monk, superior of the convent of Bobbio, in Italy, archbishop of Rheims, tutor to Robert I., king of France, and to Otho III., emperor of Germany, who appointed him to the see of Ravenna, Gerbert rose to the pontifical throne under the name of Sylvester II. : he died in 1003. This great man did honour to his country and to his age. He was acquainted with nearly all the dead and living languages; he was a mechanician, astronomer, physician, geometrician, algebraist, &c. He introduced the Arab numerals into France. In the seclusion of his monastic cell, as in his archiepiscopal palace, his favourite relaxation was the study of mechanics. He was skilled in making sun-dials, water-clocks, hour-glasses, and hydraulic organs. It was he who first applied weight as a motive power to horology; and, in all probability, he is the inventor of that admirable mechanism called escapement—the most beautiful, as well as the most essential, of all the inventions which have been made in horology."

This is not the place to give a description of these two mechanisms, which can hardly be explained except with the assistance of purely technical drawings, but it may be remarked that weights are still the sole motive power of large clocks, and the escapement alluded to. has been alone employed throughout the world until the end of the seventeenth century. Notwithstanding the importance of these two inventions, little use was made of them during the eleventh, twelfth, and thirteenth centuries. The water-clock and hour-glass (Fig. 144) continued exclusively in use. Some were ornamented and engraved with much taste; and they contributed to the decoration of apartments, as at present do our bronzes and clocks more or less costly.

History does not inform us who was the inventor of the striking machinery; but it is at least averred that it existed at the commencement

Fig. 144.—An Hour-glass of the Sixteenth Century,—French Work.

of the twelfth century. The first mention of it is found in the " Usages de l'Ordre de Cîteaux," compiled about 1120. It is there prescribed to the sacristan so to regulate the clock, that it " sounds and awakens him before matins;" in another chapter the monk is ordered to prolong the lecture until "the clock strikes." At first, in the monasteries, the monks took it in turn to watch, and warn the community of the hours for prayer; and, in the towns, there were night watchmen, who, moreover, were maintained in many places to announce in the streets the hour denoted by the clocks, the water-clocks, or the hour-glasses.

The machinery for striking once invented, we do not find that horology had attained to any perfection before the end of the thirteenth century; but, in the commencement of the following it received its impulse, and the art from that time continued to progress.

To give an idea of what was effected at that time, we will borrow a passage from the earliest writings in which horology is mentioned; that is, from an unpublished book by Philip de Maizières, entitled "Le Songe du Vieil Pélerin:"—"It is known that in Italy there is at present (about 1350) a man generally celebrated in philosophy, in medicine, and in astronomy; in his station, by common report, singular and grave, excelling in the above three sciences, and of the city of Padua. His surname is lost, and he is called 'Maistre Jehan des Orloges,' residing at present with the Comte de Vertus; and, for the treble sciences, he has for yearly wages and perquisites two thousand florins, or thereabouts. This Maistre Jean des Orloges has made an instrument, by some called a *sphere* or clock, of the movement of the heavens, in which instrument are all the motions of the signs (zodiacal), and of the planets, with their circles and epicycles, and multiplied differences, wheels (*roes*) without number, with all their parts, and each planet in the said sphere, distinctly. On any given night, we see clearly in what sign and degree are the planets and the stars of the heavens; and this sphere is so cunningly made, that notwithstanding the multitude of wheels, which cannot well be numbered without taking the machinery to pieces, their entire mechanism is governed by one single counterpoise, so mar-vellous that the grave astronomers from distant regions come with great reverence to visit the said Maistre Jean and the work of his hands; and all the great clerks of astronomy, of philosophy, and of medicine, declare that there is no recollection of a man, either in written document or otherwise, who in this world has made so ingenious or so important an instrument of the heavenly movements as the said clock. . . . . . Maistre Jean made the said clock with his own hands, all of brass and of copper, without the assistance of any other person, and did nothing else during sixteen entire years, if the writer of the book, who had a great friendship for the said Maistre Jean, has been rightly informed."

It is known, on the other hand, that the famous clockmaker, whose real name Maizières assumes to be lost, was called Jaques de Dondis; and that, in spite of the assertion of the writer, he had only to arrange the clock, the parts of which had been executed by an excellent workman named Antoine. However this may be, placed at the top of one of the towers of the palace of Padua, the clock of Jaques de Dondis, or of "Maistre Jean des Orloges," excited general admiration, and several princes of Europe being desirous to have similar clocks, many workmen tried to imitate it. In fact, churches or monasteries were soon able to pride themselves on possessing similar *chefs-d'œuvre*.

Among the most remarkable clocks of that period, we must refer to that of which Froissart speaks, and which was carried away from the town of Courtray by Philip the Bold after the battle of Rosbecque in 1382. "The Duke of Burgundy," says our author, "caused to be carried away from the market-place a clock that struck the hours, one of the finest which could be found on either side the sea; and he conveyed it piece by piece in carts, and the bell also. Which clock was brought and carted into the town of Dijon, in Burgundy, was there deposited and put up, and there strikes the twenty-four hours between day and night."

It is the celebrated clock of Dijon which then as now was surmounted by two automata of iron, a man and a woman, striking the hours on the bell. The origin of the name of *Jacquemart* given to these figures has been much disputed. Ménage believes that the word is derived from the Latin *jaccomarchiardus* (coat of mail—attire of war); and he reminds us that, in the Middle Ages, it was the custom to station, on the summit of the towers, men (soldiers wearing the *jacque*) to give warning of the approach of the enemy, of fires, &c. Ménage adds that, when more efficient watchers occasioned the discontinuance of these nocturnal sentinels, it was probably considered desirable to preserve the remembrance of them by putting in the place they had occupied iron figures which struck the hours. Other writers trace the name even to the inventor of this description of clocks, who, according to them, lived in the fourteenth century, and was called Jacques Marck. Finally, Gabriel Peignot, who has written a dissertation on the *jacquemart* of Dijon, asserts that in 1422 a person named Jacquemart, clockmaker and locksmith, residing in the town of Lille, received twenty-two livres from the Duke of Burgundy, for repairing the clock of Dijon; and from that he concludes, seeing how short the distance is from Lille to Courtray, whence the clock of Dijon had been taken, that this Jacquemart might well be the son or the grandson of the clockmaker who .had constructed it about 1360; consequently the name

Fig. 145.—Jacquemart of Notre-Dame at Dijon, made at Courtray in the Fourteenth Century.

of the *jacquemart* of Dijon is derived from that of its maker, old Jacquemart, the clockmaker of Lille (Fig. 145).

Giving to each of these opinions its due weight, we confine ourselves to stating that, from the end of the fourteenth century to the beginning of the fifteenth, numerous churches in Germany, Italy, and France already had *jacquemarts*.

The first clock possessed by Paris was that in the turret of the Palais de Justice. Charles V. had it constructed in 1370 by a German artisan, Henri de Vic. It contained a weight for moving power, an oscillating piece for regulator, and an escapement. It was adorned with carvings by Germain Pilon, and was destroyed in the eighteenth century.

In 1389, the clockmaker Jean Jouvence made one for the Castle of Montargis. Those of Sens and of Auxerre, as well as that of Lund

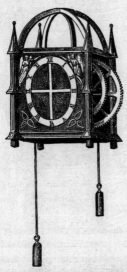

Fig. 146.—Clock with Wheels and Weights. Fifteenth Century.
(Cabinet of Antiquities, Bibl. Imp., Paris.)

in Sweden, date from the same period. In the last, every hour two cavaliers met and gave each other as many blows as the hours to be struck: then a door opened, and the Virgin Mary appeared sitting on a throne, with the Infant Jesus in her arms, receiving the visit of the Magi followed by their retinue; the Magi prostrating themselves and tendering their presents. During the ceremony two trumpets sounded: then all vanished, to re-appear the following hour.

Until the end of the thirteenth century, clocks were destined exclusively to public buildings; or they at least affected, if we may say so, a monumental character which precluded their admission into private houses. The first clocks with weights and the flywheel made for private use appeared in

Fig. 147.—A portable Clock of the time of the Valois.

France, in Italy, and in Germany, about the commencement of the four-teenth century; but naturally they were at first so costly that only nobles and wealthy persons could obtain them. But an impulse was given which led to the manufacture of these objects more economically. In fact, it was not long before portable clocks were seen in the most unpretentious abodes. This of course did not prevent the production of expensive examples, either as regards ornamentation or carving, or in placing the clock on costly pedestals or cases, within which were suspended the weights (Fig. 146).

The fifteenth century has distinctly left its mark on the progress of horology. In 1401 the Cathedral of Seville was enriched with a magnificent clock which struck the hours. In 1404, Lazare, a Servian by birth, constructed a similar one for Moscow. That of Lubeck, which was embellished with the figures of the twelve Apostles, dates from 1405. It is proper to notice also the famous clock which Jean-Galeas Visconti had made for Pavia; and more especially that of St. Marc of Venice, which was not executed until 1495.

The spiral spring was invented in the time of Charles VII.: a band of very fine steel, rolled up into a small drum or barrel, produced, in unrolling, the effect of the weights on the primitive movements. To the possibility of enclosing that moving power in a confined space is due the facility of manufacturing very small clocks. In fact, one finds in certain collections, clocks of the time of Louis XI., remarkable not only for the artistic richness of their decoration, but still more so for the small space they occupy, although they are generally of very complicated mechanism; some marking the date of the month, striking the hour, and serving also as alarm-clocks.

It is difficult, if not impossible, to determine the exact date of the invention of watches. But, in truth, we ought perhaps to regard the watch, especially after the invention of the spiral spring, as only the last step taken towards a portable form of clock. It is however true, according to the statements found in Pancirole and Du Verdier by the authors of the "Encyclopædia of Sciences," that at the end of the fifteenth century watches were made no larger than an almond. Even the names Myrmécides and Carovagius are cited as those of two celebrated artisans in such work. It was said that the latter made an alarm-watch which not only sounded the hour required, but even struck a light to ignite a candle. Besides, we know for certain that, in the time of Louis XI., there were watches very small yet perfectly manufactured; and it is proved that, in 1500, at Nuremberg, Peter Hele made them of the form of an egg, and consequently the watches of that country were long known as *Nuremberg eggs.*

We learn, moreover, from history that in 1542, a watch which struck the hours, set in a ring, was offered to Guidobaldo of Rovere; and that in 1575, Parker, Archbishop of Canterbury, bequeathed to his brother Richard a cane of Indian wood having a watch placed in its head; and, finally, that Henry VIII. of England wore a very small watch requiring to be wound up only every eighth day.

It is not inappropriate here to remark that the time kept by these little machines was not regular until an ingenious workman, whose name has not come down to us, invented the fusee, a kind of truncated cone; to the base of this was attached a small piece of catgut which, spirally rolling itself up to the top, became fastened to the barrel that enclosed the spring. The advantage of this arrangement is, that owing to the conical form of the fusee, the traction of the spring acting as it relaxes on a greater radius of the cone, it results in establishing equilibrium of power between the first and the last movements of the spring. Subsequently a clockmaker named Gruet substituted jointed (*articulées*) chains for catgut; the latter having the great disadvantage of being hygrometric and varying in tension with the state of the atmosphere.

The use of watches spread rapidly in France. In the reigns of the Valois, a large number were made of very diminutive size, to which the clockmakers gave all sorts of forms, especially those of an acorn, an almond, a Latin cross, a shell (Figs. 148 to 150). They were engraved, chased, enamelled; the hand which marked the hour was very frequently of delicate workmanship, and sometimes ornamented with precious stones. Some of these watches set in motion symbolic figures, as well as Time, Apollo, Diana, the Virgin, the Apostles, and the saints.

It may be conceived that all these complicated works required numerous craftsmen. It was therefore considered proper to unite these artisans in a community. The statutes which they had received from Louis XI. in 1483 were confirmed by Francis I. They contained a succession of laws, intended to protect at the same time the interests of members of the corporation and the dignity of their profession.

No one was admitted as master but on proof of having served eight years of apprenticeship, and after having produced a *chef-d'œuvre* in the

CLOCK OF DAMASCENED IRON AND WATCHES

Of the Fifteenth and Sixteenth Centuries.

house, or under the supervision, of one of the inspectors of the corporation. The visiting inspectors, elected by all the members, as well as by the trustees and the syndics, were authorised when introducing themselves into the workshops, to look after the proper construction of watches and clocks ; and if it happened that they found such as did not appear to be made according to the rules of art, they could not only seize and destroy them,

Figs. 148 to 150.—Watches of the Valois Epoch. (Sixteenth Century.).

but also impose a fine on the maker for the benefit of the corporation. The statutes also gave exclusive right to the accredited masters to trade, directly or otherwise, with all the stock, new or second-hand, finished or unfinished.

"Under the influence of these wise institutions," M. Dubois remarks, "the master-clockmakers had no fear of the competition of persons not

belonging to the corporation. If they were affected by the artistic
superiority of some of their colleagues, it was with the laudable desire to
contend with them for the first places. The work of one day, superior to
that of the preceding, was surpassed by that of the day following. It was
by this incessant competition of intelligence and knowledge, by this legitimate and invigorating rivalry of all the members of the same industrious
community, that science itself attained by degrees the zenith of the excellent and the sublime of the beautiful. The ambition of workmen was to
rise to the mastership, and they attained that only by force of labour
and assiduous efforts. The ambition of the masters was to acquire the
honours of the syndicate—that consular magistracy the most honourable
of all, for it was the result of election, and the recompense of services
rendered to art and to the community."

Having thus reached the middle of the sixteenth century, and not wishing
to exceed the compass assigned to this sketch, we may limit ourselves to the
mention of some of the remarkable works produced during a century
by an art that had already manifested itself with a power never to be
diminished.

The clock which Henry II. had constructed for the château of Anet has
long been regarded as very curious. Every time the hand denotes the hour,
a stag appears from the inside of the clock, and darts away followed by a
pack of hounds; but soon the pack and the stag stop, and the latter, by
means of very ingenious mechanism, strikes the hours with one of his feet.

The clock of Jena (Fig. 151), which is still in existence, is not less
famous. Above the dial is a bronze head presumed to represent a buffoon
of Ernest, Elector of Saxony, who died in 1486. When the hour is
about to strike, the head—so remarkably ugly as to have given the clock
the name of the *monstrous head*—opens its very large mouth. A figure
representing an old pilgrim offers it a golden apple on the end of a stick;
but just when poor Hans (so was the fool called) is about to close his
mouth to masticate and swallow the apple, the pilgrim suddenly withdraws
it. On the left of the head is an angel singing (the arms of the city of
Jena), holding in one hand a book, which he raises towards his eyes whenever the hours strike, and with the other he rings a hand-bell.

The town of Niort, in Poitou, possessed also an extraordinary clock,
ornamented with a great number of allegorical figures—the work of Bouhain,

in 1570. A much more famous clock was that of Strasburg (Fig. 152), constructed in 1573, and which was long considered to be the greatest of all wonders. It was entirely restored in 1842 by M. Schwilgué. Angelo Rocca, in his "Commentarium de Campanis," gives a description of it. Its most important feature was a moving sphere, whereon were represented the planets and the constellations, and which completed its rotation in

Fig. 151.—Clock of Jena, in Germany. (Fifteenth Century.)

three hundred and sixty-five days. On two sides of the dial and below it the principal festivals of the year and the solemnities of the Church were represented by allegorical figures. Other dials, distributed symmetrically on the façade of the tower in which the clock is situated, marked the days of the week, the date of the month, the signs of the zodiac, the phases of the moon, the rising and setting of the sun, &c. Every hour two angels

Fig. 152.— Astronomical Clock of the Cathedral at Strasburg, constructed in 1573.

sounded the trumpet. When the concert was finished, the bell tolled; then immediately a cock, perched on the summit, spread his wings noisily, and made his crowing to be heard. The striking machinery, by means of movable trap-doors, cylinders, and springs concealed in the interior of the clock, set in motion a considerable number of automata, executed with much skill. Angelo Rocca adds that the completion of this *chef-d'œuvre* was attributed to Nicolas Copernicus; and that when this able mechanician had finished his work, the sheriffs and consuls of the city had his eyes put out in order to render it impossible for him to execute a similar clock for any other city. This last statement is the more deserving to rank among mere legends from the fact that, independent of existing proof of the clock being made by Conrad Dasypodius, it would be very difficult to prove that Copernicus ever visited Alsace, or had his eyes put out.

A similar tradition is attached to the history of another clock still in existence, and which was not less celebrated than that of Strasburg. We refer to that of the Church of St. John at Lyons, made in 1598 by Nicholas Lippius, a clockmaker of Basle; repaired and enlarged subsequently by Nourisson, an artisan of Lyons. Only the horary mechanism now acts; but the clock is not on that account neglected by visitors, to whom the worthy attendants still repeat, in perfect faith, that Lippius was put to death as soon as he had finished his *chef-d'œuvre*. To show the improbability of this pretended penalty it is sufficient to remark, with M. Dubois, that even in the sixteenth century persons were not killed for the crime of making *chefs-d'œuvre;* and there is, besides, proof that Lippius died in peace, and honoured, in his native country.

To these famous clocks must be added those of St. Lambert at Liège, of Nuremberg, of Augsburg, and of Basle; that of Medina del Campo, in Spain, and those which, in the reign of Charles I., or during the Protectorship of Cromwell, were manufactured and placed in England, at St. Dunstan's in London,[*] and in the Cathedral of Canterbury, in Edinburgh, and in Glasgow, &c.

Before concluding, and to do justice to a century to which we have assigned a period of decline, we are bound to acknowledge that some years before the death of Cardinal Richelieu—that is to say, from 1630 to 1640

---

[*] This clock, as many readers doubtless know, was removed some years ago, when St. Dunstan's Church, in Fleet Street, was rebuilt.—[ED.]

—artists of ability made praiseworthy efforts to create a new era in
horology. But the improvements they had in view were directed much
more to the processes of the construction of the several parts composing the
clockwork of watches and clocks than to the beauty and ingenuity of the
workmanship. This was progress of a purely professional character, in
order to create a more ready and inexpensive supply ; a progress which we
may regard as services rendered by art to trade. The period of great
constructions and delicate marvels was past. Ornamental *Jacquemarts* were
no longer placed in belfries. Mechanical *chefs-d'œuvre* were no longer set
in frail gems. The time was still far off when, laying down the sceptre
of that empire on which "the sun never sets," the conqueror of Francis I.,
retiring to a cloister, employed himself in the construction of the most
complicated clockwork. Charles V. had as assistant, if not as teacher, in
his work the learned mathematician, Jannellus Turianus, whom he had
induced to join him in his retreat. It is said that he enjoyed nothing so
much as seeing the monks of Saint-Just standing amazed before his alarum
watches and automaton clocks ; but it is also stated that he manifested the
greatest despair when obliged to admit it was as impossible to establish
perfect concord among clocks as among men.

In truth, Galileo had not yet arrived to observe and formulate the laws
of the pendulum, which Huygens was happily to apply to the movements
of horology.

Fig. 153.—Top of an Hour-Glass, engraved and gilt. (A French Work of the Sixteenth Century.)

MUSICAL INSTRUMENTS.

Music in the Middle Ages.—Musical Instrumen's from the Fourth to the Thirteenth Century.—
Wind Instruments: the Single and Double Flute, the Pandean Pipes, the Reed-pipe, the
Hautboy, the Flageolet, Trumpets, Horns, *Olifants*, the Hydraulic Organ, the Bellows-
Organ.—Instruments of Percussion: the Bell, the Hand-bell, Cymbals, the Timbrel, the
Triangle, the *Bombulum*, Drums.—Stringed Instruments: the Lyre, the Cithern, the Harp,
the Psaltery, the *Nable*, the *Chorus*, the *Organistrum*, the Lute and the Guitar, the *Crout*, the
Rote, the Viola, the *Gigue*, the Monochord.

HE history of Music in the Middle Ages would commence about the fourth century of our era. In the
sixth century, Isidore of Seville, in his "Sentiments
sur la Musique," writes as follows:—"Music is a modula-
tion of the voice, and also an accordance of several sounds
and their simultaneous union."

About 384, St. Ambrose, who built the Cathedral
of Milan, regulated the mode in which psalms, hymns,
and anthems should be performed, by selecting from Greek chants those
melodies he considered best adapted to the Latin Church.

In 590, Gregory the Great, in order to remedy the disorder which had
crept into ecclesiastical singing, collected all that remained of the ancient
Greek melodies, with those of St. Ambrose and others, and formed the
antiphonary which is called the *Centonien*, because it is composed of chants
of his selection. Henceforward, ecclesiastical chanting obtained the name
of *Gregorian;* it was adopted into the whole of the Western Church,
and maintained its position almost unaltered down to the middle of the
eleventh century.

It is thought that originally the music of the antiphonary was noted
in accordance with Greek and Roman usage—a notation known as the
Boethian, from the name of Boethius the philosopher, by whom we are
informed that in his time (that is, about the end of the fifth century) the
notation was composed of the first fifteen letters of the alphabet.

The sounds of the octave were represented—the major by *capital* letters, the minor by *small* letters, as follows :—

Major mode . . . . . . A B C D E F G
Minor mode . . . . . . a b c d e f g

Some fragments of music of the eleventh century are still preserved, in which the notation is represented by letters having above them the signs of another kind of notation called *neumes* (Fig. 154).

Fig. 154.—Lament composed shortly after the Death of Charlemagne, probably about 814 or 815, and attributed to Colomban, Abbot of Saint-Tron. (MS. de la Bibl. Imp., No. 1,154.)

Musical Notation expressed in Modern Signs, the Text and Translation of the Lament on Charlemagne.

ti ti a Te ti git in gens cum er ro re ni mi o

Heu me do lens plan go!

Fran ci Ro ma ni at que cun cti cre du li, Luc tu pun

gun tur et mag na mo les ti a in fan tes, se nes

glo ri o si prin ci pes Nam clan git or bis de trimentum Ka ro li

Heu mi hi mi se ro!

A solis ortu usque ad occidua
Littora maris, planctus pulsat pectora;
Ultra marina agmina tristitia
    Tetigit ingens cum errore nimio.
      Heu! me dolens, plango.

Franci, Romani, atque cuncti creduli,
Luctu punguntur et magna molestia,
Infantes, senes, gloriosi principes;
    Nam clangit orbis detrimentum Karoli.
      Heu! mihi misero!

From the East to the Western shores,
sorrow agitates every heart; and inland,
this vast grief saddens armies.
    Alas! in my grief, I, too, weep.

French, Romans, and all believers are
plunged into mourning and profound
grief: children, old men, and illustrious
princes; for the whole world deplores the
loss of Charlemagne.
    Alas! miserable me!

About the fourth century the *neumes* were in use in the Greek Church; they are spoken of by St. Gregory of Nazianzus. Certain modifications in them were introduced by the Lombards and Saxons.

"They were specially in use from the eighth to the twelfth century," says M. Coussemaker, in his learned work, "Histoire de l'Harmonie au Moyen Age," "and consisted of two sorts of signs: some formed like commas, dots, or small inclined or horizontal strokes, which represented isolated sounds; others in the shape of hooks, and strokes variously twisted and joined, expressing groups of sound composed of various intervals.

"These commas, dots, and inclined or horizontal strokes were the origin of the long notes, the breve and the semibreve, and afterwards of the square notation still in use in the *plain-chant* of the Church. The hook-shaped signs and the variously twisted and joined strokes gave rise to the ligatures and connections of notes.

"From the eighth to the end of the twelfth century—that is, during one of the brightest periods of musical liturgy—the *neumes* were the notation exclusively adopted over the whole of Europe, both in ecclesiastical singing and also in secular music. From the end of the eleventh century, this system of notation was established in France, Italy, Germany, England, and Spain."

The chief modification to which the notation of music was subject at the end of the eleventh century is due to the monk Guido, of Arezzo. In order to facilitate the reading of the *neumes*, he invented placing them on lines, and these lines he distinguished by colours. The second, that of the *fa*, was red; the fourth, that of the *ut*, was green; the first and the third are only traced on the vellum with a pen. In order that the seven notes should be better impressed upon the memory, he gave as an example the three first lines of the Hymn of St. John the Baptist, in which the syllables *ut, re, mi, fa, sol, la*, corresponded to the signs of the gamut :—

> " *Ut* queant laxis *Re*sonare fibris
> *Mi*ra gestorum *Fa*muli tuorum,
> *Sol*ve polluti *La*bii reatum,
> Sancte Joannes."

The choristers, in singing this hymn, slightly raised the intonation of each of the italicised syllables, which were soon adopted for indicating six of the notes of the gamut. To supply the seventh, which was not named in this system, the barbarous theory of *muances* (divisions) was introduced, and it was not until the seventeenth century the term *si* was applied in France.

But after the commencement of the tenth century many individuals, and especially poets, had invented rhythmical songs, which were entirely different from those of the Church. "Harmony formed by successions of various intervals," as we are told by the author whom we have before quoted, "obtained in the eleventh century the name of *discantus*, in old French *déchant*. Francon de Cologne is the most ancient author who makes use of this word. During the whole course of the eleventh century the composition of melody was independent of harmony, and henceforth the composition of music was divided into two very distinct parts. The people, and poets and persons in high life, constructed the melody and the words; but being ignorant of the science of music, they resorted to a professional musician to have their inspirations written down. The first were very justly called *trouvères* (*trobadori*), the others the *déchanteurs*, or harmonisers. Harmony was then only adapted for two voices—a combination of fifths, and of movements in unison.

"In the twelfth century, the construction of melody continued to be in the hands of poets. The *déchanteurs* or harmonisers were the professional musicians. Popular songs became very numerous. Troubadours multiplied all over Europe, and the greatest lords deemed it an honour to cultivate both poetry and music. Germany had her 'master-singers,' who were in request at every court. In France, the Châtelain de Coucy, the King of Navarre, the Comte de Béthune, the Comte d'Anjou, and a hundred others acquired a brilliant reputation by songs, of which they composed both the words and the melody. The most celebrated of these *trouvères* was Adam de la Halle, who flourished in 1260."

In the fourteenth century, the name of *counterpoint* was substituted for that of *déchant;* and in 1364, at the coronation of Charles V. at Rheims, a mass was sung which was written in four parts, composed by Guillaume de Machault, poet and musician.

Among the ancients the number of musical instruments was considerable, but their names were even still more numerous, because derived from the shape, the material, the nature and character of the instruments, all of which varied infinitely, according to the whim of the maker or the musician. Added to this, every country had its national instruments; and as each in its own language designated them by descriptive names, the same instrument appeared under ten different denominations, and a similar name was applied to ten instruments. However, having nothing but monumental representation to guide us, and in the absence of the instruments themselves, an almost inextricable confusion arises.

The Romans carried back to their own country, as the results of conquest, specimens of most of the musical instruments they found in use in the countries subdued by them. Thus Greece supplied Rome with nearly all the soft instruments of the class of lyres and flutes. Germany and the northern provinces, being inhabited by warlike races, gave to their conquerors the taste for loud-sounding instruments, such as trumpets and drums. Asia, and Judæa especially, which had multiplied various kinds of metal-instruments for use in their religious ceremonies, were the means of naturalising in Roman music deep-toned instruments of the class of bells and tom-toms (a kind of drum). Egypt introduced into Italy the timbrel along with the worship of Isis. Byzantium had no sooner invented the first pneumatic organs than the new religion of Christ took possession of them for exclusive consecration to its service, both in the East and in the West.

All the musical instruments of the known world had therefore taken refuge, as it were, in the capital of the Roman empire; but their fate was only to disappear and sink into oblivion after they had played their part in the last pomps of that falling empire, and in the final festivals of the ancient mythology. In a letter in which he specially treats of "various kinds of musical instruments," St. Jerome, who lived from 331 to 420, speaks of those which were in use in his time for the requirements of religion, war, ceremonial, and art. He mentions, in the first place, the organ, and describes it as composed of fifteen brazen pipes, two air-reservoirs of elephant's skin, and twelve large sets of bellows, "to imitate the voice of thunder." He next specifies, under the generic name of *tuba*, several kinds of trumpets : that which called the people together, that which directed the march of troops, that which proclaimed the victory, that which sounded the charge against the enemy, that which announced the closing of the gates, &c. One of these trumpets, the shape of which is rather difficult to gather from his description, had three brazen bells, and *roared through four air-conduits*. Another instrument, the *bombulum*, which must have made a frightful uproar, was, as far as we can conjecture from the text of the pious writer, a kind of peal of bells attached to a hollow metallic column which, by the assistance of twelve pipes, reverberated the sounds of twenty-four bells, that were set in motion by one another. Next come the *cithara* of the Hebrews, in the shape of a triangle, furnished with twenty-four strings ; the sackbut, of Chaldæan origin, a trumpet formed of several movable tubes of wood, fitting one into the other ; the psaltery, a small harp provided with ten strings ; and lastly, the *tympanum*, also called the *chorus*, a hand-drum to which were fixed two metal flute-tubes.

A nomenclature of a similar kind, applying to the ninth century, exists in a history of Charlemagne, in Latin verse, by Aymeric de Peyrac. This shows us that, during the lapse of four centuries, the number of instruments had been nearly doubled, and that the musical influence of Charlemagne's

Fig. 155.—Concert; a Bas-relief taken rom a Capital in Saint-Georges de Boscherville, Normandy. (A Work of the Eleventh Century.)

reign had made itself felt in the revival and improvement of several instruments which had been formerly abandoned. This curious metrical composition enumerates all the stringed, wind, and pulsatile instruments which celebrated the praise of the great emperor, the protector and restorer of music.   The number of instruments specified are twenty-four in number, among which we find nearly all those mentioned by St. Jerome.

The names, therefore, of musical instruments had passed through seven or eight centuries without undergoing any kind of change than that naturally resulting from variations in the language.   But the instruments themselves, during this long interval of time, had been often modified to such extent that the primitive denomination not unfrequently appeared to contradict the musical characteristics of the instrument to which it still continued to be attached.   Thus, the *chorus*, which had been a four-stringed harp, and from its name seems to indicate a collection of instruments, had

Fig. 156.—Concert and Musical Instruments.   From a Miniature in a Manuscript of the Thirteenth Century.

become a wind-instrument.*   So also the psaltery, which was originally touched by a *plectrum* (stick) or with the fingers, now only gave forth its notes under the influence of a bow; an instrument that had had twenty strings now only retained eight; another, the name of which seemed to refer to a square shape, was rounded; those primitively made of wood were now constructed of metal.   There is reason to believe that, generally speaking, these changes were made not so much with the view of any musical improvement, properly so called, as with an idea of gratifying the

---

* The reader will notice a discrepancy between this description of the *chorus* and that given in a preceding paragraph.   We have retained both, mainly because it is now impossible to determine what the instrument really was: no mention of it appears in any book we have consulted.—[ED.]

fancy of the eye (Figs. 155 to 157). Scarcely any fixed rules for the construction of musical instruments existed before the sixteenth century, when learned musicians applied mathematical principles to the theory of manufacture. Down to 1589 musical instruments were made in Paris

Fig. 157.—The Tree of Jesse. The ancestors of Jesus Christ are represented with Musical Instruments, and as forming a Celestial Concert. (Fac-simile from a Miniature in a Manuscript Breviary of the Fifteenth Century. Royal Library, Brussels.)

by workmen who were organ-makers, lute-makers, or even coppersmiths, under the inspection and guarantee of the community of musicians; but at this epoch the makers of musical instruments were united in a trade corporation, and obtained, through the goodwill of Henry III., certain privileges and special statutes.

As musical instruments have always been divided into three particular classes,—stringed, pulsatile, and wind instruments,—we shall adopt this natural division in passing under review the various kinds in use during the Middle Ages and the Renaissance. We shall not, however, pretend to be always able to point out the precise musical value of these instruments, for in several instances we have no knowledge of them, except from representations more or less truthful.

The class of wind instruments comprised flutes, trumpets, and organs; each of these was, however, subdivided into several very distinct kinds. In the division of flutes alone, for instance, we find the straight flute, the double flute, the side-mouthed or German flute, the Pandean pipes, the *chorus*, the *calamus*, the bagpipes (*muse* or *mousette*), the *doucine* or hautboy, the *flaïos* or flageolet, &c.

The flute is the most ancient of musical instruments; even in the Middle Ages no orchestra was considered complete which did not contain an entire order of flutes, differing both in shape and tone. In principle, the simple flute, or *flûte à bec*, consisted of a straight pipe of hard and sounding wood, made in one piece, and pierced with four or six holes. But the number of holes being successively increased to eleven, and the pipe being enlarged to a length of seven or eight feet, the result was that the fingers were unable to act simultaneously upon all the openings; thus, in order to close the two holes farthest from the mouthpiece, keys were attached to the body of the flute which the instrumentalist acted on with his foot.

The simple flute, of greater or less length, is seen on the figured monuments of every epoch. The double flute, which was equally in use, had, as its name indicates, two pipes, generally of unequal lengths; the *left-hand* tube, which was the shortest and therefore called the *feminine*, produced shrill sounds, while the *right-hand*, or *masculine*, gave the low notes. Whether these two tubes were united or were separate, this flute had always two distinct mouths—although they were often very close together —on which the musician played alternately. The double flute (Fig. 158) was the instrument employed in the eleventh century by the *jongleurs* or jugglers as an accompaniment.

The side-mouthed flute, which was at first very little used, owed its celebrity in the sixteenth century to the improvements it received from the Germans, hence it acquired the name of the *German flute* (Fig. 160).

The *syrinx* was nothing but the ancient Pandean pipes, composed generally of seven tubes of wood or metal, gradually decreasing in length; they were closed at the bottom, and at the top took the form of a horizontal plane, which was touched by the lip of the musician as it passed along (Fig. 159). In the eleventh and twelfth centuries, the syrinx, which must have produced very shrill and discordant music, was generally made in the shape of a semicircle, and contained nine tubes in a metallic case pierced with the same number of holes.

Fig. 158.—Double Flute, Fourteenth Century.
(From Willemin's "French Monuments.")

Fig. 159.—Seven-tubed *Syrinx*, Ninth or Tenth Century. (Angers MS.)

The *chorus*, which in the time of St. Jerome was composed of a skin and two tubes, one forming the mouth, the other the bell-end (Fig. 161), must have presented a very great similarity to the modern bagpipes. In the ninth century its shape had changed but little, except that we sometimes find two bell-ends, and the membranous air-reservoir is in some examples replaced by a kind of case made of metal or resonant wood (*bois sonore*). Subsequently this instrument was transformed into a simple dulcimer.

The *calamus*, called the *chalemelle* or *chalemie*, which derived its origin from the *calamus* or reed-pipe of the ancients, became in the sixteenth century a treble to the hautboy, the *bombarde* being its counter-bass and tenor, and the bass being executed on the *cromorne*. There was, however, quite a group of hautboys. The *douçaine* or *doucine*, a soft flute, the great hautboy of Poitou, played the parts of tenor or of fifth. The length of the hautboy having been found inconvenient, it was divided into pieces united in a movable cluster (*faisceau*) known by the name of *fagot*. This instrument was afterwards called *courtaut* in France, and *sourdeline* or *sampogne* in Italy, where it had become a kind of bagpipe, like the *muse* or *estive*. The *muse de blé* was a

Fig. 160.—German Musicians playing on the Flute and Goat's Horn
(Drawn and Engraved by J. Amman)

simple reed-pipe, but the *muse d'Aussay* (or *d'Ausçois*, district of Auch) was certainly a hautboy. With regard to the bagpipes, properly so called, they generally bore the name of *chevrette, chevrie,* or *chièvre,* on account of the skin of which the bag was made. They were also designated by the names of *pythaule* and *cornemuse,* drone-pipe (Fig. 162).

The *flaïos de saus,* or reed-flutes, were nothing but mere whistles, such as village children are still in the habit of making in the spring; but there were, says an ancient author, more than twenty kinds, "as many loud as soft," which were coupled by pairs in an orchestra. The *fistule,* the *souffle,* the *pipe,* and the *fretiau* or *galoubet,* were all small flageolets played on by the left hand while the right marked the time on a tambourine or with the cymbals. The *pandorium*, which has been classed among the flutes without its shape and character of tone being rightly determined, must have presented, at least at its origin, some similarity of sound to the stringed instrument called *pandore* (*pandora*).

Trumpets formed a much more numerous class than the flutes. In Latin they were called *tuba, lituus, buccina, taurea, cornu, claro, salpinx,* &c.; in French, *trompe, corne, olifant, cornet, buisine, sambute,* &c. In most cases,

Fig. 161.—*Chorus* with single Bell-end with Holes. (Ninth Century, MS. of Saint-Blaise.)

Fig. 162.—Bagpiper, Thirteenth Century. (Sculpture on the Musicians' Hall at Rheims.)

however, they derived their name either from their shape, the sound which they produced, the material whereof they were made, or the use for which they were specially intended. Thus, among military trumpets of copper or brass, the names of some (*claro, clarasius*) indicated the piercing sound which they produced; the names of others seem rather to refer to the appearance of their bell-ends (Fig. 164), which imitated the head of a bird, a horn, a serpent, &c. Some of these trumpets were so long and heavy that a foot or stand was required to support them, while the performer took the end in his mouth and blew through it with full power of breath (Fig. 163).

The shepherds' horns, made of wood rimmed with brass, were a heavy and powerful kind of speaking-trumpet, which in the eighth century the Welsh herdsmen and those of the *landes* of Cornouaille always carried with them (Fig. 165). When the barons or knights desired to convey any signals rendered necessary either in war or hunting, they were in the habit of using horns of a much more portable character, which were suspended at their girdles; they used them, also, as drinking vessels when occasion required. At first these instruments were generally made of nothing but buffalo's or goat's horns; but when the fashion arose of working delicately

Fig. 163.—Straight Trumpet with Stand.　　　Fig. 164.—Curved Trumpet.
(Eleventh Century.　Cotton MS., British Museum.)　　(Eleventh Century.　Cotton MS., British Museum.)

in ivory, they took the name of *olifant*, an appellation destined to become famous in the old romances of chivalry, in which the *olifant* played a very important part (Fig. 166). To cite only one example among a thousand, Roland, when overwhelmed by numbers in the valley of Ronceveaux, sounded the *olifant* in order to call Charlemagne's army to his aid.

In the fourteenth century, according to a passage in a manuscript in the Library of Berne, quoted by M. Jubinal, there were in bodies of troops *corneurs*, *trompeurs*, and *buisineurs*, who played under certain special circumstances. The *trompes* sounded for the movements of the knights, or men-at-arms; the *cornes* for the movements of the banners or the foot-soldiers, and the *buisines*, or clarions, when the entire camp (*ost*) was to march. The heralds-at-arms, whose duty it was to make the announcements or proclamations in the public ways, were in the habit of using either long trumpets, called *à potence*, on account of the forked stick whereon they were supported, or trumpets *à tortilles* (serpentine), the name of which sufficiently indicates their shape. Added to this, the sound of the trumpet or horn accompanied or signalised the principal acts of the citizens both in public and private life. During the meals of great men, the water, the wine, and the bread, were heralded by sound of trumpet. In towns this instrument

Fig. 165.—Shepherd's Horn. Eighth Century.
(MS., British Museum.)

Fig. 166.—Horn, or *Olifant*, Fourteenth Century.
(From Willemin's "French Monuments.")

announced the opening and closing of the gates, the opening and closing of the markets, and the time of curfew, till the time when the horn and the copper trumpet were superseded in this function by the bells in church-towers.

Polybius and Ammianus Marcellinus tell us that the ancient Gauls and Germans had a great passion for large, hoarse-sounding trumpets. At the time of Charlemagne, and still more in the days of the Crusades, the intercourse that took place between the men of the West and the African and Asiatic races introduced among the former the use of musical instruments of a harsh and piercing tone. Then it was that the Saracen-horns, made of

copper, replaced the wooden or horn trumpets. At the same period sackbuts,
or *sambutes* (Fig. 167), made their appearance in Italy: in those of the
ninth century, we find the principle of the modern trombone. About the
same epoch the Germans introduced great improvements into the trumpet

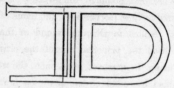

Fig. 167.—*Sambute*, or Sackbut, of the Ninth Century.   (Boulogne MS.)

by adapting to it the system of holes, which up to that time had been the
characteristic of flutes (Fig. 168).

But among all the wind instruments of the Middle Ages, the
organ was the one most imposing in its nature, and destined to the most

Fig. 168.—German Musician sounding the Military Trumpet.   Drawn and Engraved by J. Amman.

glorious career. The only instrument of this kind known by the ancients
was the water-organ, in which a key-board of twenty-six keys corresponded
to the same number of pipes; and the air, acted upon by the pressure of

water, produced most varied sounds. Nero, it is said, spent a whole day examining and admiring the mechanism of an instrument of this kind.

The water-organ, although described and commended by Vitruvius, was not much in use in the Middle Ages. Eginhard speaks of one constructed, in 826, by a Venetian priest; and the last of which mention is made existed at Malmesbury in the twelfth century. But this latter might be regarded more in the light of a steam-organ; for, like the warning whistles of our locomotives, it was worked by the effects of the steam of boiling water rushing into brass pipes.

The water-organ was, in very early times, superseded by the pneumatic or wind-organ (Fig. 169), the description of which given by St. Jerome agrees with the representations on the obelisk erected at Constantinople in the time of Theodosius the Great. We must, however, fix a date as late as the eighth century for the introduction of this instrument into the

Fig. 169.—Pneumatic Organ of the Fourth Century. (Sculpture of that date at Constantinople.)

West, or at least into France. In 757, Constantine Copronymus, Emperor of the East, sent to King Pépin a number of presents, among which was an organ that excited the admiration of the court. Charlemagne, who received a similar present from the same monarch, had several organs made from this model. These were provided, according to the statement of the monk of Saint-Gall, with "brazen pipes which were acted on by bellows made of bull's hide, and imitated the roaring of thunder, the accents of the lyre, and the clang of cymbals." These primitive organs, notwithstanding the power and richness of their musical resources, were of dimensions which rendered them quite portable. It was, in fact, only in consequence of its almost exclusive application to the solemnities of Catholic worship that the organ became developed on an almost gigantic scale. In 951, there existed in Winchester Cathedral an organ which was divided into two parts, each provided with its apparatus of bellows, its key-board, and its organist.

Twelve bellows above, and fourteen below, were worked by seventy strong men, and the air was distributed by means of forty valves into four hundred pipes, arranged in groups or choirs of ten, each group corresponding with one of the twenty-four keys of each key-board (Fig. 170).

In the ninth century, the German organ-makers acquired great renown. The monk Gerbert, who, as we have already remarked, became pope under the name of Sylvester II., and co-operated so efficiently in the progress of the horological art, established in the monastery of which he was abbot a workshop for the manufacture of organs. We must add, that all the musical treatises written from the ninth to the twelfth century entered into very

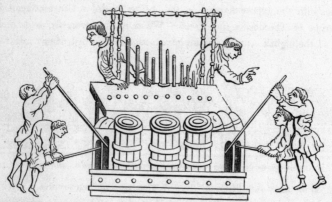

Fig. 170.—Great Organ, with Bellows and double Key-board, of the Twelfth Century. (MS. at Cambridge.)

considerable details concerning the arrangement and working of this instrument. Nevertheless, the admission of the organ into churches did not fail to meet with earnest opponents among the bishops and priests of the day. But while some complained of the thunder and rumbling of the organs, others appealed to the examples of king David and the prophet Elisha. Finally, in the thirteenth century, the right of placing organs in all churches was no longer disputed, and the only question was, who could build the most powerful and most magnificent instruments. At Milan was an organ the pipes of which were of silver; at Venice some were made of pure gold. The number of these pipes was varied and multiplied to an infinite extent, according to the effects the instrument was required to produce. The

mechanism was, generally speaking, rather complicated, and the working of
the bellows very laborious. In large organs the key-board was made up
of key-plates five or six inches wide, which the organist, his hands defended
by thickly padded gloves, had to strike with his clenched fist in order to
bring out the notes (Fig. 171).

Fig. 171.—Organ with single Key-board of the Fourteenth Century.
(Miniature from a Latin Psalter, No. 175, Bibl. Imp., Paris.)

The organ, which, as we have seen, was at first of a portable nature,
in some cases resumed its original dimensions (Fig. 172). It was then
sometimes called simply *portatif* (hand-organ), and sometimes *régale* or *positif*

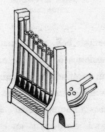

Fig. 172.—Portable Organ of the Fifteenth Century.
(Miniature in Vincent de Beauvais' "Miroir Historial," MS. in the Bibl. Imp., Paris.)

(choir-organ). Raphael, in one of his famous pictures, represents St. Cecilia
singing sacred hymns, and accompanying herself on a choir-organ.

The class of pulsatile instruments was formed of bells, cymbals, and drums.

There can be no doubt that the ancients were acquainted with large bells, hand-bells, and strung-bells (*grelots*). But we must ascribe to the requirements of Christian worship the first introduction of the bell, properly so called, formed of cast-metal (*campana* or *nola*, the first having been made, it is said, at Nola), which was employed from the first in summoning the faithful to the public services. In the first instance the bell was merely held in the hand and shaken by some monk or ecclesiastic who stood in front of the church-door, or mounted a raised platform for the purpose. This *tintin-*

Fig. 173.—*Tintinnabulum* or Hand-Bell of the Ninth Century. (Boulogne MS.)

Fig. 174.—The *Saufang* of St. Cecilia's at Cologne. (Sixth Century.)

Fig. 175.—Bell in a Tower of Siena. (Twelfth Century.)

nabulum (Fig. 173), or portable bell, subsequently passed into the hands of the public criers, the societies of ringers, and those who rang knells for the dead, at a time when most of the churches were provided with *campaniles* or bell-towers, wherein were hung the parish bells, which daily assumed dimensions of increasing importance. These great bells, of which the *Saufang* of Cologne (sixth century) is an example (Fig. 174), were at first made of wrought-iron plates laid one over the other, and riveted together. But in the eighth century they began to cast bells of copper and even of silver. One of the most ancient still existing is that in the tower of Bisdomini at Siena (Fig. 175). It bears the date of 1159, and is formed in the shape of a cask, being rather more than a yard high : the sound it produces is very sharp. The combination of several bells of various sizes naturally produced the peal or chime ; this at first consisted of an arch of wood or iron whereon were suspended the bells, which the player struck with a small hammer (Fig. 176). The number and classification of the bells becoming subsequently rather more complicated, the hand of the chimer was superseded by a mechanical arrangement. This was the origin of those peals of bells for which there was such a demand in the Middle Ages, and of which certain towns are still so proud.

The designations of *cymbalum* and *flagellum* were, in the first instance, applied to small hand-chimes ; but there were also regular cymbals (*cymbala* or *acetabula*), spherical or hollowed plates of silver, brass, or copper. Some of these were shaken at the ends of the fingers, or fastened to the knees or feet, so as to be put in motion by the movement of the body. These small cymbals, or *crotales*, were a kind of rattle (*grelots*), causing the dancers to make a noise in their performance, as do the Spanish castanets, which in the sixteenth century were called in France *maronnettes*, and were the same as the *cliquettes*, or snappers, used by lepers in former days. Small strung-bells became so much the fashion at a certain epoch that not only was the harness of horses adorned with them, but they were suspended to the clothes both of men and women, who at the slightest movement made a ringing, tinkling noise, sounding like so many perambulating chimes.

The use of pulsatile instruments producing a metallic sound increased greatly in Europe, especially after the return from the Crusades. But even before this date the Egyptian timbrel was used in religious and festival music ; this instrument was composed of a circle whereon rings were hung, which tinkled as they struck together when the timbrel was shaken. The Oriental triangle was also used on these occasions ; this was almost the same then as it is at the present day.

The drum has always been a hollow case covered with a stretched skin but the shape and size of this instrument have caused great variations in its name, and also in the way in which it was used. In the Middle Ages it was called *taborellus*, *tabornum*, and *tympanum*. It generally made its appearance in festal music and especially in processions ; but it was not until the fourteenth century that it began to take a place in military bands, at least in France ; the Arabians, however, have used it from the earliest ages. In the thirteenth century the *taburel* was a kind of tambourine, played on with only a drum-stick; in the *tabornum* we may recognise the military drum of the present day; and the *tympanum* was equivalent to our tambourine. Sometimes, as seen in a sculpture in the Musicians' Hall at Rheims, this instrument was attached to the right shoulder of the performer, who played upon it by striking it with his head, while at the

Fig. 176.—Chime of Bells of the Ninth Century.   Fig. 177.—*Tympanum* of the Thirteenth Century.
(MS. de Saint-Blaise.)   (Sculpture on the Musicians' Hall, Rheims.)

same time he blew through two metal flutes communicating with the inside of the drum (Fig. 177).

We have now to speak of stringed instruments, the whole of which may be divided into three principal classes: those played on by the fingers, those that are struck, and those which are rubbed (*frottées*) by means of some appliance.

As a matter of fact, there are some stringed instruments which may be said to belong to all three of these classes, as all three modes of playing upon them has been adopted either simultaneously or in succession.

The most ancient are doubtless those that are played on by the fingers, first among which, in right of its antiquity, we must name the lyre; from this have sprung the cithern, the harp, the psaltery, the *nabulon*, &c. In the Middle Ages, however, considerable confusion arose from the fact that these original names were at the time often diverted from their real acceptation.

The lyre, the stringed instrument *par excellence* of the Greeks and Romans, preserved its primitive form as late as the tenth century. The strings were generally of twisted gut, but sometimes also of brass wire, and varied in number from three to eight. The sounding-box, which was always placed at the lower part of the instrument, was more often made of wood than of either metal or tortoise-shell (Fig. 178).

The lyre was held upon the knees, and the performer touched or rubbed

Fig. 178.—Ancient Lyre. (Angers MS.) Fig. 179.—Lyre of the North. (Ninth Century.)

the strings with one hand, either with the fingers or by means of a *plectrum*. The lyre specified as "Northern" (Fig. 179) was certainly the origin of the violin, to the shape of which it even then bore some resemblance; it was fastened at the top, and had a *cordier* at the end of the sounding-board, as well as a bridge in the centre of the face of the instrument.

The lyre was superseded by the psaltery and the cithern. The psaltery, which never was furnished with fewer than ten, or more than twenty, strings, differed essentially from the lyre and the cithern by the sounding-board being placed at the top of the instrument. Psalteries were made of a round, square, oblong, or buckler-shaped form (Fig. 181); and sometimes the sounding-box was lengthened so as to rest upon the shoulder of the musician (Fig. 180). The psaltery disappeared in the tenth century and gave place to the cithern (*cithara*), a name which had been at first applied to all kinds of stringed instruments. The shape of the cithern, which in the days of St. Jerome resembled a Greek *delta* (Δ), varied in different countries, as is proved by the epithets — *barbarica, Teutonica, Anglica,* which we find at different times coupled with its generic name.

Fig. 180.—Psaltery to produce a prolonged sound. Ninth Century.
(MS. in the Bibl. Imp., Paris.)

In other places, in consequence of these local transformations, it became the *nabulum,* the *chorus,* and the *salterion* or *psalterion* (which latter must not be confounded with the psaltery, a primary derivative of the lyre).

The *nabulum** (Fig. 182) was made either in the shape of a triangle with truncated corners, or of a semicircle joined at the two extremities; its

---

* *Nabulum*—a name evidently derived from the Hebrew word *nebel,* generally translated in the Scriptures as a psaltery.—[ED.]

sounding-board occupied the whole of the rounded part, and left but a very limited space for the twelve strings. The *chorus* or *choron*, the imperfect representation of which in the manuscripts of the ninth and tenth

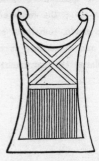

Fig. 181.—Buckler-shaped Psaltery with many Strings. (Ninth Century. Boulogne MS.)

Fig. 182.—*Nabulum*. Ninth Century. (MS. d'Angers.)

centuries calls to mind the appearance of a long semicircular window or of a Gothic capital **Ω**, generally had one of its sides prolonged, on which

Fig. 183.—*Choron*. Ninth Century. (Boulogne MS.)

Fig. 184.—*Psalterion*. Twelfth Century.

the performer leaned so as to hold the instrument in the same way as a harp (Fig. 183).

The *psalterion*, which was in use all over Europe after the twelfth century, and is thought to have originated in the East, where it was found by the Crusaders, was at first composed of a flat box of sounding wood, with two oblique sides; it assumed the shape of a triangle truncated at its top, with twelve or sixteen metallic strings either of gold or silver, which were played upon by means of a small bow of wood, ivory, or horn (Fig. 184); subsequently the strings were made more slender, the number being increased to as many as twenty-two; the three angles of the sounding-box were cut off, and holes were made, sometimes one only in the middle, sometimes one at each angle, and sometimes as many as five, symmetrically arranged. The performer placed the instrument against

Fig. 185.—Performer on the *Psalterion*.   Fourteenth Century.   (MS. No. 703 in the Bibl. Imp. of Paris.)

his chest, and held it so as to touch the strings either with the fingers of the two hands, or with a pen or *plectrum* (Fig. 185). This instrument, which in the representations of poets and painters never failed to figure in celestial concerts, produced tones of incomparable softness. The old romances of chivalry exhausted all the phrases of admiration in describing the *psalterion*. But the highest eulogium which can be passed on this instrument is that it formed the starting-point of the harpsichord, or of the stringed instruments struck or played on by means of mechanism.

It is, in fact, thought that a kind of harpsichord with four octaves, which in the fourteenth century was called *dulcimer* or *dulcemelos*, and is but imperfectly described, was nothing else than a *psalterion*, with a sounding apparatus that assumed the proportions of a large box, to which also a key-board had been adapted. This instrument, when it had but three octaves, was called *clavicord* or *manicordion*, and in the sixteenth century produced forty-two to fifty tones or semi-tones: one string expressed several notes, and this was effected by means of plates of metal which, serving as a movable bridge to each string, either increased or diminished the intensity of its vibration. The grand-pianos of the present day unquestionably have their key-boards placed in the same position as they were in the *dulcimer* and *clavicorde*. The earliest improvements in metallic stringed instruments constructed with a key-board are due to the

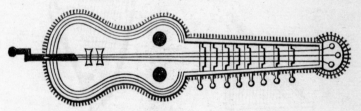

Fig. 186.—*Organistrum*. Ninth Century. (MS. de Saint-Blaise).

Italians; these improvements soon had the effect of throwing the *psalterion* into oblivion.

In the ninth century a stringed instrument was in use the mechanism of which, although not very perfect, evidently tended to an imitation of the key-board applied to organs: this was the *organistrum* (Fig. 186), an enormous guitar pierced with two sound-holes, and provided with three strings set in vibration by a small winch; eight movable screws, rising or falling at will along the finger-board, formed so many keys which served to vary the tones. In the first instance two persons performed on the *organistrum*—one turning the winch while the other touched the keys. When its size was decreased it became the *vielle* (hurdy-gurdy) properly so called, which could be managed by one musician. It was at first called *rubelle*, *rebel*, and *symphonie;* subsequently this last name was corrupted into *chifonie* and *sifonie*, and we may remark that even now in certain districts of central France the *vielle* still bears the popular name of *chinforgne*. The *chifonie* never found a place in musical concerts, and fell almost immediately into the hands of the mendicants, who solicited alms accompanied by the doleful and somewhat discordant notes of this instrument, and thence obtained the name of *chifoniens*.

Notwithstanding all the efforts which were made to substitute wheels and key-boards for the action of the fingers on the strings of instruments, still those that were played on by the hand only, such as harps and lutes, did not fail to maintain the preference among skilful musicians.

The harp was certainly Saxon in its origin, although some have imagined they could discover traces of it in Greek, Roman, and even Egyptian antiquities. This instrument was at first nothing but a triangular cithern

Fig. 187.—Triangular Saxon Harp of the Ninth
Century. (Bible of Charles le Chauve.)

Fig. 188.—Fifteen-stringed Harp of the Twelfth
Century. (MS. in the Bibl. Imp., Paris.)

(Fig. 187), in which the sounding-board occupied the whole of one side from top to bottom, instead of being limited to the lower angle, as in the primitive *cithara*, or confined to the upper part as in the psaltery. The English harp (*cithara Anglica*) of the ninth century differed but little from the modern instrument; the simplicity and good judgment shown in its shape bear witness to the perfection it had already attained (Fig. 188). The number of strings and the shape of this instrument varied constantly from time to time. The sounding-box was sometimes made square, some-times elongated, and sometimes round. The arms were sometimes straight and sometimes curved; the upper side was often lengthened so as to represent an animal's head (Fig. 189), and the lower angle, on which the instrument rested on the ground, terminated in a griffin's claw. According to the miniatures in manuscripts, the harp was of a size that the top of it did not extend higher than the head of the performer, who played upon it in a sitting posture (Fig. 190). There were, however, harps of a lighter character, which the musician bore suspended from his neck by a strap, and played upon while standing up. This portable harp was the one that may *par excellence* be called noble, and was the instrument on which the *trouvères* accompanied their voices when reciting ballads and metrical tales (Fig. 191).

Fig. 189.—Harpers of the Twelfth Century, from a Miniature in a Bible. (MS. in the Bibl. Imp., Paris.).

Fig. 190.—Harp-player of the Fifteenth Century. From an Enamelled Dish found near Soissons, and preserved in the Bibl. Imp., Paris.

In the romances of chivalry harpers are constantly introduced, and their harps are ever tuned to some lay of love or war; we find this taking place as well in the north as in the south. "The harp," says Guillaume de Machaut—

> "tous instruments passe,
> Quand sagement bien en joue et compasse."

In the sixteenth century, however, it began to fall into disfavour; it was supplanted by the lute (Fig. 192), an instrument much used in the thirteenth century, and by the guitar, which was brought into fashion in France from Spain and Italy, and formed the delight both of the court and private circles. At that time every great lord, imitating kings and princesses, wished to have his lute or guitar player, and the poet Bonaventure des Périers, *valet de chambre* of Marguerite de Navarre, composed for her "La Manière de bien et justement entoucher les Lucs et Guiternes." The lute and the guitar, which for about two centuries were in high favour in what was called "chamber music," have since the above-named epoch scarcely been altered in shape. With certain modifications, however, they gave rise to the *theorbo* and the *mandolin*, which never attained more than a transient or local favour.

Stringed instruments that were played on by means of bows were not known before the fifth century, and belonged to the northern races; they

Fig. 191.—Minstrel's Harp, of the Fifteenth Century.
(MS. in the *Miroir Historial* of Vincent de Beauvais.)

Fig. 192.—Five-stringed Lute. Thirteenth Century
(MS. in the Bibl. Imp., Paris.)

did not become prevalent in Europe generally until after the Norman invasion. At first they were but roughly made and rendered indifferent service to musical art; but from the twelfth to the sixteenth century, these instruments were subject to many changes both in form and name, and were brought to perfection according as the execution of musicians also improved. The most ancient of these instruments is the *crout* (Fig. 193), which must have produced the *rote*, so dear to the minstrels and the *trouvères* of the thirteenth century. The *crout*, which is the instrument placed by tradition in the hands of the Armorican, Breton, and Scotch bards,* was

* The Welsh or Scotch *Crwd.*—[Tr.]

composed of an oblong sounding-box, more or less hollowed out at the two sides, with a handle fixed in the body of the instrument, in which were made two openings that allowed the performer to hold it by the left hand and at the same time to touch the strings; these, as a matter of principle, were only three in number. Subsequently it had four strings, and then six—two of which were played open (*à vide*). The musician

Fig. 193.—Three-stringed *Crout* of the Ninth Century. From a Miniature.

played on it with a straight or convex bow, provided with a single thread either of iron wire or of twisted hair. Except in England, where the *crout* was national, it did not last beyond the eleventh century. It was replaced by the *rote*, which was not, as its name (apparently derived from *rota*, a wheel) would seem to intimate, a *vielle* or *symphonie*. It would be useless to seek for the derivation of the name of *rota*, except in the word *crotta*, the Latin form of the term *crout*.

In the earliest *rotes* (Fig. 194), those made in the thirteenth century,
there is an evident intention of combining the two modes of playing
on the strings—rubbing with a bow and touching with the fingers.   The
box, which was not hollowed out and rounded at the two ends, was much
deeper at the lower end, where the strings commenced, than higher up,
near the pegs, where these strings are sounded open under the action of
the finger, which reaches them through an aperture ; the bow acting on

Fig. 194.—King David playing on a *Rote*.   From a Painted Window of the Thirteenth Century.
(Chapel of the Virgin, Cathedral of Troyes.)

them near the string-bridge in front of the sounding-holes.   It must have
been difficult to touch with the bow one string alone, but it should be
remarked that the harmonic ideal of this instrument consisted in forming
accords by consonances of thirds, fifths, and eighths.   The *rote* was soon
developed into a new instrument, assuming the form that our violoncellos
have almost exactly retained.   The box was increased in size, the handle was
lengthened beyond the body of the instrument, the number of strings

was reduced to three or four, stretched over a bridge, and the sounding-holes were made in the shape of a crescent. From this time the *rote* acquired a special character it had not lost even in the sixteenth century, when it became the bass-viol. This was its true destination. The size of the instrument dictated the manner in which it was held, either on the knees, or on the ground between the legs (Fig. 195).

The *vielle* or *viole*, which had no affinity except in shape with the *vielle* (hurdy-gurdy) of the present day, was at first a small *rote* held by the

Fig. 195.—German Musicians playing on the Violin and Bass-Viol.
Drawn and Engraved by J. Amman.

performer against his chin or his breast, in much the same way as the violin is now used (Fig. 196). The box, which was at first conical and convex, became gradually oval in shape, and the handle remained short and wide. It was, perhaps, this handle which terminated in a kind of ornamental scroll, in the shape of a violet (*viola*), that originated the name of the instrument. The *viole*, just as the *rote*, formed the accompaniment *obligato* of certain songs; and among the jugglers who played upon it good performers were rare (Figs. 197, 198). Improvements in the *vielle* came for the most part from Italy, where the co-operation of a number of skilful lute-players was the means of gradually forming the violin.   Even before the famous Dnifloprugar, born in the Italian Tyrol, had hit upon the model of his admirable violins, the handle of the *vielle* had been lengthened,

Fig. 196.—Oval *Vielle* with Three Strings, of the Thirteenth Century.
(Sculpture on the Cathedral of Amiens.)

Fig. 197.—Juggler playing on a *Vielle*, hollowed out at the Sides.   Fifteenth Century.
("Heures du Roi René," MS. No. 159 in the Bibl. Imp. of the Arsenal, Paris.)

its sides hollowed out, and its strings had received a more extended field of action by removing the stringer (*cordier*) from the centre of the sounding-

Fig. 198—Player on the *Vielle*. Thirteenth Century.
(Taken from an Enamelled Dish at Soissons.)

Fig. 199.—Angel Playing on a Three-stringed Fiddle.   Thirteenth Century.
(Sculpture in the Cathedral of Amiens.)

board.   Henceforth the play of the board became more free and easy, the performer was able to touch every string singly, and was in a position to substitute effects more characteristic instead of the former monotonous consonances.

England was the birthplace of the *crout;* France invented the *rote,* and Italy the *viole;* Germany originated the *gigue,** the name of which may perhaps be derived from the similarity presented by the shape of the instrument to the thigh of a kid. The *gigue* was provided with three strings (Fig. 199), and its special distinction from the *viole* was, that instead of the handle being as it were independent of the body of the instrument, it was a

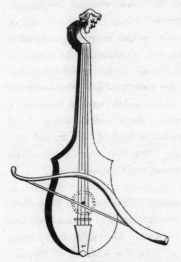

Fig. 200.—Rebec, of the Sixteenth Century.
From Willemin.

Fig. 201.—Long Monochord played on with a Bow.
Fifteenth Century.
(MS. of Froissart, in the Bibl. Imp., Paris.)

kind of prolongation of the sounding-board. The *gigue,* which bore a considerable resemblance to the modern mandolin, was an instrument on which the Germans were accustomed to work wonders in the way of performance; according, at least, to the statement of Adenès, the *trouvère,* who speaks with admiration of the "*gigueours* of Germany." The *gigue,* however, entirely disappeared, at least in France, in the fifteenth century; but its name still remained as the designation of a joyous dance, which for a considerable period was enlivened by the sound of this instrument.

* In German *Geige,* "fiddle."—[Tr.]

Among the musical instruments of this class in the Middle Ages, we have still to mention the rebec (Fig. 200), which was so often quoted by the authors of the day, and yet is so little known, although it figured in the court concerts in the time of Rabelais, who specifies it by the term *aulique*, in contrast to the rustic *cornemuse* (bagpipes).

We must, in conclusion, speak of the monochord (*monocordium*), which is always mentioned by the authors of the Middle Ages with feelings of pleasure, although it appears to have been nothing more than the most simple and primitive expression of all the other stringed instruments (Fig. 201). It was composed of a narrow oblong box, on each end of the front-board were fixed two immovable bridges supporting a metallic string stretched from one to the other, and corresponding to a scale of notes traced out on the instrument. A movable bridge, which was shifted up and down between the string and the scale, produced whatever notes the performer wished to bring out. In the eighth century there was a kind of violin or mandolin furnished with a single metallic string played on with a metallic bow. Later still, we find a kind of harp formed of a long sounding-box traversed by a single string, over which the musician moved a small bow handled with a sudden and rapid movement.

The instruments we have named do not, however, embrace all those in use in the Middle Ages and the Renaissance. There certainly were others which, in spite of the most intelligent investigations, and the most judicious deductions, are now known to us only by name. As regards, for instance, the nature and appearance of the *éles* or *celes*, the *échaqueil* or *échequier*, the *enmorache*, and the *micamon*, we are left to the vaguest conjectures.

Fig. 202.—Triangle of the Ninth Century. (MS. of Saint-Emmeran.)

PLAYING-CARDS.

 HE origin of playing-cards has for many years
past formed a special subject of investigation
among scholars and antiquarians. For, however
trifling the matter may appear in itself, this
curious point is connected with two of the most
important inventions of modern times—engraving
and printing.

We must not, however, take upon ourselves to
assert too positively that all the profound researches, persevering study, and
ingenious deductions which have been applied to the subject have entirely
succeeded in elucidating the question. Nevertheless, a certain degree of
light has been thrown upon it, by which we shall endeavour to profit.

The question is, at what date are we to fix the invention of playing-
cards, and to whom are we to attribute it? In order to solve these queries,
they must be divided; for, although the introduction of playing-cards into
Europe may not date back beyond the fourteenth century, and the invention
of our game of piquet may not have been prior to the reign of Charles VII.,
it is at least asserted—(1st), that playing-cards existed in India in the
twelfth century; (2nd), that the ancients played at games in which certain
figures and numbers were represented on dice or tablets; (3rd), that in
comparatively recent times the game of chess and the game of cards presented striking affinities, proving the common origin of these two games
—one connected with painting, the other with sculpture.

If we are to believe Herodotus, the Lydians, in order to beguile the sufferings of hunger during a long and cruel famine, invented nearly every game, especially that of dice.   Later authors ascribe the honour of these inventions to the Greeks, when irritated at the tedious delays of the siege of Troy.   Cicero even mentions by name Pyrrhus and Palamedes as the originators of the " games in use in camps " (*ludos castrenses*).   What were these games ?   Some say, chess ; others, dice or knuckle-bones.

Certain very ancient specimens prove unquestionably that the Indian cards were nothing but a transformation of the game of chess ; for the principal pieces in this game are reproduced on the cards, but in such a way that eight players instead of two could take part in it.   In the game of chess there were only two armies of pawns, each having at its head a king, a vizier (who was afterwards turned into a "queen"), a knight, an elephant (which became a "bishop"), and a dromedary (afterwards a "castle ").   There can be no doubt that the course and arrangement of these games were very different ; but in both may be found an original affinity in the fact that they recalled to mind the terrible game of war, in which each adversary had to attack by means of stratagems, combinations, and vigilance.

We have now learned from certain authority (Abel de Rémusat, *Journal Asiatique*, September, 1822) that playing-cards, proceeding from India and China, were, like the game of chess (Fig. 203), in the hands of the Arabians and the Saracens at the commencement of the twelfth century. It is therefore almost certain they must have been brought into Europe after the Crusades, with the arts, traditions, and customs which the men of the West then derived from their Oriental antagonists.   There is, however, every reason to believe that the use of cards spread but slowly ; for, at an epoch when the civil and ecclesiastical authorities were constantly issuing ordinances against games of chance, we do not find that cards were ever the subject of legal proceedings, like dice and chess.

The first formal mention made of playing-cards is found in a manuscript chronicle of Nicolas de Covelluzzo, preserved in the archives of Viterbo. "In the year 1379," says the chronicler, "there was introduced at Viterbo the game of cards, which comes from the country of the Saracens, and is called by the latter *naïb*."   There is, in fact, a German book, the "Jeu d'Or," printed at Augsbourg in 1472, which testifies to the fact that cards existed in Germany in the year 1300.   But, in the first place, this evidence is not contemporary with the fact alleged ; and, besides, we may well suppose that the vanity of the Germans, which had attributed to themselves the discovery of printing, desired, with about as much reason, to appropriate also the invention of cards—that is, of wood-engraving. We shall, therefore, act judiciously in paying but little attention to this doubtful assertion, and hold to the account given by the chronicler of Viterbo. But the latter, unfortunately, furnishes us with no details as to the nature of these cards. Was the game similar to that which is still

Fig. 203.—Chess-Players, Fac-simile of a Miniature of the Thirteenth Century. (MS. 7,266, Bibl. Imp., Paris.)

extant in India? Or was it one peculiar to the Arabs? These are questions which must remain unsolved. The only facts presented to our notice are, that in 1379 cards made their appearance in Europe, brought from Arabia, or the country of the Saracens, and that their original name is given. The Italians for a long time gave to cards the name of *naïbi*. In Spain they are still called *naypes*. If it be understood that the word *naïb* in Arabic signifies "captain," we shall see that the game in question was one of a military character, like that of chess, and we shall be led to recognise in these primitive cards the *tarots* which were for a long time current in the south of Europe.

In 1387, John I., King of Castile, issued an ordinance prohibiting to play with dice, *naypes,* or at chess.

In the archives of the Audit Office, in Paris, there formerly existed an account of the treasurer, Poupart, who states that, in 1392, he had "paid to Jacquemin Gringonneur, painter, for three packs of cards in gold and various colours, ornamented with numerous devices, to lay before the lord the king (Charles VI.) for his amusement, 50 sols of Paris." This game, which seemed at first intended only for the amusement of the king in his mental derangement, subsequently spread so much among the people, that the provost of Paris, in an ordinance of January 22, 1397, issued a prohibition "to persons engaged in trade from playing at tennis, bowls, dice, *cards,* and skittles, except on feast-days." We must remark that, twenty-eight years previously, Charles V., in a celebrated ordinance which enumerates all the games of chance, did not mention cards.

The "Red Book" of the town of Ulm, a manuscript register preserved in the archives of that town, contains an ordinance dated in 1397, in which is conveyed a prohibition of games with cards.

These facts are the only authenticated evidence which can be brought forward with a view of fixing the approximate period of the introduction of cards into Europe. Some authors have certainly imagined they were in a position to determine an earlier epoch, but they have gone upon data the value of which has since been destroyed by more thorough investigation.

In the fifteenth century there are evident traces both of the existence and popularity of cards in Italy, Spain, Germany, and France. Their names, colours, and emblems, their number and forms, were indeed constantly changing, according to the country in which they were used and the fancy of the players. But whether called *tarots* or "French cards," they were in fact nothing but modifications of the primitive Oriental cards, and an imitation more or less faithful of the ancient game of chess.

Reckoning from the fifteenth century, we meet with cards in every enumeration of games of chance; we find them also proscribed and condemned in ecclesiastical and royal ordinances. The clergy, too, raised their voices against them; but these measures did not prevent the trade in them from increasing, nor great attention to their improved manufacture. Poets and romance-writers vied with each other in speaking of them; they

Figs. 204 and 205.—Jean Dunois, King Alexander, Julius Cæsar, King Arthur, Charles the Great, and Godefroi de Bouillon. From ancient coloured Wood-Engravings; prints analogous to the first Playing-Cards of the Fifteenth Century. (Bibl. Imp., Paris, Department of Manuscripts.)

appeared in the miniatures in manuscripts, and also in the first attempts at engraving on wood and copper (Figs. 204 and 205). And, notwithstanding the fragile nature of the cards themselves, some have been preserved which belong to the earliest years of the fifteenth century.

As we have already seen, cards had, in principle, been classed among the number of childish games; but it may be safely asserted that this could not have long been the case, else how could we explain the legal strictures and the ecclesiastical anathemas of which they were the subject?

St. Bernard, for example, speaking on the 5th of March, 1423, to the crowd assembled in front of a church at Siena, inveighed with so much energy, and fulminated with so much persuasion, against games of chance, that all who heard ran at once and fetched their dice, chess, and *cards*, and burnt them on the very spot. But, adds the chronicle, there was a card-maker who, being ruined by the sermon of the saint, went to seek him, and with a flood of tears said to him: "Father, I am a maker of cards, and I have no other trade by which to live. By preventing me from following my trade, you condemn me to die of hunger." "If painting is all you are capable of," replied the preacher, "paint this picture." And he showed him an image of a radiating sun, in the centre of which shone the monogram of Christ—I. H. S. The artisan followed his advice, and soon made his fortune by painting this representation, which was adopted by St. Bernard as his device.

Although in every direction similar censures were directed against cards, they nevertheless did not fail to come much into fashion, especially in Italy; and to have a considerable sale. Thus, in 1441, we find the master card-makers at Venice, "who formed a rather numerous association," claiming and obtaining from the senate a kind of prohibitory order against "the large quantity of *painted* and *printed* cards which were made out of Venice and were introduced into the town, to the great detriment of their art." It is important to notice that mention is made here of *printed* as well as of painted cards. The fact is, that at this date, not only did all the cities in Italy make their own cards, but, in consequence of the invention of wood-engraving, Germany and Holland exported a large quantity of them. We must also point out that documents of the same date appear to establish a distinction between the primitive *naïbi* and cards properly so called, without, however, affording any detailed characteristics of either. It is, however, known that prior to the year 1419, one François Fibbia, a noble of Pisa who died in exile at Bologna, obtained from the "reformers" of this city, on the score of his being the inventor of the game of *tarrochino*, the right of placing his escutcheon of arms on the "queen *de bâton*," and that of his wife's arms on the "queen *de denier*." *Bâtons, deniers*, with *coupes* and *épées*, were then the suits of the Italian cards, as *carreau* (diamond), *trèfle* (club), *cœur* (heart), and *pique* (spade), were those of the French cards.

No original specimen has been preserved of the *tarots* (*tarrochi, tarrochini*) or Italian cards of this epoch; but we possess a pack engraved about 1460, which is known to be an exact copy of them. Added to this, Raphael Maffei, who lived at the end of the fifteenth century, has left in his "Commentaries" a description of *tarots*, which were, he says, "a new invention,"—in comparison, doubtless, with the origin of playing-cards. From these two documents—though they present some differences—we may gather that the pack of *tarots* was then composed of four or five series or suits, each of ten cards, bearing consecutive numbers, and presenting so many *deniers, bâtons, coupes*, and *épées*, equal in number to that of the card. To these series we must add a whole assortment of figures, representing the *King*, the *Queen*, the *Knight*, the *Foot-traveller*, the *World*, *Justice*, an *Angel*, the *Sun*, the *Devil*, a *Castle*, *Death*, a *Gibbet*, the *Pope*, *Love*, a *Buffoon* (Fig. 206), &c.

It is evident that *tarots* were current in France long before the invention of the game of piquet, which is unquestionably of French origin; and among these *tarots* we must class the cards that are called those of Charles VI. (Figs. 207 and 208), and are now preserved in the Print-Room of the Bibliothèque Impériale in Paris; these may be considered as the oldest to be found in any collection, either public or private. The Abbé de Longuerue states that he saw the pack with all its cards complete; but only seventeen have been preserved to our day. These cards are painted with delicacy, like the miniatures in manuscripts, on a gilt ground, filled with dots forming a perforated ornamentation; they are also surrounded by a silvered border in which a similar dotting depicts a spirally twisted ribbon. This dotting is doubtless the *tare*, a kind of goffering produced by small holes pricked out and arranged in compartments, to which the *tarots* owe their names, and of which our present cards still retain a kind of reminiscence, in their backs being covered with arabesques or dotted over in black or various colours. These cards were about seven inches long and three and a half inches wide, and were painted in distemper on cardboard ·039 inch thick. The composition of them is ingenious and to some extent skilful, the drawing correct and full of character, and the colouring or illumination brilliant.

Among the subjects they represent are some which deserve all the more attention, because they can hardly fail to recall to mind a conception somewhat similar to that of the "Dance of Death," that terrible

Fig. 206.—The Buffoon, a Card from a Pack of *Tarots*. Fifteenth Century.

"morality" which, dating from this epoch, was destined to increase more and more in popularity. Thus, for instance, by the side of the *Emperor*, who is covered with silver armour and holds the globe and the sceptre, a *Hermit* makes his appearance as an old man muffled in a cowl and holding up an hour-glass, an emblem of the rapidity of time. Then we have the *Pope*, who, with the tiara on his head, sits between two cardinals; but *Death* is also there, mounted on a grey horse with a rough

and shaggy coat, and sweeping down with his scythe kings, popes, bishops,
and other great men of the earth. If we see *Love*, represented by three
couples of lovers who embrace as they converse, while two cupids dart
at them their arrows from a cloud above; we also see a *Gibbet*,
on which hangs a gambler suspended by one foot, and still holding in
his hand a bag of money. An *Esquire*, clothed in gold and scarlet,

Fig. 207.—The Moon.   Fig. 208.—Justice.
(Cards taken from the Pack, said to be of Charles VI., preserved in the Bibl. Imp., Paris.)

rides gallantly along, proudly waving his sword; a *Chariot* bears in
triumph an officer in full armour; a *Fool* places his cap and bells under
his arm that he may count upon his fingers. Finally, the last trumpets
are waking up the dead, who come out of their graves to appear at the
Last Judgment.

Most of these allegorical subjects have been retained in the *tarots*, which
include, independent of the sixteen figures of our piquet-pack, twenty-two

cards, representing the *Emperor*, the *Lover*, the *Chariot*, the *Hermit*, the *Gibbet*, *Death*, the *House of God*, the *End of the World*, &c.

We should scarcely be justified in imagining that these *tarots*, presenting as they did a picture of life so gloomily philosophical, regarded from a Christian point of view, could have enjoyed any great favour in the centre of a frivolous and corrupt court, devoted to little else but *fêtes*, masquerades, and singing; this, too, at a time when the State, a prey to every kind of intrigue, was falling into ruin, and the voice of insurrection was surging up among a people burdened by taxes, and decimated by pestilence and famine. On the other hand, these *tarots* might well please the imagination of certain good people who, having been deprived of their property in some of the disturbances incidental to these times, could not fail to accept as a consolation such emblematical representations of life and death. Artists of every kind tried their best to reproduce them in all forms; and as these designs found a place even in the ornaments of the female sex, it was scarcely probable that playing-cards would form an exception.

We are in possession of the remains of two ancient packs of cards, produced by means of engraved plates; they were discovered, like most cards of this date which have come to light, in the bindings of books of the fifteenth century. These cards, which belong to the reign of Charles VII., are essentially French in their character. We find in them the king, the queen, and the knave of each suit, as in our present pack of piquet cards. In one of these ancient packs we notice, however, traces of the Saracenic origin of the *naïbi;* the Mussulman "crescent" being substituted for the "diamond," while the "club" is depicted in the Arabian or Moorish fashion; that is, with four similar branches. There is also another peculiarity; the "king of hearts" is represented by a kind of savage, or hairy ape, leaning upon a knotty stick. The "queen" of the same suit is likewise covered with hair, and holds a torch in her hand. The "knave of clubs," who is well fitted to serve as an escort to the "king" and "queen of hearts," is also covered with hair, and carries a knotty stick on his shoulder. We may, besides, notice the legs of a fourth hairy personage among those which have been separated from their bodies by the knife of the bookbinder. But, with the exception of these, all the other personages are clothed according to the fashion or the etiquette which prevailed at the court of Charles VII. The "queen of crescents" is represented in a costume similar to that of

Mary of Anjou, the wife of the king; or in that of Gérarde Gassinel, his mistress. The representations of the kings, the hairy one excepted, are

Fig. 209.—Charles VI. on his Throne, from a Miniature in the MS. of the Kings of France. (Bibl. Imp., Paris.)

identical with those we have of Charles VII. himself, or the nobles of his suite. Their costume was a velvet hat surmounted by the crown ornamented with fleurs-de-lis; a robe open in front and lined with ermine or *menu vair,* a tight doublet, and close stockings. The "knaves" are copied from the pages and sergeants-at-arms of the period; one wears the plumed flat cap and long cloak; another, on the contrary, is clad in a short dress, and stands erect in his close-fitting doublet and tightly-drawn breeches. The latter displays, written on a streamer which he is unrolling, the name of the card-maker, "F. Clerc." These are certainly cards of French invention, or, at any rate, of French manufacture; but what explanation are we to give of the presence of the savage "king" and "queen," and the "hairy knave," among the kings, queens, and knaves all dressed according to the fashion of the time of Charles VII.? We may, perhaps, find a satisfactory reply by referring to the chronicles of the preceding reign.

On the 29th of January, 1392, there was a grand *fête* at the mansion of Queen Blanche in honour of the marriage of a Chevalier de Vermandois with one of the queen's ladies. The king, Charles VI., had only just recovered from his mental malady. One of his favourites, Hugonin de Janzay, projected an entertainment in which the king and five lords were to take a part. "It was," says Juvénal des Ursins, "a masquerade of wild men chained together, and all shaggy; their dress was made to fit close to their body, and was rendered rough by flax and tow fastened on by resinous pitch, greased so as to shine the better." Froissart, who was an eye-witness of this *fête*, says that the six actors in the *ballet* entered the hall yelling and shaking their chains. As it was not known who these maskers were, the Duke of Orleans, brother of the king, wishing to find out, took a lighted torch from the hands of his servant, and held it so close to one of these strange personages that "the heat of the fire caught the flax." The king was fortunately separated from his companions, who were all burned, with the exception of one only, who threw himself into a tub full of water. Although Charles VI. escaped from this peril, he was deeply affected by the thought of the danger to which he had been exposed, and the result was a relapse into his former insanity.

This fearful *ballet des ardents* left such an impression on the minds of people generally, that seventy years afterwards a German engraver made it the subject of a print. Should we, then, be venturing on an inadmissible hypothesis if we attribute to a cardmaker of this epoch the idea of intro-ducing the same subject in a pack of cards? which, as is abundantly proved, was modified according to the whim of the artist. In order to justify the costume of a female savage and the torch which are given to the "queen of hearts," we must not forget that Isabel of Bavaria, consort of Charles VI., is accused of having assisted in devising this fatal masquerade, which was intended to get rid of the king; and of having taken as her accomplice the Duke of Orleans, her brother-in-law, who is said to have purposely set fire to the clothing of these pretended wild men, among whom was the king.

The second pack, or fragment of a pack, which is dated back to this epoch, presents a similarity to our present cards of a yet more striking nature, at least in the characters and costumes of the figures; although the names and devices of the personages still are suggestive of their Saracenic origin. We must remark, under this head, that for several centuries the names coupled with the different personages were incessantly varying. In this pack we find "kings," "queens," and "knaves" of clubs, hearts, spades, and diamonds; the Saracenic crescent has disappeared. The "kings" are all holding sceptres, and the "queens" carry flowers. Everything in the representations is not only in harmony with the fashions of the period, but in addition to this, there are no violations either of the laws of heraldry or of the usages of chivalry.

According to tradition, this pack, the true piquet-pack, which superseded the Italian *tarots* and the cards of Charles VI., and soon became generally used in France, was the invention of Etienne Vignoles, called La Hire, one of the bravest and most active soldiers of that period. The tradition has a right to our respect, for the mere examination of this piquet-pack proves that it must have been the work of some accomplished *chevalier*, or at least of a mind profoundly imbued with the manners and customs of chivalry. But, without any wish to exclude La Hire, who, as the historians say, "always had his helmet on his head and his lance in his hand, ready to attack the English, and never rested until he died of his wounds," we are led rather to ascribe the honour of this ingenious invention to one of his contemporaries, Etienne Chevalier, secretary and treasurer to the king, who was distinguished by his skill in designing. Jacques Cœur, whose commercial relations with the East brought upon him the accusation of having "sent arms to the Saracens," might well have become the importer of Asiatic cards into France, and Chevalier might then have amused himself by applying devices to them, or, as was then said, by *moralising* or symbolising them. In India it had been the game of the vizier and of war; the royal treasurer turned it into a pack having reference to the knight and chivalry. In the first place he placed on it his own armorial bearings, the unicorn, which figures in several ancient packs of cards. He did not forget the allusive arms of Jacques Cœur, and substituted "hearts" for the *coupes*. He made the "clubs" imitate the heraldic flower of Agnes Sorel; and also changed the *deniers* into diamonds, or arrow-heads (Fig. 210), and the *épées* into spades,

Fig. 210.—Ancient French Card of the Fifteenth Century. (Bibl. Imp., Paris.)

Fig. 211.—Specimen of a Pack of Cards of the Sixteenth Century. (Bibl. Imp., Paris.)

to do honour to the two brothers Jean and Gaspard Bureau, grand-masters of artillery in France.

Etienne Chevalier, as the most skilful designer of emblems of the period, was eminently capable of substituting, in playing-cards, ladies or queens for the Oriental "viziers" or Italian "knights" which, on the *tarots*, figured alone among the "kings" and "knaves." We must, however, repeat that we have no intention of depriving La Hire of the honour of the invention, and only hazard a supposition in addition to the opinion generally received.

These cards, which bear all the characteristics of the reign of Charles VII., must be looked upon as the first attempts at wood-engraving, and at printing by means of engraved blocks. They were probably executed between 1420 and 1440, that is to say, prior to most of the known xylographic productions. Playing-cards, therefore, served as a kind of introduction or prelude to printing from engraved blocks, an invention which considerably preceded the printing from movable characters.

When, however, we observe that so early as the middle of the fifteenth century playing-cards were spread all over Europe, it is but natural to imagine that some economical plan of manufacture had been discovered and employed. Thus, as we have already mentioned, Jacquemin Gringonneur, in 1392, was paid fifty-six sols of Paris, that is about £7 1s. 8d. of our present money, for three packs of *tarots*, painted for the King of France. One single pack of *tarots*, admirably painted, about the year 1415, by Marziano, secretary to the Duke of Milan, cost one thousand five hundred golden crowns (about £625); but in 1454, a pack of cards intended for the Dauphin of France cost no more than five *sous of Tours* (about eleven or twelve shillings). In the interval between 1392 and 1454 means had been discovered of making playing-cards at a cheap rate, and of converting them into an object of trade; mercers were accustomed to sell them together with the "pins," which then took the place of copper and silver counters; hence the French proverb, "Tirer son épingle du jeu" (to get out of a scrape).

Although the use of playing-cards continued to extend more and more, we must not imagine that they had ceased to be the subject of prohibitory and condemnatory ordinances on the part of the civil and ecclesiastical authorities. On the contrary, a long list might be made of the decrees launched against cards themselves and those that used them. Princes and lords, as a matter of right, felt themselves above these prohibitions; the lower orders and the dissolute did not fail to infringe them. It was nevertheless the case, that in the face of these constantly-renewed prohibitions, the manufacture of playing-cards could only be developed, or rather perhaps be carried on, in some indirect mode. Thus, we find the business at first was concealed, as it were, under that of a stationer or illuminator. Not until December, 1581—that is, in the reign of Henry III.—do we find the first regulation fixing the statutes of the "master-cardmakers." These statutes, confirmed by letters patent in 1584 and 1613, remained in force down to the (French) Revolution. In the confirmation of corporate privileges granted at the latter date, it is laid down as a rule that henceforth master-cardmakers should be bound to place their names, surnames, signs, and devices on the "knave of clubs" (Figs. 212, 213), of every pack of cards. This prescription appears to have done nothing more than legalise an old custom—a fact which may be proved by an examination

Figs. 212 and 213.—The "Knave of Clubs" in the Packs of Cards of R. Passerel and R. Le Cornu. (Sixteenth Century. Bibl. Imp., Paris.)

of the curious collection of ancient cards in the Print-Room of the Bibliothèque Impériale. We have already stated that for a period of many years the names given to the various personages in the pack varied constantly, according to the fancy of the cardmaker; a mere glance at the collection just mentioned will confirm this assertion.

The cards that might be styled those of Charles VII., which appear to us to convey some reminiscence of the *ballet des ardents,* have no inscription but the name of the cardmaker. But in the other pack of the same date the "knave of clubs" bears as a legend the word *Rolan ;* the "king of clubs," *Sans Souci ;* the "queen of clubs," *Tromperie ;* the "king of diamonds," *Corsube ;* the "queen of diamonds," *En toi te fie ;* the "king of spades," *Apollin,* &c. This collection of names reveals to us the threefold influence of the Saracenic origin of playing-cards, the ideas conveyed at that period to the mind by the reading of the old romances of chivalry, and the effect of contemporary events. In fact, in the ancient epics, *Apollin* (or Apollo) is a deity by whom the Saracens were accustomed to swear ; *Corsube* is a knight of Cordova (*Corsuba*). *Sans Souci* is evidently one of those *sobriquets* which squires acquired the habit of adopting at the time they were proving themselves worthy of the title of knight. Roland, the mighty Paladin who died at Roncevaux fighting against the Saracens, seems to have been placed upon the cards in order to oppose the memory of his glory to that of the infidel kings. The queen "*En toi te fie*" might well allude to Joan of Arc. The queen "*Tromperie*" recalls to mind Isabel of Bavaria, who was an unfaithful wife and a cruel mother ; and, moreover, had betrayed France to England. All these ideas are doubtless mere suppositions, but such as a critical examination of a more minute and extended character would perhaps succeed in changing into unquestionable certainties.

Next after the cards of the time of Charles VII. follow, as the most ancient in point of date, two packs which certainly belong to the reign of Louis XII. One of these packs does not bear any kind of legend ; in the other the "king of hearts" is called *Charles ;* the "king of diamonds," *Cæsar ;* the "king of clubs," *Arthur ;* the "king of spades," *David ;* the "queen of hearts," *Héleine ;* the "queen of diamonds," *Judith ;* the "queen of clubs," *Rachel ;* the "queen of spades," *Persabée* (doubtless for Bathsheba).

In a pack of cards belonging to the reign of Francis I., the "king of clubs" becomes *Alexander,* and the name of *Judith* is transferred to the "queen of hearts ;" and for the first time (at least in the specimens which have been preserved) some of the "knaves" bear special names—the "knave of hearts" is *La Hire,* and the "knave of diamonds" *Hector of Trois* (*sic*).

A few years later, about the time of the battle of Pavia and of the king's captivity, the influence of Spanish and Italian fashions begins to affect the legends on packs of cards. It is remarked that the "knave of spades," which presents nothing in the way of a legend but the name of the cardmaker, is made to resemble Charles-Quint (Fig. 211). The three other knaves bear the singular denominations of *Prien Roman*, *Capita Fili*, and *Capitane Vallant*. The kings are: "hearts," *Julius Cæsar;* "diamonds," *Charles;* "clubs," *Hector;* "spades," *David.* The queens are: "hearts," *Héleine;* "diamonds," *Lucresse;* "clubs," *Pentaxlée* (Penthesilea); "spades," *Beciabée* (Bathsheba).

In the reign of Henry II., the names given to the personages come much nearer to the arrangement observed in our present cards. *Cæsar* is the "king of diamonds;" *David*, the "king of spades;" *Alexander*, the "king of clubs." *Rachel* is the "queen of diamonds;" *Argine*, of "clubs;" *Pallas*, of "spades." *Hogier*, *Hector of Troy*, and *La Hire*, are the "knaves" of "spades," "diamonds," and "hearts," respectively.

At the time of Henry III., who devoted himself much more to regulating the fashions than to governing his kingdom, and was the first to grant statutes to the association of cardmakers, the pack of cards became the mirror of the extravagant fashions of this effeminate reign. The "kings" have the pointed beard, the starched collar, the plumed hat, the breeches puffing out round the loins, the slashed doublet, and the tight-fitting hose. The "queens" have their hair drawn back and crisped, the dress close round the body, and made *à vertugarde* (in the form of a hoop-petticoat). We see a *Dido*, an *Elizabeth*, and a *Clotilde*, make their appearance in the respective characters of "queens" of "diamonds," "hearts," and "spades." Among the kings figure *Constantine*, *Clovis*, *Augustus*, and *Solomon.*

The valiant Béarnais * mounts the throne, and the cards still reflect the aspect of his court. But soon *Astrea* and a whole *cortége* of tender and gallant heroes begin to assume an influence over refined minds, and we then find *Cyrus* and *Semiramis* as "king and queen" of diamonds; *Roxana* is the "queen of hearts" (Fig. 214), *Ninus* the "king of spades," &c.

In the regency of Marie de Medicis, in the reign of Louis XIII., or rather of Richelieu, in the time of Anne of Austria and Louis XIV., playing-cards continued to assume the character of the period, following the whim of the court, or the fancy of the cardmaker. At a certain time they began to take an Italian character. The "king of diamonds" was called *Carel;* his queen, *Lucresi;* the "queen of spades," *Barbera;* the "queen of clubs," *Penthamée;* the "knave of diamonds," *capit. Melu.*

* Henry IV., born at Pau, in the Béarn.—[ED.]

A vast field of investigation would lie before us if, in tracing out the detailed history of these numerous variations, we were to endeavour to distinguish and settle the different causes which gave rise to them. One fact must certainly strike any one devoting himself to such inquiry; he would see that, in contradistinction to the changes which have affected the personages on the cards and their names, a continuous state of stability has been the characteristic of the four suits in the French cards or the piquet-pack, which were adopted from the very commencement, and that no attempt has ever been made against their arrangement and nature. *Cœur* (hearts), *carreau* (diamonds), *trèfle* (clubs), and *pique* (spades)—these were the divisions established by La Hire or Chevalier, and they are still faithfully maintained in the present day, although at various times endeavours have been made to define their symbolical signification.

For a long time the opinion of Father Menestrier was the prevalent one; that "hearts" were an emblem of the clergy or the choir (*chœur*); "diamonds," of the citizens, who had their rooms paved with square tiles; "clubs," of labourers; and "spades," of military men. But Menestrier was in egregious error. A much clearer view of the matter was taken by Father Daniel, who, like all sensible interpreters, recognising in cards a game of an essentially military character, asserted that "hearts" denoted the courage of the commanders and soldiers; "clubs" (*trèfle*— "trefoil*") the stores of forage; "spades" and "diamonds," the magazines of arms. This was a view which, as we think, comes much closer to the real interpretation of the suits; and Bullet was still nearer the mark when he recognised *offensive* arms in "clubs" and "spades," and *defensive* arms in "hearts" and "diamonds." The first were the sword and the lance; the second, the target and the shield.

But in order to do full honour to French cards, we must not exclude from our attention the *tarots*, which preceded our game of piquet, and continued to be simultaneously used even in France.

The Spanish and Italian cardmakers, who had been nearly always established in France, made a large quantity of *tarots* (Fig. 215); but they made a certain concession to French politeness by substituting "queens" for the "cavaliers" of their national game. We must remark here, that even at the epoch of the conquests of Charles VIII. and Louis XII., French cards with the four "queens" replacing the "cavaliers" never succeeded in nationalising themselves in Italy, and still less in Spain; on the contrary, the fact was that as regards this point of fashion, the vanquished people obtained the advantage over their conquerors, and the *tarots* came into full favour among the victorious soldiery.

The Spaniards must certainly have received the Oriental *naïb* from the Moors and Saracens a long time prior to the introduction of this game into Europe at Viterbo; but we have no written proofs which certify to the existence of cards among the Saracens of Spain. The first document

Fig. 214.—Roxana, Queen of Hearts.
(Specimen of the Cards of the time
of Henry IV.

Fig. 215.—Card of Italian *Tarots*, from the Pack of the
minchiate.
(Collection of Playing-Cards, Bibl. Imp., Paris.)

in which they are mentioned is the edict of John I., of the date of 1387, to which reference has been made. Certain *savants* have endeavoured to ascertain the signification of the four suits of the Spanish *naypes*, and have fancied that they could distinguish in them a special symbolism. In their view, the *dineros*, *copas*, *bastos*, and *spadas*, denoted the four estates which composed the population: the merchants, who have the money; the priests, who hold the chalice or cup; the peasantry, who handle the staff; and the nobles, who wear the sword. This explanation, although ingenious, does not appear to us to be based on any very solid foundation. The signs or suits of the numeral cards were fixed upon in the East, and Spain as well as Italy merely adopted them without taking much trouble to penetrate into their allegorical meaning. The Spaniards became so addicted to this game that they soon preferred it to any other recreation; and we know that when the companions of Christopher Columbus, who had just discovered

 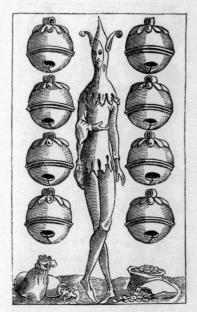

Figs. 216 and 217.—The "Three" and "Eight" of "Bells." German Cards of the Sixteenth Century. (Bibl. Imp. of Paris. Print-Room.)

America, formed their first settlement at St. Domingo, they almost instantly set to work to make playing-cards out of the leaves of trees.

There can be no doubt that playing-cards very soon made their way from Italy into Germany; but as they advanced towards the North they almost immediately lost their Oriental characteristics and Saracenic name. There is, in fact, no longer any etymological trace to be found in the old German language of the words *naïb, naïbi,* or *naypes.* Cards were called

Briefe, that is, letters; the game itself *Spielbriefe*, game of letters; the earliest cardmakers were *Briefmaler*, painters of letters. The four suits of the *Briefe* were neither Italian nor French in character; they bore the name of *schellen*, "bells" (Figs. 216, 217, 218), or *roth* (red), *grün* (green), and *eicheln* (acorns) (Fig. 219). The Germans, in their love of symbolism, had comprehended the real original signification of the game of cards, and although they introduced many marked changes, they made it their study,

Figs. 218 and 219.—The "Two of Bells" and the "King of Acorns," taken from a Pack of Cards of the Sixteenth Century, designed and engraved by a German Master.
(Bibl. Imp. of Paris. Print-Room.)

at least in principle, to preserve its military characteristics. Their suits depicted, it is said, the triumphs or the honours of war—the crowns of oak-leaves or ivy, the bells were the bright insignia of the German nobility, and the purple was the recompense of their valiant warriors. The Germans were careful not to admit ladies into the thoroughly warlike company of kings, captains (*ober*), and officers (*unter*). The ace was always the flag, the warlike emblem *par excellence;* in addition to this, the oldest game was the *Landsknecht,* or lansquenet (Fig. 220), the distinctive term of the soldier.

We are speaking here only of the earliest German cards, for, after a certain date, the essential form and emblematical rules of the pack depended on nothing but the fancy and whim of the maker or the engraver. The figures were but seldom designated by a proper name, but often bore devices in German or Latin. Among the collections of ancient cards we find one pack half German and half French, with the names of the Pagan gods.

Fig. 220.—The "Two" of a Pack of German Lansquenet Cards.
(Bibl. Imp. of Paris.)

Fig. 221.—Card from a Game of " Logic," invented
by Th. Murner, and copied from his " Charti-
ludium Logices." (Cracow, 1507.)

There are also several sets of cards with five suits (of fourteen cards each), among others those of " roses " and "pomegranates."

The Germans were the first who entertained the idea of applying cards to the instruction of youth; and, as it were, of moralising a game of chance by making it express all the categories of scholastic science. Thomas Murner, a Franciscan monk, and professor of philosophy, made in 1507 an attempt of this kind (Fig. 221). He designed a pack of fifty-two cards, divided into sixteen suits, corresponding to the same number of scholastic treatises; each card is covered with so many symbols that a description would resemble the setting forth of some obscure riddle (*ténébreux logogriphe*). The German universities, which were far from being dismayed at a little mysticism, were only the more eager to study the arcana of grammar and logic while playing at cards. Imitations of Murner's cards were multiplied *ad infinitum*.

A game and pack of cards attributed to the celebrated Martin Schœngauer, or to one of his pupils, must also be dated in the fifteenth century. The cards are distinguished by their form, number, and design; they are round in shape, and much resemble Persian cards, are painted on ivory and covered with arabesques, flowers, and birds. This pack, only a few pieces of which now exist in some of the German collections, was composed of fifty-two cards divided into four numeral series of nine cards each, and with four figures in each series—the king, the queen, the squire, and the knave. The suits or marks are the "Hare," the "Parrot," the "Carnation," and the "Columbine." Each of the aces represents the type of the suit, and they bear philosophical devices in Latin. The four figures of the "Parrot" suit are of African character; those of the "Hare" are Asiatic or Turkish; those of the "Carnation" and the "Columbine" belong to Europe. The "kings" and "queens" are on horseback; the "squires" and "knaves" are so similar that it is difficult to distinguish them, with the exception of the knaves of "Columbine" and "Carnation" (Figs. 222 to 227).

The English also were in possession of playing-cards at an early date, obtaining them through the medium of the trade which they carried on with the Hanseatic towns and Holland; but they did not manufacture cards before the end of the sixteenth century; for we know that in the reign of Queen Elizabeth the Government retained in its own hands the monopoly of playing-cards, "which were imported from abroad." The English, while adopting indiscriminately cards of a German, French, Italian, or Spanish character, gave to the *valet* the characteristic appellation of "knave." *

---

* The English "knave" is only our old equivalent for the German *knabe*, and had originally the same meaning of *servant*; it is also nearly similar in sense to the French *valet*.—[Tr.]

Figs. 222 to 227.—German Round-shaped Cards, with the Monogram T.W.

1. "King of Parrots."   2. "Queen of Carnations."   3. "Knave of Columbine."   4. "Knave of Hares."
5. "Three of Parrots."   6. "Ace of Carnations."

(Bibl. Imp. of Paris.)

Wood-engraving, which was invented at the commencement of the fifteenth century, and perhaps even before, must have been applied at the very first and almost simultaneously to the reproduction of sacred pictures and the manufacture of playing-cards.   Holland and Germany

Fig. 228.—*La Damoiselle*, from a Pack of Cards engraved by "The Master of 1466." (Bibl. Imp. of Paris.   Print-Room.)

have contended for the honour of having been the cradle of this invention. Taking advantage of this, they have also even thought themselves warranted in laying claim to the credit of the original manufacture of cards ;

whereas the fact is that all they can claim is to have been the first to produce them by some more expeditious method of making. According to the opinion of several *savants*, Laurent Coster of Haerlem was only an engraver of wood-blocks for cards and pictures, before he became a printer

Fig. 229.—The Knight, from a Pack of Cards engraved by " The Master of 1466." (Bibl. Imp. of Paris.)

of books. It certainly is a fact that wood-engraving, which was for a long time limited to a few studios in Holland and Upper Germany, owed a large share of its progress to the trade in playing-cards—one which was carried on with such activity that, as we read in an old chronicle of the city of Ulm, about the year 1397, "they were in the habit of sending playing-cards in bales to Italy, Sicily, and other southern countries, to exchange for groceries and various merchandise."

A few years later, engraving on metal or copper-plate was employed in producing playing-cards of a really artistic character, among which we may mention those of "The Master of 1466" (Figs. 228 and 229), and by his anonymous rivals. The pack of cards of this engraver exists only in a small number of print-collections, and it is in every case incomplete. As far as we can judge, it must have been composed of sixty cards, consisting of forty numeral cards divided into five series, and twenty picture-cards, being four to each series. The figures are the king, queen, knight, and knave. The suits, or marks, present rather a strange selection of wild men, ferocious quadrupeds, deer, birds of prey, and various flowers. These objects are numerically grouped and tolerably well arranged, so as to allow the numbers indicated to be distinguished at first sight.

Thus, as we have seen, playing-cards made their way through Arabia from India to Europe, where they first arrived about the year 1370. Within a few years they spread from the south to the north of the latter country ; but those who, under the influence of a passion for play, had so eagerly welcomed them, were far indeed from suspecting that this new game contained within itself the germ of two of the most beautiful inventions ever devised by the human mind—those of engraving and printing. There can be no doubt that playing-cards were in use for many a long year, ere the public voice had proclaimed the almost simultaneous discovery of the arts of engraving on wood and metal, and of printing.

Fig. 230.—Coat of Arms of the Cardmakers of Paris.

GLASS-PAINTING.

Painting on Glass mentioned by Historians in the Third Century of our Era.—Glazed Windows at Brioude in the Sixth Century.—Coloured Glass at St. John Lateran and St. Peter's in Rome.—Church-Windows of the Twelfth and Thirteenth Centuries in France: Saint-Denis, Sens, Poitiers, Chartres, Rheims, &c.—In the Fourteenth and Fifteenth Centuries the Art was at its Zenith.—Jean Cousin.—The Célestins of Paris; Saint-Gervais.—Robert Pinaigrier and his Sons.—Bernard Palissy decorates the Chapel of the Castle of Ecouen.—Foreign Art; Albert Dürer.

E have already established the fact that the art of manufacturing and colouring glass was known to the most ancient nations; and, says Champollion-Figeac, "if we study the various fragments of this fragile substance that have been handed down to our time, if we take into consideration the varied ornamentation with which they are covered, even the human figures which some of them represent, it would be difficult to assert that antiquity was unacquainted with the means of combining glass with painting. If antiquity did not produce what are now called painted-windows, the real cause doubtless was because the custom of employing glass in windows did not then exist." Some few specimens of it have, however, been found in the windows of the houses exhumed at Pompeii; but this must have been an exception, for the third century of our era is the earliest date in which traces are found in history of window-glass being used in buildings; and we must bring down our researches as late as the times of St. John Chrysostom and St. Jerome (the fourth century) in order to find any reliable affirmation as to its adoption.

In the sixth century Gregory of Tours relates that a soldier broke the glass-window of a church at Brioude in order to enter it secretly and commit robbery; and we know that when this prelate caused the restora-

tion of the Church of St. Martin of Tours, he took care to fill its windows
with glass "of varied colours." About the same time Fortunatus, the
poet-bishop of Poitiers, highly extols the splendour of the glass-window
of a church in Paris, the name of which he does not mention; but the
learned investigations of Foncemagne with reference to the first kings of
France inform us that the church built at Paris by Childebert I. in honour
of the Holy Cross and St. Vincent, as well as the churches of Lyons and
Bourges, were closed in with glass-windows. Du Cange, in his "Constantinople Chrétienne," describes the glass-windows of the basilica of St. Sophia,
rebuilt by Justinian; and Paul, the Silentiary,* dwells with enthusiasm on
the marvellous effect produced by the rays of the sun upon this assemblage
of various coloured glasses.

In the eighth century, the epoch at which the use of glass-windows
was becoming general, the basilica of St. John Lateran and the Church
of St. Peter at Rome possessed coloured glass-windows; and Charlemagne,
who had caused mosaics of coloured glass to be made in a large number
of churches, did not fail to avail himself of this kind of ornament in the
cathedral erected by him at Aix-la-Chapelle.

Up to this time the only method of making glass was in small pieces,
generally round, and designated by the name of *cives*, a number of which,
by means of a network of plaster, wooden frames, or strips of lead, were
used to fill up the windows. This material being, however, very costly, it
could only be introduced into edifices of great importance. Added to this,
it can scarcely be a source of wonder if, at a time when all branches of
art had relapsed into a sort of barbarism, and glass was only exceptionally
employed in ordinary purposes, no one thought of decorating it with painted
figures and ornaments.

With regard to mosaic, either in marble or coloured glass, Martial,
Lucretius, and other writers of antiquity mention it in their works. Egypt
had a knowledge of it even before Greece; the Romans were accustomed to
employ it in ornamenting the roofs and pavement of their temples, and
even their columns and streets. Some magnificent specimens of these

---

* *Paul, the Silentiary*, is so named from holding in the court of Justinian the office of chief of
the Silentiarii, persons who had the care of the palace. He wrote a poem on the rebuilding of
St. Sophia, at Constantinople, which was translated from Greek into Latin, and published with
notes, by Du Cange, of Paris, in 1670. It is this to which M. Lecroix refers in the text.—[ED.]

decorations have remained to our time, and they are considered as insepar-able from the architecture of the emperors.

Some have desired to attribute the custom of employing coloured glass in mosaics to the rarity of coloured marbles. Would it not be a more probable hypothesis that the simultaneous use of marble and glass for this purpose was the result of improvements in the art of making mosaics? for glass that, by metallic mixtures, may be brought to a variety of colours, is much more easily adapted to pictorial combinations than marble, the tints of which are the result of the caprices of nature. Seneca, alluding to the use of coloured glasses in mosaic, complains of people not being able "to walk except on precious stones;" this shows how prevalent the use of rich mosaics had become in Rome. But this art must have singularly fallen into decay, for the few examples of the kind we now possess, which date from the first centuries of Christianity, are marked with a character of simplicity that fully harmonises with the rudeness of the artists of those times. Among these specimens must be mentioned a pavement discovered at Rheims, upon which are represented the twelve signs of the zodiac, the seasons of the year, and Abraham's Sacrifice; another on which are depicted Theseus and the labyrinth of Crete, in juxtaposition with David and Goliath. It is, moreover, known that there existed in the Forum of Naples a portrait in mosaic of Theodoric, king of the Goths, who had caused a representa-tion of the Baptism of Christ to be executed, in the church of Ravenna, by the same process. Sidonius Apollinaris, describing the excessive luxury of Consentius at Narbonne, speaks of arches and pavements ornamented with mosaics. The churches of St. John Lateran, St. Clement, and St. George in Velabro, at Rome, still display mosaics of this period. Lastly, Charle-magne caused the greater part of the churches constructed by him to be ornamented with mosaics.

To return to glass-work, we find that in the time of Charles the Bald, in 863, mention is made of two artisans, Ragenat and Balderic, who became as it were the heads of the race of French glass-makers. We also learn from the chronicle of St. Benignus of Dijon, that in 1052 there existed in that church a "very ancient painted window," representing St. Paschasie, which was said to have been taken from the earlier church. We have therefore a right to conclude that at this period the custom of painting on glass had long been common.

In the tenth century glass-makers must have acquired some degree of
importance, for the reigning Dukes of Normandy of that era established
certain privileges in their favour; but, says Champollion-Figeac, "as all
privilege was the prerogative of the order of nobility, they contrived to
give them to noble families whose fortunes were precarious. Four Norman
families obtained this distinction. But although it was understood that in
devoting themselves to the trade these titled individuals incurred no
degradation, it was never said, as is commonly believed, that the profession
of this art conferred nobility; on the contrary, a proverb arose which
long continued in use, namely, that 'in order to make a gentleman glass-
maker, you must first take a gentleman.'"

Although painting on glass was from that time carried on with considerable activity, in many cases it was still very far from being accomplished by
the processes which were destined to make it one of the most remarkable
productions of art. The application of the brush to vitrifiable colours
was not generally adopted. In the examples of this period that remain
to our days, we indeed find large *cives* cast in white glass, upon which
characters were painted by the artist; but, as the colour was not designed
to be incorporated with the glass by the action of fire, with a view to
ensure the preservation of the painting, another transparent but thick
cive was placed over the first, and closely soldered to it.

While glass-painting was thus seeking to perfect its processes, mosaic
work gradually declined. Only a very small number of mosaics of the tenth
and eleventh centuries exist at the present day, and these, moreover, are
very incorrect in design, and entirely wanting in taste and colour.

In the twelfth century, all the arts began to revive. The fear of the end
of the world, which had thrown mankind into a strange state of perturbation,
was dissipated. The Christian faith everywhere stirred up the zeal of its
disciples. Magnificent cathedrals with imposing arches sprang up in various
places, and the art of the glass-maker came to the aid of architecture in
order to diffuse over the interiors consecrated to worship the light, both
prismatic and harmonious, which affords the calm necessary for holy medita-
tion. But though, in the painted windows of this period, we are forced to
admire the ingenious combination of colours for the rose-work (rose-
windows), the case is very different as regards the drawing and colouring
of the designs. The figures are generally traced in rough, stiff lines on

glass of a dull tint, which absorbs all the expression of the heads; the
entire drapery of the costume is heavy; the figure is spoilt by the folds of

Fig. 231.—St. Timothy the Martyr, Coloured Glass of the end of the Eleventh Century, found in the
Church of Neuwiller (Bas-Rhin) by M. Bœswillwald.
(From the "History of Glass-Painting," by M. Lasteyrie.)

its vestments as if it were enclosed in a long sheath. This is the general
character of the examples of that period as they are known to us (Fig. 231).

The painted windows which Suger made to adorn the abbey-church of St. Denis, some of which exist in our days, date from the twelfth century. The abbot made inquiries in every country, and gathered together at a great expense the best artists he could find, in order to assist in this decoration. The Adoration of the Magi, the Annunciation, the History of Moses, and various allegories, are there represented in the chapel of the Virgin and those of St. Osman and St. Hilary. Among the principal pictures may be also observed a portrait of Suger himself at the feet of the Virgin. The borders surrounding the subjects may be considered as models of harmony and good arrangement of effect; but still, the taste shown in the selection and combination of colours is carried to the highest point in the subjects themselves, the designs of which are very excellent.

In the Church of St. Maurice, at Angers, we find examples of a rather earlier date—perhaps the most ancient specimens of painted windows in France; these are the history of St. Catherine and that of the Virgin, which, in truth, are not equal in merit, as regards execution and taste, to the ancient windows of the Church of St. Denis.

We still have to mention some fragments contained in the Church of St. Serge, and the chapel of the Hospital, in the town of Angers; also a glass-window in the Abbey of Fontevrault; another in the Church of St. Peter, at Dreux, in which is represented Queen Anne of Brittany. We will, in conclusion, mention one of the windows of the choir in the Church of the Trinity, at Vendôme; it represents the Glorification of the Virgin, who bears on her forehead an aureola, the shape of which, called *amandaire*,* has furnished archæologists with a subject for long discussions; some being desirous of proving that this aureola, which does not appear to be depicted in the same way on any other painted window, tends to show that the works of the Poitevine glass-makers, to whom it is attributed, had been subject to the influence of the Byzantine school; others assert that the almond-shaped crown is a symbol exclusively reserved for the Virgin. Before we proceed to the examples handed down to us from the twelfth century, we must mention some remains of glass to be seen at Chartres, Mans, Sens, and Bourges (Fig. 232), &c. We may also add, as an incident

---

* *Amandaire*—almond-shaped. Strictly speaking, the aureola is the nimbus of the whole body, as the nimbus is the aureola of the head. In Fairholt's " Dictionary of Terms in Art " is an engraving showing a saint standing in the centre of an almond-shaped aureola.—[ED.]

not without interest, that a chapter of the order of the Cistercians, considering the great expense to which the acquisition of painted windows led, prohibited the use of them in churches under the rule of St. Bernard.

Fig. 232.—Fragment of a Church-window, representing the "Prodigal Son." Thirteenth Century.
(Presented to the Cathedral of Bourges by the Guild of Tanners.)

"The architecture of the thirteenth century," according to the judicious remarks of Champollion-Figeac, "by its style of moulding, which is more slender and graceful than the massive forms of Roman art, opened a wider

and more favourable field for artists in glass. The small pillars then projected and extended themselves with a novel elegance, and the tapering and
delicate spires of the steeples lost themselves in the clouds. The windows
occupied more space, and likewise had the appearance of springing lightly
and gracefully upwards. They were adorned with symbolical ornaments,
griffins, and other fantastic animals; leaves and boughs cross and intertwine
with one another, producing that varied rose-work which is the admiration
of modern glass-makers. The colours are more skilfully combined and better
blended than in the windows of the preceding century; and although some
of the figures are still wanting in expression, and have not thrown off all
the stiffness which characterised them, the draperies, at least, are lighter
and better drawn." Examples of the thirteenth century which have
remained to our time are very numerous. There is at Poitiers some painted
glass composed of small roses, and chiefly placed in one of the windows in
the centre of the church and in the " Calvary " of the apse; at Sens, the
legend of St. Thomas of Canterbury is represented in a number of small
medallions, called *verrières legendaires;* at Mans is glass representing the
corporations of trades; at Chartres, the painted glass in the cathedral,
a work both magnificent and extensive, contains no fewer than one thousand
three hundred and fifty subjects, distributed throughout one hundred
and forty-three windows. At Rheims, the painted glass is perhaps less
important, but it is remarkable both for the brilliancy of its colours and
also for its characteristic fitness to the style of the edifice. Bourges, Tours,
Angers, and Notre-Dame in Paris, present very beautiful specimens. The
Cathedral of Rouen possesses, to this day, a window which bears the name
of Clement of Chartres, *master glazier*, the first artist of this kind who has
left behind him any work bearing his signature. We must, in conclusion,
mention the Sainte-Chapelle, Paris, which is unquestionably the highest
representation of what the art is capable of producing. The designs of the
windows in this last edifice are *legendary*, and although some few inaccuracies
may be noticed in the figures, the fault is redeemed by the studied
elegance of the ornamentation and the harmony of colours, which combine
to render them one of the most consistent and perfect works of painting
on glass.

In the thirteenth century "*grisaille*" first made its appearance; it was
quite a new style, and has been often since employed in the borders and

ornaments of painted windows. "*Grisaille*,"* the name of which is to some extent sufficient to describe its aspect, was used simultaneously with the mosaics of variegated glass, as we see in the Church of St. Thomas, Strasbourg, in the Cathedral of Freybourg in Brisgau, and in many churches of Bourges.

The large number of paintings on glass belonging to the thirteenth century, which may still be studied in various churches, has given rise to the idea of classifying all these monuments, and arranging them under certain schools, which have been designated by the names of *Franco-Norman*, *Germanic*, &c. Some have even gone further, and desired to recognise in the style peculiar to the artists of ancient France a Norman style, a Poitevin style (the latter recognisable, it is said, by the want of harmony in the colours), &c. We can hardly admit these last distinctions, and are the less inclined to do so, as those who propound them seem to base their theories rather on the defects than the good qualities of the artists. Besides, at a period in which a nobleman sometimes possessed several provinces very distant from each other—as, for example, Anjou and Provence—it might so happen that the artists he took with him to his different residences could scarcely fail, by the union of their various works, to cause any provincial influences to disappear, and would finally reduce the distinction between what is called the Poitevin style, the Norman style, &c., to a question of a more or less skilful manufacture, or of a more or less advanced improvement.

In the fourteenth century the artist in glass became separated from the architect; although naturally subordinate to the designer of the edifice, in which the windows were to be only an accessory ornament, he wished to give effect to his own inspiration. The whole of the building was subjected by him to the effect of his more learned and correct drawing, and his purer and more striking colouring. It mattered little to him should some part of the church have too much light, or not light enough, if a flood of radiance deluged the apse or the choir, instead of being gradually diffused everywhere, as in earlier buildings. He desired his labour to recommend him, and his work to do him honour.

The court-poets, Guillaume de Machaut and Eustache Deschamps, celebrate in their poems several works in painted glass of their time, and even give some details in verse on the mode of fabricating them.

* *Grisaille*—white and black.—[ED.]

In 1347 a royal ordinance was proclaimed in favour of the workmen of

Fig. 233.—Legend of the Jew of the Rue des Billettes, Paris, piercing the Holy Wafer with his Knife.
(From a Window of the Church of St. Alpin, at Châlons-sur-Marne.   Fourteenth Century.)

Lyons.   The custom existed at that time of adorning with painted windows royal and lordly habitations. The artists produced their own designs, adapting them to the use that was made, in private life, of the halls for which they were intended. Some of these windows representing familiar legends adorned even the churches (Fig. 233).

Among the most important works of the fourteenth century, we must mention in the first place the windows of the cathedrals of Mans, Beauvais, Évreux (Fig. 234), and the rose-windows of St. Thomas at Strasbourg. Next come the windows of the Church of St. Nazaire at Carcassonne and of the Cathedral of Narbonne. There are, besides, in the Church of St. John at Lyons, in Notre-Dame of Semur, in Aix in Provence, at Bourges, and at Metz, church-windows in every respect worthy of attention.

The fifteenth century only continues the traditions of the preceding one. The principal works dating from this epoch begin, according to the order of merit, with the window of the Cathedral of Mans, which represents Yolande* of Aragon, and Louis II., King of Naples and Sicily, ancestors of the good King René; after them we shall place the windows of the Sainte-Chapelle, Riom; St. Vincent, Rouen; the Cathedral of Tours; and that of Bourges, representing a memorial of Jacques Cœur, &c.

The sixteenth century, although bringing with it, owing to religious troubles, many ravages of new iconoclasts, has handed down to us a variety of numerous and remarkable church-windows. We are, of course, unable to mention them all; but it seems expedient—adopting the rule of most archæologists—to divide them into three branches or schools, which are actually formed by the different styles of the artists of that epoch; the French

Fig. 234.—Fragment of a Window presented to the Cathedral of Evreux by the Bishop Guillaume de Cantiers. Fourteenth Century.

* Probably Alfonso is thus designated.—[Ed.]

school, the German school, and the Lorraine school (Fig. 235), which partakes of the characteristics of the two preceding.

Fig. 235.—Allegorical Window, representing the "Citadel of Pallas."
(Lorraine work of the Sixteenth Century, preserved in the Library at Strasbourg.)

At the head of the French school figures the celebrated Jean Cousin, who decorated the chapel of Vincennes; he also made for the Célestins monastery,

Paris, a representation of Calvary; for St. Gervais, in 1587, the windows representing the "Martyrdom of St. Lawrence," the "Samaritan conversing with Christ," and the "Paralytic." In these works, which belong to a high style of painting, the best method of arrangement, vigorous drawing, and powerful colouring, seem to reflect the work of Raphael. Windows in "*grisaille*," made from the cartoons of Jean Cousin, also decorated the Castle of Anet.

Another artist, named Robert Pinaigrier, who, although inferior to Cousin, was much more fertile in production, assisted by his sons Jean, Nicholas, and Louis, and several of his pupils, executed a number of windows for the churches of Paris, of which the greater part have disappeared: Saint-Jacques la Boucherie, the Madeleine, Sainte-Croix en la Cité, Saint-Barthélemy, &c. Magnificent specimens of his work still remain at Saint-Merry, Saint-Gervais, Saint-Etienne du Mont, and in the Cathedral of Chartres. Pinaigrier's works in the decorations of châteaux and the mansions of the nobility are perhaps equally numerous.

At this period several windows were made from the drawings of Raphael, Leonardo da Vinci, and Parmigiano; it may also be remarked that two patterns of the latter's work were used by Bernard Palissy, who was a glass-maker before he became an enameller, in forming windows in "*grisaille*" for the chapel of the Château of Ecouen. For the same place, following the style of Raphael, and from the drawings of Rosso, called *Maître Roux*, Bernard Palissy executed thirty pictures on glass, representing the history of Psyche, which are justly considered as ranking among the most beautiful compositions of the epoch; but it is not now known what has become of these valuable windows, which at the Revolution were transported to the Museum of French Monuments.

They were, it is said, executed under the direction of Leonard of Limoges, who, like all the masters of that school (Fig. 236), applied to painting on glass the processes of enamelling, and *vice versâ*. In the collections of the Louvre and of several amateurs, there are still examples of his composition, on which he employed the best glass-painters of his time; for he could not himself work on all the objects that proceeded from his studios, and which were almost exclusively destined for the king's palace.

The French art of glass-working became cosmopolitan. It was introduced into Spain and also into the Low Countries under the protection of

Charles V. and the Duke of Alba. It even appears to have crossed the
Alps; for we know that in 1512 a glass-painter of the name of Claude
adorned with his works the large windows of the Vatican; and Julius II.
summoned Guillaume of Marseilles to the Eternal City, the pontiff when

Fig. 236.—St. Paul, an Enamel of Limoges, by Etienne Mercier.

occupying the sees of Carpentras and Avignon having appreciated his talent.
We must not omit to mention, among the Flemish artists who escaped this
foreign influence, the name of Dirk of Haarlem (Fig. 237), the most
celebrated master in this art at the close of the fifteenth century.

While French art was thus spreading over the continent, foreign art was being introduced into France. Albert Dürer employed his pencil in painting twenty windows in the church of the Old Temple, in Paris, and produced a collection of pictures characterised by vigorous drawing, and

Fig. 237.—Flemish Window (Fifteenth Century), half life-size. Painted in Monochrome, relieved with yellow, by Dirk of Haarlem. (Collection of M. Benoni-Verhelst, Ghent.)

warm and intense colouring. The celebrated German did not work alone— other artists assisted him ; and, notwithstanding the devastations which took place during the Revolution, in many a church and mansion traces of these skilful masters may still be found; their compositions, which are generally as well arranged as they are executed, are marked with a tinge of German simplicity very suitable to the pious nature of the subjects they represent.

In 1600, Nicholas Pinaigrier placed in the windows of the Castle of La Briffe seven pictures in "*grisaille*," copied from the designs of Francis Floris, a Flemish master, who was born in 1520. At this same period Van Haeck, Herreyn, John Dox, and Pelgrin Rösen, all belonging to the school of Antwerp, and other artists who had decorated the windows of most of the churches in Belgium, especially St. Gudule in Brussels, influenced either directly or indirectly the glass-painters of the east and north of France. Another group of artists, the Provençals, imitators of the Italian style, or rather perhaps inspired by the same luminary, the sun of Michael Angelo, trod a similar path to that which Jean Cousin, Pinaigrier, and Palissy had followed with so much renown. The chiefs of this school were Claude, and Guillaume of Marseilles, who, as we have just mentioned, carried their talent and their works into Italy, where they succeeded in educating some clever pupils.

With regard to the school of Messin or Lorraine, it is principally represented by a disciple of Michael Angelo, Valentin Bousch, the Alsatian, who died in 1541 at Metz, where he had executed, since 1521, an immense number of works. The windows of the churches of St. Barbe, St. Nicolas du Port, Autrey, and Flavigny-sur-Moselle, are due to the same school, in which Israel Henriet was also brought up; he became the chief of a school exclusively belonging to Lorraine, at the time when Charles III. had invited the arts to unite under the patronage of the ducal throne. Thierry Alix, in a "Description inédite de la Lorraine," written in 1590, and mentioned by M. Bégin, speaks of "large plates of glass of all colours," made in his time in the mountains of Vosges, where "all the herbs and other things necessary to painting" were found. M. Bégin, after having quoted this curious statement, adds that the windows which at that era were produced in the studios of Vosges, and subsequently carried to all parts of Europe, constituted a very active branch of commerce.

"Nevertheless," says Champollion-Figeac, "art was declining. Christian art especially was disappearing, and had almost come to an end, when Protestantism stepped in and gave it the last blow; this is proved by the window in the cathedral church of Berne, in which the artist, Frederic

FRANCIS I. AND ELEONORA AT THEIR DEVOTIONS.

Portion of a Stained Glass Window in the Church of St. Gudule at Brussels.

"FRANCIS I. AND ELEANOR HIS WIFE AT PRAYERS."

PART OF A WINDOW IN THE CHURCH OF ST. GUDULE IN BRUSSELS.

FROM "L'HISTOIRE DE LA PEINTURE SUR VERRE EN EUROPE."

This magnificent window was given to the Church of St. Gudule by Francis I. and Eleanor of Spain, his wife, sister of Charles V., and widow by her first marriage of Emmanuel the Great, King of Portugal.

The donors are represented kneeling, each one protected by his or her patron saint; the king is attended by St. Francis of Assisi, who is receiving in a vision the impress of the stigmata of Jesus on the Cross; the queen is accompanied by St. Eleanor, who holds in her hand the palm of the elect. This window is from a design by Bernard van Orley.

Francis I. and Eleanor expended on the window two hundred and twenty-two crowns, or four hundred florins, an important sum in those days (1515-47).

Walter, dared to launch his satire against doctrine itself, and to ridicule transubstantiation by representing a pope shovelling four evangelists into a mill, from which come forth a number of wafers; these a bishop is receiving into a cup in order to distribute them to the wondering people. Any edification of the masses by the powerful effect of transparent images placed, so to speak, between the earth and heaven, soon ceased to be possible, and glass-painting, henceforth alienated from the special aim of its origin, was destined also to disappear."

Fig. 238.—Temptation of St. Mars, a Hermit of Auvergne, by the Devil disguised as a Woman. Fragment of a Window of the Sainte-Chapelle of Riom. Fifteenth Century.
(From " Histoire de la Peinture sur Verre," by M. F. de Lasteyrie.)

FRESCO-PAINTING.

 OO frequently in conversational language and even in the writings of grave authors," says M. Ernest Breton, "the word *fresco* is made synonymous with mural painting in general. This confusion of terms has sometimes caused the most fatal errors. The etymology of the word is the best definition of the subject. The Italians give the name of paintings *in fresco* or *a fresco*, that is to say, *à frais*, or *sur le frais*, to those works executed upon damp stucco into which the colour penetrates to a certain depth. The ancient French authors, preserving the difference existing between the Italian *fresco* and the French *frais*, wrote the word *fraisque*. At the present day Italian orthography has prevailed, and with us this word has now more relation to its etymology than its real signification."

Whatever may be the common acceptation of the word, we must, in order to keep within the limits of our subject, here only take into consideration real frescoes, or in other words, works of art executed upon a bare wall, properly prepared for the purpose, with which they are as it were incorporated; for in the roll of art all are excluded from the catalogue of mural paintings, rightly so called, which, although applied to walls either directly or by the aid of panels or fixed canvas, are produced otherwise than with water-colours, and used in such a manner as to penetrate the special kind of plaster with which the wall had been previously covered.

We will mention as a striking example of this the famous "Lord's Supper" of Leonardo da Vinci, which has many times been called a fresco (it is well known to have been painted upon the wall of the refectory of Santa Maria della Gratia, at Milan), but is nothing but a painting in distemper * on a dry partition—a circumstance, by-the-bye, which has not a little contributed to the deterioration of this magnificent work.

Fresco has long been considered the most ancient style of painting. Vasari, who wrote in the middle of the sixteenth century, says in apt terms that "the ancients generally practised painting *in fresco*, and the first painters of the modern schools have only followed the antique methods;" and, in our own day, Millin, in his "Dictionnaire des Beaux-Arts," asserts that the great paintings in the "Pœcile" of Athens and the "Lesche" of Delphi, by Panænus and Polygnotus, spoken of by Pausanias, were executed by this process; the same author also ranks among frescoes the numerous paintings left by the Egyptians in their temples and catacombs. "It was," he remarks, "what the Romans called *in udo pariete pingere* (to paint on a damp wall); they say *in cretula pingere* (to paint on chalk) to designate water-colour painting on a dry ground."

Some persons have considered the paintings found at Herculaneum and Pompeii to be frescoes; nevertheless Winckelmann, who is an authority in these matters, said, a hundred years ago, in speaking of those works, "It is to be remarked that the greater part of these pictures were not painted on damp lime, but upon a dry ground, which is rendered very evident by several of the figures having scaled off in such a way as to show distinctly the ground upon which they rest."

The whole mistake has arisen from taking the expression "*in udo pariete,*" found in Pliny, in too literal a sense; the error, which might at all events have been dissipated by an attentive examination of the examples themselves, would not have lasted long if the passage from Pliny had

---

* This is obviously a misconception. Lanzi, alluding to the picture, says, "Had Leonardo desired to follow the practice of his age in painting in distemper, the art at this time would have been in possession of this treasure. But being always fond of attempting new methods, he painted this masterpiece upon a peculiar ground, formed of distilled oils, which was the reason that it gradually detached itself from the wall," &c. And a later authority, Kugler, thus writes: "The determination of Leonardo to execute the work in oil-colours instead of fresco, in order to have the power of finishing the minutest details in so great an undertaking, appears to have been unfortunate." Distemper differs from fresco in that it is painted on a dry, and not a damp, wall but in both the vehicle used is of an aqueous, and not an oily, nature.—[ED.]

been compared with a statement of Vitruvius, which informs us that they applied to fresh walls uniform tints of black, blue, yellow, or red, which were destined to form the grounds of paintings, or even allowed them to remain plain, like our present coloured walls. The employment of this process may also be easily recognised in the paintings of Pompeii, where this uniform colouring has sometimes penetrated nearly an inch into the stucco of the wall. On this ground, when it was perfectly dry, ornamental subjects were painted either in distemper or encaustic.

Thus, therefore, it is shown that the process of painting *in fresco* was unknown to the ancients, and was invented by artists of succeeding times; but it would be difficult to assign any precise date to this invention; for however far we go back, we do not find any authors who fix the epoch at which the new method was for the first time followed. We are, therefore, compelled to notice the age of some particular example which shows that the discovery had then taken place, without being able to determine the exact date of its commencement.

Painting, which with the Greeks attained its greatest height in the reign of Alexander, fell, says M. Breton, " with the power of Greece. In losing its liberty, the country of the Fine Arts lost, too, the perception of the beautiful." At Rome, painting never reached the same degree of perfection as it did in Greece; for a long time it was only practised by men of the lowest rank and by slaves. A few patricians, such as Amulius, Fabius *Pictor* (painter), and Cornelius Pinus, were, at the best, able to bring about only some slight revival. After the twelve Cæsars, painting followed the movement of decadence which carried away with it all the arts; like them, it received its death-blow in the fourth century, on the day when Constantine, quitting Rome in order to establish the seat of empire at Byzantium, took with him into his new capital not only the best artists, but also a prodigious number of their productions, and of those of the artists who preceded them. Several other causes may also be mentioned as having led to the decline of art, or to the destruction of examples which would now bear witness to its power in remote ages. In the first place, there was the birth of Christian Art, which rose on the ruins of Paganism; then, the invasion of barbarians which took place in the fifth century; lastly, in the eighth and ninth centuries, the fury of the Iconoclasts, or Image-breakers, a sect at the head of which figured several emperors of the East, from Leo

the Isaurian, who reigned in 717, down to Michael the Stammerer and
Theophilus, who respectively ascended the imperial throne in 820 and 829.

Even among the ignorant masses, to whom we owe the loss of so many
chefs-d'œuvre, were some individuals who formed honourable exceptions,
not only by opposing the devastations, but also by manifesting a laudable
conservative instinct. Cassiodorus tells us that Theodoric, king of the
Goths, re-established the office of centurio nitentium rerum (guardian of
beautiful objects), instituted by the emperor Constantius ; and we know that
the Lombard kings who succeeded this prince and reigned in Italy for 218
years, although less zealous in the culture of the arts, did not fail to honour
and protect them. In Paul the Deacon * we read that, in the sixth century,
queen Teudelinde, wife of Autharis and afterwards of Agilulphus, caused
the valorous deeds of the first Lombard kings to be painted on the basilica
that she had consecrated at Monza under the name of St. John. Other
paintings of the same epoch may still be seen at Pavia. The Church of
St. Nazaire at Verona possesses in its crypt paintings spoken of by Maffei,
which have been engraved by Ciampini and Frisi : these must date back to
the sixth and seventh centuries. Lastly, they have recently found in the
subterranean chapel of the basilica of St. Clement, in Rome, some admirable
mural paintings, which archæologists refer to the same epoch.

The Eastern artists, driven away by the persecutions of the Iconoclasts,
sought an asylum in Italy, where the Latin Church, obedient to the
prescriptions of the Council of Nice, seemed determined to multiply sacred
images as much as possible. The arrival of the Grecian artists in the West
was also singularly promoted by the commercial relations which from that
time were established between all points of the Mediterranean shore and the
maritime or mercantile towns of Italy—Pisa, Genoa, and Venice. Thus
was brought about the movement which, although taking place on Italian
soil, drew from an entirely Eastern source the inspiration of the revival of
the Fine Arts ; thus was continued the so-called Byzantine school, destined
to be the foundation of all modern art.

In 817 some Greek artists, by order of Pope Pascal I., executed under
the portico of the Church of St. Cecilia in Rome a series of frescoes, the
subjects of which were taken from the life of the saint. To the same school

---

* Deacon of the church at Aquila, and afterwards attached to the court of Charlemagne.
Paul, who died about the year 799, was distinguished as a poet and historian.—[Ed.]

we are indebted for the sitting figures of Christ and His mother (Fig. 239), in the old Church of Santa-Maria Trans-Tiberia, in Rome; the large Madonna painted on the walls of Santa-Maria della Scala, Milan, which, at the time when this church was destroyed and replaced by the theatre of La Scala, was taken away and carried to the Church of Santa-Fidelia, where it still remains; a series of portraits of the Popes after St. Leo, a collection of which a large portion perished in the fire of St. Paul-extra-Muros, Rome

Fig. 239.—Christ and His Mother. Fresco-Painting of the Ninth Century, in the Apse of Santa-Maria Trans-Tiberia, Rome.

(Fig. 240); and lastly, the paintings in the vaults of the Cathedral of Aquila.

"The works of these earliest painters," observes M. Breton, "seem to mark the transition from painting to sculpture: they are long figures as stiff as columns, single or arranged symmetrically, forming neither groups nor compositions, without perspective or effects of light and shade, and having nothing to express their meaning than a sort of legend proceeding out of the mouths of the characters. These frescoes, which are so weak when looked at in an artistic point of view, are remarkable for their material execution, being extremely solid in their workmanship. It is astonishing to see the wonderful preservation of some pictures of saints that adorn the pilasters of St. Nicolas in Treviso and the walls of the church in Fiesole, whereon are preserved the frescoes of Fra Angelico."

Among the paintings remaining to our time, the first in which the authors departed from the uniform style of the Byzantine masters are those which adorn the interior of the ancient temple of Bacchus, now the Church

Fig. 240.—Portrait of the Pope Sylvester I. Fresco-Painting in Mosaic, on a gold ground, in the Basilica of St. Paul-extra-Muros, Rome.

of St. Urban, in the Campagna of Rome: there is nothing Grecian either in the figures or draperies, and it is impossible not to recognise in them an Italian pencil; the date, however, is 1011. Pesaro, Aquila, Orvieto, and Fiesole, possess examples of the same epoch.

At last, in the thirteenth century, notwithstanding its fierce intestine struggles, Italy, and especially Tuscany, witnessed the dawn of the sun of the Fine Arts, which, after a long period of darkness, was to shine with so much brilliancy over the whole world. Pisa and Siena, earliest in the

revival, gave birth respectively to Giunta and Guido (Palmerucci), each of
whom in his time acquired great renown; but the only works of these artists

Fig. 241. – The Apostles in the Garden of Gethsemane. Fresco by Berna, at San-Geminiano.
(Fourteenth Century.)

which remain now, in the Cathedral of Assisi, seem but to indicate a desire
of progress without manifesting any real advancement in art.

To Guido of Siena succeeds, but not immediately, the friend of Petrarch,

Simon Memmi, whose frescoes in the Campo Santo of Pisa testify to his powerful genius, and denote the first remarkable stage of art.

In the collegiate church of San-Geminiano * may be still seen a fresco by Berna (Fig. 241), an eminent master in the school of Siena, who died in 1370.

Passing, but not without mention, Margaritone and Bonaventura Berlinghieri, who were only the timid harbingers of a great individuality, the Florentine school places in the first rank of its celebrities Cimabue (1240—1300), justly regarded by the artistic world as the true restorer of painting. Cimabue pointed out the path; Giotto, his pupil, trod it. He took nature for his guide, and has been surnamed "nature's pupil." Real imitation was the object of his endeavour, and as he found this system marvellously applied in the beautiful antique marbles which had already inspired, in the preceding century, the sculptors John and Nicolas of Pisa, he made an earnest study of these ancient *chefs-d'œuvre*. The impulse was given, and the Campo Santo of Pisa shows us its first results in "The Dream of Life."

For two centuries there was a slow but always progressive improvement, owing to the industry of Buffamalco, Taddeo Gaddi, Orcagna, Spinello of Lucca, and Masolino of Panicale. With the fifteenth century appeared Fra Angelico of Fiesole (Figs. 242 and 246), and Benozzo Gozzoli; then Masaccio, Pisanello, Mantegna, Zingaro, Pinturicchio, and lastly Perugino, the master of the divine Raphael. In the sixteenth century art attained its culminating point. At this epoch Raphael and his pupils painted the "Farnesina" and the "Stanze" and "Loggie" of the Vatican (it is known that the two first pictures of the "Loggie" (Fig. 243) were painted solely by the hand of Raphael); Michael Angelo alone executed the immense expanse of the "Last Judgment," and Paul Veronese painted the ceilings of the palace of the Doges at Venice. Then Giulio Romano covered with his works the walls of the Te palace at Mantua; Andrea del Sarto, those of the "Annunziata" and "Dello Scalzo" at Florence. Daniel of Volterra painted his famous "Descent from the Cross" for the Trinité du Mont, Rome; at Parma, the pencil of Correggio worked marvels on the circle of the dome of the cathedral. Leonardo da Vinci, besides the picture of the "Lord's Supper," which we before mentioned only to exclude it from the

* Or San-Gemignano, a small town between Florence and Siena.—[ED.]

THE DREAM OF LIFE.

(After a Copy made for the Library of M. Ambroise Firmin Didot.)

From a Fresco Painting by Orcagna, in the Cloister of the Campo Santo of Pisa. Fourteenth Century.

"THE DREAM OF LIFE."

FRESCO-PAINTING, BY ORCAGNA, IN THE CLOISTER OF THE CAMPO SANTO OF PISA.

(FOURTEENTH CENTURY.)

This fresco is by Andrea Cione, called Orcagna, a Florentine painter of the fourteenth century, who executed for the Campo Santo of Pisa a series of paintings which are still admired, representing the four destinies of man:—"Death," "Judgment," "Hell," and "Paradise." Each of these large compositions embraces several scenes; that which we give belongs to the "Triumph of Death."

Petrarch had just given to the world the concluding notes of his funereal song, and the wish of the painter seems to have been to call to life, in his fresco, the strange vision of the poet. The happy of this world are here represented gathered together under cool shades and upon carpets of verdure; gay lords are murmuring magic words into the ears of the young ladies of Florence. Even quiet falcons on the wrists of the lords seem captivated by this delicious music. Everything appears to invite forgetfulness of the miseries of life,—the richness of the vestments, the beautiful sky of Italy, the perfumes, the love-songs. . . . This is the "Dream of Life," which "Death" is destined to dispel with one sweep of his mighty wing.

number of frescoes, endowed the monastery of St. Onofrio at Rome with a magnificent Madonna, and the palace of Caravaggio, near Bergamo,

Fig. 242.—Group of Saints, taken from the large Fresco of " The Passion " in the Convent of St. Mark. Painted by Fra Angelico of Fiesole.

with a colossal Virgin. It was, in short, the age of splendid productions in mural painting, that in which the great Buonarotti exclaimed when engaged in enthusiastic labour on one of his sublime conceptions—" Fresco is the only painting; painting in oils is only the art of women and idle and unenergetic men." And yet, at least as regards improvements in the process of execution, fresco had hardly reached its climax.

In the seventeenth century the school of Bologna, after having for a long time maintained a merely imitative style of art, shone forth with independent light under the influence of the Carracci, who, summoned to Rome, covered the walls of the Farnesian gallery with frescoes, to which none others could be compared for brilliancy and powerful effect. As

Fig. 243.—First Picture of the Loggie of Raphael—" God creating the Heaven and the Earth."

much must be said of the works of their pupils: the "Martyrdom of St. Sebastian," in the Church of St. Mary of the Angels; the "Miracles of St. Nil," at Grotta-Ferrata, near Rome; the "Death of St. Cecilia," at Saint-Louis-des-Français, by Domenichino; "Aurora," by Guercino, at the Villa Ludovici; the "Chariot of the Sun," by Guido, in the Rospigliosi Palace, &c.

Luca Giordano, a Neapolitan painter, founder of the gallery of the Ricciardi Palace at Florence, and author of the frescoes in numerous churches in Italy and Spain, must not be forgotten; and with him must be mentioned Pietro da Cortona, of the Roman school, who especially distinguished himself in the ceilings of the Barberini Palace, at Rome.

We still have to mention the fertile painters of the Genoese and Parmesan schools—Lanfranc, Carloni, and Francavilla; but the hour of decadence had come when these artists appeared; they had more boldness than talent, they aimed at the majestic, but only succeeded in attaining to the gigantic; their pencils were skilful, but their soul lacked fervour and conviction; in spite of their efforts, fresco-painting declined under their hands, and since that time has only decayed and gradually sunk into oblivion.

We must not quit the classical ground of the Fine Arts without mentioning a process of painting which is closely allied to fresco, and bears the characteristic name of *sgraffito* (literally, a scratch). This style of painting, or rather of drawing (for the works had the appearance of a large drawing in black crayon), was more generally used for the exterior of buildings, and was produced by covering the wall first with black stucco, then with a second layer of white, and afterwards by removing with an iron instrument the second layer so as to lay bare, in places, the black ground. The most important work executed in this style is the ornamentation of the monastic house of the knights of St. Stephen, at Pisa; this work is by Vasari, to whom also has been attributed—but wrongfully—the invention of *sgraffito*, which was used long before his time.

Hitherto we have chiefly confined our remarks to Italy and Italian artists; however, in the consideration of them we have nearly summed up our brief history of fresco. If we would look to France for any remarkable works of this kind, we must refer to the epochs in which Italy sent Simon Memmi to decorate the palace of the popes at Avignon, and Rosso and Primaticcio to adorn that of the kings at Fontainebleau. Prior to this, all we meet with are, at the most, a few primitive, not to say barbarous, subjects, painted here and there, in distemper, by unknown artists, on the walls of churches or monasteries. Among these conventional examples it is, however, only just to distinguish some pictures of powerful effect, if not in execution, at least for the ideas they are intended to convey; we would speak of the "Dance of Death," or "Dance of the Dead," like that which existed at Paris in the Cemetery of the Innocents, and another still to be seen in the Abbey of Chaise-Dieu, in Auvergne; legends more than pictures, and philosophical compositions rather than manifestations of art. Spain, too, has no reason to be proud of her national productions; for,

Fig. 244.—" Fraternity of the Cross-bowmen."
(Fresco-Painting of the Fifteenth Century, in the ancient Chapel of St. John and St. Paul, Ghent.)

with the exception of the Gothic frescoes still existing in the Cathedral of Toledo, representing the combats between the Moors and the Toledans (pictures specially worthy of the attention of archæologists), the only frescoes of Spanish origin we can mention are the paintings of a few ceilings in the Escurial and in a chapter-room in the Cathedral of Toledo; all the other frescoes must be attributed to Italian artists.

Whenever the northern artists, usually so cold and methodical in their mode of operation, devoted themselves to mural painting, it seems to have been necessary that they should enliven their temperament in the sunny

Fig. 245.—" Death and the Jew."
An episode from the " Dance of Death." Painted in 1441, in the Cemetery of the Dominicans, Basle.
(Facsimile from the Engraving of M. Mérian.)

rays of a southern sky; for while in Holland and Belgium we notice but few walls covered with decorative painting, we find a large number of Italian churches and palaces which contain frescoes bearing the signature of Flemish masters.

There was considerable excitement manifested a few years ago at the discovery of the mural paintings in the ancient Chapel of St. John and St. Paul, in Ghent (Fig. 244). These works are of the fifteenth century, and although satisfactory enough as regards the design, they derive more importance from the subjects which they represent than from any merit of execution.

In speaking of Germany, we should not omit to mention the ancient "Dance of Death" (Fig. 245), at Basle, in the cemetery of the Dominicans, painted in the middle of the fifteenth century; also another "Dance of Death" much more famous, and the façades of several houses, painted at Basle by Holbein. We must also indicate the paintings with which (in 1466) Israel de Meckenheim covered the walls of a chapel of St. Mary of the Capitol, at Cologne; and the frescoes of St. Etienne and St. Augustine, at Vienna. But it does not follow, from this limited enumeration of works, that Germany either created or followed any special school.

Fig. 246.—Fra Angelico, of Fiesole.

PAINTING ON WOOD, CANVAS, ETC.

The Rise of Christian Painting.—The Byzantine School.—First Revival in Italy.—Cimabue, Giotto, Fra Angelico.—Florentine School: Leonardo da Vinci, Michael Angelo.—Roman School: Perugino, Raphael.—Venetian School: Titian, Tintoretto, Veronese.—Lombard School: Correggio, Parmigianino.—Spanish School.—German and Flemish Schools: Stephan of Cologne, John of Bruges, Lucas van Leyden, Albert Dürer, Lucas van Cranach, Holbein.—Painting in France during the Middle Ages.—Italian Masters in France.—Jean Cousin.

AFTER its first weak manifestations in the dark shadows of the Catacombs—the place of refuge to which the earliest believers had to resort to celebrate their holy mysteries—Christian painting made its first attempt to display itself in open day at the time when the new faith found in Constantine the high protection of a crowned disciple. But this art felt an instinctive repugnance to draw its inspirations from works which had been created under the empire of decayed and contemned creeds. In the completely spiritual worship of the true God, it seemed but natural to seek for other types than those which had been consecrated by the fancies of materialistic mythologies.

The school of *idea*, which was substituted for the school of *form*, desired to owe nothing to its frivolous predecessor. It would have considered it a reproach to give even the semblance of permanence to reprobated traditions, and it set itself to work to create an art completely new in all its features. The rule it laid down, therefore, was to regard as non-existent the *chefs-d'œuvre* which recalled to mind the days of moral error; rejecting the inspiration to be derived from the magnificent relics of the past, it resolved to commence an era of its own, and to exist on its own ideas. Hence that principle of energetic simplicity which, although it may have hindered art from elevating itself to the perfection we call classical, had at least this advantage, that it sought by gradual development to imprint on

Christian art a stamp of individuality from which it was to derive both its power and its glory.

Thus, by the enthusiasm of faith, was called into existence that really primitive School of Painting which has received the name of *Byzantine;* because at the very time when it obtained the liberty of displaying itself, Constantine, transferring the seat of empire to Byzantium, necessarily took with him the body of artists of whom he was the protector; because, too, as we have before observed, Byzantium henceforth became for many centuries the sole focus whence light radiated towards the West, which was now plunged in barbarism. We must, therefore, go back to the Byzantine school, if we wish to trace to their origin all the forms of European painting.

"Allegory," says M. Michiels, "was the first language of Christian painting; not only did it express typically the Evangelical teachings, but the Divine personages themselves were metamorphosed into symbols. Sometimes, for instance, Christ appeared in the form of a young shepherd, bearing on his shoulders and carrying back to the fold a wandering sheep; sometimes He was represented as the Orpheus of the new faith, charming and taming ferocious animals by the sound of His lute. . . . He also was made to assume the form of the lamb without spot, or of a phœnix spreading its wings, the conqueror of death and the spirits of darkness. Thus was the transition softened down; thus did they escape the raillery of Pagans who would have turned into ridicule the heroic sufferings and the glorious humiliations of the Son of man. But this timidity could not long continue.

. . The council held at Constantinople in 692 commanded that allegory should be repudiated, and that the objects of their veneration should be displayed to the faithful without the veil hitherto employed. Now was exhibited to view a spectacle new indeed to men; a Deity crowned with thorns, enduring the outrages of a vile populace, or stretched upon a cross and pierced with a lance, turning His sad glance to heaven and wrestling with His agony. The Greeks and Latins were but slow in adopting this mode of representation, and did so with regret. . . . But the perception of moral dignity was destined to eclipse the vain pomp of Pagan grandeur. The generous sufferings of sacrifice were to become the greatest of all glories."

"Christian painting, when once established as an art on the banks of the Bosphorus, assumed a certain immobility of character. Forms, attitudes, groups, and vestments—all were regulated by ecclesiastical prescription. There was, as it were, an inflexible text-book, to which artists were bound to submit. Delicacy of colouring and nobility of attitude were the only things to recall the beauty of ancient art. Even in our days the Greek and Russian painters follow a similar plan, drawing and arranging their figures in the same manner as their ancestors of the time of Honorius and the Palæologi."

Even in the West the case was nearly the same, so long as the practice of painting remained almost exclusively confined to artists coming from Constantinople. Thus, in some celebrated manuscripts of the eighth and ninth centuries we find compositions that give a very exact representation of the state of the art in these remote times, though the paintings themselves have been destroyed by the Iconoclasts. In fact, during ten centuries it seemed that the Western races resisted any expression of artistic individuality or invention. Throughout this long period we find Greek painters the supreme arbiters of taste and knowledge in the countries of Western Europe, forcing upon them their own barren style, and teaching them their contracted perceptions. Art among them seemed always to be but a mere instinct. Constant immigrations took place which were continually leading them to every point in Western Europe, but none of them ever brought anything novel in art beyond what their predecessors had already introduced. If they took root in a new country, the son repeated the works of his father. The pupil took no means to enlarge his thoughts; he adopted as his model and his ideal nothing but the work of his master, and the poor form of tradition was continued without enthusiasm and without progress (Fig. 247). Genius is altogether wanting, or if its sacred spark sprung forth from heaven, it was soon extinguished when it reached the earth for want of a soul which could receive it, and be kindled by its fire. The Greek masters doubtless affected some pride in the grandeur of their native name, but they were none the less living proofs that the sources from which flowed the inspiration of a Zeuxis, a Protogenes, or an Apelles, had since those far-distant days been long dried up. The East had for ever terminated its ancient character of artistic creation, and the most it seemed destined to achieve during the Middle Ages was to preserve the germ which the West was to bring again into active life.

Italy, and more particularly Tuscany, may lay claim to the honour of having witnessed, about the end of the thirteenth and the beginning of the fourteenth century, the dawn of the great revival of artistic light.   The

Fig. 247.—" Baptism of King Clovis."
Fragment of a Painting on Canvas at Rheims.   Fifteenth Century.)

names of Giunta of Pisa, Guido of Siena, and Duccio, had, however, already commenced the glorious list of Italian artists, who were the first to endeavour to modify the immutable Greek manner. Their attempts, no doubt, seem but insignificant, looking at the immense progress subsequently accomplished; but, however slight it may appear to be, the first step made beyond the beaten path which has been trodden for centuries is often evidence of the most courageous daring.

The year 1240 witnessed the birth of Cimabue: as a young man, he became enamoured of art by watching the labours of the Greek painters who had been summoned to Florence to decorate the chapel of the Gondi. It was purposed to make him a *savant* and a lawyer; but he succeeded in abandoning the pen in favour of the pencil, and, from the lessons of the timid Byzantines, he soon became a master whose every thought was henceforth devoted to the emancipation of an art that he found condemned to a kind of immobility. Thanks to him, the expression of faces, which up to that time had been entirely conventional in character, was animated by a truer sentiment; the lines of drawing, which had been hard and stiff, were broken up into well-ordered grace; the colouring, hitherto dull and gloomy, assumed soft brilliancy and harmonious relief. It is said that Cimabue's *chef-d'œuvre*, the "Madonna" which is still to be seen in the Church of Santa-Maria-Novella, was carried in procession by the crowd to the place which it now occupies; the painter was received with shouts, and, it is added, the joy of the people at the sight of the picture was so great that the part of the city wherein Cimabue's studio was situated received, after this event, the name of *Borgo Allegro* (the Joyous Town). One day when Cimabue was in the country, he noticed a young shepherd-boy who was amusing himself by sketching on a rock the sheep he tended. The painter took charge of the boy; he became his favourite pupil, and was the celebrated Giotto, who happily persevered in the reform commenced by Cimabue. Giotto, the first among the artists of his time, ventured to paint portraits, and succeeded well in them. To him we owe our acquaintance with the real features of his friend Dante; and we still admire, at least as manifestations of an adventurous genius, the paintings he left in the Church of Santa Clara at Naples, in the Cathedral of Assisi, and especially in the Campo Santo at Pisa, where he painted in fresco the history of Job.

Giotto died in 1336, but he left behind him to continue his work, Taddeo Gaddi, Giottino, Stefano, Andrea Orcagna, and Simon Memmi, who were each destined to open out some new path in art. In the Campo Santo at Pisa we may see how great was the power of the genius of these masters, especially of Andrea Orcagna (1329—1389), who has there represented, with an equal measure of beauty and of sombre and terrible energy, the "Dream of Life," facing the "Triumph of Death." Taddeo Gaddi remained a fervent disciple of his master, and continued his delicate accuracy of design, and the living freshness of his colouring. Stefano succeeded him in the boldness of his compositions, in his studious knowledge of the nude, and of perspective effect which had been hitherto neglected. Giottino inherited his serious inspirations. Memmi endeavoured to recall his mystical and graceful sentiment. Orcagna, who was at once painter, sculptor, architect, and poet, seemed to possess in turn all the qualities which his fellow-disciples had shared among them, and could represent with equal success the terrors of the infernal regions and the visions of heaven.

The progress of which these painters had constituted themselves the apostles was not carried out without exciting some opposition. In addition to the Greek masters, who naturally felt compelled to contend with the innovators, certain individuals were found among the Italian artists who energetically embraced the party of the past. We will only mention one, Margaritone of Arezzo, who wore out his long life in a useless devotion to a cause which was already lost; even his name we should not have particularised, if it had not been that the art owed him some gratitude for the service he rendered it, by substituting the use of canvas prepared for painting instead of panels of wood, which had hitherto been exclusively employed.

The Florentine school (for thus we call the group of artists who trod in the footsteps of Cimabue and Giotto) had for its representative, at the beginning of the fifteenth century, Giovanni of Fiesole, surnamed *Fra Angelico*, the personification of enthusiasm in artistic sublimity; whose works, too, resemble so many hymns of adoration. Born in the year 1387, and inheriting great wealth, he was endowed with a contemplative mind, and, ignorant of the talent which inspired him, he sought oblivion from the world in the garb of a Dominican, little suspecting that glory awaited him in the very depth of his humility. At first, as a kind of pious recreation, he covered with miniatures several pages of manuscripts; next, his companions in the cloister requested him to paint a picture. He obeyed, feeling convinced that the inspiration which stirred within him was a manifestation of the Divine spirit, and it was with the most artless simplicity that he referred to this celestial origin the *chef-d'œuvre* which proceeded from his hands. His reputation spread far and wide. At the invitation of the head of the Christian Church, he repaired to Rome in order to paint one of the chapels of the Vatican. And when the pontiff, full of enthusiasm at his talent, wished to confer upon him as a reward the dignity of archbishop, Angelico retired modestly to his cell in order to devote himself without interruption to that art which was to him a continual prayer, and a perpetual soaring up to that heavenly country on which he unceasingly meditated with all the unutterable feelings of the elect.

About the same era as the "seraphic monk," who died full of years in 1455, appeared Tomaso Guidi, for whom a kind of unconsciousness of everyday life had obtained the ironical *sobriquet* of Masaccio (the Stupid); who, however, astonished the world by his works to such extent that it was said concerning them, "those of his predecessors were *painted*, but his were *living*." Masaccio was one of the first (and this fact shows how slowly art may progress even in bold hands) to place in his pictures firmly on the soles of their feet figures presenting a full front, instead of making them stand upon their great-toes, as his predecessors had done from a want of knowledge of the requisite foreshortening. Masaccio died in 1443.

Philippo Lippi, who devoted himself more specially to the study of nature, both in the human physiognomy and also in the accessory details of his works, marks as it were the last stage of the art, when it approached the state of full vigour in which it was to manifest the whole extent of its power. We are now at the end of the fifteenth century, and the masters of the *great masters* are in existence. It was Andrea Verrochio who, at the sight of an angel which Leonardo da Vinci, his pupil, had painted in one of his works, for ever abandoned his pencil. It was Domenico Ghirlandajo who, jealous of the superior qualities which he recognised in his pupil, the youthful Buonarotti, not only endeavoured, but succeeded in diverting his talents, at least for a time, to sculpture. It was Fra Bartolommeo (1469—1517) who was affected with such profound grief at the death of his friend Savonarola, that he embraced a monastic life. Baccio della Porta (such was the name of the Brother) was a very great painter (Fig. 248); the vigour and

Fig. 248.—"The Patriarch Job." A Painting on Panel, by Fra Bartolommeo. Fifteenth Century.
(In the Gallery at Florence.)

harmony of colouring which he showed, especially in his last productions, has sometimes caused them to be attributed to Raphael, with whom
he was for some time united in the bonds of friendship. But we must
not confine ourselves to characterising the works of one single group of
artists; for, although the revival took its rise on the banks of the Arno, it
spread far and wide beyond those limits. Added to this, Giotto, when
visiting Verona, Padua, and Rome, left in each place the still resplendent
traces of his presence. When Fra Angelico went to adorn the Vatican,
his genius spread around it a fruitful irradiation which everywhere dimmed
the ancient renown of the Byzantine painters who had hitherto prevailed
in the Italian cities.

At Rome we find flourishing in succession Pietro Cavallini, whom Giotto
had instructed during the sojourn of the latter in the Eternal City; Gentile
da Fabriano, who drew his inspiration from Fra Angelico; and Pietro della
Francesca, who has been regarded as the originator of perspective. We
next meet with Pietro Vannucci, called Perugino, who was born in 1446;
it was owing to nothing but the force of his genius and his character that he
became one of the most celebrated masters of his time. At the close of his
career, Perugino had the honour of initiating into the practice of his art
Raphael Sanzio of Urbino, who was in his own day, as he still is, the prince
of painting.

At Venice a body of pioneers, still more numerous and compact, prepared
the way for the new era, destined to be made illustrious by Titian,
Tintoretto, and Paul Veronese. We will mention also Gentile and Jacopo
Bellini; the former was incessantly absorbed in investigating the theories of
an art which he nevertheless exercised with all the *abandon* of an inspired
genius; the latter constantly devoted himself to the combination of power
and grace; and, at the age of seventy-five years, seemed to regain a second
youth in following with happy boldness the example of his pupil Giorgione.*
This painter, who was born in 1477, and died in 1511, introduced all kinds
of innovations in respect to design and colouring. and was the master of
Giovanni da Udine, Sebastian del Piombo, Jacques Palma, and Pordenone,

* Giorgione studied under Giovanni Bellini, younger brother of Gentile, and son of Jacopo.
M. Lacroix does not even mention Giovanni Bellini, though he is generally esteemed before his
father and brother, besides being the master of two of the greatest painters of the Venetian school,
Titian and Giorgione; who, however, soon cast aside the antiquated style of their early
instructor.—[ED.]

fellow-pupils and sometimes rivals of the three great artists by whose works the Venetian school was to mark its individuality.

At Parma a local school was represented by Antonio Allegri, called Correggio, born in 1494; and by Francesco Mazzuoli, called Parmigianino, born in 1503.

In other places, too, talents of a vigorous or of a graceful character were developed, but we can only cast a comprehensive glance on this memorable

Fig. 249.—Portrait of Leonardo da Vinci, from a Venetian Engraving of the Sixteenth Century.

artistic epoch, and are unable to offer a detailed review of the artists and their works. And what further luminaries of art could we wish to embrace in our summary after having displayed in it, shining, so to speak, at one and the same epoch, Leonardo da Vinci (Fig. 249), Michael Angelo, Raphael, Titian, Tintoretto, Veronese, Correggio, and Parmigianino?

Four principal schools compete with one another—the Florentine school, the characteristics of which are truth of design, energy of colouring, and grandeur of conception; the Roman school, which seeks its ideal in the skilful and sober judgment of its lines, the dignity of its compositions, propriety of expression and beauty of form; the Venetian school, which occasionally neglected correctness of drawing, and devoted itself more to the brilliancy and magical effect of colour; lastly, the school of Parma, which is distinguished especially by its softness of touch and by its knowledge of light and shade. All such estimations of the different qualities of these various groups must not, however, be looked upon as in any way absolute.

As chiefs of the first school we have two men, each of whom presents to us one of the richest organisations and the most widely-extending genius which human nature has, perhaps, ever produced; these were Leonardo da Vinci and Michael Angelo, both of whom were sculptors as well as painters; and also architects, musicians, and poets. We will first speak of Leonardo da Vinci, whose style presents two very distinct epochs; the first tending to vigour in the shadows, to a mistiness in reflected lights, to a general effect produced by a certain oddness, or rather by a strange representation of truth; a combination of qualities which, as M. Michiels says, makes Leonardo the "most northerly of the Italian painters" (Fig. 250). His second style, "clear, serene, and precise," transports us into a "completely southern sphere." But some secret influence drew the artist so forcibly towards his earlier manner, that he returned to it at an advanced age in painting the famous portrait of Mona Lisa, which adorns the gallery of the Louvre. We must not forget the fact that we have to attribute to Pope Leo X. the great revival of the arts, and especially of painting, in Italy at the commencement of the sixteenth century.

"In Michael Angelo," still to quote the words of M. Michiels, "science, power, grandeur, and all the more severe qualities are combined. No vulgar artifice and no affectation. The painter was imbued with a sublime ideal of majestic types from which nothing was able to divert him. He felt as if there were existing in himself a whole population of heroes, whom, by the aid of painting and sculpture, he endeavoured to withdraw from their mental concealment, and to embody in incarnate forms. His personages scarcely seem to belong to our race; they appear to be creatures worthy of some more spacious world, to the proportions of which their physical vigour and their moral energy would well respond. The very women do not possess the grace of their sex; we might fancy them valiant Amazons well capable of mastering a horse or of crushing an enemy. This great man's object was neither to charm nor to please; his delight rather was to astonish and to strike with admiration or terror; but it is this very excess of power which enabled him to win the approbation of all."

Fig. 250.—The Holy Family, by Leonardo da Vinci, from the Picture in the Museum at St. Petersburg.

Next we have Raphael, *il divino Sanzio,* as he was called by his numerous admirers, whose genius was constantly attaining to grandeur by means of simplicity, and to power by means of reserve. Michael Angelo always seems as if he were only able to represent a limited portion of his gigantic conceptions on the wall he covered with his designs; but it was sufficient for Raphael to place some tranquil figure on a narrow square of canvas, and we have before us the bright image of the most perfect and delicious inspiration. He created for himself a heaven which he peopled with the purest and most venerated types of the human race; and a light, as from on high, beams with regal splendour on these graceful visions. In Raphael, even more than in Leonardo da Vinci, it seemed as if two artists of equal sublimity succeeded one another. At first we have the charming dreamer who, in the fresh enthusiasm of his early youth, creates Madonnas, artless daughters of the earth in whose look and countenance a sacred light shines in all its ineffable purity; next he is the master full of the deepest science, for whom the real beauties of creation have no concealment; who, in representing nature, succeeded in transforming to her the magnificent ideal of which his own soul appears to have received the impression from association with the divine regions.

"The principal characteristic of Raphael," still following the very just remarks of M. Michiels, "is the universality of his fame. It becomes almost painful to hear the vulgar crowd constantly repeating a magic name, the true signification of which they do not understand." As the spoiled child of fortune, the creator of Virgins and "The Transfiguration," he is almost without detractors from his fame; and it is impossible to reckon the number of his admirers. "One circumstance in his life affords us an emblem of his destiny. Having sent to Palermo the famous canvas of the 'Spasimo,'* a tempest overwhelmed the ship which carried it; but the waves seemed to respect the *chef-d'œuvre*. After having drifted more than fifty leagues through the sea, the box which enclosed the precious production floated gently on shore at the port of Genoa. The picture was in no way injured. The Sicilian monks, for whom it was intended, did not fail to claim it; and since that time, thanks to the mercy of the waves, it attracts to the foot of Etna numerous pilgrims to the shrine of genius."

At Venice, we first have Titian, the painter of Charles V. and Francis I. "The genius of Titian," says Alexander Lenoir, "is always great and noble. No painter has ever produced flesh-colours so beautiful and life-like. In Titian there is no apparent tone; the colouring of his flesh is so well

---

* The famous picture, an altar-piece, representing "Christ bearing his Cross," known by the name of *Lo Spasimo di Sicilia*, from its having been painted for the convent of Santa Maria della Spasimo at Palermo, in Sicily. It is now in the Museum of Madrid.—[ED.]

blended that it seems as difficult to imitate as the model itself. Add to his pictures their truth and expression of action, and the elegance and richness of the drapery, and we shall have some idea of the great works which he left behind him."

Next Jacques Robusti presents himself, who, from the profession of his father was surnamed Tintoretto (the Dyer). He was at first a pupil of Titian, who, it is said, from motives of jealousy, dismissed him from his studio; but the fervour of uninterrupted labour was all that Tintoretto required in order to mature the most productive talent. "The drawing of Michael Angelo, and the colouring of Titian"—such was the ambitious motto he wrote over the door of his humble *atelier*, and we are almost justified in stating that he was enabled, by force of study and labour, to fulfil his aspirations, if we look only at some of his pieces executed before a certain fever of exuberant production had seized upon and necessarily weakened his vigorous talents. To form some estimate of the extent to which Tintoretto was impelled by this impulse of creation, we may recollect that even Paul Veronese reproached him with being unable to restrain himself—Veronese, the most indefatigable of producers!

With regard to the latter, his works are characterised not only by the number of figures in them, but also by the striking brilliancy of the *mise en scène*. Although he multiplies his actors, they are grouped in perfect order; although he paints a multitude, he knows how to avoid a crowd. Notice how a feeling of life profusely pervades the whole of his vast pictures of important events; an idea of space is everywhere given; everywhere light plays a powerful part, and imagination has full scope. He is the painter *par excellence* of feasts and ceremonies: at once pompous and natural, his copiousness is only equalled by his dazzling facility; and we are compelled to forgive the errors with which he mingles on the same canvas the religious ideas of sacred subjects and the profane splendour of modern times.

What shall we say about Correggio? There is no methodical scale by which to measure grace; and there is no formula laid down of delicious softness. But if, at the Louvre, we examine his "Antiope asleep," we shall not soon forget the fascinating power of the old Allegri (Correggio).

From Correggio to Parmigianino the distance is of the kind that admiration can easily fill up. It was said of the latter that he had more the appearance of an angel than of a man ; and the Romans of his own day used to add that the spirit of Raphael had passed into his body. In more than one instance his genius was kindled by the sun of Correggio, and ripened in the studios of Michael Angelo and Raphael; but in addition to this, his flexible and varied talent enabled him to find a place by himself between these two masters. "St. Francis receiving the Stigmata," and "The Marriage of St. Catherine," which he painted before he had attained his eighteenth year, are still regarded as equal to the *chefs-d'œuvre* signed by Allegri. It is well-known that a "St. Margaret," executed by Parmigianino fifteen years later for a church at Bologna, was placed by Guido in the same rank as the "St. Cecilia" of Raphael.

By the side of, or after, these famous men, in whom the glory of Italian painting seems to have brilliantly culminated, how many noble names still remain to be cited ; how many remarkable names are there still to mention, even among those who, in following the glorious path opened out for them by the great masters, began to show glimpses of the earliest symptoms of decay, exhaustion, and lassitude ! It does not form a part of our plan to dwell upon the various phases of this decadence ; but before we glance at the last sparks of light which were shed forth, we must not forget the fact that the Italian pleiades were not exclusively privileged to illumine the artistic horizon.

It is certainly the case that all over Europe the Byzantine tradition had been the sole possessor of the throne of art since the earliest centuries of the Middle Ages. In Germany as in Italy, in France as in the countries bounding it on the north, we find nothing but the same school displaying the dead level of its inflexibility. At various epochs, however, certain feeble attempts at independence were here and there manifested ; but these aspirations were at first generally isolated, and therefore transient in their character. Finally, however, as if the hour of revival had been simultaneously agreed upon at all points of the intellectual world, these desires for emancipation manifested themselves in a corresponding effort to reject the former too absolute form, and to substitute the element of life for the principle of conventionality.

In Spain a strange combat was waging on the soil itself, for the possession of which two hostile races, two irreconcilable faiths, were in fierce contention. The Mahometan built the Alhambra, the halls of which were destined to be subsequently adorned by a Christian pencil. In the paintings that enliven the arches of this marvellous edifice an art is manifested which is both simple and grand in its character; but in this one undertaking it appears to have exhausted the share of vitality time had awarded to it; for immediately afterwards it seems to have died away. If, however, any fresh masters of the art of painting appeared on the Iberian soil, they had sought in Italy the flame of inspiration, or some mighty art-pilgrim visited their country. We must come down to a later epoch, from the consideration of which we are now precluded, in order to meet with an Herrera, a Ribera, a Velasquez, or a Murillo, the glory of whom, although comparatively late, may perhaps hold its own by the side of the great Italian schools, but cannot pretend to eclipse them. Among the predecessors of these real and distinct individualities, we will, however, mention the following:—Alonzo Berruguete, born in 1480, at once painter. architect, and sculptor; he was a pupil of Michael Angelo, in whose works he often took a share; Pedro Campagna, born in 1503, who studied under the same master—his *chef-d'œuvre* is still admired in the Cathedral of Seville; Luis de Vargas, born in 1502, who was able in many points to appropriate the secrets of Sanzio, from whom he appeared to have received lessons; Morales, whose paintings are still admired for the harmony of their lines and the delicacy of their touch; Vicente Juanes, whose purity of design and sober vigour of colouring obtained for him the title (certainly by some exaggeration of praise) of the "Raphael of Valentia;" lastly, Fernandez Navarette, born in 1526, who, perhaps less hyperbolically, was surnamed the "Spanish Titian;" and Sanchez Coello, born about 1500, who, excelling in portraits, has handed down the likenesses of some celebrated personages of his time.

In Germany and the Low Countries we find similar traces of the feeling of regeneration actuating the minds of artists at a much earlier period. The first name which presents itself to us beyond the Rhine is that mentioned in the Chronicle of Limburg, of the date of 1380. "There was then at Cologne," says the chronicler, "a painter named Wilhelm. According to the masters, he was the best in all the countries of Germany; he has painted men of every description as if they were alive." We have nothing left of the works of this artist except some panels without signature, which, in consideration of the date they bear, are attributed to him; an examination shows that, considering the epoch at which he lived, Wilhelm might justly be looked upon as a creative genius. He was succeeded by his most talented pupil, *Maître* Stephan. A triptych of his work may be seen at the Cathedral of Cologne, representing "The Adoration of the Magi," "St. Gereon," "St. Ursula," and "The Annunciation." This work, which exhibits charming finish as well as harmonious simplicity, is sufficient evidence that its author was possessed of much natural ability as well as a certain extent of knowledge; and if we make it our study to seek out the relics of the artistic movement of the period, we can in no way feel surprise at seeing that the influence of this early master made itself felt in a very extended radius.

But at this epoch, that is, at the commencement of the fifteenth century, in a city of Flanders, a new luminary made its appearance, which was destined to eclipse the brilliancy of the somewhat weak German innovation. Two brothers, Hubert and John van Eyck, together with their sister Margaret, established themselves in the "triumphant city of Bruges," as it is called by an historian; and very soon all the Flemish and Rhenish regions resounded with the name of Van Eyck, their works being the only representations which were admired and followed; and even in those early days it was a title of glory to form a part of their brilliant school.

John, the younger of the two brothers, was the one to whom renown more particularly attached (Fig. 251). He is reputed to have been the inventor of oil-painting; but all he did was to improve the methods employed. Nevertheless, tradition tells us that an Italian master, Antonello of Messina, made a journey to Flanders, with the object of finding out the secret of John of Bruges (by which name Van Eyck is often called); and that he subsequently circulated it throughout the Italian schools. Be this as it may, John of Bruges, apart from any similarity in manner (for it was by the force of his colouring, as much as by his new theories of composition, that he succeeded in revolutionising the old school of painting), may be considered as the Giotto of the North; but we must add that the effects of his attempts were much more rapidly decisive. At one leap, so to speak, the somewhat cold painting of the Gothic school decked itself with a splendour which left but little for the future Venetian school to achieve beyond it; with one flight of genius, stiff and methodical conceptions became imbued with suppleness and vital action. Finally, we have the first notable sign of the true feeling of an art combining science and grace—a knowledge of anatomy is shown in the life-like flesh and under the brilliant draperies. There is, however, a considerable distance, which cannot fail to be remarked, separating the two reformers of art whose names we have just brought together. One, Giotto, desired to grasp the real in order to make it conduce to the triumph of the ideal; while Van Eyck only accepted the ideal because he had as yet been unable to apprehend the deepest secrets of the real. All the other masters are but as the fruit yielded by the school of the great Florentine, and by those which the

Fig. 251.—" The Holy Virgin, St. George, and St. Donat." By John van Eyck. (Museum of Antwerp.)

descendants of the Flemish masters were destined to produce. At Ghent, we still have as an object of admiration, an altar-piece, a *chef-d'œuvre* of Van Eyck; it is an immense composition, some portions of which have been removed; but at first it did not contain less than three hundred figures, representing the "Adoration of the Paschal Lamb by the Virgins of the Apocalypse."

John van Eyck resided for some time at the court of Portugal, whither he had been sent by Philip the Good, Duke of Burgundy, to delineate the

ST. CATHERINE AND ST. AGNES.

Painting attributed to Margaret Van Eyck. (M. Quedeville's Collection.)

"ST. CATHERINE AND ST. AGNES."

A PICTURE ATTRIBUTED TO MARGARET VAN EYCK.

On the left of the picture is seen St. Catherine of Alexandria holding in her hands the instruments of her punishment—the *wheel*, which is broken into fragments, and the *sword* which decapitated her; below her is the head of the Emperor Maximilian II., who ordered her martyrdom.

On the right is St. Agnes, and a *lamb*, the emblem of her innocence and gentleness.

The *ring* St. Agnes is presenting to St. Catherine denotes the bond which unites the two virgin-martyrs, and attests that both are worthy to be spouses of Jesus Christ.

features of his *fiancée*, the Princess Elizabeth (1428).   The influence exercised by his labours is thought to have brought about that tendency to brilliancy and realism which, after its first manifestation in the earliest Spanish manner, gave way before the encroachments of Italian genius, only to reappear in all its power in the great national school.

Among the best pupils that Van Eyck left behind him at Bruges, we must not omit the name of Hugo van der Goes, whose works are rare.

Roger van der Weyden, of whose paintings but few are now extant, was the favourite pupil of John of Bruges, and the master of Hemling, whose reputation was destined to equal, if not to surpass, that of the chief of his school. "Hemling," says M. Michiels, so eminent a judge on this subject, "whose most ancient picture bears the date 1450, possesses more sweetness and grace than the Van Eycks. His figures charm by an ideal elegance; his expression never exceeds the limits of tranquil feeling and agreeable emotion.   Quite contrary to John van Eyck, he prefers the slender and rich character of the Gothic (Fig. 252) to the heaviness and scanty detail of Roman architecture.   His colouring, although less vigorous, is softer; the water, the woods, the sites, the grass, and the distances of his pictures cause a dream-like feeling."

A kind of instinctive reaction was manifested in the pupil, but the master was not altogether forgotten.   We shall, however, find elsewhere the effects of his direct influence; but in order not to have to return to the school of Bruges, we will first mention Jerome Bosch, who, contrary to his countryman Hemling, sought after opposition of effects and singularities of invention; and next Erasmus, the great thinker and writer, who was also a painter in his day;* lastly, Cornelius Engelbrechtsen, the master of Lucas van Leyden, born in 1494.   The latter was as famous with the pencil as with the graving tool, and introduced into all his works a powerful and sometimes strange originality which caused him to be looked upon as the first painter of "*genre*."   Lucas van Leyden must close our list of the artists who opened out the paths which were destined to be followed, though with many a diversity of method and of style, by Breughel, Teniers, Van Ostade, Porbus, and Schellincks.   At the head of these masters was subsequently to rise the magnificent Rubens, and the energetic Rembrandt, the king of the palette, the great chief of the school, who

---

* We can find no authority to support this statement.—[ED.]

Fig. 252.—" St. Ursula."   By Hemling.

towers loftily over all his pupils, Gerard Dow, Ferdinand Bol, Van Eckhout, Govaert Flinck, &c., as well as over his imitators and contemporaries— Abraham Bloemaert, Gerard Honthorst, Adrian Brauwer, Seghers, &c.

When the Van Eycks made their appearance, German art—which, under the impulse of Stephan of Cologne had appeared as if destined to direct the movement—allowed itself to be led away and influenced by the Flemish school, without, however, entirely divesting itself of the individual characteristics which are, to some extent, inherent in the region wherein it flourished. In Alsatia, we see the style peculiar to the school of Bruges showing itself in Martin Schön (1460); in Suabia, it had as its interpreter Frederick Herlen (1467); at Augsburg, it was old Holbein; at Nuremberg, it was first Michael Wohlgemuth, and after him Albert Dürer (1471), whose vigorous individuality did not fail to reflect the temperament of the Van Eycks.

"The works of Albert Dürer present a singular combination of the fantastic and the real (Fig. 253). The principal tendencies peculiar to the character of the northern mind are always to be found in them. The thoughts of the artist are always transporting him into a world of abstraction and chimeras; but the ever-present consciousness of the difficulties of life under the cold northern sky always draws him back to the details of existence. On the one hand, therefore, he seems to love philosophical, and even supernatural subjects; but, on the other, the minute details of his execution bind him down to earth. His models, his action, his positions, the muscular development of his nude subjects, the innumerable folds of his draperies, the expression which he gives to joy, grief, and hatred, all seem to bear a manifest character of exaggeration. Added to this, he is deficient in grace; a rudeness entirely northern in its character closes the path to any of the softer qualities of art. The panels of Albert Dürer all seem to have a touch of the antique barbarism of the Germanic hordes. He himself was in the habit of wearing his hair long, like the ancient German kings. Upon the whole, however, his beautiful colouring, the skilful firmness of his drawing, his grand characteristics, his depth of thought, the poetry, often terrible, of his composition, place him in the first rank of masters" (Michiels).

While Albert Dürer was endeavouring to combine in his works every type of the strangest character, Lucas van Cranach made it his study

Fig. 253.—" Jesus Crowned with Thorns," painted on Wood by Albert Dürer ; a Fac-simile traced from the
original of the same size.   (In the Collection of M. de Quedeville.)

to represent with no less success pleasant legends or the most charming realities. He is the painter of artless youths, aerially veiled, and of sportive and enchanting virgins; and if some antique scene is created by his delicate and original pencil, it seems to be metamorphosed by a happy

Fig. 254.—" Princess Sibylla of Saxony," by Lucas van Cranach. (Suermondt Collection.)

facility into something that appears to have the character of a German reminiscence (Fig. 254).

Between these two masters, so equally endowed with power in their respective lines of art, the great Holbein takes his place, as if embodying the rather abrupt vigour of the one, and the sentimental delicacy of the other. This painter's artistic career was carried out almost entirely in England, but the character of his genius belongs unquestionably to the country where he left behind him his "Dance of Death," a piece of tragic raillery justly held to be the most wonderful among all the creations of fancy.

Albert Dürer, who died in 1528, and Lucas van Cranach, and Holbein, who died in 1553,* were destined to create a race of painters, and a host of successors were soon at work. But the movement, which was impeded by troubles of a religious character, died away in the terrbile convulsions of the Thirty Years' War, and was never again renewed.

The era in which German art seemed all at once to decline was that wherein the Italian school flourished in full splendour, and exercised an unrivalled influence over every European country occupied by the Latin races. France yielded all the more readily to this foreign influence, because the Papal court at Avignon had already given an asylum to Giotto in the first place, and afterwards to Simon Memmi; both of whom, and especially the last, have left master-like traces of their presence on French soil.

As a matter of fact, although French painting, regarded in the light of a national art, cannot boast of having spontaneously produced, as a thing of home-growth, any of those essays of complete independence of which Germany and Italy are so proud; the memorials of French art at least bear witness that, during the long reign of Byzantine tradition, it never ceased to struggle with some force under the yoke; at a time, indeed, when Italy and Germany themselves seemed, on the contrary, to bear the burden with the most submissive servitude.

The tenth century, in becoming subject to the influence of a foolish but heartfelt terror (the fear of the end of the world), marked a period of fatal obstruction to every kind of effort, and progress died away; but if we look beyond this we shall perceive that, from the earliest days of the monarchy, painting was held in honour, and painters themselves afforded proofs of power, if not of genius. We shall, for instance, find that the basilica of St. Germain-des-Prés, built by Childebert I., had its walls decorated with "elegant paintings." We shall find Gondebaud, the son of

---

* Holbein died of the plague which prevailed in London in 1554.—[ED.]

Clotaire, himself handling the pencil and "painting the walls and roofs of oratories." In the reign of Charlemagne, we discover the texts which the bishops and priests were compelled to paint on "the whole interior surface" of their churches, in order that the charm of the colouring and of the compositions might aid the fervour of faith in the congregations. But all this is but evidence recorded in the pages of the ancient chronicles. We have other testimony derived from works still existing, on which a judgment may be practically passed. Some frescoes discovered at St. Savin, in the department of Vienne, and at Nohant-Vicq, in the department of Indre, which must be attributed to the eleventh and twelfth centuries, attest, in all their rude simplicity, the efforts of a thoughtful art, and specially bear the stamp of a true spirit of independence.

The Sainte-Chapelle, in Paris, by its painted windows and the mural paintings of its crypt, asserts the real vitality of an artistic feeling, which only waited for the signal of a bolder spirit to rise to loftier things. Moreover, if other examples are wanting, there are manuscripts, on the ornamentation of which the most skilful painters have concentrated their powers, that would suffice to point out the tendencies and artistic standard of every succeeding age. (See the article on MINIATURE-PAINTING.) However little we may consult history, we scarcely ever fail to discover traces of certain groups of artists whose names or works have survived. Thus, a series of paintings preserved in the Cathedral of Amiens, as well as the "Sacre de Louis XII." and the "Vierge au Froment," in the museum at Cluny, prove to us the existence, at the end of the fifteenth century, of the school of Picardy, which possessed skill in composition, combined with a feeling for colour and a certain knowledge of handling. Thus, too, the researches of the learned have traced out the laborious career of the Clouet family, sung by Ronsard and others, but whose works are almost entirely lost; thus, also, we find the names of Bourdichon, Perréal, Foucquet, who worked for Louis XI. and Charles VIII., and that of the peaceful King René of Provence, who thought it not beneath his dignity to make himself the practical chief of a school whose nameless productions are still scattered over the south of France.

With the sixteenth century commenced the age of the great Italian painters. In 1515, Francis I. persuaded Leonardo da Vinci to come to France, and to afford the example of his wonderful genius. But the illustrious creator of "La Gioconda" (the famous portrait of Mona Lisa), burthened with years and worn out with work, visited France as if only to draw his last breath (1519). Andrea del Sarto, the graceful pupil of the severe Michael Angelo, came to France in 1517; but, after having painted for his royal protector a few pictures, among which was the magnificent "Charity" in the Louvre, he again repaired to the Italian soil, to which his unhappy marriage recalled him to his doom.

In 1520 Raphael died, at the age of only thirty-seven years. Giulio Pippi (called *Giulio Romano*), Francis Penni, (called *il Fattore*), and Perino del Vaga, whom he named as his heirs and charged with the completion of his unfinished works, did their best to replace the illustrious dead. For a short time it might have been thought that the inspiration of the master still remained with his pupils; but soon a separation of this group of artists, who had found their principal power in unity of thought, took place; and, fifteen or twenty years after the tomb had closed on Raphael, the tradition of his school was nothing more than a glorious ruin.

Michael Angelo, who died in 1563, was destined to have a longer career; but it was only to become a witness of the rapid decadence of the great movement he had helped to call forth. After Daniele di Volterra, the painter of the "Descent from the Cross," which is classed among the three most beautiful works that Rome possesses; after Vasari, who possessed a double title to celebrity as a skilful painter and the historian of the Italian schools; after Rosso, whose renown subsequently suffered at the court of France; and Bronzino, who sought success in taste and delicacy; the school of the great Buonarotti produced nothing but works which seemed to wander from exaggeration to bad taste. The dwarfs who attempted to walk in the footsteps of the giant were soon exhausted, and only succeeded in rendering themselves ridiculous.

The Venetian school, the great masters of which did not become extinct before the end of the sixteenth century, had its period of decadence at a later epoch; this will not come under our consideration. The Lombard school, which, by the deaths of Correggio and Parmigianino, had been left without its chiefs before the middle of this century (1534 and 1540), seemed for a moment as if it would disappear as it had risen. But in Michael Angelo Caravaggio (Fig. 255) it met with a powerful master, who was able for some time to arrest the progress of its decadence.

Fig. 255.—"The Tribute Money." Picture by Caravaggio (Sixteenth Century), in the Florence Gallery.

We have as yet done little more than hint at the presence of Rosso, or *Maître Roux*, at the court of France. He came in 1530, at the invitation of Francis I., to decorate the Palace of Fontainebleau. "His engraved work," says M. Michiels, "shows him to be a feeble and pretentious man, devoid both of taste and inspiration, who exhibited laboured refinement in the place of vigour, mistaking want of proportion for grandeur, and absence of truth for originality. Being nominated by the king as Canon of the Sainte-Chapelle, he had as his assistants Leonard, a Fleming, the Frenchmen Michel Samson and Louis Dubreuil, and the Italians Lucca Penni, Bartolommeo Miniati, &c. But in 1531, Primaticcio arrived from Mantua, and a contest arose henceforth between them. . . . Le Rosso having ended his days by suicide, Primaticcio remained master of the field. His most talented pupil decorated under his direction the magnificent ball-room. Primaticcio painted with less exaggeration and more delicacy and elegance than Rosso; but still he formed one of that troop of awkward and affected copyists who exaggerated the errors of Caravaggio. . . . His empire of forty years' duration, in the midst of a foreign population, was, however, an undisturbed one. Henry II., Francis II., Charles IX., and Catherine de Medicis, showed him no less favour than Francis I. He died in 1570, loaded with honours and riches.

"The number of French artists who allowed themselves to be influenced by the Italian method was considerable. At last a man of more vigorous character arose who would not permit false taste to rule him, and adopted all the improvements of modern art, without following in the footsteps of court favourites. His talents inaugurated a new period in the history of French painting. We are speaking of Jean Cousin, who was born at Soucy, about 1530 ; he adorned with his compositions both glass and canvas, and was, in addition, a skilful sculptor. His famous picture of the "Last Judgment," in the Louvre, suggests a high opinion of him. The colouring is harsh and monotonous, but the drawing of the figures and the arrangement of the piece prove that he had the habit of thought and also of reckoning on his own powers and of seeking out novel dispositions, producing effects hitherto unknown."

The beautiful composition we introduce here (Fig. 256) is taken from M. A. Firmin Didot's "Notice sur Jean Cousin," in which a large number of other subjects are reproduced ; some of them may have been engraved by the painter himself. Like Albert Dürer and Holbein, Jean

Fig. 256.—Composition by Jean Cousin. First Sketch of his, "Last Judgment," from a Wood-Engraving
in the Romance of "Gérard d'Euphrate." Paris, 1549. (Cabinet of M. A. F. Didot.)

Cousin did not disdain to apply his talents to the ornamentation of books.

Jean Cousin is generally looked upon as the real chief of the French school. After him, and by his side, we must place the Janets,* who although of Flemish origin, are actually French in their style and the character of their pictures. The most celebrated of them, François Clouet, portrayed, with a realism full of elegance and distinction, the nobles and beautiful ladies of the court of Valois.

We should here close our remarks, were it not that we might be accused of an important omission in this review of the principal schools. For nothing has been said of the Bolognese school, whose origin, though not its

Fig. 257.—Sketch of the Virgin of Alba.   Chalk-drawing by Raphael.

maturity, belongs to the epoch we have made our study. But the material circumstances we now mention must be our justification : although the school of Bologna gave signs of its existence in the thirteenth century, and under the impulse of Guido, Ventura, and Ursone, showed itself to be industrious, active, and numerous ; and also in the fourteenth century, under that of Jacopo d'Avanzo and Lippodi Dalmasio ; yet it died away, reviving only at the commencement of the sixteenth century, again to become extinct after the death of the poetic Raibolini, called *Francia*, without having produced

---

* This name is generally written Jeannet, and, according to Wornum's "Epochs of Painting," seems to have been applied indiscriminately almost to the two painters, Jehannet or Jehan Clouet, father and son. M. Lacroix appears also to include François under the same general cognomen ; which, indeed, appears to have been a species of surname.—[ED.]

any of those great individualities to whose glory alone we are compelled to devote our attention.

We must, however, confess that this school, which suddenly retrieved its position at a time when all other schools were in a state of complete decadence, found three illustrious chiefs instead of one, and acquired the singular glory of resuscitating, by a kind of potent eclecticism, the *ensemble* of the noblest traditions. But it was not till the latter part of the sixteenth century that Bologna witnessed the opening by the Carracci of that studio whence were destined to proceed Guido, Albano, Domenichino, Guercino, Caravaggio, Pietro of Cortona and Luca Giordano—a magnificent phalanx of men who, by their own works and the force of their example, were to become the honour of an age into which it does not form a portion of our task to follow them.

ENGRAVING.

LMOST all authors who have devoted themselves to investigate this subject have asserted, but doubtless very erroneously, that engraving on metal was naturally derived from engraving on wood. Nevertheless, any one who gives but a slight consideration to the difference existing between the two processes must be led to the belief that the two arts must result from two distinct inventions. In wood-engraving, the impression is, in fact, formed by the portions of the block which are in relief; while in engraving on metal, the incised strokes give the lines of the print. Now, no one who has any knowledge of professional matters can for a moment doubt that, in spite of the similar appearance of the productions, there is a radical difference in the starting-points and modes of execution of these two methods.

We certainly must consider it probable that the appearance of prints produced by wood-engraving may have suggested the idea of seeking to obtain a similar or better result by some other process; but that a process should be assimilated, as if by affiliation, to another diametrically opposed to it is a view we do not feel called upon to accept without reservation.

Be this as it may, certain authors look upon wood-engraving as having been invented in Germany at the commencement of the fifteenth century. Others have derived it from China, where it was in use in the year 1000 of our era. Others, again, propound the opinion that the art of printing stuffs

by means of engraved blocks was employed in different parts of Asia, to
which it had been imported from ancient Egypt, at a period long before it
was first thought of in Europe.   These hypotheses being admitted, the
whole question reduces itself into an inquiry as to the way in which the art

Fig. 258.—" The Virgin and Infant Jesus."   Fac-simile of a Wood-Engraving of the Fifteenth Century.
(Bibl. Imp., Paris.)

made its entrance into Western Europe in the first half of the fifteenth
century ; this being the earliest date at which we find engravings made in
Germany, France, and the Low Countries.

The most ancient *dated* impression known of a cut engraved on wood is a St. Christopher, without either mark or name of its author, bearing a Latin inscription and the date of 1423. This specimen is so roughly engraved, and in drawing is so faulty, that it is only natural to assume it must be one of the earliest attempts at wood-engraving. There is, however, an engraving in the Imperial Library, Paris, representing the Virgin holding the Child Jesus seated in her arms (Fig. 258), which may perhaps be considered an earlier specimen than the St. Christopher. The back of the niche is a kind of mosaic, formed of diamond-shaped quadrilaterals; the *aureolæ* and ornaments of the niche are coloured a yellowish-brown. There is, however, one singularity in this engraving which testifies to its great antiquity; it is printed on paper made of cotton, and is unsized, and the impression sinks so deeply into it that it may be seen nearly as well on the back of the print as on the front. We must not omit to mention another engraving, preserved in the Royal Library, Brussels; this is also a "Virgin with the Child Jesus," surrounded by four saints (Fig. 259). It is a composition of a somewhat grand style, and does not agree very well with the date, MCCCCXVIII., which is seen at the foot of the print.

We must, doubtless, attribute to nearly the same time some specimens of playing-cards,—these we have already mentioned when dealing specially with this subject; and also a series of figures of the Twelve Apostles with Latin legends, underneath which are the same number of phrases in French, or rather in the ancient dialect of Picardy, reproducing the whole text of the Decalogue; one of these xylographic plates may be seen in the chapter on "PRINTING." In these engravings each figure is standing up, clothed in a long tunic, and covered with a wide mantle; the ink, so to speak, is bistre, and the mantles are coloured, red and green alternately. The Apostles all bear the symbolical sign which distinguishes them, and are surrounded with a long fillet, whereon is traced in Latin the sentence of the Creed attributed to each, and one of the ten Commandments. St. Peter, for instance, has for his motto this French sentence, "Gardeis Dieu le roy moult sain;" St. Andrew, "Ne jurets point son nome en vain;" St. John, "Père et Mère tosjours honoras;" St. James the Greater, "Les fiestes et dymeng. garderas," &c.

There are other engravings belonging to the middle of the fifteenth century which make known the fact that the art of engraving was practised by several artists in France; and that without doing any injustice

Fig. 259.—"The Virgin and Child." A Wood-Engraving of the Fifteenth Century (?).
(Bibl. Roy., Brussels.)

to Germany we can attribute several anonymous works to French masters.

But we must in any case claim the very characteristic works of an engraver named Bernard Milnet. In the engravings of this master there are neither lines nor cross-hatching; the ground of the print is black; the lights are

Fig. 260.—"St. Catherine on her Knees." Fac-simile of an Engraving on Wood, by Bernard Milnet, called the ' Master with the dotted backgrounds." (Bibl. Imp., Paris.)

formed by an infinite number of white dots varying in size according to the requirement and taste of the artist. This engraver does not appear to have had any imitators; and, to tell the truth, his mode of operation must have presented many difficulties in execution. There are only six known specimens of his work—a "Virgin with the Child Jesus," "St. Catherine Kneeling" (Fig. 260), the "Scourging of Christ," a group of "St. John, St. Paul, and St. Veronica," a "St. George," and a "St. Bernard."

Although engravings of this time are now extremely rare, it does not necessarily follow that they were equally scarce at the dates when they were executed. M. Michiels, in his "Histoire de la Peinture en Flandre," says that, "according to ancient custom, on feast-days the Lazarists, and others belonging to religious orders who were accustomed to nurse the sick, carried in the streets a large wax candle ornamented with mouldings and glass-trinkets, and distributed to the children wood-engravings illuminated with brilliant colours, and representing sacred subjects. There must, therefore, have been a considerable number of these engravings."

In the sixteenth century wood-engraving, improved by the pupils of Albert Dürer, and especially by John Burgkmair (Fig. 261), was very extensively developed; and the art was then practised with a superiority of style which left far behind the timid attempts of the preceding century.

The works of most of the wood-engravers of this period are anonymous; nevertheless, the names of a few of these artists have survived. But it is only by an error that, in the nomenclature of the latter, certain painters and designers, such as Albert Dürer, Lucas van Leyden, and Lucas van Cranach, have long been made to figure. There are wood-engravings which do actually bear the signatures or monograms of these masters; but the fact is, that the latter were often in the habit of drawing their designs on the wood, as is frequently the practice with artists in our own day; and the engraver (or rather the *formschneider*, form-cutter, to employ the usual expression), in reproducing the composition drawn with a pencil or pen, has copied also the signature which the designer of the subject added. An error [often committed by writers may be thus easily set right.

We must not quit the subject of wood-engraving without mentioning engraving in *camaïeu;* a process of Italian origin, in which three or four blocks, applying in succession to the print uniform tints of more or less intense tones, ultimately produced engravings of a very remarkable effect, imitating drawings with the stump or the pencil. At the commencement of the sixteenth century several artists distinguished themselves in this

Fig. 261.—The Archdukes and High Barons of Germany assisting, in State Costume, at the Coronation of the Emperor Maximilian. A fragment taken from a large collection of Engravings, entitled the "Triumph of Maximilian I.," by J. Burgkmair. (Sixteenth Century.)

mode of engraving, especially Ugo di Carpi, who worked at Modena about the year 1518 ; Antonio Fantuzzi, a pupil of Francis Parmigianino, who accompanied and assisted Primaticcio at Fontainebleau ; Gaultier, and Andrew Andreani ; and, lastly, Bartholomew Coriolano, of Bologna, who would have been the last engraver in this style, were it not for Antonio M. Zanetti, a celebrated Venetian amateur, who was still nearer to us in point of date. Two or three Germans, John Ulrich in the sixteenth, and Louis Buring* in the seventeenth, century, also made some engravings in *camaïeu*, but only with two blocks : one giving the design of the subject with the outline and cross-hatching, the other introducing a colour, usually bistre, on which all the lights were taken out, so as to leave the ground of the paper white. These specimens imitated a pen-and-ink drawing on coloured paper, and finished with the brush or pencil.

We must now go back to the year 1452, which is generally fixed upon as the date of the invention of engraving on metal (Fig. 262).† When discussing the subject of " Goldsmith's Work," we mentioned, among the pupils of the illustrious Ghiberti, Maso Finiguerra, and stated that this artist had engraved on silver a "Pax" intended for the treasury of the Church of St. John. Certain writers having recognised in a print now in the Imperial Library of Paris, and also in another print in the Library of the Arsenal, an exact impression of this engraving, were led to attribute to the celebrated Florentine goldsmith the honour of an invention in which he might perhaps have had no share at all. Possibly this process of printing off an impression, which was a very natural thing to do, had been actually practised by goldsmiths long before Finiguerra ; they wished, doubtless, to preserve a pattern of their *niello-work*, or to see how it progressed in its various stages. The proofs, thus taken off by hand, having been lost, Finiguerra may have been considered the originator of a method which he only applied as a matter of course to his goldsmith's work. The two circumstances—that the plate is made of silver and not of any common metal, and that it may be classed among the numerous *nielli*, engraved plates of decorative goldsmith's work, which have been handed down to us and are of even earlier dates—will alone suffice, in our opinion, to dispose of the

---

* *Businck* is the name by which this old wood-engraver is generally known.—[ED.]

† The legend which accompanies this engraving is in old Italian ; it relates to the famous prophecy of Isaiah as to the birth of Christ (Isaiah vii. 14).

·ISAIA·

PROFETA

ECCHO LAVERGIN CHECHONCEPERA
EPO PATORIRA VERGINE STNDO
ELNOME DEL FIGLVOL SI CHIAMERA
EMANVEL CHEDETTO INTERPETRANDO
IDDIE CHONESSO NOI EMAGERA
BITVRO EMELE ACCIO CHERIPRONDO
SAPPI FVGGIRE ELMAL CHEE VISIOSQ
EELEGGERE ELBEN CHEVIRTVOSO

Fig. 262.—The Prophet Isaiah, holding in his hand the saw which was the instrument of his martyrdom.
(Fac-simile from an Engraving on Copper by an unknown Italian Master of the Fifteenth Century.)

idea that this work was expressly executed in order to furnish impressions on paper. It was nothing but chance that in this case introduced the name of Finiguerra, which would not have become known in this connection, if it had not been for the preservation of two ancient impressions of his *niello-work;* while those taken from other and perhaps older plates had been destroyed. Thus the date, or the asserted date, of the invention of engraving on metal was fixed by the ascertained date of the piece of goldsmith's work.

Be this as it may, the print of the "Pax," or rather of the "Assumption," engraved by Finiguerra, does not fail, in the opinion of all writers and amateurs, to bear the title of the earliest print from metal; a title to which it has a perfect right, and in thus regarding it we are induced to give a brief description of the subject represented in the engraving. Jesus Christ, seated on a lofty throne and wearing a cap similar to that of the Doges, places, with both his hands, a crown on the head of the Virgin, who, with her hands crossed upon her breast, is seated upon the same throne; St. Augustine and St. Ambrose are kneeling; in the centre, below, and on the right, several saints are standing, among whom we can distinguish St. Catherine and St. Agnes; on the left, in the rear of St. Augustine, we see St. John the Baptist and other saints; lastly, on both sides of the throne a number of angels are blowing trumpets; and, above, are others holding a streamer, on which we read: "ASSVMPTA . EST . MARIA . IN . CELVM . AVE . EXERCITVS . ANGELORVM;" "Mary is taken up into Heaven. Hail, army of angels!"

The first of the impressions of this *niello* found its way into the Royal Library with the Marolles Collection, bought by Louis XIV. in 1667: the other was discovered only in 1841, by M. Robert Dumesnil, who, in the Library of the Arsenal, was turning over the leaves of a volume containing engravings by Callot and Sebastian Le Clerc. This latter impression, though taken on inferior paper, is nevertheless in a much better state of preservation than the other; but the ink is of a greyer hue, and one might readily fancy that, as M. Duchesne, the learned writer, asserts, it was printed before the final completion of the plate.

In support of the opinion which we before indirectly expressed, that the practice of taking impressions from engraved plates of metal might well be a kind of fortuitous result of a mere professional tradition incidental to the goldsmith's art, we may remark that most of the engravings which have been handed down to us as belonging to the era fixed upon for the invention of engraving, are the work of Italian goldsmith-engravers. More than four hundred specimens of this date have been preserved; among the artists we must mention Amerighi, Michael Angelo Bandinelli, and Philippo Brunelleschi, of Florence; Forzoni Spinelli, of Arezzo; Furnio, Gesso, Rossi, and Raibolini, of Bologna; Teucreo, of Siena; Caradosso and Arcioni, of Milan; Nicholas Rosex, of Modena, of whose work we have three *nielli* and more than sixty engravings; Antonio Pollajuolo, who engraved a print called

Fig. 263.—Fac-simile of a *Niello* executed on Ivory, from the original design of Stradan, representing
Columbus on board his Ship, during his first Voyage to the West.

the "Fight with Cutlasses," representing ten naked men fighting; lastly, the most skilful of the metal-chasing goldsmiths after Finiguerra, Peregrino of Cesena, who has left his name and his mark on sixty-six *nielli*.

More special mention must be made of Bartholomew Baldini, better known under the name of Baccio, to whom we owe, in addition to some large engravings both of a sacred and of a mythological character, twenty vignettes designed for the folio edition (1481) of Dante's "Inferno;" of Andrea Mantegna, a renowned painter, who himself engraved many of his own compositions; and of John van der Straet, called *Stradan* (Fig. 263), who executed at Florence many remarkable plates.

We find in Germany an engraver who dates several of his works in the year 1466, but on none of them has he left more than his initials, E. S. This has not failed to tax the ingenuity of those who would establish his individuality in some authentic way. Some have agreed to call him Edward Schön or Stern, on account of the stars he frequently introduces into the borders of the vestments of his figures; one asserts that he was born in Bavaria, because in a specimen of his works is the figure of a woman holding a shield emblazoned with the arms of that country; another believes him to have been a Swiss, because he twice engraved the "Pilgrimage of St. Mary of Einsiedeln," the most celebrated in the country. But those amateurs who, upon the whole, think more of the work than the workman, are content to designate him as *the Master of* 1466.

This engraver has left behind him three hundred examples, most of them of small dimensions, among which, independently of sundry very curious compositions, we must notice two important series, namely, an *Alphabet* composed of grotesque figures (Fig. 264), and a pack of *Numeral Cards*, the greater part of which are in the Imperial Library.

At almost the same epoch Holland also presents us with an anonymous engraver, who might be called *the Master of* 1486, from the date on one only of his engravings. The works of this artist, whose manner exhibits a powerful and original style, are very rare in any collections not belonging to the country in which he worked. The Cabinet of Engravings at Amsterdam possesses seventy-six of them, while that of Vienna has but two, that of Berlin one only, and that of Paris six, among which we may remark "Samson sleeping on the knees of Delilah," and "St. George," on foot, piercing with his sword the throat of the dragon which menaced the life of the Queen of Lydia.

We have still three comparatively celebrated engravers to mention before reaching the epoch at which Marc Antonio Raimondi in Italy, Albert Dürer in Germany, and Lucas van Leyden in Holland, all simultaneously flourished.

Martin Schöngauer, for some time designated by the name of Martin Schön, who died at Colmar in 1488, was a good painter as well as a skilful engraver. More than one hundred and twenty specimens of his work are known, the most important of which are—"Christ bearing his Cross," "The Battle of the Christians" (waged against the infidels by the apostle

St. James), both very rare compositions of large size; the "Passion of Jesus Christ," the "Death of the Virgin," and "St. Anthony tormented by Demons," one proof of which, it is said, was coloured by Michael Angelo. We must add (and this circumstance shows again the kind of direct

Fig. 264.—Fac-simile of the letter N from the "Grotesque Alphabet," engraved by the "Master of 1466."

relation which we have already noted as existing between engraving and goldsmith's work), that Martin Schöngauer also engraved a pastoral staff and a censer, both of very beautiful workmanship.

Israel van Mecken (or Meckenem), supposed to be a pupil of Francis van Bocholt, as he worked át Bocholt previous to the year 1500, is, of all German engravers of this epoch, the one whose works are most extensively known.   The Cabinet of Engravings in the Imperial Library, Paris, possesses three volumes of his engravings, containing two hundred and twenty-eight superb examples; among these we must especially notice a composition engraved on two plates of the same height, "St. Gregory perceiving the Man of Sorrows at the Moment of the Mass." We must confine ourselves to the mention, in addition, of his "St. Luke painting the Portrait of the Virgin;" "St. Odile releasing from Purgatory, by his prayers, the Soul of his Father, Duke Etichon;" "Herodias" (Fig. 265); and "Lucretia killing herself in the presence of Collatinus and others," which last is the only subject this artist has taken from profane history.

We mention Wenceslaus of Olmutz, who was engaged in engraving from the year 1481 to 1497, with the especial object of describing an allegorical print due to his *burin;* it may serve to give a notion of the fantastic tendency impressed on the ideas of the day by the religious dissensions which arose at this epoch between several princes of Germany and the court of Rome.   This print, or rather this graphic satire, most of the allusions in which are now lost to us, represents the monstrous figure of a woman entirely naked, seen in profile and turning to the left, her body covered with scales, with the head and mane of an ass; her right leg terminates in a cloven foot, and the left in a bird's claw; her right arm is terminated by the paw of a lion, and the left by a woman's hand.   The back of this fantastic being is covered with a hairy mask, and in the place of a tail she has the neck of a chimera, with a deformed head from which darts a serpent's tongue.   Above the engraving is written, "*Roma Caput Mundi*" ("Rome the head of the world").   On the left hand is a three-storied tower, upon which a flag adorned with the keys of St. Peter is floating.   On the château is written, "*Castelagno*" (Castle of St. Angelo); in the foreground is a river, upon whose waves is traced the word "*Tevere*" (the Tiber); lower still is the word "*Ianvarii*" (January), below the date 1496; on the right, in the background, is a square tower, upon which is written, "*Tore Di Nona*" (Tower of the Nones); on the same side, in front, is a vase with two handles, and in the centre of the lower part the letter W, the monogrammatic signature of the engraver.   Our interest in this plate is increased by the date it bears; for, being engraved by means of

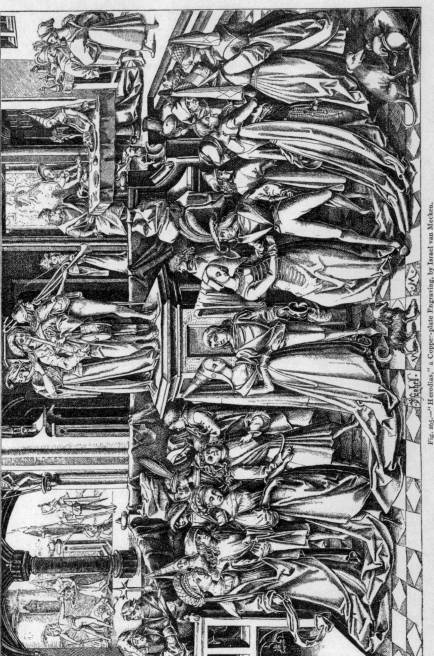

Fig. 265.—"Herodias," a Copper-plate Engraving, by Israel van Mecken.

aquafortis, it proves that Albert Dürer is wrongfully regarded as the inventor of this mode of engraving, more expeditious than with the *burin*, as the oldest *aquafortis* work of Albert Dürer is dated 1515, that is to say, nineteen years later than that of Wenceslaus of Olmutz.

We now come to three great artists who, at a period in which the art of engraving had made the most remarkable progress, availed themselves of it for producing works which eminently characterise each master respectively.

Albert Dürer, born at Nuremberg in 1471, was a vigorous painter, and was not less remarkable for the productions of his *burin* and etching-needle. We do not intend to describe all his works, though all are worthy of notice, but must content ourselves with mentioning " Adam and Eve standing by the Tree of Knowledge of Good and Evil," a small plate of delicate workmanship and admirable perfectness of design; the "Passion of Jesus Christ," in a series of sixteen plates; "Christ praying in the Garden of Gethsemane," the first work executed by this master by means of *aquafortis*, then a new method, which, being less soft than the *burin*, gave rise to an idea not dispelled for some time, that this print and several others were engraved on iron or tin; several figures of the "Virgin with the Infant Jesus," which are all remarkable for expression and simplicity, and have received odd *sobriquets* on account of some accessory object which accompanies them (for instance, the "Virgin with the pear, butterfly, ape," &c.); the "Prodigal Son keeping Swine," a composition in which the painter himself is represented; "St. Hubert praying before the Cross borne by a Stag" (Fig. 266), a very rare and beautiful plate; the "Chevalier and his Lady;" lastly, the "Chevalier of Death," a *chef-d'œuvre*, dated 1515, and representing Francis of Sickingen, who was destined to be the firmest supporter of Luther's Reformation.*

Marc Antonio Raimondi, born at Bologna about the year 1475, was first a pupil of Francis Raibolini, and afterwards of Raphael,† whose style he often

---

* We presume this plate to be that commonly known among collectors of prints as "Death's Horse;" it represents a knight on horseback followed by Death. The best impressions of this plate are prior to the date 1513. It is also called "The Christian Knight," and "The Knight, Death, and the Devil."—[ED.]

† That Marc Antonio studied painting under Raphael, as is here implied, is more than doubtful, though he engraved a very large number of his various compositions, and was highly esteemed by the great master.—[ED.]

Fig. 266.—" St. Hubert praying before the Cross borne by a Stag."   Engraved by Albert Dürer.

followed, and in his compositions did his utmost to imitate his pure and noble manner. Everything in his designs is ideally true, and all is harmonious in the *ensemble* of his works. Most of his engravings still existing are very much sought after, and as any description we could give would only convey but an imperfect idea of the excellence of these works, the strongest testimony in favour of their merit will be to mention the high prices given for certain prints by this master at the public sale which took place in 1844. For example:—"Adam and Eve," a print after Raphael, 1,010 francs (£40); "God commanding Noah to build the Ark," from the same master, 700 francs (£28); the "Massacre of the Innocents," 1,200 francs (£48); "St. Paul preaching at Athens," 2,500 francs (£100); the "Lord's Supper," 2,900 francs (£116); the "Judgment of Paris," which is regarded as the *chef-d'œuvre* of Marc Antonio, 3,350 francs (£134); three pendentives of the "Farnesina," 1,620 francs (£64 10*s.*), &c. Subsequently, these enormous prices have been even exceeded.

Lucas van Leyden, born in 1494, and, like Albert Dürer, a clever painter as well as skilful engraver, has left about eighty plates, the most remarkable of which are "David playing the Harp before Saul;" the "Adoration of the Magi;" a large "Ecce Homo," engraved by the artist at the age of sixteen; a "Peasant and Peasant-woman with a Cow;" the "Monk Sergius killed by Mahomet;" the "Seven Virtues;" a plate called the "Little Milkmaid," very rare; lastly, a "Poor Family travelling," of which only five proofs are known; they were bought for sixteen louis d'or by the Abbot of Marolles, when he formed his cabinet of prints, which became one of the richest additions to the Imperial Library.

In a befitting rank below these famous artists we may class a French engraver, Jean Duret, born at Langres in 1488, who was goldsmith to Henri II., and executed several beautiful allegorical plates on the intrigues of the king and Diana of Poitiers, as well as twenty-four compositions taken from the Apocalypse; also Pierre Woeiriot (or Voeiriot), an engraver and goldsmith of Lorraine, born in 1531, who produced numerous fine works down to the end of the century; the most famous of them, designated by the name of the "Bull of Phalaris" (Fig. 267), represents the tyrant of Agrigentum shutting up human victims destined to be burnt alive in a brazen bull.

There were at work in Italy at the same epoch Augustine of Musi

Fig. 267.—" Phalaris, Tyrant of Agrigentum, causing Victims destined to be burnt alive to be shut up in a Brazen Bull."
Engraved by P. Woeiriot. (French School of the Sixteenth Century.)

(Agustino de Musis, called the Venetian), Giacomo Caraglio, the Ghisis,* Eneas Vico ; in Germany, Altdorfer (Fig. 268), George Pencz,† Aldegrever,

Fig. 268.—" Repose of the Holy Family."
Engraved by A. Altdorfer.

Jacque Binck, Bartel and Hans Sebald Beham (Fig. 269), who are designated under the collective name of the " Little Masters ;" in Holland, Thierry (Dirk) van Staren.

In the course of the sixteenth century engraving reached its culminating point, and at that time Italy and Germany no longer took the lead in this branch of art, for the most skilful and renowned masters then belonged to Holland and France.

Those of Holland were Henry Goltzius (or Goltz), born in 1558, and his pupils Matham and the Mullers, whose vigorous gravers might remind one of brilliant effects of colour without any loss of purity of design ; the two brothers, Boetius and Scheltius Bolswaert, so called from their native town Bolswaert, born in 1580 and 1586 respectively ; Paul Pontius and Lucas Vorsterman, both born in 1590, whose engravings so well represent the *chiar-oscuro* and colour of Van Dyck and Jordaens.

In France was Jacques Callot, born in 1594, whose works were both numerous and original, and enjoyed a somewhat popular celebrity ; among them the most worthy of remark are the " Temptation of St. Anthony," the "Fair of the Madonna d'Imprunette," "The Garden" and the " Parterre," both scenes in Nancy ; as well as several series, such as the " Miseries of War," &c. There were also Michael Lasne, born in 1596, who engraved a number of historical portraits ; and Etienne (Stephen) Baudet, who reproduced eight large landscapes after Poussin.

---

* Giovanni B. B. Ghisi ; Giorgio and Adams, his two sons ; and Diana, his daughter.—[ED.]

† This engraver, generally known by the single name of George, usually signed his plates with the surname Peins or Pentz.—[ED.]

Fig. 269.—" Ferdinand I., Brother of Charles V."   Engraved by Bart. Beham in 1531.

A separate notice is reserved for Jonas Suyderoef, born at Leyden in 1600, who, by combining the graver, the etching-needle, and aquafortis, gave an exceptional character to his works. Among the two hundred engravings by this master the most admired are the "Treaty of Munster," after Terburg; and the "Burgomasters of Amsterdam receiving the News of the Arrival of Queen Mary of Medicis," after De Keyser.

We are now touching closely upon, even if we have not already exceeded, the limits to which we are prescribed by the scope of our notices; but as the history of engraving does not present, like that of so many other arts, the spectacle of a grievous decadence after a period of brilliancy, we cannot without regret come to a conclusion, when mention might still be made of many distinguished names among the engravers of every country.

We should also scarcely be able to pass on to another subject without having alluded to those men whose works belong, indeed, to the following epoch, but the date of whose birth connects them with that we are considering. We could not, in fact, assume to have treated of engraving had we passed over in silence Van Dyck, Claude Lorraine, and Rembrandt (Fig. 270), those greatest of masters who were equally celebrated for painting and engraving. In truth, perhaps, we could not say anything of them which would not be superfluous.

Who is not acquainted with at least some few works by Van Dyck? This celebrated pupil of Rubens has left in painting as many masterpieces as canvases; and in engraving he knew how to give to his etching-needle so much *verve* and spirit, that his prints are perfect models to follow, and have never been surpassed. Who is there that does not admire the landscapes of Claude Lorraine, which are equally remarkable for the light diffused over them, and the misty atmosphere that tempers its brilliancy? We all know this master produced, as if for recreation, certain engravings which for truth and melancholy (*mélancolie*) are hardly surpassed by his marvellous paintings. And how can we speak of Rembrandt without seeming to be commonplace? For his fertile and varied talent no difficulty ever seemed to exist; a theme, the most simple and common in appearance, becomes in his hands the basis of a masterly conception; nature, to which he seemed to lend a new life, while seizing upon its most striking realities, was for him an inexhaustible source of powerful compositions.

The mention of these artists on the threshold of an epoch into which we are precluded from following them, must suffice to convey some idea of the height that art had attained during this century. We will, however, enumerate after them a few names among foreign engravers. The Flemish artists, Nicolas Berghem and Paul Potter, both great animal-painters, have

Fig. 270.—" Portrait of John Lutma, Goldsmith of Groningen." Designed and Engraved in aquafortis by Rembrandt.

left some prints in aquafortis for the possession of which amateurs contend; Wenceslaus Hollar, the Englishman,* engraved "The Queen of Sheba," after Veronese; to Cornelius Visscher, a Dutchman, we owe the famous

* He was born at Prague, although most of his works were executed in England.—[Tr.]

" Seller of Ratsbane ;" and to Stefano della Bella, of Florence, the " View from the Pont-Neuf, Paris." Rupert, the Prince-Palatine (nephew of Charles I. of England), was the inventor of the mezzo-tinto, or black style of engraving ; and William Faithorne, an Englishman, engraved several portraits after Van Dyck. France also presents to our notice some justly-celebrated names. The views of towns by Israel Silvestre, of Nancy, are very beautiful ; François de Poilly, of Abbeville, reproduced several pictures by Raphael ; Jean Pesne, of Rouen, himself a painter, engraved especially after Poussin ; Antoine Masson, of Orleans, has left a print of the " Pilgrims of Emmaus," after the picture by Titian, which is regarded as a *chef-d'œuvre.* Lastly, Robert Nanteuil, of Rheims, the famous portrait-painter, engraved Péréfixe, Archbishop of Paris, four times ; the Archbishop of Rheims five times ; Colbert six times ; Michel Le Tellier, Chancellor of France, ten times ; Louis XIV. eleven times, and Cardinal Mazarin fourteen times.

Fig. 271.—" The Holy Virgin." Engraved by Aldegrever in 1527.

SCULPTURE.

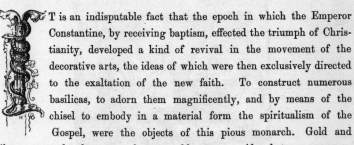

T is an indisputable fact that the epoch in which the Emperor Constantine, by receiving baptism, effected the triumph of Christianity, developed a kind of revival in the movement of the decorative arts, the ideas of which were then exclusively directed to the exaltation of the new faith. To construct numerous basilicas, to adorn them magnificently, and by means of the chisel to embody in a material form the spiritualism of the Gospel, were the objects of this pious monarch. Gold and silver were the less spared, as marble was considered too common a substance in which to represent the sacred personages of the divine hierarchy. At Constantinople, in the basilica constructed by Constantine, there was represented, on one side of the apse, a seated figure of our Saviour surrounded by His twelve disciples; on the other side, Christ was represented also sitting on a throne and accompanied by four angels, who had precious stones of Alabanda, inlaid, to represent their eyes. All these figures were life-size, and made of silver *repoussé;* each one weighing from ninety to a hundred and ten pounds. In the same church, a canopy representing the Apostles and cherubim in relief, of polished silver, weighed more than two thousand pounds. But these splendours were even eclipsed by those of the font of porphyry in which Constantine received baptism from the hands of Bishop Sylvester. The part whence the water flowed away was adorned with massive silver over an extent of five feet, and for the purpose three thousand pounds of this precious metal were employed. In the centre, columns of gold supported a lamp of the same metal weighing fifty-two pounds, in which, during the feast of Easter, two hundred pounds of perfumed oil were burnt. The water was poured into the font through the image of a lamb of solid gold, weighing thirty pounds. On the right was a life-size representation of our Saviour, weighing a hundred and seventy pounds; on the left was a statue of John the Baptist of the same size; while seven hinds of silver placed around the font, and pouring water into the basin, harmonised in their dimensions and materials with the other figures.

We would not assert that these works, pompously enumerated by Anastasius, the Librarian, corresponded in purity and elevation of style

Fig. 272. - Altar of Castor (a Gallo-Roman Sculpture), discovered in 1711 under the Choir of Notre-Dame, Paris.

with the richness of the materials employed; for we know, on the contrary, that in order to comply with the wishes of the powerful emperor, artists were found who, by simple substitution of heads, attributes, or inscriptions, converted without any scruple a Jupiter into God the Father, or a Venus into a Virgin. The large cities were not as yet depopulated of the innumerable crowd of statues which adorned them; and it was only in provinces far from the metropolis that the images of the false gods were buried under the fragments of their overthrown temples (Figs. 272 and 273).

In fact, before the art had adopted, or rather created, the system of Christian symbolism, it was absolutely necessary to borrow the elements of its existence from the glorious materials of the past, and even to imitate the works of Pagan art.

In Greece more than elsewhere—and by Greece we include Constantinople—statuary preserved, under Constantine and his earliest successors, a certain degree of power which we might call original. The design still adhered to beautiful forms, and, in the arrangement of subjects, the principles of the ancients were for a long time applied, as if instinctively. Although artists no longer studied nature, they were, at all events, surrounded by excellent models, which guided them with somewhat imperious rule.

We have already seen that, among the barbaric chiefs who invaded the empire of the Cæsars and seated themselves on the Imperial throne of Rome, were some who, at a certain period, professed to be, if not the protectors of the Fine Arts, which had then sunk into torpor, at least

Fig. 273.—Altar of Jupiter Ceraunus (Gallo-Roman Sculpture), discovered in 1711, under the Choir of Notre-Dame, Paris.

the preservers of the Greek and Roman monuments belonging to the noblest epoch of Art. The statues were no longer broken down; the inscriptions and bas-reliefs ceased to be mutilated; the triumphal arches (Fig. 274), the palaces, and the theatres, were respected, or rather, were left standing. But a kind of deadness had come over the artistic world, and a few sympathetic manifestations of this kind were not sufficient to reanimate its enervated spirit; it was necessary that the period of repose should be fully accomplished—a period which, in the views of Providence, was perhaps a phase of profound contemplation or preparatory development.

Nevertheless, although the art which gives life to marble and bronze—a high style of sculpture—was in a stationary or retrograde state, the lower kind, which we may call domestic, preserved some degree of activity.

For instance, it was then the custom for great personages to send as presents diptychs of ivory, on the outer face of which were carved bas-reliefs recalling some memorable event. Monarchs, on their accession, were in the habit of conferring diptychs of this kind on the governors of provinces and bishops; and the latter, in order to testify to the good understanding existing between the civil and religious authorities, placed the diptych on the altar. A marriage, a baptism, or any success, gave occasion for the

Fig. 274.— Restoration of a Roman Triumphal Arch, with its Bas-reliefs.

presentation of diptychs. For two centuries artists lived on nothing but this kind of work. It needed events of some very extraordinary character to cause the production of any monument of real sculpture.

In the sixth century the cathedrals of Rome, Trèves, Metz, Lyons, Rhodez, Arles, Bourges, and the abbeys of St. Médard at Soissons, St. Ouen at Rouen, and St. Martin at Tours, are mentioned as remarkable; and yet the walls of these edifices were nothing but bare stone, without either ornament or sculpture. "To become living stones," says M. J. Duseigneur, "they had to wait for another age. The whole of the ornamentation was exclusively applied to the altar and the baptismal font. The tombs even of great personages present the most primitive simplicity." (Fig. 275.)

Ancient Gaul, in spite of its disasters, still retained, in certain parts of its territory, men, or rather groups of men, in whose hearts the cultivation of Art still remained a living principle. This was the case in Provence, round the archbishops of Arles; in Austrasia (Metz), near the throne of Brunehaut; in Burgundy, at the court of King Gontran. Most of the works and even the names of these artists are now lost; but history has recorded the movement, which was, as it were, a happy link destined to abbreviate the solution of continuity in artistic tradition.

At the time when Greek art, in its degenerate state, had sunk down into a department of mere goldsmith's work, casting over Europe only a pale and feeble light; when artists, in representing sacred or profane subjects,

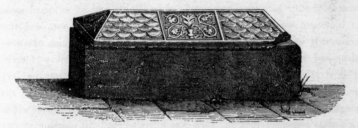

Fig. 275.—A Stone Tomb, of one of the first Abbots of St. Germain-des-Prés, Paris.

contented themselves with simple medallions of bronze, gold, or silver, which were generally inserted in a shrine, or suspended on the walls; across the seas Byzantine art was springing into life; an art which blended Hellenic reminiscences with Christian sentiment.

In the eighth century, the epoch of the uprising of the Iconoclasts against images of all kinds, Byzantine sculpture had acquired certain well-marked characteristics: rigidness of outline, meagreness of form, elongation of the proportions, combined with great profuseness of costume; all was the expression of saddened resignation and costly grandeur. The monumental statuary of this age has, however, almost entirely disappeared, and we should be nearly destitute of any accurate record as to the state of Art for a period of several centuries, were it not for numerous diptychs which, to some extent, supply this want. Many of these sacred diptychs were exquisitely wrought.

Gori, in his "Trésor des Diptyques," written in Latin and published at
Florence in 1759, divides these monuments into four classes: diptychs
intended to receive the names of the newly baptised; those wherein were
written the names of the benefactors of the church, sovereigns, and popes;
and those destined to preserve the memory of the faithful who had died in
the bosom of the church (Fig. 276). Their outward surface generally
represented some scene taken from the Evangelists, in which Christ was
especially depicted as young and beardless, his head glorified with a nimbus
without a cross. The more these representations were condemned, the more
they who paid respect to them endeavoured to perpetuate their use. The
Greek artists, being unable to find a livelihood in their own country, made
their way into Italy in such numbers that the popes Paul I., Adrian I.,
and Pascal I., erected monasteries to receive them. Owing to the influence
of this immigration, Art, which in the West was germinating in an
undecided state between a weak style of originality and an awkward mode
of imitation, was compelled to assume a character of its own, and this
necessarily was the Byzantine character; that is, a manner which was firm,
clear, and, in general, impressed with a certain imposing nobility of style.
This style attained all the more success by its being illustrated by very
eminent artists, whom Charlemagne patronised as fully adequate to the
magnificence of his ideas; and also because the richness of ornament which
this style combined with its work was likely to render it pleasing to the
populace.

The royal palaces of Aix-la-Chapelle, Goddinga, Attiniacum, and
Theodonis Villa, and the monasteries of St. Arnulph, Trèves, St. Gall,
Salzbourg, and Prüm felt the salutary influence which Charlemagne
exercised on all kinds of Art. Prior to 1793, in these various localities
precious remains were still to be seen, reaching back to the eighth century;
they testified to the fact that, apart from Byzantine influence, and bearing
the impress of a simple Christian sentiment, sculpture still clung, owing to
Lombard ascendancy, to some of the grand traditions of antiquity.

This union of principles gave rise to a number of works bearing
a remarkable character. The foundation of the abbeys of St. Mihiel
(Lorraine), Isle-Barbe (near Lyons), of Ambernay and Romans; the erection
of several of the great monasteries in Alsace, Soissonnais, Brittany,
Normandy, Provence, Languedoc, and Aquitaine; the construction of the

Fig. 276.—Diptychs in Carved Ivory of the Eleventh Century. (M. Rigollot's Collection, Amiens.)

The first compartment represents St. Remy, Bishop of Rheims, healing a paralytic; the second, St. Remy healing a sick man by the invocation of the sacrament on the altar; the third, St. Remy, assisted by a holy bishop, baptising King Clovis in the presence of Queen Clotilda, and receiving from the Holy Spirit the sacred *ampulla*.

important churches of Metz, Toul, Verdun, Rheims, Autun, &c.; the restorations which took place at the abbeys of Bèze, St. Gall, St. Benignus of Dijon, Remiremont, St. Arnulphe-lès-Metz, and Luxeuil, were of sufficient importance to occupy an immense number of artists, architects, and sculptors, who, like the monk Gundelandus, abbot of Lauresheim, handled the compasses and the mallet with as much authority as the crucifix. Nothing could equal the splendour of some of the monasteries, which were perfect centres of genius and skill, in which all the Fine Arts united were a mutual assistance to one another; directed, perhaps, by a master who was himself inspired by a feeling for elevated production (Fig. 277).

Nevertheless, the smaller examples of sculpture and carving constituted the principal work of the artists of the eighth century. In the execution of any larger objects they were deterred by a dread of the Iconoclasts, who still continued their course of destruction, neither was it much less after the death of Charlemagne, owing to the civil wars and invasions which, in every direction, put a stop to or ruined architectural works. A shrine or an altar might perhaps be saved, but a church-front or doorway could not be protected; and the hereditary hatred with which princes pursued one another did not fail to be wreaked on their effigies. At that time there were neither artists nor monks; every one became a soldier, and the common peril gave some energy to our alarmed ancestors.

When these invasions had almost come to an end in Europe, the very disasters they had caused assisted to some extent the progress both of architecture and sculpture. In the first place there sprang up a complete order of new buildings, originated by the need that arose for fresh edifices for the purpose of public worship; the Church, having a thousand disasters to repair, built or restored a number of monasteries which assumed a decided character of individuality. The cathedrals of Auxerre, Clermont, Toul, the Church of St. Paul at Verdun, the abbeys of Montier-en-Der and of Gorze, of Munster, Cluny, Celles-sur-Cher, &c., were specially adorned with the sculptural characteristics of this epoch. Crucifixes in high relief were multiplied, the introduction of which into monumental sculpture did not take place before the pontificate of Leo III. In the arched recesses over doorways representations of the good and the bad were placed opposite to one another; the worship of the Virgin was celebrated in all

kinds of artistic productions; and, in short, sculpture was displayed everywhere with an extraordinary amount of richness. Nothing escaped, so
to speak, its luxurious growth: *ambons,** seats, arches, baptismal fonts,
columns, cornices, bell-turrets, and gargoyles—everything, in short, testified
that sculpture and stone were now in full harmony. Almost all the

Fig. 277.—Bas-relief in the Abbey-Church of St. Denis; a reproduction of the ancient Statue of
Dagobert I., destroyed in the Ninth Century.

figures were then represented as clothed in the Roman style, with a
short tunic, and the chlamys clasped upon the shoulder; this still continued to be the court-costume, and consequently the only one suitable
to the representation of the exalted followers of Christianity.

* *Ambons*—a kind of pulpit in the early Christian churches.—[ED.]

It is worthy of remark that the monuments of this age are generally wanting both in dates and the name of the sculptor. Not more than five or six of the principal artists or directors of artistic works of the period are mentioned by name in any historical records. Among them, however, are Tutilon, a monk of Saint-Gall, who, at once poet, sculptor, and painter, ornamented with his works the churches of Mayence and Metz; Hugues, Abbot of Montier-en-Der; Austée, Abbot of St. Arnulph, in the diocese of Metz; Morard, who, with the co-operation of King Robert, rebuilt, towards the end of the tenth century, the old church of St. Germain-des-Prés, at Paris; lastly, Guillaume, Abbot of St. Benignus, at Dijon, who took under his direction forty monasteries, and became chief of a school of Art, as well as their head on religious matters. The doorways of the churches of Avallon, Nantua, and Vermanton, executed at this epoch, bear witness to the rigour of an improved taste; and it may be well said that this abbot Guillaume, who for a long series of years directed a number of artists, who also in their turn became chiefs of schools, exercised as powerful an influence on French art as Nicholas of Pisa on Tuscan art in the following century.

But although it embraced within its influence a very extended sphere, the school of Burgundy did not fail to find on the ancient Gallic soil very skilful and industrious rivals. The districts of Messin, Lorraine, Alsace, Champagne, Normandy, and the Ile-de-France, in short all the various centres of the South, possessed numerous artists, each of whom impressed on their works their own special character of individuality.

While all this activity was prevailing in France, Italy had as yet taken so insignificant a part in the revival of Art, that in 976 Peter Orseolo, Doge of Venice, having formed the idea of rebuilding the basilica of St. Mark, was compelled to summon from Constantinople both architects and artists.

A period of check to any progress took place in France, however, just as in all the rest of Europe, when, at the approach of the year 1000, the whole population became subject to an ideal dread that the end of the world was at hand; but when this date was once passed, every school of art set vigorously to work, and the most remarkable monuments of Romanesque architecture sprang up throughout Europe in every direction.

Then it was that the artists of Burgundy built and ornamented, among other churches and monasteries, the Abbey of Cluny, the apse of which consisted of a bold cupola, supported by six columns thirty-six feet in height, of

Fig. 278.—Tomb of Dagobert, executed by order of St. Louis, in the Abbey-Church of St. Denis. It represents
the King carried away by Demons, after his death, towards the Infernal Bark, from which he is rescued by
Angels and the Fathers of the Church. (Thirteenth Century.)

Cipolin and Pentelican marble, with capitals, cornices, and friezes, carved, painted, and decorated with bronze. In Lorraine they worked at the cathedrals of Toul and Verdun, and the abbey of St. Viton. In the diocese of Metz Gontran and Adélard, celebrated abbots of St. Trudon, covered Hasbaye with new buildings. "Adélard," says a chronicler, "superintended the construction of fourteen churches, and his outlay was so great that the imperial treasury would scarcely have sufficed for it." In Alsace, the cathedral at Strasbourg and the two churches of Colmar and Schelestadt simultaneously arose, and in Switzerland the Cathedral of Basle. These magnificent edifices are still standing to show the vigour and majestic simplicity with which the art of sculpture was then able to embody its ideas; and, by lending its aid to architecture, to manifest, so to speak, the faith which actuated it. It was in this century that Fulbert, Bishop of Chartres, who was doubtless a sculptor also, superintended the restoration of his church, the splendour of which is still open to the admiration of all. Art, too, did not less distinguish herself in the decoration of certain additions made at that time to edifices already existing. The doorways of the churches of Laon, Châteaudun, and St. Ayoult of Provins, grand works of the earliest years of the twelfth century, yield the palm only to the splendid external ornamentation of the Abbey of St. Denis, executed between the years 1137 and 1180. The Abbot Suger, who was himself an eminent artist, does not name any of the sculptors to whose care this important task was committed. We are equally ignorant as to the sculptors of the statues of Dagobert and of Queen Nanthilde, his wife; and also as to the artists of a large golden crucifix, the foot of which was enriched with bas-reliefs, and the figure of Christ, that presented, says Suger, "an expression really divine." The names of the sculptors of the cathedral church of Paris are likewise concealed from our admiration. One might suppose that a body of artists fired with the same inspiration, and with a common sentiment both in thought and action, had there assembled to design their works; some sculpturing in marble the sarcophagus of Philip of France; some peopling the rood-loft and the apse with tall figures and a long gallery of Biblical subjects; others decorating the façade and exterior with statues, all of very diversified character, but yet all appearing to unite in the expression of the same feelings and the same faith (Fig. 279).

In the twelfth century, the Burgundian artists continued their marvellous work. The tomb of Hugues, Abbot of Cluny; the doorway of the monastery

Fig. 279.—External Bas-relief of Notre-Dame, in Paris, representing Citizens relieving Poor Scholars.
(The work of Jean de Chelles. Date 1257.)

of St. Jean, that of the Church of St. Lazare at Autun; the nave and the
west front of Semur-en-Auxois, are all of this school, and of this epoch.

The school of Champagne raised to the memory of Count Henry I., in the Church of St. Etienne, at Troyes, a tomb surrounded with forty-four columns of gilded bronze, surmounted by a slab of silver on which were placed, in a recumbent position, the statues of the Count and of one of his sons; bas-reliefs, in bronze and silver, representing the Holy Family, the celestial court, angels, and prophets, surrounded this monument. The tomb of Count Henry was a triumph of sculpture in metal; and, at that time, surpassed all other tombs in France, just as the Cathedral of Rheims was destined, ere long, to excel all others.

In Normandy we find the same enthusiasm, the same zeal, the same skill in Art; and there, at least, we learn the names of some of the artists: Otho, the builder of the Cathedral of Séez; Garnier, of Fécamp; Anquetil, of Petit-Ville, &c. The masons and sculptors, too, formed at this epoch a numerous and powerful corporation.

In the South, Asquilinus, Abbot of Moissac, near Cahors, ornamented with fine statues the cloister and front of his church, and affixed to the sides of the apse a Crucifixion so skilfully carved, that it was believed to have emanated from some divine hand ("ut non humano, sed divino artificio facta"). In Auvergne, Provence, and Languedoc, many other important works of sculpture were executed. But the chief masterpiece of all, which combines the different styles of the southern schools, is the famous Church of St. Trophimus of Arles, the front of which, where the breadth and grace of the Greek style is allied with the purest Christian simplicity, carries back the imagination to the brightest epochs of the art.

Towards the end of the eleventh and the commencement of the twelfth century, the sculptors' studios of the districts of Messin and Lorraine were in full activity. Several magnificent churches having been destroyed by fire, particularly that of Verdun, the whole population assisted, either with money or labour, in the restoration of these edifices. It was a perfect artistic crusade, in which several bishops and abbots, who were clever artists as well as spiritual chiefs, took the lead in the movement.

In Alsace, art asserted its position in the magnificent Cathedral of Strasbourg,* a kind of challenge thrown out to the artists on the other side of the Rhine, who were unable, even at Cologne, to carry an edifice to such an

---

* Strasbourg spire is 468 feet in height, the highest in the world. Amiens, the next, a mere *flèche*, is 422 feet.—[TR.]

CLOVIS I. AND CLOTILDE HIS WIFE.

Statues formerly at the Entrance of the Church of Notre Dame at Corbeil. Twelfth Century.

enormous height, or to adorn it with such a diversified multitude of statues. Although belonging more especially to the thirteenth century, it may be taken as the starting-point of the prodigious works executed by an association of freemasons, who have marked with their hieroglyphic signatures the stones of this edifice, as of all others executed by them in the valley of the Rhine, from Dusseldorf to the Alps.

We are, however, led to believe that Germany also did not fail to be subject to the influence of this artistic school, for among contemporary monuments are several in a style which manifestly testifies to the effects of the neighbouring country of Alsace.

Flemish art of that time is exemplified by the Church of St. Gudule at Brussels, the style of which is especially rich with decorations borrowed from churches on the banks of the Rhine, the Moselle, the Sarre, and the Upper Meuse.

If we include in one comprehensive glance French, German, and Flemish sculptural works, we shall recognise in all, notwithstanding the predominance of any particular school, one original and special type. The characteristics of this are elongated faces with a calm, contemplative, and penitent expression; stiffness of attitude, and a kind of ecstatic immobility, rather than any glow of animation; draperies with small narrow folds and close-fitting, as if wetted; pearled fringes or ribbons, set off with gems (Fig. 280). We see statues of lofty proportions reared up; representations of various personages are multiplied on the tombs; Greek art is disappearing and its learned theories are giving way before Christian sentiment; thought

Fig. 280.—Statue said to be of Clovis I., formerly in the porch of St. Germain-des-Prés, Paris.
(Twelfth Century.)

is obtaining the mastery over mere form; symbolism makes its appearance and becomes a science.

But let us turn our eyes towards Italy. Venice had scarcely raised her lofty dome ere Pisa aspired to have one also. Many a Tuscan ship, launched upon the sea for conquests of a new kind, brought from Greece an infinity of monuments, statues, bas-reliefs, capitals, friezes, and various fragments; and the Tuscan people, the best organised race in Europe for fully appreciating all the beauty of form, were called upon to draw their inspiration from the relics of ancient works of Art. The enthusiasm became general. In 1016, Buschetto, regarded as the first architect of his time, undertook the building of the Cathedral of Pisa, where ancient fragments are still conspicuous amid the works of more modern creation: a kind of holographic testament the benefit of which the followers of the art of Phidias have thus handed down to posterity. The pupils of Buschetto, accepting the impulse of his masterly hand and reproducing his ideas, soon spread all over the peninsula, and the cathedrals of Amalfi, Pistoia, Siena, and Lucca arose, the Byzantine character of which differed from the Lombard style presented by the Cathedral of Milan. One might almost have fancied that the bosom of the earth brought forth statues which, as if by enchantment, peopled every pedestal; and that from heaven descended the ray which animated them with their sublime expression. The art of casting in bronze, hitherto almost unknown in Italy, became naturalised there as much as the art of carving in stone.

While in the West the Arts were making such a spring, in the East they had relapsed into the lowest stage of debasement, at the period when Byzantium was simultaneously threatened by the Bulgarians and the Crusaders; although for a time they had appeared to revive, owing to the zeal of Basil the Macedonian, Constantine VIII., and some of their successors. Eastern sculpture disappeared when the Latins sacked the ancient capital of the first Christian emperor (1204).

At the approach of the thirteenth century, which was destined to be the great age of Christian architecture and sculpture, artists no longer looked, as they had hitherto done, towards Byzantium, they depended on themselves; and although some hesitation might still be felt, they found all round them models they could imitate, traditions they could follow, and masters to whom they could listen. Christian art had now an independent existence, and the various schools asserted their styles in a way which became every day more clear, more powerful, and more original.

"The style of the head of Christ at Amiens" (Fig. 281), says M.

Viollet-le-Duc, writing on this subject, "fully deserves the attention of

Fig. 281.—"The *Beau Dieu d'Amiens;*" a Statue of Christ in the Front of the Cathedral of Amiens.
(Thirteenth Century.)

sculptors. This carving is treated in the same way as the Greek heads

called Eginetic. There is the same simplicity of model, the same purity
of outline, the same style of execution, at once broad and delicate. It well
represents the features of Christ as a man : a blending of sweetness with
firmness, a gravity devoid of sadness."

This is not the place to assert any minute comparisons between
different manners and styles ; even the bare enumeration of the many
monuments to which this fervent age gave birth might prove wearisome.
We call it a "fervent age," and fully are we justified, for, at a time
when a whole world of artist-sculptors of ornaments and figures were
devoting themselves to the most delicate and marvellous works of sculpture
(Fig. 282), none seemed desirous of displaying his own personal distinction. We find, for instance, numerous sculptors setting aside all claim
to individual merit, and carrying this self-denial so far that, instead of
their own names, they inscribed that of the Virgin Mary on the carvings
of the churches which they had enriched with their finest works : " Hoc
panthema pia cælaverat ipsa Maria."

In Germany, Christian art became specially enthroned in Saxony ; and
Dresden, which has been justly styled the German Athens, can date back
her architecto-sculptural adornments to the tenth century. On the banks
of the Rhine, at Cologne, Coblentz, and Mayence, we find again the school of
Saint-Gall, which, having been planted in 971, under the auspices of
Notker, Bishop of Laodicea, left its stamp, during a period of two centuries,
in a series of remarkable works.

England, as early as the seventh century, had called to her aid some of
the French "masters in stone " and best workmen, and she subsequently
continued to do so for the building and ornamentation of her finest religious
edifices. William of Sens, a very skilful artist (*artifex subtilissimus*), proceeded, in 1176, to rebuild Canterbury Cathedral. Norman and French
artists also restored the abbeys of Croyland and Wearmouth, and York
Cathedral, already enriched with Byzantine and French sculpture.

Spain and Portugal, the soil of which had long been the theatre of an
inveterate conflict between two races embracing two irreconcilable religions,
were destined to inherit from these very struggles the creation of a singularly characteristic style of art. In adopting the Byzantine style, the
Moors had deprived it of its character of simple earnestness, and made
it to harmonise with the tendencies of their refined sensualism. Even when

Christian art was able to exercise an undivided rule, it could not fail to be influenced by the buildings erected by the Moors; and the fact that

Fig. 282.—Statues in the South Porch of Bourges Cathedral. (Twelfth Century.)

this alliance of architectural and sculptural styles succeeded in producing masterpieces is well attested by the cathedrals of Cuenca, Vittoria, and some portions of those of Seville, Barcelona, and Lugo in Galicia.

Sicily and the kingdom of Naples followed the movement made in other countries of Europe; but here, again, was felt the influence of various foreign importations. Some of them were of Greek origin, coming from Byzantium; some northern, from Normandy, and perhaps also from Germany; most, however, from Spain, and especially from the important school of Aragon.

"Nicolas of Pisa," says Emeric David, "was born towards the end of the twelfth century, in a town then peopled with Greek masters and the pupils of those masters, and full of Greek monuments of every age; a town which might be called altogether Greek. He had the good sense to disdain the productions of his own time and to devote himself to the more elevated contemplation of the *chefs-d'œuvre* of ancient Greece. This proof of undoubted discernment, and a high degree of taste on his part, could not but lead to very marked progress. But a premature study of the antique is not so sure a guide to the desired end as the contemplation of nature, to which Guido of Siena, his contemporary, and a little later Cimabue and Giotto, taught perhaps by his errors, assiduously applied themselves." There can, however, be no doubt that the first development of Christian sculpture in Italy must unquestionably be referred to Nicolas of Pisa. He had, nevertheless, some rivals who were well worthy of competing with him. Among these were Fuccio, sculptor of the magnificent tomb of the Queen of Cyprus, in the Church of San Francesco at Florence; and also Marchione of Arezzo, who in 1216 carved his name over the doorway of the church of that town. Giovanni of Pisa, son of Nicolas, who sculptured many beautiful works at Arezzo, Pistoia, and Florence, and even surpassed himself in the Campo Santo at Pisa, perhaps the most remarkable monument in Christian Europe, has been placed by some far below his father in rank as a sculptor, on account of an accusation made against him of having abandoned the Greek style. But this renunciation was, in fact, a real trait of genius, and actually constitutes his glory; for, by neglecting form to some extent, he was enabled to carry religious idealism and power of expression to its very highest limits. We must, therefore, consider Giovanni and Margaritone, pupils of Nicolas; Andrea Ugolino, pupil of Giovanni; Agnolo and Agostino of Siena; and the celebrated Giotto, who was at once architect, sculptor, and painter, as real regenerators of the art. Indeed, we might call these great artists the creators of Christian sculpture in Italy—that art in which simultaneously shone forth seriousness of composition, grace and ease of attitude, simplicity of imitation, elevation of sentiment; in short, all the great harmonies of a style which seemed to breathe forth a hymn of love and faith.

Thanks to the studios of Agnolo and Agostino, Siena, a small town which calls to mind the ancient Sicyone, so weak in a political point of view and yet so learned and polished, was for some time the rival of Pisa, up to the period when Florence absorbed the artistic splendour of the two cities. Florence, as the home of the Arts, became the centre of radiation, whence artists took their flight over the whole of Italy, and from Italy spread among all the nations of Europe.

Towards the end of the thirteenth century, the churches of Florence, on which the fraternities combined their efforts, and some of the civil buildings of this rich and flourishing city, were filled with statues. The foundation of the municipal palace in 1282, and that of the cathedral in 1298, made these two wonderful edifices real museums of sculpture, in which, among the works of Eastern artists, those of Giovanni of Arezzo and Giotto are distinguished. Agostino and Agnolo of Pisa executed at that time some magnificent examples at Santa Maria in Orvieto, San Francisco in Bologna, and in the subterranean Church of Assisi, &c. Lastly, Andrea of Pisa, a contemporary of Giotto, as he died only in 1345, extracted from antiquity all that Christian sculpture could borrow from it; that is, he combined sublimity both of form and expression. At Pisa, the chancel of Santa Maria a Ponte; at Florence, the campanile and the high-altar of Santa Maria de' Fiori, and a door of San Giovanni; in the Cathedral of Pistoia, the tomb of Cino, are all of them so many masterpieces; above which, however, the old Pisan master proudly classed the works of his son Nino. This young artist, who carved the monument of the Scaligers at Verona, became, in fact, the worthy follower of the school which recognised Andrea as its chief. Jacopo della Quercia and Niccolo Aretino enriched also with magnificent works the towns of Siena, Lucca, Bologna, Arezzo, and Milan, as well as Florence. But when, in 1424, the tomb closed over Jacopo della Quercia, the lofty destinies of the art seemed to come to a termination, and soon rapidly declined. In Venice, at the death of Filippo Calendario, which occurred in 1355, Italian sculpture had already lost much of its nobility and vigour of style.

Italian sculpture (Fig. 283), as remarked by Emeric David, raised itself to the height of the sublime by merely striving after a simple and exact imitation of nature. It was by the same course of action that French sculpture always emulated its Transalpine rival; but, in order to attain the same end, the imitation followed a different path. In Italy, Art raised itself to the ideal by an attentive study of Greek forms; while on this side of the Alps, when sentiment required it, form was, if not sacrificed, at least neglected. French art showed more respect for the orthodoxy of Christian

Fig. 283.—Bas-relief on one of the Bronze Gates of St. Peter's at Rome, representing the Coronation of the Emperor Sigismund by Pope Eugène IV., in 1433. (Sculpture of the Fifteenth Century.)

thought; she did not introduce into the sanctuary of the Holy of Holies any of those profane and material ideas that might have been inspired by the marbles of Greece. In spite of the pointed architecture which everywhere prevailed, French sculpture, replete with a certain eloquent unction, preserved for a considerable period the Byzantine style in the appearance of the head and in the delicacy of draperies; without, however, altogether renouncing its individuality of character, and without ceasing to seek for models peculiar to its own soil.

Unfortunately for the personal glory of the French sculptors, the historians of the time have scarcely taken the trouble to record their names. In order to discover but a few of them, learned men of modern days have been compelled to undertake laborious researches; while many, and those the most remarkable—worthy, no doubt, to be compared with the greatest Italian artists—are and must remain ever unknown (Fig. 284). The Italians were more fortunate; to them Vasari, their rival and contemporary, has raised a lasting monument. In French art, the list of the sculptors of so many

Fig. 284.—Statuette of St. Avit, in the Church of Notre-Dame de Corbeil, demolished in 1820. (Eleventh Century.)

masterpieces must come to a close when we have mentioned Enguerrand, who, from 1201 to 1212, commenced the Cathedral and the Church du Buc, at Rouen, and had for his successor Gautier de Meulan; Robert de Coucy, chief of the body of artists who, in 1211, caused the Cathedral of Rheims to rise loftily from the earth; Hugues Libergier, who rebuilt the ancient basilica of St. Jovin; Robert de Luzarches, the founder, in 1220, of the Cathedral of Amiens, continued after his death by Thomas de Cormont and his son Regnault; Jean, Abbot of St. Germain-des-Prés, who in 1212 undertook the Church of St. Cosme, Paris; that of St. Julien le Pauvre being restored and adorned with sculpture at the same date, from the designs of the abbot and the "brethren" of Longpont (Fig. 285); Jean des Champs, who in 1248 worked at the ancient Cathedral of Clermont; lastly, the two Jeans de Montereau, who at one time as military architects, at another as sculptors of sacred subjects, were at the command of St. Louis, and produced some extraordinary works both of construction and sculpture.

Alsace manifested no less enthusiasm than France for the new architectural system, and sculpture was also subject to a similar development. From Basle to Mayence, the slopes of the Vosges and the long valley of

Fig. 285.—Bas-relief formerly over the Doorway of St. Julien le Pauvre, Paris, representing St. Julien and St. Basilissa, his wife, conveying in their boat Jesus Christ under the figure of a Leper. (Thirteenth Century.)

the Rhine became full of edifices enriched with sculpture and peopled with statues. Erwin of Steinbach (who died in 1318), assisted by Sabina, his daughter, and William of Marbourg, were the most renowned masters in these parts.

The extraordinary advance that French sculpture made in this age was assisted,—if not as regards the higher style of work, which could do without this help, at least in respect to the minor details of the art,— by the institution of the fraternities of the *Conception Notre-Dame*. In many towns the sculptors of images and the painters, the moulders, the *bahutiers,* or carvers in wood, horn, and ivory (Fig. 286), were all united under the same banner. In Germany and Belgium also existed *hanses,* or guilds, which were in direct communication with those of Alsace, and who accepted as guides French artists of known ability; as, for instance, Volbert and Gérard, architect-sculptors, who were simultaneously engaged in the construction of the Church of the Holy Apostles, Cologne.

With respect to the works commenced or finished in the fourteenth

Fig. 286.—Fragment of a small Reredos, in carved Bone (Fourteenth Century). Presented by Jean, Duc de Berry, Brother of Charles V., to the church of the ancient Abbey of Poissy. (Museum of the Louvre.)

century, the only difficulty is to make a choice among these wonderful monuments of Art; which, however, must be looked upon as the last manifestations of Christian art, properly so-called. We must, however, point out the polychrome sculptures of Chartres, of St. Remy, Rheims; St. Martin, Laon; St. Yved, Braisne; St. Jean des Vignes, Soissons; of the Chartreux, Dijon. In this ducal city we find, in 1357, Guy le Maçon, a celebrated

sculptor; at Bourges, about the same date, Aguillon, of Droues; at Montpellier, between 1331 and 1360, the two Alamans, John and Henry; at
Troyes, Denisot and Drouin of Mantes, &c. Beyond France, Matthias of
Arras, in 1343, laid the foundations of the Cathedral of Prague, which was
to be continued and finished by another French artist, Pierre of Boulogne.

Fig. 287.—" Le Bon Dieu," in the old Chapel of the Charnier des Innocents, Paris.
(Fifteenth Century.)

Arrested as our attention must be by the statues and bas-reliefs which were
multiplied under the porches, in the niches (Fig. 287), and on all the tombs,
we can cast but a very cursory glance on the immense number of wood-
carvings, figures in ivory, and movable pieces of sculpture, executed by

artists who may be divided into two very distinct classes, the Norman and the Rhenish; all of other schools appear to have been nothing but imitators of these.

In 1400 the *Maître* Pierre Pérat, architect of three cathedrals, who was at once both civil engineer and sculptor, and one of the greatest masters of whom France can boast, died at Metz, where he was interred with all the honours due to his wonderful talents. Just at the same time a memorable competition was opened at Florence. The object in view was to finish the doors of the Baptistery of St. John. The formal announcement of the competition, which was made all over Italy, did not fail to call forth the most skilful artists. Seven of these were selected, on account of their renown, to furnish designs: they consisted of three Florentines—Filippo Brunelleschi, Donatello, and the goldsmith, Lorenzo Ghiberti; Jacopo della Quercia of Siena; Nicolo Lamberti d'Arezzo; Francesco da Valdambrina; and Simone da Colle, called *de' Bronzi*. To each of these competitors the republic granted one year's salary, on condition that, at the end of the period, each of them should furnish a panel of wrought bronze of the same size as those of which the doors of St. John were to be composed. On the day fixed for the examination of the works, the most celebrated artists of Italy were summoned. Thirty-four judges were selected, and before this tribunal the seven models were exhibited, in the presence of the magistracy and the public. After the judges had audibly discussed the respective merits of the works, those of Ghiberti, Brunelleschi, and Donatello were preferred. But to whom of the three was the palm to be awarded? They hesitated. Then Brunelleschi and Donatello retired apart and exchanged a few words; after which one of them, commencing to address the assembly, said:—"Magistrates and citizens, we declare to you that in our own judgment Ghiberti has surpassed us. Award him the preference, for our country will thus acquire the greater glory. It is less discredit to us to make known our opinion than to keep silence."

These doors, at which Ghiberti worked for forty years, with the assistance of his father, his sons, and his pupils, are perhaps the finest work we have in sculptured metal.

At the date when Lorenzo Ghiberti, Donatello, Brunelleschi, and their pupils were the representatives of Florentine sculpture, the French school also produced its masters and its works of Art. Nicholas Flamel, the famous writer (*écrivain*) of the parish of St. Jacques la Boucherie, ornamented the churches and mortuary chapels of Paris with mystical and alchemical (*alchimiques*) sculptures, of which he was the designer if not the actual artist. Thury executed the tombs of Charles VI. and Isabelle of Bavaria; Claux Sluter, author of the "Puits de Moïse," at Dijon, assisted by James

Fig. 288.—" St. Eloi, Patron of Goldsmiths and Farriers." A Sculpture of the Fifteenth Century, in the Church of Notre-Dame d'Armançon, at Semur, Burgundy.

de la Barre, multiplied the works of monumental sculpture in Burgundy (Fig. 288). In Alsace, under the impulse of King René, himself an artist, the sculptor's art produced examples bearing the impress of a remarkable individuality. In the district of Messin, Henry de Ranconval, his son Jehan, and Clausse, were distinguished. In Touraine, Michael Columb executed the tomb of Francis II., Duke of Brittany; Jehan Juste, that of the children of Charles VIII., as introductory to the mausoleum of Louis XII., which he executed between 1518 and 1530, for the basilica of St. Denis; a German, Conrad of Cologne, assisted by Laurent Wrine, master of the ordnance to the king, cast in metal the effigy for the tomb of Louis XI. In Champagne appeared Jean de Vitry, sculptor of the stalls of the Church of St. Claude (Jura); in Berry, Jacquet Gendre, *master-mason* and *figure-maker* for the Hôtel de Ville, Bourges, &c.

At the end of the same century, Peter Brucy, of Brussels, exercised his art at Toulouse; the inspiration of the Alsacian artists was developed in the magnificent sculpture of Thann, Kaisersberg, and Dusenbach; while Germany, achieving but a late independence, sheltered the faults of her early genius under the illustrious names of Lucas Moser, Peter Vischer, Schühlein, Michel Wohlgemuth, Albert Dürer (Fig. 289), &c.

In sculptural works, as in every other branch of art, historical sentiment and faith seemed to die out with the fifteenth century. Mediæval art was subjected to protest; the desire seemed to be to re-create beauty of form by going back to the antique; but the emphatically Christian individuality was no longer reached, and this pretended *renaissance*, in which even earnest minds were induced to gratify themselves, only served to exhibit the feeble efforts of an epoch that sought to reproduce the glories of a vanished age. In the time of Charles VIII. and Louis XII., Lombardo-Venetian art, the affected and ingenious imitation of the Greek style, was introduced into France; it suited the common people and pleased mediocre intellect. The sculptors who came at that period to seek their fortunes at the court of the French kings worked exclusively for the aristocracy, and vied with one another in adorning, with an ardent infatuation for Italian art, the royal and aristocratic palaces which were being built or restored in every direction, such as the Châteaux of Amboise and Gaillon. But they failed to do any injury to French artists, who still remained charged with the works of sacred sculptures; and their style became but slightly, if at all, influenced by this foreign immigration. Even Benvenuto Cellini himself failed to exercise much effect on the vigorous schools of Tours, Troyes, Metz, Dijon, and Angers; his reputation and his works never passed, so to speak, beyond the limits of the court of France, and the brilliant traces they left behind them were confined to the school of Fontainebleau. Ere long, some zealous artists from all the principal centres of the French schools left their country and betook themselves to Italy; among these were

Fig. 289.—" St. John the Baptist preaching in the Desert." Bas-relief in Carved Wood by Albert Dürer. (Brunswick Gallery.)

Bachelier of Languedoc, Simon and Ligier Richier of Lorraine, Valentine Bousch of Alsace, and Jacques of Angoulême, who had the honour of a victory over his master, Michael Angelo, in a competition of statuary (many of the former artist's works now exist in the Vatican) ; Jean de Boulogne, and several others. Some of them, after they had become celebrated on the other side of the Alps, returned to their native country, bringing back to it their own native genius matured by the lessons of the Italians. There was, therefore, always a French school that preserved its individual character-istics, its generic good qualities and defects, which are so well represented in the sculptures of the Hôtel du Bourgtheroulde, Rouen (Fig. 290).

Michael Angelo was born on the 6th of March, 1475, and died on the 17th of February, 1564, without having shown any signs of decadence; greater, possibly, by his genius than by his works, he is the personifica-

Fig. 290.—Bas-relief of the Hôtel du Bourgtheroulde, Rouen, representing a Scene in the Interview between Francis I. and Henry VIII., on the Field of the Cloth of Gold.

tion of the Renaissance. It would be, perhaps, irreverent to say that this age was an age of decay; we might fear of desecrating the tomb of Buonarotti if we laid to his charge that his grand boldness led ordinary talents astray; and it is not a pleasant subject of thought that, influenced by two currents of ideas—one coming from Italy, the other from Germany—the art of the century operated to its own suicide. When the very soil itself seemed to be shaken, and the Christian pedestal which had formed both its grandeur and power overturned, what could be done

in the way of opposition to the downfall of Art by Jean Goujon, Jean
Cousin (Fig. 291), Germain Pilon, François Marchand, Pierre Bontemps,
those stars of French sculpture in the sixteenth century?

A final manifestation of the old religious feeling was, however, apparent in the tombs in the Church of Brou, designed by Jean Perréal, the
great painter of Lyons, executed by Conrad Meyt, and carved by Gourat and
Michael Columb; also in the mausoleum of Francis II., carved by Columb
and his family; in the sepulchre of St. Mihiel (Fig. 292) by Richier;
of the *Saints de Solesme*, in the tombs of Langey du Bellay, and of
the Chancellor De Birague, by Germain Pilon, &c.   But fashion and

Fig. 291.—Statue in Alabaster of Philip Chabot, Admiral of France, by Jean Cousin.   Formerly in the
Church of the Célestins, Paris, now in the Museum of the Louvre.

the prevailing taste now required from artists nothing but profane and
voluptuous compositions, and they adopted this line of Art all the more
readily, seeing, as they did every day, most beautiful works of Christian
sculpture mutilated by a new tribe of Iconoclasts, the Huguenots, who
seldom showed mercy to the figured monuments in Catholic churches.
The stalls of the Cathedral of Amiens, by Jean Rupin, the rood-loft by
Jean Boudin, and a number of other works of the same kind, testify to the
irruption of the Greek style, its implantation in religious art, and its hybrid
association with pointed architecture.   It is, however, only due to our
sculptors of the sixteenth century to say, that when they sacrificed them-

selves to the requirements of their age in imitating the masterpieces of Italy, they approached the natural grace of Raphael much closer than

Fig. 292.—"The Entombment," by Richier, in the Church of St. Mihiel (Meuse). (Sixteenth Century.)

Cellini, Primaticcio, or any of the other Italian artists who were settled in France; that they combined in the best possible way the mythological expression of the ancients with our modern ideas, and that, thanks to them, France is enabled to point with pride to a natural art, original and independent, which has been handed down to our days in direct succession by Sarrazain, Puget, Girardon, and Coyscvox.

Figs. 293, 294.—Gargoyles on the Palace of Justice, Rouen. (Fifteenth Century.

ARCHITECTURE.

The Basilica the first Christian Church.—Modification of Ancient Architecture.—Byzantine Style.
—Formation of the Norman Style.—Principal Norman Churches.—Age of the Transition from
Norman to Gothic.—Origin and Importance of the *Ogive.*—Principal Edifices in the pure
Gothic Style.—The Gothic Church, an Emblem of the Religious Spirit in the Middle Ages.—
Florid Gothic.—Flamboyant Gothic.—Decadency.—Civil and Military Architecture: Castles,
Fortified Enclosures, Private Houses, Town-Halls.—Italian Renaissance: Pisa, Florence,
Rome.—French Renaissance : Mansions and Palaces.

HEN the Christian family, humble and per-
secuted, was beginning to form itself into congregations; when it was forbidden to consecrate any
special edifice to the performance of the services of its
religion—a religion which opposed to the gorgeous
ceremonies of polytheism the most austere simplicity
—any refuge might have seemed good enough which
offered to the faithful the means of assembling themselves together in security; any retreat must have appeared sufficiently
ornamented which would recall to the disciples of the crucified
Saviour the mournful events preceding the glorification of that Divine
sacrifice. But when the religion proscribed one day found itself on the
next the religion of the State, things changed.

Constantine, in the mighty ardour of his zeal, wished to see the worship
of the true God efface in pomp and in magnificence all the solemnities of
the heathen world. In expelling the idols from their temples, the idea
could not have suggested itself of using these buildings for the new religion,
because they were generally of excessively limited dimensions, and the
plan on which they were built would have but indifferently answered the
requirements of the Christian ceremonial. What was necessary for these
services was principally a spacious nave, in which a large congregation
could assemble to hear the same word, to join in the same prayer, and
to intone the same chants. The Christians sought, therefore, among the

edifices then in existence (Fig. 295), for such as would best answer
these purposes. The *basilicas* presented themselves; these buildings served
at once as law-courts and places of assembly for tradesmen and money-
changers, and were generally composed of one immense hall, with lateral
galleries and tribunes adjoining it. The name of *basilica*, derived from the
Greek word *basileus* (a king), was given them, according to some writers,
from the fact that formerly the kings themselves used to administer justice
within their walls; according to others, because the basilica of Athens
served as a tribunal of the second archon, who bore the title of king;

Fig. 295.—Basilica of Constantine, at Trèves, transformed into a Fortress in the Middle Ages.

whence the edifice was called *stoa basiliké* (royal porch), a designation of
which the Romans preserved only the adjective, the substantive being
understood.

"The Christian basilica," says M. Vaudoyer, in his learned treatise on
architecture in France, "was most certainly an imitation of the heathen
basilica; but it is of importance to observe that from one cause or
another the Christians, in the construction of their basilicas, very soon
substituted for the Grecian architecture of the ancient basilicas a system of
arches reposing directly on isolated columns, which served as their supports;
a perfectly new contrivance, of which there existed no previous example.

This new mode of construction, which has generally been attributed to the want of skill in the builders of this period, or to the nature of the materials they had at their disposal, was, however, to become the fundamental principle of Christian art; a principle characterised by the breaking up of the range of arches, and by the abandonment of the system of rectilinear construction of the Greeks and Romans.

" Indeed, the arcade, which had become the dominant element of Roman architecture, had nevertheless remained subject to the proportions of the Greek orders, of which the entablature served as an indispensable accompaniment; and from this medley of elements so diverse was produced the mixed style which characterises the Greco-Roman architecture. But the Christians, in separating or breaking up the arcade, in abandoning the use of the ancient orders, and in making the column the real support of the arch, laid the foundations of a new style, which led to the exclusive employment of arches and vaults in Christian edifices. The Church of St. Sophia at Constantinople, built by Justinian in the middle of the sixth century, affords the most ancient example of this system of construction by arches and vaults in a Christian church of large dimensions."

Transported to the East, the Latin style there assumed a new character, owing especially to the adoption and generalisation of the cupola, of which there were some examples in Roman architecture, but only as an accessory; whereas, in what is called Byzantine architecture, this form became dominant, and, as it were, fundamental; thus, at all periods and at each time that the architectural influence of the East made itself felt in the West, we see the cupola introduced into buildings. The Church of St. Vital at Ravenna affords, in its plan (Fig. 296) and in its general appearance, an example of this influence, which is quite Byzantine.

Edifices of Latin architecture, properly so called, are rare, we might almost say that they have all disappeared (Figs. 297 and 298); but if some churches in Rome, whose foundation dates back to the fifth and sixth centuries, can be considered as specimens of this first period of Christian art, it is in the arrangement of the plan much more than in the details of execution, which for a long subsequent time since have been united with the work of later periods.

In the days when Christianity was so triumphantly established as to have no fear nor scruple to utilise, in the construction of its churches, the ruins of the ancient temples, it generally happened that the architect, conforming himself to new requirements, endeavoured, by a prudent return towards the traditions of the past, to avoid those striking incongruities which would have deprived of all their value the magnificent materials he had at his disposal. Hence arose a style still undecided; hence mixed creations, which it will suffice merely to mention. Then we must not forget—to say nothing of the case in

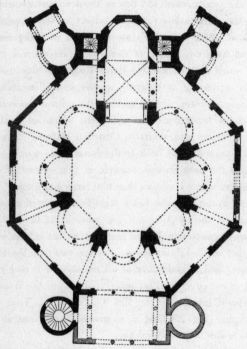

Fig. 296.—Church of St. Vital, at Ravenna. Byzantine style. (Sixth Century.)

which, as in the old Roman city, Christian basilicas might be built with the marble of heathen sanctuaries—the monuments of this same Rome were still the only models that presented themselves for imitation. Finally, for this architecture which the Christian religion was to create as its own, it was obvious there would be an infancy, an age of groping in the dark and of uncertainty; and at length that there should be a separation from the past, and a gradually experienced feeling of individual strength. (Fig. 299.)

This infancy lasted about five or six centuries; for it was only about
the year 1000 that the new style—which we see at first made up of "recollections" and weak innovations—assumed an almost determinate form.
This is the period called Norman,* which, according to M. Vaudoyer, has
left us some monuments that are "the noblest, the simplest, and the
severest expression of the Christian temple."

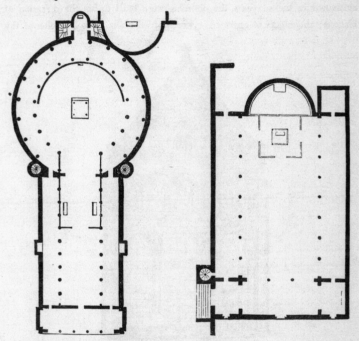

Fig. 297.—The Church of St. Agnes, at Rome, Latin
style (Fifth Century). Restored and debased in
the Seventeenth Century.

Fig. 298.—The Church of St. Martin, at Tours
(Sixth Century). Rebuilt or restored in the
Eleventh Century.

"Three years after the year 1000, which was supposed was to be the
last year of the world," says the monk Raoul Glaber, "churches were
renewed in nearly every part of the universe, especially in Italy and in Gaul,
although the greater number were still in a condition good enough to require

* M. Lacroix uses the word *Romane* throughout, with reference to this style of architecture:
we have adopted *Norman* as that most commonly associated with it, and because it is a generic term
comprehending Romanesque, Lombardic, and even Byzantine.—[ED.]

no repairs." "It was to this period, that is to say, the eleventh century," adds M. Vaudoyer, "must be assigned the greater number of the ancient churches of France, grander and more magnificent than all those of preceding centuries; it was then, also, the first associations of builders were formed, whereof the abbots and the prelates themselves formed a portion, and which were essentially composed of men bound by a religious vow; the Arts were cultivated in the convents, the churches were built under the direction of bishops; the monks co-operated in works of all kinds. . . . . The plan of the

Fig. 299.—Remains of the Church of Mouen, in Normandy. Architecture of the Fifth or Sixth Century.

Western churches preserved the primitive arrangement of the Latin basilica —that is, the elongated form and the lateral galleries; the most important modifications were the lengthening of the choir and of the galleries, or of the cross, a free passage established round the apse (Fig. 300); and, lastly, the combination of chapels, which grouped themselves around the sanctuary. In the construction the isolated columns of the nave are sometimes replaced by pillars, the spaces between which are filled up with semicircular arches, and a general system of vaulted roofs is substituted for the ceilings and timber roofs of the ancient Latin basilicas. . . . . The use of bells, which

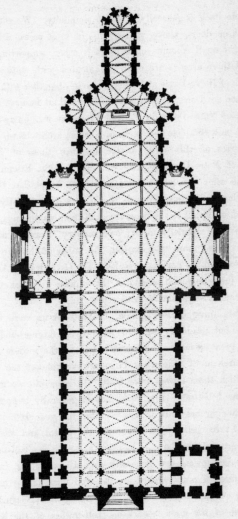

Fig. 300.—Notre-Dame, Rouen, ogival style. (Thirteenth Century.)

was but sparingly adopted in the East, contributed to give to the churches of the West a character and an appearance quite their own, and which they owe particularly to those lofty towers that had become the essential part of their façade."

The façade itself is generally of great simplicity. We enter the edifice by one or three doors, above which runs, in most cases, a little gallery formed of very small columns close to each other, supporting a range of arcades; and these arcades are often ornamented with statues, as we find in the church of Notre-Dame at Poitiers, which—together with the churches of Notre-Dame des Doms, at Avignon; of St. Paul, at Issoire; of St. Sernin, at Toulouse; of Notre-Dame du Port, at Clermont, &c.—may be considered as one of the most complete specimens of Norman architecture.

In churches of this style, as for instance those of St. Front, at Périgueux; of Notre-Dame, at Puy en Velay; of St. Etienne, at Nevers, are seen also some cupolas; but we must not forget that the Byzantine architects, whose migrations towards the West were constantly taking place at this period, could not fail to leave traces of their wanderings, and we must acknowledge that, especially in our own country (France), where Oriental influence was never more than partial, the union of the two architectonic principles produced the happiest results. The Cathedral of Angoulême, for example, is justly regarded as one of the edifices in which Oriental taste harmonises the best with the Norman style.

At the beginning of this period, the bell-towers were of very little importance; but gradually we find them rising higher and higher, and attaining to great elevations. Some cathedrals on the borders of the Rhine, and the Church of St. Etienne at Caen, are examples of the extraordinary height to which these towers were built. In principle, we may add, there was only one bell-tower (Fig. 301); but it generally happened that two were given to churches built or restored after the year 1000 : St. Germain-des-Prés had three bell-towers—one over the portal, and one at each side of the transept; certain churches had four and even five bell-towers.

Norman bell-towers are generally square, exhibiting, in stories, two or three ranges of round-arched arcades, and terminating in a pyramidal roof resting on an octagonal base. The Abbey of St. Germain d'Auxerre possesses one of the most remarkable bell-towers of the Norman style; then come, although built subsequently to the principal edifice, those of the Abbaye aux Hommes, at Caen.

The sun's rays penetrated into the Norman church first through the *oculus*,* a vast round opening intended to admit light into the nave, and

Fig. 301.—Ancient Church of St. Paul-des-Champs, at Paris, founded, in the Seventh Century, by St. Eloi. Restored and in part rebuilt in the Thirteenth Century.

situated above the façade, which generally rose in the form of a gable

* *Oculus* (eye).—This word is not known in the vocabulary of English architects; but it is evidently intended to signify a circular window.—[Ed.]

above one or several rows of small columns on the exterior. A series of
lateral windows opened on the side-aisles of the edifice; another was
pierced on a level with the galleries; and a third between the vaulted
arches of the nave.

The crypt, a sort of subterranean sanctuary, which generally contained
the tomb of some beatified saint, or of some martyr to whom the edifice was
dedicated, formed very often an integral part of the Norman church. The
architecture of the crypt, which had for its ideal object to recall to the mind
the period when the offices of the Christian religion were performed in
caverns and in catacombs, was generally of a massive and imposing severity,
well suited to express the sentiment which must have presided over the
earliest Christian buildings.

The Norman style, that is to say, the primitive idea of Christian
architecture, freed from its remaining servility to the antique, seems to
have caught a glimpse of the definitive formula of Christian art. Many a
majestic monument already attested the austere power of this style; and
perhaps a final and masterly inspiration would have sufficed, perfection
being attained, to cause the researches of the *maîtres d'œuvre*,* made
as they felt their way forward, to cease of themselves. Already, too, as
a sign of maturity, Norman edifices, instead of remaining in the somewhat
too unadorned simplicity of the first period, became gradually ornamented,
till in time they resembled, from their base to the summit, a delicate work
of embroidery. It is to this florid Norman style, which in France reigns
especially to the south of the Loire, that the charming façade of the Church
of Notre-Dame de Poitiers (Fig. 302) belongs, which we have already cited
as a perfect type of the Norman style itself; the façade of St. Trophimus, at
Arles (Figs. 303 and 304), an example in the general arrangement of
which the same character of original unity does not prevail; and that of
the Church of St. Gilles, which M. Mérimée cites as the most elegant
expression of the florid Norman.

In short, let us repeat it, the Norman style, grandiose in its austerity,
still quiet and compact even in its richest phantasy, was on the eve of
individualising for ever, perhaps, Christian architecture; its rounded arches,
uniting their full soft curves to the simple profiles of columns, robust even
in their lightness, seemed to characterise at one and the same time the

* Officers who had jurisdiction over, and were inspectors of, works of masonry and carpentry.

Fig. 302.—Notre-Dame la Grande of Poitiers (Twelfth Century).

elevated calm of hope and the humble gravity of faith. But lo! the *ogive* sprang up; not, indeed, as certain authors have thought they were right in affirming, from an outburst of spontaneous invention, for we find the principle and the application of it not only in many edifices of the Norman period, but even in the architectural contrivances of the most remote times. And it happened that this simple breaking up of the round arch, this "sharpness" of the arch, if we may use the expression, which the Norman builders had skilfully utilised, giving more of slenderness or graceful strength to vaults of great extent, became the fundamental element of a style which, in less than a century, was to shut the future to a tradition

Fig. 303.—Tympanum of the Portal of St. Trophimus, at Arles (Twelfth Century).

dating from six or eight centuries, and which could with justice pride itself on the most beautiful architectural conceptions. (Fig. 305.)

From the twelfth to the thirteenth century the transition took place. The Norman style, which is distinguished by its round arch, maintained the struggle with the Gothic style, of which the ogive is the original mark. In the churches of this period we find also, with regard to the ground-plan of edifices, the choir assuming larger dimensions, necessitated no doubt by increased ceremonials in the services. The Latin cross, which was the ground-plan whereon up to this time the greater number of sanctuaries were built, ceased to indicate as precisely as heretofore its outlines; the nave was raised considerably in height, the lateral chapels were multiplied, and often broke the perspective of the side-aisles; bell-towers assumed greater importance, and the placing of immense organs above the principal

Fig. 304.—Details of the Portal of St. Trophimus, at Arles. (Twelfth Century.)

entrance gave rise to a new system of elevated galleries in this part of the building.

The churches of St. Remy, Rheims; of the Abbey of St. Denis; of

St. Nicholas, Blois; the Abbey of Jumiéges; and the Cathedral of Châlons-sur-Marne, are the principal examples of the architecture of the mixed style.

It should be remarked that for a long while, in the north of France, the pointed arch had prevailed almost entirely over the round arch, at the time when, in the south, Norman tradition, blended with the Byzantine,

Fig. 305.—Cloister of the Abbey of Moissac, Guyenne. (Twelfth Century.)

still continued to inspire the builders. Nevertheless, the demarcation cannot be rigorously established, for, at the time when edifices of the purest Norman style showed themselves in our (French) northern counties (as, for example, the Church of St. Germain-des-Prés, and the apse of

DECORATION OF LA SAINTE CHAPELLE, PARIS.

Thirteenth Century.

St. Martin-des-Champs, Paris), we find, at Toulouse, at Carcassonne, at Montpellier, the most remarkable specimens of the Gothic style. At last Gothic architecture gained the day. "Its principle," says M. Vitet, "is in emancipation, in liberty, in the spirit of association and commerce, in sentiments quite indigenous and quite national : it is homely, and more than that, it is French, English, Teutonic, &c. Norman architecture, on the contrary, is sacerdotal."

And M. Vaudoyer adds : "The rounded arch is the determinate and invariable form ; the pointed arch is the free and indefinite form which lends itself to unlimited modifications. If, then, the Pointed style has no longer the austerity of the Norman, it is because it belongs to that second phase of all civilisation, in which elegance and richness replace the strength and the severity of primordial types."

It was, moreover, at this period that architecture, like all the other arts, left the monasteries to pass into the hands of lay architects organised into confraternities, who travelled from place to place, and thus transmitted the traditional types ; the result of this was that buildings raised at very great distances from each other presented a striking analogy, and often even a complete similitude to each other.

There has been much discussion not only on the origin of the pointed arch, but also as to the beauty and excellence of its form. According to some it was suggested by the sight of many arches interlaced, and only constituted one of those fantastical forms which an art in quest of novelty adopts ; others, among whom is M. Vaudoyer, attribute to it the most remote origin, by making it result quite naturally in the first attempts at building in stone,— "from a succession of courses of stone so arranged that each overhung the other ;" or else in wooden constructions, "from the greater facility there was in forming with beams a pointed rather than a perfectly rounded arch ;" others consider the adoption of the Pointed style, as we said above, as nothing but a proof of the religious independence succeeding the rigid faith of earlier days. A third opinion, again, is that of M. Michiels, who looks on the Pointed style as in some sort an inevitable result of the boldness of the Norman, and who considers the Gothic, of which it is the characteristic, as "expressing the spirit of a period when religious feeling had attained its most perfect maturity, and Catholic civilisation produced its sweetest and most agreeable fruits."

Fig. 306.—Mayence Cathedral. Rhenish Norman. (Twelfth and Thirteenth Centuries).

Whatever may be the merits of these different opinions, into the discussion of which we need not enter, it is now generally assumed that the Pointed style, properly so called, sprang up first within the limits of the ancient Ile-de-France, whence it propagated itself by degrees towards the southern and eastern provinces.

M. Michiels, agreeing on this point with the celebrated architect Lassus, points out that it would be as difficult to attribute the creation of this style to Germany as to Spain. It was in the thirteenth century that the finest Gothic buildings appeared in France; while in Germany, except the churches built, as it were, on the French frontier, we find nothing at that period but Norman churches (Fig. 306); and it is reasonable to suppose that, if we owed the general adoption of the pointed arch to Spain, the introduction of it would have been gradually made through that part of the country situated beyond the Loire, where, however, the Norman style continued to be in great favour when it was almost entirely abandoned in the north of France.

A century sufficed to bring the Pointed style to its highest perfection. Notre-Dame (Fig. 307) and the Sainte-Chapelle, in Paris; Notre-Dame, Chartres; the cathedrals of Amiens (Fig. 308), Sens, Bourges, Coutances, in France; those of Strasbourg, Fribourg, Altenberg, and Cologne, in Germany, the dates of whose construction succeed each other at intervals from the first half of the twelfth to the middle of the thirteenth century, are so many admirable specimens or types of this art, which we may here call relatively new.

To know to what marvellous variety of combinations and effects, by merely modifying it in height and breadth from its original type, this pointed arch, which, taken by itself, might appear the simplest of forms, can attain, one must have passed some time in dividing into the different parts of which it is composed, by an accurate examination of its *tout ensemble*, such an edifice as Notre-Dame, Paris, or as the Cathedral of Strasbourg; the first of which attracts attention by the sustained boldness of its lines, strong as they are graceful; the second, by its perfectly bold independence, seeming, as it does, to taper away as by enchantment, in order to bear to a surprising height the evidence of its incomprehensible temerity.

We must rise in thought above the edifice to grasp the plan of its first conception; we must, from below, study it on all sides to perceive

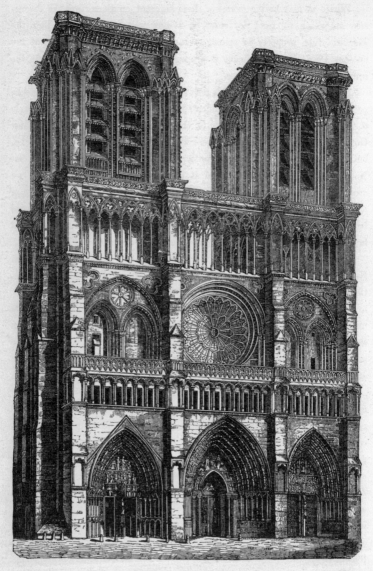

Fig. 307.—Notre-Dame, Paris (Twelfth and Thirteenth Centuries).
View of the principal Façade before the restoration executed by Messrs. Lassus and Viollet-le-Duc,

Fig. 308.—Interior of Amiens Cathedral   (Thirteenth Century.)

with what art its various parts are arranged, grouped, placed at certain
intervals from each other; we must seek to discover the contrivance by
virtue of which the immense *évidage* (sloping) of numerous buttresses, the
height of the towers, the retiring of the laterals, and the curve of the apse
are harmonised; we must enter the church and stand in its nave, with its
interminable delicate ribs—how many clusters of small columns extend
above the slender pillars!—we must contemplate the beautiful fancies of the
rose-windows, which by their many-coloured glass sober down the glare
of the light passing through them; we must gain the summit of those
towers, those spires, and from them command the dizzy extent of aërial

Fig. 309.—Capital of a Column in the Abbey of
St. Geneviève (destroyed), Paris.
(Eleventh Century.)

Fig. 310.—Capital of a Column in the Church of
St. Julien the Poor (destroyed), Paris.
(Twelfth Century.)

space, and the landscape stretching out around them below; we must follow
attentively with our eye the strikingly bold outlines which the turrets,
the ornamented gables, the *guivres*, the tops of the bell-towers trace upon
the sky.   This done, we should yet have paid but a brief tribute of
attention to these prodigious edifices.   What, then, if we wished to devote
sufficient time to the ornamentation of the details (Figs. 309 to 312)? if
we desired to obtain a tolerably exact idea of the people from the statues
which swarm from the porch to the pinnacle, and of the *flora* and *fauna*,
real or ideal, that give movement to every projection or animate every
wall? if one counted on success in finding out the key to all the crossings

and intersections of the lines, of the well-adjusted conceptions which, while they deceive the eye, contribute to the majesty or the solidity of the whole ? if, finally, we were most careful not to lose any one of the multifarious thoughts that have been fixed in the stones of the gigantic edifice ? The mind becomes confused ; and certainly the effect produced by so much imagination and so much enterprise, by so much skill and taste, wonderfully elevates the soul, which searches with more love after the Creator when it sees such a work proceeding from the hands of the creature.

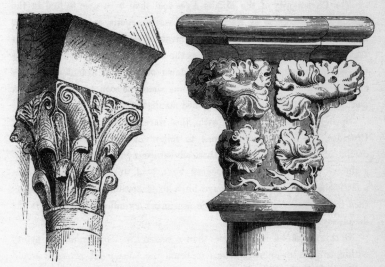

Fig. 311.—Vestige of the Architecture of the Goths at Toledo. (Seventh Century.)

Fig. 312.—Capital in the Church of the Célestins (destroyed), Paris. Fourteenth Century.

When you approach the Gothic church, when you stand beneath its lofty roof, it is as if a new country were receiving you, possessing you, casting around you an atmosphere of subduing reverie in which you feel your wretched servitude to worldly interests vanishing away, and you become conscious of more solid, more important ties, springing up in you. The Deity whom our finite nature can figure to ourselves seems in fact to inhabit this immense building, to be willing to put himself in direct communion with the humble Christian who approaches to bow down before Him. There is nothing in it of the human dwelling-place—all relating to our poor and miserable existence is here forgotten; He for whom this residence was constructed is the Strong, the Great, the Magnificent, and it is from a paternal condescension that He receives us into His holy habitation, as weak, little, miserable. It is the ideal of the faith which is realised; all the articles of the belief in which we have been brought up are here embodied before our eyes; it is, lastly, the chosen spot where the meeting of mortal nothingness and Divine Majesty is quietly accomplished.

The Christianity of the Middle Ages had then been able to find in the Gothic style a tongue as tractable as it was energetic, as simple as it was ingenious, which, for the pious excitement of souls, was to declare to the senses all its ineffable poetry. But as the unbounded faith, of which it was the faithful organ, was on the next dawn of its most ardent aspirations about to decline, so this splendid style was almost as soon to lose its vigour, and to exhaust itself in the unrestrained manifestation of its power.

Springing into existence with the warm enthusiasm of the first Crusades, the Pointed style seems to follow in its different phases the decline of faith in the time of these adventurous enterprises. It began by a sincere outburst, and was produced by a bold, unshackled genius; then a factitious or reflected ardour gave birth to elaborateness and mannerism; then the fervent zeal and the artistic sentiment dwindled away: this is the decadency.

Gothic art raised itself in less than a century to its culminating point; within two centuries more it was to reach the fatal point where it would begin to decline. The thirteenth century saw it in all its glory, with the edifices we have mentioned; in the fourteenth it had become the Florid or *Rayonnant* Gothic, which produced the churches of St. Ouen at Rouen, and of St. Etienne at Metz. "Then," says M. A. Lefèvre, one of the latest historians of architecture, "no more walls; everywhere open screen-work supported by slender arcades; no more capitals, rows of foliage imitated directly from nature; no more columns, lofty pillars ornamented with round or bevelled mouldings. As yet, however, there was nothing weakly in its extreme elegance; slim and delicate without being gaunt, the Florid style did not in the least disfigure the churches of the thirteenth century, which it bounded and decorated.

"But after the *Rayonnant* Gothic came the *Flamboyant*, which, always under the pretext of lightness and grace, denaturalises the ornaments, the forms, and even the proportions of the architectural members. It effaces the horizontal lines which used to give two stories to the windows of the nave, fills up the nave with irregular compartments, *cœurs, soufflets,* and *flammes;* suppresses the angles of the pillars, and sharpens the mouldings; leaves even to the most massive supports nothing but an undulating, vanishing, impalpable form, where shadow cannot fix itself; changes the lancet-arches into braces, or into flat-arched vaults more or less depressed, and the florid ornamentation of the pinnacles into whimsical scrolls. It reserved all its riches for accessory or exterior decorations, stalls, pulpits, hanging key-stones, running friezes, rood-screens, and bell-towers. Visible decadency of the whole corresponds with great progress in details." (Fig. 313.)

The churches of St. Wulfran, Abbeville; of Notre-Dame, Cléry-sur-Loire; of St. Riquier; of Corbiel; and the cathedrals of Orleans and of Nantes, may be cited as the principal specimens of the *Flamboyant* style, and as the last notable manifestations of an art which thenceforward diverged more and more from its original inspiration. The middle of the fifteenth century is generally fixed as the limit beyond which the handsome Gothic buildings that still rose were no longer, in any degree, the normal productions of their period, but were felicitous copies or imitations of works already consecrated by the history of the art.

A remark may here be made showing to what extent religious feeling predominated in the Middle Ages; it is that at the very moment when the Norman and Gothic architects were designing and producing so many marvellous habitations for the Deity, they seemed to bestow scarcely any attention on the construction of comfortable or luxurious dwellings for man, even those destined for the most exalted personages of the State. In proportion as this sentiment of original faith lost its intensity, art occupied itself more and more with princely and lordly habitations. The middle class was the last favoured by this progress, and the feeling of their position as citizens had taken the place of a zeal exclusively pious; so we find the "town-halls" absorbing the splendour and elegance of which private houses remained destitute; these being generally built of wood and plaster, and in the heart of the towns, so close together that they seemed to be disputing for light and air.

Fig. 313.—Saloon of the Schools, Oxford. (Fourteenth Century.)

Everywhere, during the Middle Ages, rose the church—the home of peace; but everywhere also towered up at the same time the castle, that characterised the permanent state of war in which feudal society lived, delighted, and gloried.

"The castles of the richest and most powerful nobles," says M. Vaudoyer, "consisted of irregular, uncomfortable buildings, pierced with a few narrow windows, standing within one or two fortified enclosures, and surrounded by moats. The donjon, a large high tower, generally occupied the centre,

Fig. 314.—Ancient Castle of Marcoussis, near Rambouillet. (Thirteenth Century.)

and other towers, more or less numerous, flanked the walls, and served for the defence of the place." (Fig. 314.) "These castles," adds M. Mérimée, "generally present the same characteristics as the ancient *castellum;* but a certain ruggedness a striking quaintness in plan and execution, bear witness to a personal will, and that tendency to isolation which is the instinctive sentiment of the feudal system."

In most of the buildings destined for the privileged classes, it seems as if it were deemed unnecessary that care should be taken to secure harmony

of form. The decorative style of the period showed itself chiefly in the
interior of some of the principal apartments, the habitable quarters of
the lord of the castle and of his family. There were vast fireplaces with
enormous chimney-corners surmounted by projecting mantelpieces; the
vaulted roof was ornamented with pendents of various devices, and with
painted or carved escutcheons. Narrow closets, contrived in the walls,
served as sleeping-places. The embrasures of the windows pierced in the
excessively-thick walls formed so many little chambers, raised a few steps
above the floor of the room to which they admitted light. Stone seats ran
along each side of these embrasures. Here the inmates of the tower

Fig. 315.—Staircase of a Tower. Fig. 316.—Pointed Window with Stone Seats.
(Thirteenth Century.)

generally sat when the cold did not oblige them to draw near to the
fireplaces. (Figs. 315 and 316.)

With the exception of these slight sacrifices made to the comforts of
life, everything in the castle was arranged, contrived, and disposed with a
view to strength and resistance; and yet it cannot be denied that,
unintentionally, the builders of these silent (*taciturnes*) edifices have many a
time—aided often, it is true, by the picturesque sites which encircle their
works—attained to a majesty of height and a grandeur of form truly
extraordinary.

If the Norman church expresses with gentle severity, and the Gothic

church with sumptuous fancy, the important and sublime doctrines of
the Gospel, we must equally allow that the castle, in some sort, loudly
proclaims the stern and uncivilised notions of the feudal authority of which
it was at once the instrument and the symbol.

Placed, in most cases, on natural or artificial eminences, it is not with-

Fig. 317.—The Castle of Coucy in its ancient state.
(From a Miniature taken from a Manuscript of the Thirteenth Century.)

out a sort of eloquent boldness that the towers and the donjons shoot into
the air, succeed each other at intervals, command and support each other.
It is frequently not without a sort of fantastic grace that the walls scale
the rising ground, making an infinity of the strangest bends, or coiling
themselves about with the supple ease of a serpent.

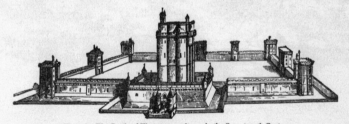

Fig. 318.—The Castle of Vincennes, as it was in the Seventeenth Century.

Evidently, if the castle raises its gloomy head high into the air, it has no
other object in doing so than to secure to itself the advantages of distance
and height; but not the less on that account does it stand out on the sky
a grand object. The masses of its walls unsymmetrically pierced with
sombre loop-holes present an abrupt and naked appearance; but the mono-

tony of their lines is picturesquely broken by the projection of overhanging turrets, by the corbels of the machicolated arches, and by the embrasures of the battlements.

A vast amount of civilisation still exists for him who recalls the past in the multitude of ruins which were the witnesses of bloody feudal divisions; and we must add to the system of isolated castles that often commanded

Fig. 319.—Tour de Nesle, which occupied the site of the Exchange on the banks of the Seine, Paris.
(From an Engraving of the Seventeenth Century.)

the most deserted valleys, the apparatus of strength and defence of cities and towns—gates, ramparts, towers, citadels, &c., immense works which, although inspired solely by the genius of strife and dissension, did not fail nevertheless, in many instances, to combine harmony and variety of detail with the general grandeur of the whole.

We may cite, as examples of architecture purely feudal, the castles of

Coucy (Fig. 317), Vincennes (Fig. 318), Pierrefonds, the old Louvre, the Bastille, the Tour de Nesle (Fig. 319), the Palais de Justice, Plessis-les-Tours, &c. ; and as specimens of the fortified town in the Middle Ages, Avignon and the city of Carcassonne. Let us add that Aigues-Mortes, in Provence; Narbonne, Thann (Haut-Rhin), Vendôme, Villeneuve-le-Roi, Moulins, Moret (Fig. 320), Provins (Fig. 321), afford yet again the most characteristic remains of analogous fortifications.

While the nobles, jealous and suspicious, sheltered themselves in the

Fig. 320.—Gate of Moret. (Twelfth Century.)

shadow of their donjons built with many strategetical contrivances and of substantial materials; while the large and small towns were surrounded with deep moats, high walls, impregnable towers, the most primitive simplicity presided over the construction of private dwellings. Stone hardly ever, and brick but seldom, figured among the number of the materials employed. Sawed or squared timbers serving as ribs, mud or clay filling up the interstices, were all that was at first required for the erection of houses as small as they were comfortless, and following each other in irregular lines along the narrow streets. The beams of the corbels, it is true, began to be adorned with carvings and paintings, the façades with panes (glass) of different colours; but we must reach the last half of the fifteenth century before we see the resources of architecture applied to the erection and ornamentation of private houses. Moreover, faith was already growing weak; and no longer was it possible to direct all the resources of an entire province to the honour of the Deity by the erection of a church; the use of gunpowder, by revolutionising the art of war, came to lessen, if it did not annihilate, the vast strength of walls; the decline of

Fig. 321.—Gate of St. John, with Drawbridge, Provins. (Fourteenth Century.)

feudalism itself had commenced; and, lastly, the enfranchisement of corporations gave rise to a perfectly new order of individuals who took their place in history. We must refer to this period the house of Jacques Cœur, Bourges; the Hôtel de Sens, Paris (Fig. 322); the Palais de Justice, Rouen; and those town-halls in which the belfry was then considered as a sort of palladium, in whose shade the sacred rights of the community sheltered themselves. It is in our (French) northern towns—St. Quentin, Arras, Noyon; and in the ancient cities of Belgium—Brussels (Fig. 323), Louvain, Ypres, that these edifices assume the most sumptuous character.

In Germany, where for a time it reigned almost exclusively, Gothic art established the cathedrals of Erfurt, of Cologne, Fribourg, and of Vienna ; then it died away in the growth of the *Flamboyant* style. In England, after having left some magnificent examples of pure inspiration, it found its decline in the attenuated meagreness and the complicated ornamentation of the style called *Perpendicular ogival.* If it penetrated also into Spain, it was to contend with difficulty against the mighty Moorish school, which had too many imposing *chefs-d'œuvre* in the past to surrender without resistance the country of its former triumphs. (Fig. 324.) In Italy it clashed not only with the Latin and Byzantine schools, but also with a style that, just beginning to form itself, was soon to dispute with it the empire of taste,

Fig. 322.—Doorways of the Hôtel de Sens, at Paris ; the last remaining portion of the Hôtel Royal de Saint-Pol, built in the reign of Charles V. (Fourteenth Century.)

and to dethrone it in that very land which had been its cradle. The cathedrals of Assisi, of Siena, of Milan, are the splendid works in which its influence triumphed over local traditions and over the *Renaissance* that was preparing to follow ; yet we must not think that it succeeded even there in rendering itself absolutely the master, as it had done on the Rhenish or British territories. Sacrifices were made in its favour ; but these sacrifices did not amount to an entire immolation.

When we use the word *Renaissance*, we seem to be speaking of a return to an age already gone by, of the resurrection of a period that had passed

away. It is not strictly in this sense that the word must be understood
in the present instance.

Inheriting from of old the artistic temperament of Greece, rather than

Fig. 323.—Belfry of Brussels (Fifteenth Century), from an engraving or the Seventeenth Century.

spontaneously creating of herself any style, Italy, among all the nations of
Europe, was the country which had most successfully resisted the profound

Fig. 324.—Interior of the Palace of the Alhambra, at Granada. (Thirteenth Century.)

darkness of barbarism, and the first on which the light of modern civilisation shone.

At the period of this new dawn of genius, Italy had only to ransack the ruins its first magnificence had bequeathed it to find among them examples it might follow; moreover, it was the time when the active rivalry of its republics caused all the treasures of ancient Greece to flow into it. But while it derived inspiration from these abundant manifestations of another age, it never entertained the idea of abandoning itself exclusively to a servile imitation; it had—and in this consists its chief title to glory—while giving a peculiar direction to the revivals of the antique, the good sense to remain under the poetic influence of that simple and congenial art which had consoled the world during the whole continuance of that protracted infancy of a civilisation which was at last advancing with rapid strides towards perfect manhood.

From the twelfth century, Pisa gave an impetus to the art by building its Duomo, its Baptistery, its Leaning Tower, and the cloisters of its famous Campo Santo; so many admirable works forming an era in the history of modern art, and in a brilliant manner opening the career on which so many distinguished men were to enter, rivalling each other in invention, in science, and in genius. In these monuments the union of Oriental taste with the traditions of ages gone by created an originality as grand as it was graceful. " It is," as M. A. Lefèvre points out, "the Antique without its nudity, the Byzantine without its heaviness, the fervour of the Western Gothic without its ghastliness " (effroi).

In 1294 the magistrates of Florence passed the following decree, charging the architect, Arnolfo di Cambio, to convert into a cathedral the church, till then of little importance, of Santa Maria de' Fiori :—" Forasmuch," they said, "as it is in the highest degree prudent for a people of illustrious origin to proceed in their affairs in such manner that their public works may cause their grandeur and wisdom to be acknowledged, the order is given to Arnolfo, master-architect of our town, to make plans for repairing the Church of Santa Maria with the greatest and most lavish magnificence, so that the skill and prudence of men may never invent, nor ever be able to undertake, anything more important or more beautiful."

Arnolfo applied himself to his task, and conceived a plan which the shortness of human life did not allow him to carry out; but Giotto succeeded

Fig. 325.—Interior of the Basilica of St. Peter's, Rome.

him, and to Giotto succeeded Orcagna, and to Orcagna, Brunelleschi, who designed and almost completed that Duomo, of which Michael Angelo said it would be difficult to equal, and impossible to surpass, it.

Arnolfo, Giotto, Orcagna, Brunelleschi—does it not suffice to cite these great names for us to form an idea of the movement going on at this period? and which was soon to produce Alberti, Bramante, Michael Angelo, Jacques della Porta, Baldassare Peruzzi, Antonio and Juliano de Sangallo, Giocondo, Vignola, Serlio, and even Raphael, who, when he liked, was as mighty an architect as he was a marvellous painter. It was in Rome that these princes of the art congregated together, as the splendours of St. Peter's (Fig. 325), to mention only one of their grand creations, still attest; so, it is from this city that henceforward light and example are to come.

In the style which this masterly phalanx created, the Latin rounded arch regained all its ancient favour, and united itself to the ancient orders, which became intermingled, or at any rate, superposed. The ogive was abandoned, but the columns to decorate their capitals, and the entablatures to give more grace to their projections, borrowed a certain fantastical style which yielded in nothing to the ogival; the Grecian pediment reappeared, changing sometimes the upper lines of its triangle into a depressed semi-circle; lastly the cupola, that striking object which was the characteristic feature of the Byzantine style, became the dome, whose ample curve defied, in the daring heights whereto it rose, the wonders of the Perpendicular Gothic.

The Italian *Renaissance* was now accomplished, the Gothic age at an end. Rome and Florence sent in every direction their architects, who, as they travelled far from these metropolises of the new style, were once more subjected to certain territorial influences, but who knew how to make the tradition of which they were the apostles triumphant. It was then that France inaugurated in its turn a Renaissance peculiar to herself; it was then that, under the reign of Charles VIII., after his expedition into Italy, began, with the Château de Gaillon, a long succession of edifices, which in many cases yielded neither in richness nor in majesty to the works of the preceding period. Under Louis XII. rose the Château de Blois, and the Hôtel de la Cour des Comptes, Paris, a splendid building destroyed by fire in the eighteenth century. Under Francis I., Chambord (Fig. 326), Fontainebleau, Madrid (near Paris), magnificent royal "humours," contended in elegance and grace with the châteaux of Nantouillet, Chenonceaux, and

Fig. 326.—Château de Chambord, with its Ancient Moat. (Seventeenth Century.)

Azai-le-Rideau; and with the manor-house of Ango, near Dieppe, all sumptuous, lordly mansions; the old Louvre, the palace of kings, the cradle of monarchy, was regenerated under the care of Peter Lescot; the Hôtel de Ville, Paris, still bears witness to the varied talent of Dominique Cortona, who, as M. Vaudoyer said of him, "justly understood that, in building for France, he should act in a perfectly different manner to that in which he would have acted in Italy." Under Henry II. and Charles IX. this activity continued, and the architects who sought their inspirations in Grecian and Roman antiquity, as much as in the *souvenirs* of the Italian Renaissance, delighted in loading all the elegant and graceful buildings with ornaments, with bas-reliefs, and with statues, which they seemed to carve in the stone, as delicately wrought as a piece of goldsmith's work. Philibert

Fig. 327.—Porte de Hal, Brussels. (Fourteenth Century.)

Delorme built for Diana of Poitiers the Château d'Anet, that architectural jewel whose portico, transported piece by piece at the time of the revolutionary disorders, now decorates the court of the Ecole des Beaux-Arts; Jean Bullant built Ecouen for the Constable Anne de Montmorency; and the architect d'Anet undertook, by order of Catherine de Medicis, the construction of the Palace of the Tuileries, which, by a sort of exigency resulting from its particular destination, seemed typically to characterise the style of the French Renaissance.

We must not burden with details this summary of one of the most important branches of art. The history of architecture is among those vast domains which demand either a short epitome or a thoroughly deep investigation. The epitome being alone consistent with the plan of our work, we must confine ourselves to its limits; but we may, perhaps, be allowed to think that the few rapid pages thus devoted to the subject have inspired the reader with the desire of penetrating farther into a study which is capable of offering him so many agreeable surprises, so many rational delights.

PARCHMENT AND PAPER.

Parchment in Ancient Times.—Papyrus.—Preparation of Parchment and Vellum in the Middle Ages.—Sale of Parchment at the Fair of Lendit.—Privilege of the University of Paris on the Sale and Purchase of Parchment.—Different Applications of Parchment.—Cotton Paper imported from China.—Order of the Emperor Frederick II. concerning Paper.—The Employment of Linen Paper dating from the Twelfth Century.—Ancient Water-Marks on Paper. —Paper Manufactories in France and other parts of Europe.

ALTHOUGH most authors who speak of parchment attribute the invention of it, on the testimony of Pliny, to Eumenius, king of Pergamus (doubtlessly from the etymology of the word by which it was designated, viz., *Pergamena*), it seems to be proved, according to Peignot, that the use of it is much more ancient, and that its origin is utterly lost. Certainly, in many passages of the Old Testament we find a Hebrew word, in Latin *volumen*, which can only be understood to mean a roll formed of prepared skin or of the leaves of papyrus, and it is consequently evident that the Jews, from the time of Moses, wrote the tables of the Law on rolls of parchment.

Herodotus says that the Ionians called books *diphthera* (διφθέρα, a prepared hide), because, at a time when the *biblos* (βίβλος, the inner bark of the papyrus) was scarce, they wrote on skins of goats or of sheep. Diodorus Siculus affirms that the ancient Persians wrote their annals on skins, and we must suppose that Pliny's assertion refers only to some improvements the King of Pergamus had made in the art of preparing a material that could supply the place of papyrus, which Ptolemy Epiphanius would no longer allow to leave Egypt. The absolute deficiency of papyrus raised into activity the fabrication of parchment, and soon so large a quantity was seen to flow into Pergamus that this town was considered as the cradle of the new trade, already so flourishing. There were then books of two kinds:

the one in rolls composed of many leaves sewed together, on one side of which only was there writing; the others, square-shaped, were written upon both sides. The grammarian Crates, ambassador of Eumenius at Rome, passed as the inventor of vellum.

Ordinary parchment is the skin of a goat, sheep, or lamb, prepared in lime, dressed, scraped, and rendered smooth by pumice-stone. Its principal qualities are whiteness, thinness, and stiffness; but the work of the currier must have been formerly very imperfect, for Hildebert, Archbishop of Tours in the eleventh century, tells us that the writer, before beginning his occupation, "was in the habit of clearing away from the parchment, with the aid of a razor, the remains of fat and other gross impurities, and then with pumice-stone to make the hair and tendons disappear:" this almost amounts to affirming that the scribes bought the hide undressed, and, by an elaborate preparation, made them fit for proper use. Virgin parchment, which in its grain and colour resembles vellum, was made of the skins of those lambs and goats which had been clipped. Vellum, more polished, whiter, more transparent, is made, as its name indicates, of the hide of the calf.*

It is probable that with the Romans, papyrus, considering the facility they had of procuring it for themselves, was more frequently used than parchment, which, at first, was rare and costly. But parchment, more durable and of greater resistance than papyrus, was reserved for the transcription of the most important works. Cicero, who had many books on parchment in his magnificent library, said that he had seen the "Iliad" copied on a scroll of *pergamena* which went into a nut-shell. Many of Martial's epigrams prove to us that in the time of this poet books of such kind were still more numerous. Unfortunately, there remains to us no writing on parchment dating from this distant period. The Virgil in the Vatican, and the Terence at Florence, are of the fourth and fifth century of our era. Admitting that time destroys all, and also that the work of the rude tribes on many occasions assisted this natural cause of destruction, we must not forget that at certain periods, to supply the place of new parchment when it was scarce, a plan had been devised of making the parchment rolls which had already been used for manuscripts serve again

---

* The word is derived from *vellus*, which merely signifies the skin of any beast, not of a calf only.—[ED.]

Fig. 328.—Miniature of the Ninth Century, representing an Evangelist who is transcribing with the *Calamus*,
on Parchment, the Sacred Text, of which he is receiving the revelation.
(Bibl. de Bourgogne, Brussels.)

for a similar purpose, either by scraping and rubbing them with pumice-stone, or by boiling them in water or soaking in lime. There is no doubt but the scarceness and the dearness of parchment was the cause of the loss of very many excellent works. Muratori cites, for example, a manuscript of the Ambrosian Library, of which the writing, dating from eight or nine centuries back, had been substituted for another of more than a thousand years old; and Maffei informs us that the employment of ancient parchment scraped and washed became so general, in the fourteenth and fifteenth

Fig. 329.—View of the Ancient Abbey of St. Denis and its Dependencies.

centuries, throughout Germany, that the Emperors put a stop to this dangerous abuse by issuing an order to the notaries to use nothing but parchment "quite new."

Generally, the quality of parchment serves to determine the date of its manufacture. The vellum of manuscripts till the middle of the eleventh century is very white and thin; the parchment of the twelfth century is thick, rough, and brownish, which often shows it has been scraped or washed. The greater number of fine manuscripts are on virgin parchment, which from its nature was suited to the delicacies of calligraphy and illumination. Moreover, we see from a statute of the University of Paris, dated 1291, that the parchment trade had attained at that period to considerable development; so, as a protection against the frauds and deceptions which might result from the great competition of traders in it, and to insure a good article being furnished to students and artists, a special privilege was granted to the university, which,

Fig. 330.—Seal of the University of Paris (Fourteenth Century), after one of the Dies preserved in the Collection of Medals in the Imperial Library, Paris.

in the person of its rector, had not only the right of inspection, but also the refusal of all parchment bought in Paris, no matter whence it had come. Besides which, at the fair of Lendit, which was held every year at Saint-Denis, on the domains of the abbey (Fig. 329), and at the fair of Saint-Lazare, the rector likewise caused the parchment brought to them to be examined, and the merchants of Paris could not purchase any till the king's agents, those of the Bishop of Paris, and the masters and scholars of the university had provided themselves with what they required (Fig. 330). Let us add that the rector was paid a duty on all parchment sold, and the result of this tax was the only source of income attached to the rectorship in the seventeenth century.

Although white parchment seems to be the best suited for writing, the Middle Ages, following the example of antiquity, gave to the material various tints, especially purple and yellow. The purple was chiefly intended to receive characters of gold or silver. The Emperor Maximinius, the younger, inherited from his mother the works of Homer inscribed in gold on purple vellum; and parchment tinted in this way was, during the first centuries, one of the prerogatives reserved for princes and the great dignitaries of the Church. It is remarkable that the barbarism of the seventh and eighth centuries did not diminish the favour in which these luxurious manuscripts were held. Little by little, however, the custom (of writing the entire work in gold or colours) dwindled away. Scribes began by colouring a few pages only in each volume, then some margins or frontispieces; and lastly this decoration was restricted to the heads of chapters, or to words to which great prominence was to be given, or to capital letters. The *rubricatores* (literally, writers in red), workmen who performed this operation, came in time to be mere painters of letters or *rubrics* (so called because they were originally painted red), of whose assistance, however, the first printers availed themselves to *rubric* or colour the initials of missals, Bibles, and law books.

The dimensions or sizes of our books at the present day have their origin in the sizes of the parchment in olden times. The entire skin of the animal, cut square and folded in two, represented the "in-folio," which, moreover, varied in length and breadth; and we have every reason to suppose that paper, from the day it was invented, followed the ordinary sizes of the folded parchment.

As to the dimensions of the parchment employed for diplomas, they varied according to the time, the brevity of the matter, or the nature of its employment. Among the ancients, who wrote only on one side of the parchment, the skins were cut in bands joined together so as to form *volumes*, or rolls, which were unrolled as their contents were read. This custom was preserved for public and judicial acts for a long time after the invention of the square book (*codex*) had caused the *opisthographic* writing to be adopted, by which is to be understood writing on both sides of the page. In principle, only the final formulæ, or the signatures, were written on the back of the document. By degrees people adopted the practice of writing on the back as well as the front of the page; but it was not till the sixteenth century that this custom became general.

Judicial acts, composed sometimes of many skins sewed together, came in time to form rolls of twenty feet in length; to such extreme proportions did they reach, though at first they were so small in size that their limited dimensions are truly incredible; for in 1233 and 1252 we find contracts of sales of two inches long by five inches wide, and in 1258 a

Fig. 331.—Seal of the King of La Basoche. (This title was suppressed, with all its prerogatives, by Henry III.)

will written on a piece of parchment of two inches by three and a half· It was by way of compensating for the great cost of parchment that opisthographic writing was adopted and rolls were put aside; and the name alone remains as applied to the *rolls* of procedure. The size that leaves should assume was also fixed, according to the different uses for which they were intended. For instance, the leaves of parliamentary documents were nine inches and a half long by seven and a half wide; those of the council, ten by eight; those of finance and of private contracts, twelve and a half by nine and a half; letters of pardon, under the king's hand, were to be on entire skins squared, two feet two inches by one foot eight inches in diameter.

But while the use of parchment was still strictly employed in the chancellor's offices and the tribunals, where the *basoche* (a brotherhood of lawyers of all grades) considered it as one of their most lucrative privileges (Fig. 331), it had for a long while ceased to be used anywhere else. Paper, after having during many centuries competed with parchment, at last almost entirely replaced it (Fig. 332); for if less durable, it had the great

Fig. 332.—The Paper-Maker, drawn and engraved in the Sixteenth Century by J. Amman.

advantage of costing much less. Formerly nothing but the ancient papyrus of Egypt was known, and it was made use of concurrently with parchment till there was brought into Europe, towards the tenth century, cotton paper, which is generally believed to be a Chinese invention, and which was at first called *Grecian parchment*, because the Venetians, who introduced it into the West, had found it in use in Greece.

Actually, this paper was at first of a very inferior quality, coarse, spongy, dull, and subject to the attacks of damp and worms; so much so that the Emperor Frederick II. issued, in 1221, an order declaring null and void all documents written on it, and fixing the term at two years by which all were to be transcribed on parchment.

The use and the knowledge of the process of manufacturing paper from cotton soon led to the fabrication of paper from linen or rags. It is, however, impossible to say when and where it was accomplished—the

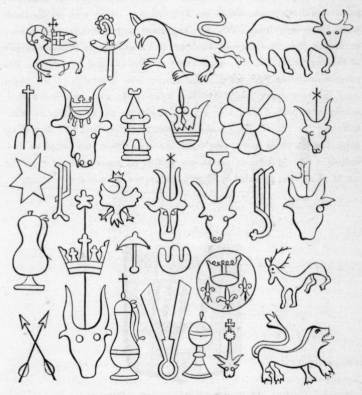

Fig. 333.—Water-Marks on Paper, from the Fourteenth to the Fifteenth Century.

assertions and the testimonies on this point are so contradictory. Some think that the paper was brought from the East by the Spanish Saracens; others say it came from China; these affirm it has been employed since the tenth century; those, that we can only find specimens of it as far back as the reign of St. Louis.

At any rate, the most ancient writing on paper made of rags known at
the present day is a letter from Joinville to Louis X., dated 1315; we
may, moreover, mention with certainty, as written on linen paper, an
inventory of goods belonging to a certain Prior Henry, who died in 1340,
which is preserved at Canterbury, and many authentic writings, dating back
as far as 1335, preserved in the British Museum, London. The first
paper-manufactory established in England was, it is said, at Hertford,
which dates only from 1588; but important paper-manufactories existed
in France from the reign of Philippe de Valois, that is, from the middle
of the fourteenth century; particularly at Essonne and at Troyes. The
paper which came from these manufactories bore generally, in the paper
itself, different marks (Fig. 333) called water-marks, such as a bull's head,
a cross, a serpent, a star, a crown, &c., according to the quality or destination of the paper. Many other countries in Europe had also flourishing
paper-manufactories in the fourteenth century. From this period we find,
indeed, a large number of documents written on paper made of rags, the
use of which thus preceded by about a century the invention of printing.

Fig. 334.—Banner of the Paper-Makers of Paris.

MANUSCRIPTS.

ET the reader refer to the chapters on PARCHMENT and BINDING, and he will find a few remarks on the purely material part of manuscripts; we may, then, here treat this question very summarily; and for that purpose we shall avail ourselves of the remarkable work of J. J. Champollion-Figeac.

When writing was once invented, and had passed into general use in civilised society, the choice of substances suited for its reception, and to fix it in a durable manner, was very diversified, although depending on the nature of the text to be written.

People wrote on stone, on metals, on the bark and leaves of many kinds of trees, on dried or baked clay, on wood, on ivory, wax, linen, the hides of quadrupeds, on parchment, the best of these preparations; on papyrus, which is the inner bark of a reed growing in the Nile; then on paper made of cotton; and lastly, on paper made from hemp and flax, called rag paper. The Roman world had adopted the use of papyrus, which was a very important branch of commerce at Alexandria. We find proof of this in the writers of antiquity: St. Jerome bears witness to it as far as regards the fifth century of our era. The Latin and Greek emperors gave their diplomas on papyrus. Popes traced their most ancient bulls upon it. The charters of the kings of France of the first race were also issued on papyrus. From the eighth century parchment contended with papyrus; a little later cotton paper also became its competitor, and the eleventh century is generally fixed on as the period when papyrus was entirely superseded by the new materials appropriated to the preservation of writing.

For writing on papyrus the brush or reed was employed, with inks of different colours; black ink was, however, most generally used. There grew on the banks of the Nile, at the time when the reed furnished papyrus, another sort of reed, stiffer and also more flexible, and admirably suited for the manufacture of the *calamus*, an instrument supplying the place of the pen, which was not adopted before the eighth century.

The size of manuscripts was in no way subject to fixed rules, there were volumes of all dimensions; the most ancient on parchment are, in general, longer than they are broad, or else are square; the writing rests on a line traced with the dry point of the *calamus*, and afterwards with black-lead; the parts making up a volume are composed of an indeterminate number of leaves; a word or a figure, placed at the bottom of the last page of each part and at the end of the volume, serves as a *catchword* from one fasciculus to another.

The emperors of Constantinople used to sign in red ink the acts of their sovereignty; their first secretary was the guardian of the vase containing the cinnabar (vermilion), which the emperor alone might use. Some diplomas of the kings of France of the second race are signed in the same manner. In valuable manuscripts, great use was made of golden ink, especially when the parchment was dyed purple; but red ink was almost always employed for capital letters or for the titles of books, and for a long time after the invention of printing the volumes still had the *rubrics* (*ruber*, red) painted or beautifully executed with the pen.

The greater number of rich manuscripts, even when they contained the text of some ancient secular author, were destined to be presented to the treasuries of churches and abbeys, and these offerings were not made without great display: the book, whatever its contents might be, was placed on the altar, and a solemn mass was celebrated on the occasion; moreover, an inscription at the end of the work mentioned the homage which had been paid for it to God and to the saints in paradise.

We must not forget that in this time of almost universal ignorance, the Church was the only depository of literature and science; she sought after those heathen authors who could instruct her in eloquence that might be employed in advancing the faith, almost as much as she sought for sacred books; it was not rare even to see Christian zeal exalting itself so far as to find prophets of the Messiah in writers very anterior to the doctrines of Christ. Thus the best Greek and Latin manuscripts of profane authors are the work of monks, as were the Bibles and the writings of the Fathers of the Church. The rules of the most ancient brotherhoods recommended the monks who could write and who wished to please God to re-copy the manuscripts, and those who were illiterate to learn to bind them. "The work of the copyist," said the learned Alcuin to his contemporaries, "is a meritorious work, which is profitable to the soul, while the work of the ploughman is profitable only to the belly."

At all periods of history we find mention made of certain celebrated manuscripts. We will not go so far back as the Greek traditions relating to the works of Homer, of which some copies were ornamented with a richness that has, probably, never been surpassed. In the fifth century St. Jerome possessed twenty-five parts of the works of Origen, which Pamphilus the Martyr had copied with his own hand. St. Ambrose, St. Fulgentius, Hincmar, Archbishop of Rheims, men as learned as they were pious, applied themselves to reproducing with their own hands the best ancient texts. A copyist by profession was called *scriba, scriptor ;* the place in which they generally worked was called *scriptorium.* The capitularies against bad copyists were frequently renewed. "We ordain that no scribe write incorrectly," we find in the collection of Baluze. We read in the same collection, in 789, "There shall be good Catholic texts in all monasteries, so that prayers shall not be made to God in faulty language." In 805, "If the Gospels, the Psalter, or the Missal are to be copied, only careful middle-aged men are to be employed : verbal errors may otherwise be introduced into the faith." There were, moreover, *correctors* who rectified the work of the copyists, and attested the work, on the volumes, by the words *contuli, emendavi* ("I have collated, I have revised "). A copy of Origen's works has been mentioned, corrected by the hand of Charlemagne himself, to whom is also attributed the introduction of full stops and commas.

The same care presided over the preparation of royal charters and diplomas ; the referendaries or chancellors drew them up and superintended their despatch ; the principal officers of the crown intervened, as guarantors or witnesses to them, and these acts were read publicly before they were signed and sealed. Notaries and witnesses guaranteed the authenticity of private charters.

As long as printing did not exist in France, the corporation of scribes, copyists of charters, and copyists of manuscripts, which counted among them booksellers, was very numerous and very influential, since it was composed of graduates of the university that patronised them and placed them among the number of its indispensable agents. He who desired to become a bookseller had to give proof of his instruction and of his ability ; he was obliged to take an oath " not to commit any deception, fraud, or evil thing which might damage or prejudice the university, its scholars and frequenters, nor to rob nor speak ill of them." Besides which he was compelled to deposit a sum of fifty francs (*livres parisis*) as caution-money.

The rules imposed on scribes and on booksellers were always very strict, and this severity was only too justly occasioned by the abuses that existed, and by the scandalous disorder of the people who exercised these professions. In the year 1324 the university published this order :—" There will be admitted only people of good conduct and morals, sufficiently acquainted with the book trade, and previously approved by the university. The book-seller may not take a clerk into his service till that clerk has sworn, before the university, to exercise his profession according to the ordinances. The bookseller must give to the university a list of the works which he sells ; he must not refuse to let a manuscript to whomsoever may wish to make a copy of it, on payment of the indemnity fixed by the university. He is forbidden to let out books that have not been corrected, and those students who find an incorrect copy are requested to denounce it publicly to the rector, so that the bookseller who has let it out may be punished, and that the copy may be corrected by *scholares* (learned men or scholars). There shall be every year four commissioners chosen to fix the price of books. One bookseller shall not sell a work to another bookseller before he has exposed the work for sale during four days. In any case the seller is obliged to register the name of the purchaser, to describe him, and to state the price for which the book was sold."

From century to century this legislation underwent variations, according to the ideas of the times : and when the printing-press came, in the middle of the fifteenth century, to change the face of the world, the corporation of *scribes* rose at first against the new art which was to ruin them. " But at last," says Champollion-Figeac, " they submitted, and temporary measures were recommended to the public authorities for the defence of an ancient order of things which could not long resist the new."

Now let us go back to the first centuries of the Middle Ages, to resume the question from a palæographic point of view.

The languages and literature of modern Europe are all Greek or Latin, Sclavonic or Gothic ; these four great families of peoples and of languages have existed in spite of the vicissitudes of politics. Such is the basis whereon must be found all the researches by which we are to establish the origin and nature of the writing peculiar to each literature.

The Greeks of Constantinople taught writing to the Sclavonic race, and with it the Christian faith. The most ancient Greek writing (we speak of the Christan era only) was the *capital* writing, regular and well-proportioned ; as it became general it was simplified more and more. After this sort of writing, examples of which are found only on stone or bronze, we come to the writing called, although we do not know why, *uncial,** which was the first step towards the Greek *cursive* (flowing).

Uncial writing was employed, in Greek manuscripts, up to the ninth century ; we may observe the transition from the *uncial* to the *half-uncial*, and from the *half-uncial* to the *minuscule.†* In the tenth century manuscripts in minuscule became very abundant—the tachygraphers (ταχύς, quick, and γράφω, I write), or the partisans of quick writing, gained the day ; the caligraphers (καλός, beautiful, and γράφω, I write) desired to follow their example. These employed a great deal of time in painting the initials of running letters : the new method, which produced more in the same space of time, easily got into favour ; the caligraphers abandoned the uncial and adopted the minuscule characters connected together, which combined good

---

* The word is derived from the Latin *uncialis,* and is applied to letters of a round or hook-shaped form : such were used by the ancients as numerals, or for words in abbreviated inscriptions.—[ED.]

† *Minuscule.*—Less or little. The term is evidently here intended to distinguish small letters from capitals.—[ED.]

forms with greater facility of execution. Thenceforward, the uncial was no longer employed except for the titles or headings of books.

Among the fine specimens of this epoch which have been preserved, we may mention, in the Imperial Library of Paris, a Book of the Gospels, called Cardinal Mazarin's, and the Commentaries of Gregory Nazianzus; at the Laurentinean Library, Florence, are a Plutarch and a Book of the Gospels, written with gold in kin large and massive minuscule cursive characters; and lastly, a book of ecclesiastical offices, belonging also to the Imperial Library in Paris, and which bears this superscription in Greek :— "Pray for Euthymus, a poor monk, priest of the monastery of St. Lazare. This volume was finished in the month of May, Convocation S, in the year 6515," a date which, according to the computation of the Greek Church, corresponds to the month of May of the year 1007 of the Christian era.

To the twelfth century is assigned the beautiful Greek manuscript which was afterwards given to Louis XIV. by Chrysanthes Noras, Patriarch of Jerusalem; to the thirteenth century belongs another manuscript, in very small cursive letters, ornamented with portraits, presented by the Emperor Palæologos to St. Louis. It was only in the fourteenth century that manuscripts half Latin and half Greek, appeared. Lastly came Ange Végèce, of Corfu, who, towards the middle of the fifteenth century, made for himself, as a Greek caligrapher, such a reputation that he gave, it is said, rise to the proverb, " *Ecrire comme un ange.*"

The Greek alphabet, when it penetrated into the countries of the north with the Christian religion and civilisation, underwent important modifications. On the right bank of the Danube, in ancient Mœsia, Ulphilas, the descendant of a Cappadocian family formerly taken prisoner by the Goths, invented, in the fourth century, the alphabet bearing, on that account, the name of *Mœso-Gothic,* and which is of Greek origin, with a mixture of Latin characters and other peculiar signs. This writing is heavy, without being elegant; differing, as if by an instinct of nationality, from the types which it imitates. The Mœso-Gothic manuscripts are, however, very rare; only two or three being known.

The Sclavonic writing, which is also a daughter of Greece, has a history nearly similar to that of the Mœso-Gothic. When the people of this family were converted to Christianity, they were brought over to it by Greek Christians, and the Patriarch Cyril, in the ninth century, became their teacher; he taught them how to write (which they never knew till then), and it was the Greek alphabet they adopted, adding to it, however, a few new signs, so that they might be able to express the sounds peculiar to their language. Sclavonic manuscripts are positively numerous in public libraries. We find them in Paris, Bologna, and Rome, but above all in Germany, and in the country under the dominion of the Muscovite. One of the most celebrated is that belonging to the town of Rheims, and which is known by the name of "Texte du Sacre," because a tradition (an erroneous one, however) asserts that the kings of France, at the time of their coronation at Rheims, took the oaths on this book, which was said to be written by the hand of St. Procopius. The Sclavonic manuscripts in general recommend themselves less by the elegance of their execution than by the richness of their bindings.

The actual Russian alphabet is but an abridgment of the alphabet called the *Cyrilian*, reduced to forty-two signs by the Emperor Peter I.; so that the Sclavonic nations knew two *Cyrilian* alphabets, the ancient Sclavonic for the liturgical writings, and the modern Sclavonic, or Russian, in general use. Of the first no manuscripts exist earlier than the eleventh century of our era.

The manuscripts of the Latins are, without doubt, more numerous and more varied, because the Latin Church is more extensive, and because Roman civilisation spread itself over a larger number of European provinces. At the head of the manuscripts of the Latin writing is placed a fragment of papyrus, found in Egypt, on which is inscribed an imperial edict for the annulment of a sale of property, agreed upon in consequence of some violence committed by a certain man named Isidore; the date of this document has been fixed as the third century. For the fourth century we have the "Virgil," with miniatures, which we mention elsewhere (Miniatures of Manuscripts), and a "Terence," both belonging to the Vatican Library, and both written in capital letters; in the latter, however, they are irregular, and called, on that account, *rustic capitals.*

To the same period we must refer the "Treatise on the Republic," by Cicero, which has but lately been found in a volume from which the previous writing had been effaced, as was often the case (see Parchment and Paper), in order to make room for the new writing. For the fifth century we have a second "Virgil," with miniatures, which passed from the library of the Abbey of St. Denis into that of the Vatican. The "Prudence," which the Imperial Library of Paris still possesses, is a very fine manuscript of the sixth century, written in rustic capitals, quaint but elegant.

Two other kinds of writing were, at the same period, in use among the Latins; this same rustic capital, ceasing to be rectangular, and rounded in its principal strokes, became the uncial; and for that very reason being much more expeditious, was reserved especially for the copying of works; while the cursive, although sometimes employed for manuscripts, was used chiefly in letter-writing. Of the first of these two writings, the uncial, we have two fine specimens of the sixth century in the "Sermons" of St. Augustine, on papyrus (Fig. 336), and in a Psalter of St. Germain-des-Prés, written in letters of silver on purple vellum, both of which now belong to the Imperial Library, Paris.

In the same century, we find a kind of writing called *half-uncial,* which became more and more expeditious by the change made in certain of its forms. There was then also a Gallican uncial, the form of which we can see in the manuscript said to be by St. Prosper (Imperial Library, Paris); and an uncial of Italy, among which figure the Bible of Mont-Amiati, at Florence; the palimpsest* Homilies of the Vatican, and the admirable Book of the Gospels at Notre-Dame, Paris (Fig. 337).

The most ancient style of cursive writing, employed in charts and diplomas, is to be seen in the deeds known by the name of *charters of Ravenna,* from the name of the town in which they were first discovered. We may consider as analogous to these the writing of the Acts of our early kings, very difficult to read on account of the exaggerated manner in which the thin strokes join the letters together, and by the indefinite forms of the up and down strokes. We give a fragment (Fig. 338) taken from an original chart, on parchment, of Childebert III. We see what the same writing had become in 784 by Fig. 339, copied from an original capitulary of Charlemagne.

To the same period belongs the employment, in ordinary use among chancellors and notaries, of a writing completely tachygraphic; it is composed of ciphers, one of which took the place of a syllable or a word. This writing was called *Tironian,* because the invention of it is attributed to

---

* *Palimpsest*—a kind of parchment from which anything written could easily be erased.—[ED.]

Tiro, Cicero's freed-man, who made use of it in tachygraphing, or, as we should now say, stenographing (short-hand), the speeches of the illustrious orator. Fig. 340 is taken from a psalter of the eighth century, of which the text is transcribed with the tachygraphic characters of that period.

The name of *Visigothic* is given to the writing of manuscripts executed in the south of France and in Spain during the rule of the Goths and the Visigoths; this writing, still rather Roman, is generally round and embellished with fanciful strokes, which render it agreeable to the eye.

We also find in Italy the *Lombardic*, in use for diplomas till the twelfth century.

The beautiful manuscripts on purple vellum are of the time of Charlemagne, when luxury in the arts showed itself in all forms. There is in the Imperial Library, Paris a magnificent volume, which came from the ancient domain of Soubise, that contains the Epistles and Gospels for all the festivals of the year: the execution of this work is perfect; the gigantic capital letters, of Anglo-Saxon form, are coloured, and rendered still richer by being dotted with gold.

A valuable manuscript of the "Tractus Temporum" of the Venerable Bede, a manuscript posterior by more than two hundred years to the author, who lived in the beginning of the eighth century, affords a specimen of one of the varieties of minuscule writings, which in France was called the *Lombardic writing of books*, because it was in use during the reign of the Lombard kings beyond the Alps; it is more difficult to read than the Roman, though similar in form, because the words are not separated. A beautiful manuscript of "Horace" (Imperial Library, Paris), which presents a mixture of the different kinds of Roman writing of the period, is attributed to the same century. We have in Fig. 341 an elegant ornamental capital, taken from a manuscript, "Commentaries of St. Jerome," also in the Imperial Library. We find specimens of writing of Anglo-Saxon origin, capital letters, and running text, in many books of the Gospel.

The diplomatic writing of the tenth century is here represented by a charter of the king Hugh Capet, from which we borrow Fig. 342; it must have been issued between 988 and 996. In this fragment, the first line only is composed of characters very elongated, close together, mixed with some capital letters and some singular forms. It bears witness to the fact that the fine Merovingian writing had then singularly degenerated.

In the eleventh century the minuscule of manuscripts was characterised
by its angular forms, which caused it to receive the name of *Capetian.* Then
the Capetian, exaggerated in its tendency towards its strokes and angles,
became the *Ludovician,* which announces the thirteenth century, and
characterises the reign of St. Louis.

However, manuscripts of the thirteenth century abound, and the history
of the writing of the period of St. Louis and of the three centuries
succeeding it, may be summed up in these words :—" The Capetian writing,
called *Ludovician,* when it had come to differ still more from the beautiful
forms of the writings of Charlemagne's time or the renovated Roman,

Fig. 335.—Scribe or Copyist, in his Work-room, surrounded by Open Manuscripts, and Writing at a Desk.
(From a Miniature of the Fifteenth Century.)

was more and more deformed, and these successive degradations became
so complicated that the writing, in the seventeenth century, resulted in
being perfectly illegible. Thus can be generalised all the precepts relative
to the state of writing, in the manuscripts and the charters in France, for
this period of three hundred years " (Fig. 343).

It was, however, the era of the richest manuscripts, that in which
was brought to perfection the art of ornamenting them, when the pencil
of the miniature-painter and the pen of the caligrapher, conjointly,
produced some masterpieces (Fig. 344). This was also the time when the
corporation of writers became numerous and powerful (Fig. 335). One of

the most distinguished members of this society was that Nicolas Flamel, about whom so many fabulous legends have been invented. We give, as a specimen of his magnificent cursive writing (Fig. 345), the fac-simile of one of the *ex libris* inscriptions he placed at the beginning of all the books belonging to Duke Jean de Berry, whose secretary and *bookseller* he was.*

In other countries than France, in Germany especially, Gothic writing was easily diffused. German manuscripts differ little from those of France. We observe only that German writing continued to be very fine till the middle of the thirteenth century, at which period it became irregular, angular, and bristling with sharp points.

That which has just been said of Germany in particular is naturally applicable to East and West Flanders, and to the Low Countries. During the fifteenth century, under the impulse given by the Dukes of Burgundy, whose influence we have already mentioned, the most important chronicles, the best histories then extant, were magnificently transcribed in that beautiful Gothic minuscule, thick, massive and angular, which was called *lettre de forme;* and we find it again in some ancient editions of the end of the fifteenth century (Fig. 346), and of the beginning of the sixteenth.

In more northern countries the *Runic* alphabet was made use of, to which for a long while a marvellous origin was attributed, but which the Benedictines justly regard it as an imitation, or rather as a corruption, of the Latin alphabet. There exist in the *Runic* language inscriptions on stone and on wood, some manuscripts on vellum, and Irish books on parchment and on paper.

In the south, the writing seems constantly to have reflected the lively and frank spirit of its inhabitants, among whom was perpetuated the profound impress of the old Roman civilisation. The minuscule continued as high as it was long, thin, and distinct; even when it was altered by the influence of the Gothic, it was still beautiful, and, above all, legible, as we may be convinced of by examining a fine manuscript entitled "Specchio della Croce" ("Mirror of the Cross"), of the thirteenth century; and a precious manuscript of Dante, of the fourteenth century, both belonging to the Imperial Library, Paris.

We may adopt for Spain the same opinions as for Italy. There was

* Librarian probably; though *libraire* means only a bookseller, *bibliothécaire* being the French for a librarian.—[Tr.]

in that country also writing of great merit, handed down from the
Romans, which received, as we have already said, the name of *Visigothic*.
The Visigothic writing of the eleventh and twelfth centuries, of the
eleventh especially, is a minuscule of the most graceful kind. But
Gothicism, by the *Capetian* and the *Ludovician* coming in as intermediate
agents, at last corrupted this elegant and delicate writing, as we see
in the collection of Spanish troubadours, formed by order of John II.,
King of Castile and Leon, about 1440; a celebrated manuscript in the
Imperial Library, Paris.

Into England, where the Anglo-Saxon type reigned supreme, the
Norman conquest introduced the French writing in charters and manuscripts. And lastly, among the writings called national, we must again
mention that of Ireland, of which there are fine examples remaining; but
upon examination they prove to be nothing but a variety of the Anglo-
Saxon. It is said to have been in use since the sixth century; and
we find that in spite of divers conquests it continued to be employed till
the fifteenth century. It was even known and employed in France, although
it by no means recommends itself by its elegance, as is attested, among
other manuscripts, by that of the "Homilies of St. Augustine," in the
Imperial Library, Paris, which is supposed to belong to the eighth century.

Here our summary review of palæographic examples at different
periods of the Middle Ages comes to an end. We might follow up our
investigations on this point, even after the time when the printing-press
was invented, since manuscripts are found of the reign of Louis XIV.;
but they were nothing but fanciful inutilities; each century, in order to
show itself in its true light, should follow the instincts and the inspirations
which belong to it.

FAC-SIMILE OF MANUSCRIPTS.

Fig. 336.—Writing of the Sixth Century, with Capital Letters, from a Manuscript, on Papyrus, of the "Sermons of St. Augustine."
(Imperial Library, Paris.)

SPESNOSTRAF

NON DEISTOTEMPORE NEQUED
MUNDOEST NEQUEINEAFELICITA

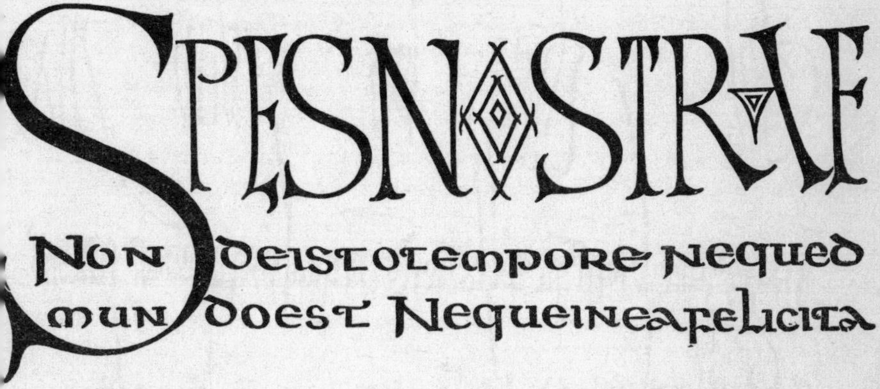

TEXT.—*Spes nostra e[st] non de isto tempore, neque de mundo est, neque in ea felicita[te. . . .*

TRANSLATION.—Our hope is not of this time, nor is it of the world, nor in that felicity.

Fig. 337.—Title and Capital Letters of the Seventh Century, from a Book of the Gospels of Notre-Dame, Paris. (Imperial Library, Paris.)

TEXT.—*Incipit præfatio.*

TRANSLATION.—Here begins the Preface.

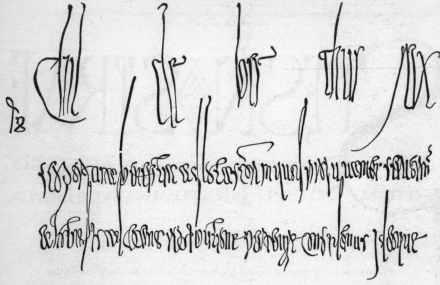

TEXT.—*Childeberthus rex*
Se oportune beneficia ad loca sanctorum quod pro juvamen servorum. . . . .
Et hoc nobis ad eterna retributione pertenire confidemus. Ideoque. . . . .

Fig 339.—Writing of the Eighth Century, from a Capitulary of Charlemagne, addressed to Pope Adrian I. in 784.
(Imperial Library, Paris.)

TEXT.—*Primo Capitulo. Salutant vos dominus noster, filius vester, Carolus rex* [*et filia vestra domna nostra Fastrada, filii et*] *filiæ domini nostri simul, et omnis domus sua.*

II. Salutant vos cuncti sacerdotes, episcopi et abbates, atque omnis congregatio illorum [*in Dei servicio constituta etiam, et universus*] *populus Francorum.*

TRANSLATION.—I. Our lord, your son, King Charles [and your daughter our Lady Fastrada, salute thee, also the sons and] daughters of our Lord, and all his house.

II. All the priests, bishops, and abbots salute thee, as also the whole congregation [of those who are established in the service of God, and the whole] of the French people.

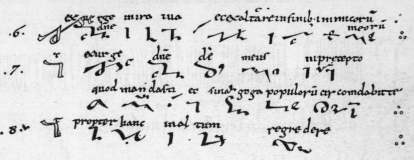

TEXT.—*Exsurge, Domine, in ira tua et exaltare in finibus inimicorum meorum, et exsurge, Domine Deus meus, in precepto quod mandasti ; et sinagoga populorum circomdabit te, et propter hanc in altum regredere.*

TRANSLATION.—Arise, O Lord, in thine anger, lift up thyself because of the rage of mine enemies : and awake for me to the judgment that thou hast commanded.

So shall the congregation of the people compass thee about: for their sakes therefore return thou on high.—(Psalm vii., 6, 7.)

Fig. 341.—Writing of the Tenth Century, after a Manuscript of the " Commentaries of St. Jerome." (Imperial Library, Paris.)

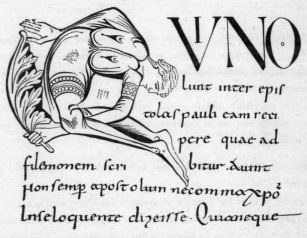

TEXT.—*Qui nolunt inter epistolas Pauli eam recipere quæ ad Filemonem scribitu, aiunt non semper apostolum nec omnia Christo in se loquente dixisse. Quia neque . . .*

TRANSLATION.—Those who are unwilling to receive among the epistles of St. Paul that which is written to Philemon, deny that the Apostles spoke everything and at all times under the inspiration of Christ. Because neither . . .

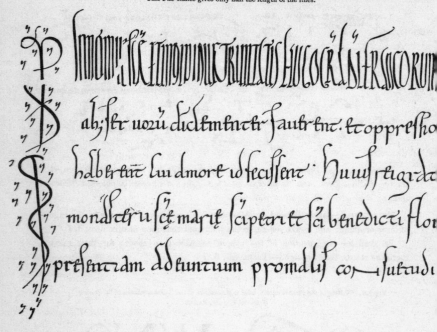

Fig. 342.—Diplomatic Writing of the Tenth Century, from a Charter of Hugh Capet. (Archives of the Empire.) This Fac-simile gives only half the length of the lines.

TEXT (completely restored).—*In nomine sanctæ et individuæ Trinitatis, Hugo gratia Dei Francorum rex.* [*Mos et consuetudo regum prædecessorum nostrorum semper exstitit ut ecclesias Dei sublimarent et justis petitioni]bus servorum Dei clementer faverent, et oppression[em eorum benigne sublevarent, ut Deum propitium*] *haberent, cujus amore id fecissent. Hujus rei grati[a, auditis clamoribus venerabilis Abbonis abbatis*] *monasterii S. Mariæ, S. Petri et S. Benedicti Flori[acensis et monachorum sub eo degentium, nostram*] *presentiam adeuntium, pro malis consuetudi[nibus et assiduis rapinis* . . .

TRANSLATION.—In the name of the holy and indivisible Trinity, Hugh, by the grace of God, King of the Francs.

The custom and habit of the kings our predecessors has always been to honour the churches of God, and to show themselves mercifully favourable to the just petitions of the servants of God, and to deliver them kindly from oppression, so that God might be propitious to them, for the love of whom they thus acted. For this cause, having heard the complaints of the venerable Abbon, Abbot of the Monastery of Our Lady, St. Peter and St. Benedict, of Fleury-sur-Loire, and those of the monks living under his direction, and who came into our presence, on account of the bad customs and continual rapines . . .

TEXT.—*Messeigneurs et freres, si tres humblement que faire puis a voz bonnes graces me recommande. Messeigneurs, j'ay receu voz lettres par le present porteur : ensemble la requeste et arrest de la court par icelle ensuivy. J'ay le tout communiqué a messeigneurs les generaulx de Langue doil et Normandie, et nous avons souuant esté ensemble. Ilz trouuent bien estrange, aussi font daultres, qui zelent le bien et honneur de la chambre ausquelz pareillement* . . .

TRANSLATION.—My lords and brothers, I commend myself as humbly as possible to your good graces. My lords, I received your letters by the bearer of this, together with the petition and the decree of the court accompanying them. I communicated the whole to my lords the generals of La Langue d'Oil and of Normandy, and we have often conferred together on the matter. They think it very strange, as do others also, who are zealous for the good and the honour of the chamber, to which equally . . .

Fig. 344.—Writing of the Fourteenth Century, after a Manuscript of "L'Histoire Romaine;" being a paraphrase of the text of Valerius Maximus. (Imperial Library, Paris.)

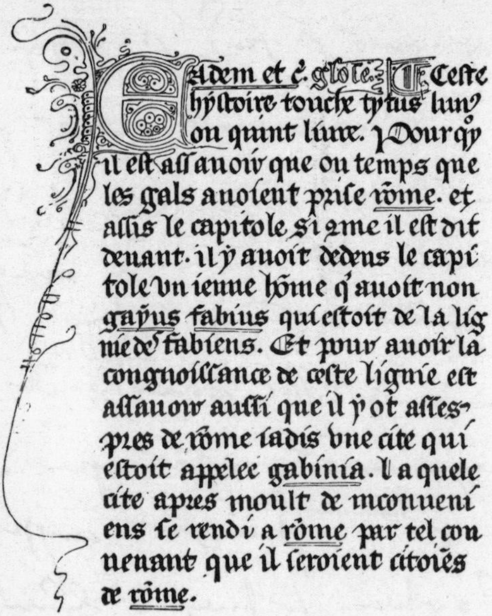
Eadem et c. glose. ¶ Ceste
hystoire touche tytus liui⁹
ou quint liure. Pourq̃y
il est assauoir que ou temps que
les gals auoient prise rõme. et
assis le capitole si cõme il est dit
deuant. il y auoit dedens le capi
tole vn ieune hõme q̃ auoit non
gayus fabius qui estoit de la lig
nie des fabiens. Et pour auoir la
congnoissance de ceste lignie est
assauoir aussi que il y ot asses
pres de rõme iadis vne cite qui
estoit appelee gabinia. la quele
cite apres moult de inconueni
ens se rendi a rõme par tel con
uenant que il seroient citoiẽs
de rõme.

Text.—*Eadem, &c.*—Glose. *Ceste histoire touche Titus Liuius ou quint liure. Pourquoy il est assauoir que ou temps que les Gals auoient prise Romme et assis le Capitole, si comme il est dit deuant, il y auoit dedens le Capitole un jeune homme qui auoit non Gayus Fabius qui estoit de la lignie des Fabiens. Et pour auoir la congnoissançe de ceste lignie est assauoir aussi que il y ot asses pres de Romme jadis une cite qui estoit appelee Gabinia: laquele cite apres moult de inconueniens se rendi a Romme par tel conuenant que il seroient citoiens de Romme.*

Translation.—Eadem, &c.—Glose. Livy, in his fifth book, touches on this history. We must know that at the time when the Gauls had taken Rome and besieged the Capitol, as was said above, there was in the Capitol a young man named Caius Fabius, and who was of the Fabian race; and to know this race we must also know that there was formerly near Rome a town called Gabinia; which town, after many vicissitudes, surrendered to Rome, on the condition that all its inhabitants should be considered as citizens of Rome.

TEXT.—*Ceste Bible est a Monseigneur le Duc de Berry.*
                                        FLAMEL.

TRANSLATION.—This Bible belongs to Monseigneur the Duke de Berry.
                                        FLAMEL.

NOTE.—The Duke de Berry, John, brother of King Charles V., and uncle to King Charles VI., was a great amateur of fine books. He spent very large sums in having manuscripts copied and illuminated. The Imperial Library, Paris, preserves a large number of the most valuable of them.

Fig. 346.—Writing of the Fifteenth Century, after the First Page of a Breviary. (Royal Library, Brussels.)

TEXT.—*Sabbato in aduentu Domini, ad vesperas, super psalmos antiphona, Benedictus, psalmus, ipsum cum ceteris antiphonis et psalmis. Infra capitulum.*

Ecce dies veniunt, dicit Dominus, et suscitabo Dauid germen.

TRANSLATION.—On Saturday in Advent, at vespers, before the psalms chanted alternately, (comes) the hymn Benedictus, with the other antiphons and psalms. After the lesson . . .

"Behold the days are coming, saith the Lord, and I will restore the seed of David."

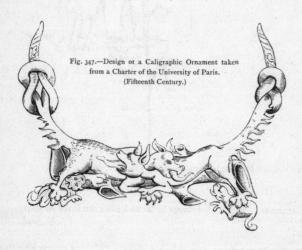

Fig. 347.—Design of a Caligraphic Ornament taken from a Charter of the University of Paris. (Fifteenth Century.)

MINIATURES IN MANUSCRIPTS.

Miniatures at the Beginning of the Middle Ages.—The two "Vatican" Virgils.—Painting of
Manuscripts under Charlemagne and Louis le Débonnaire.—Tradition of Greek Art in
Europe.—Decline of the Miniature in the Tenth Century.—Origin of Gothic Art.—Fine
Manuscript of the time of St. Louis.—Clerical and Lay Miniature-Painters.—Caricature
and the Grotesque.—Miniatures in Monochrome and in Grisaille.—Illuminators at the Court
of France and to the Dukes of Burgundy.—School of John Fouquet.—Italian Miniature-
Painters.—Giulo Clovio.—French School under Louis XII.

ONTEMPORANEOUS, almost,
with the idea which first caused
oral traditions, chronicles,
speeches, and poetry to be collected together under the form
and name of *book*, is the art of
ornamenting manuscripts with
miniatures. Our intention is
not to go back to the sources
—as obscure as they are distant—of that art, but only to
point out its principal phases
of improvement or of decay
during the Middle Ages.

The most ancient known miniatures date from the very
commencement of that period which is generally called the
Middle Ages; that is to say, from the third and fourth centuries.
These paintings, of which there exist but two or three specimens in the libraries of Europe, nevertheless offer, in their
correctness and masterly beauty, the great characteristics of
ancient Art. The most celebrated are those of the "Virgil,"
preserved in the Vatican Library (Fig. 348), a manuscript long
celebrated among learned men for the authenticity of its text.

Another "Virgil," of the date of about a century later, and which, before its presentation to the Pope, was one of the most beautiful ornaments of the ancient library of the Abbey of St. Denis, in France, contains paintings not less remarkable in respect of colour, but very inferior as far as drawing and the style of the compositions are concerned. These two

Fig. 348.—Miniature taken from the "Virgil" in the Library of the Vatican, Rome.
(Third or Fourth Century.)

incomparable examples are sufficient in themselves to show the state of the painting of manuscripts at the beginning of the Middle Ages.

The sixth and seventh centuries have left us no books with miniatures; the utmost we find at that period are some capital letters embellished by caligraphy. In the eighth century, on the contrary, the ornaments were multiplied, and some rather elegant paintings can be pointed out; the fact is, under the reign of Charlemagne a movement of renovation took place in the Arts as in literature: the Latin writing, which had become illegible,

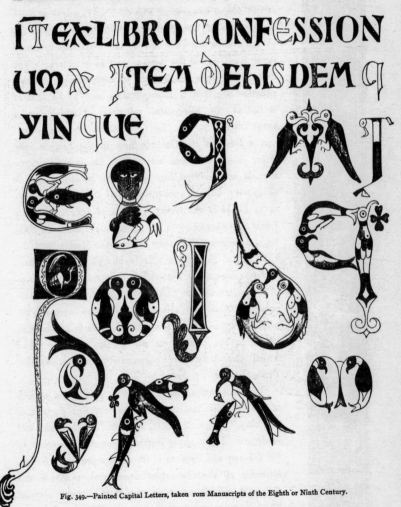

Fig. 349.—Painted Capital Letters, taken rom Manuscripts of the Eighth or Ninth Century.

was reformed, and the style of painting manuscripts assumed something of the form of the fine antique examples still extant at that period. (Fig. 350.)

Fig. 350.—Border, taken from a Book of the Gospels of the Eighth Century. (Library of Vienna.)

If we would have an idea of the heaviness and the ungraceful character of the writing and of the ornaments which accompanied it before the period of Charlemagne, it will suffice to examine Fig. 349. "It was then quite time," says M. Aimé Champollion-Figeac, "that the salutary influence exercised by the illustrious monarch made itself felt in the Arts as well as in letters." The first manuscripts which seem to bear witness to this progress are first a sacramentary, said to be that of Gellonius, the allegorical paintings of which are of great interest in the history of Christian symbolism; and a Book of the Gospels, now in the Louvre: the latter is said to have belonged to the great emperor himself, and we reproduce one of the paintings from it (Fig. 351). We may mention, as of the ninth century, many Books of the Gospels, in one of which, given by Louis le Débonnaire to the Abbey St. Médard de Soissons, the purest Byzantine style shows itself; then the Bible called the "Metz" Bible, in which are paintings of large dimensions, remarkable for the felicitous groupings of the figures and for the beauty of the draperies. One of these miniatures excites an interest quite peculiar, inasmuch as King David, who is represented in it, is but a copy of an ancient Apollo, round whom the artist has personified Courage, Justice, Prudence, &c.

Let us mention still further two Bibles and a book of prayers, the last containing a very fine portrait of the king, Charles the Bald, to whom it belonged; and lastly, two books really worth attention, on account of the delicacy and freedom of the outline drawings, for the attitudes of the characters represented, and for the draperies, which resemble those of ancient statues. These books are a "Terence," preserved in the Imperial Library, Paris, number 7,899 in the catalogue; and a "Lectionary of the Cathedral of Metz," from which the border (Fig. 352) is taken. While in France the art of painting manuscripts had progressed so much as to produce some perfect models of delicacy and

Fig. 351.—Miniature from the Book of the Gospels of Charlemagne.
(Manuscript in the Library of the Louvre.)

taste, Germany had never got beyond the simplest compositions, as we see

Fig. 352.—Border of a Lectionary in the Cathedral of Metz. (Ninth Century.)

in the "Paraphrase on the Gospels," in Theotisc (the old Teutonic language), belonging to the Library of Vienna.

The artistic traditions of the ancients in the ninth century are attested by the manuscripts of Christian Greece, whereof the Imperial Library, Paris, possesses many magnificent specimens, at the head of which we must place the "Commentaries of Gregory Nazianzus," ornamented with an infinite number of paintings, in which all the resources of ancient art are applied to the representation of Christian subjects (Fig. 353). The heads of the characters portrayed are admirably expressive, and of the finest style; the colouring of the miniatures is warm and soft; the costumes, the representations of buildings and of the accessories, offer, moreover, very interesting subjects of study. Unfortunately, these paintings were executed on a very crumbling surface, which has in many places peeled off: it is sad to see one of the most precious monuments of Greek and Christian Art in a deplorable state of dilapidation.

The masterpiece of the tenth century, which again is due to the artists of Greece, is a "Psalter, with Commentaries," belonging also to the Imperial Library (number 139 among the Greek manuscripts), a work in which the miniature-painter seems not to have been able to disengage himself from the Pagan creeds in illustrating Biblical episodes. Two celebrated manuscripts of the same time, but executed in France, and preserved in the same collection, show, by the stiffness and incorrectness of the drawing, that the impetus given by the genius of Charlemagne had abated: these are the "Bible de Noailles," and the "Bible de St. Martial," of Limoges (Fig. 355).

To speak truly, if in France there was a decadency, the Anglo-Saxon and Visigothic artists of this period

Fig. 353.—Miniature of the Ninth Century, extracted from the "Commentaries of Gregory Nazianzus," representing the consecration of a Bishop. (Large folio Manuscript in the Imperial Library, Paris.)

Fig. 355.—Border taken from the Bible of St. Martial of Limoges. (Tenth Century.)

were also very inferior, to judge from a Latin Book of the Gospels of the tenth century painted in England (Fig. 356); it, however, proves that the art of ornamenting books had degenerated less than that of drawing the human

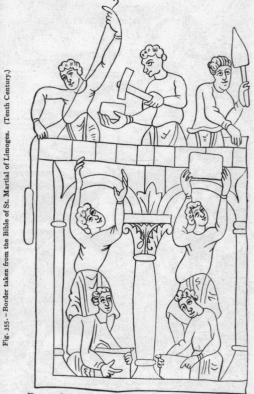

Fig. 354.—Fac-simile of a Miniature drawn with the pen, taken from a Bible of the Eleventh Century. (Imperial Library, Paris.)

figure. Another manuscript with paintings, called Visigothic, containing the Apocalypse of St. John, gives, in its fantastic ornaments and animals, an example of the strange style adopted by a certain school of miniature-painters.

Fig. 356.—Border taken from a Book of the Gospels in Latin, executed in England. (Tenth Century.)

Germany now began to improve in the art of painting miniatures. It owed this happy result to the emigration of Greek artists, who came to the German court to take refuge from the troubles of the East. The progress accomplished in this part of Europe shows itself in the drawing of the figures of a German Book of the Gospels of the beginning of the eleventh century, a work very superior to that of the Teutonic Book of the Gospels just referred to. The border of which we give a fac-simile in Fig. 357 shows also a certain degree of improvement; it is taken from a Book of the Gospels of the same period, preserved in the Royal Library, Munich.

But in France, to foreign invasions and to misfortunes of all kinds, which, since the death of Charlemagne, had afflicted the country, was added the terror caused by the general expectation that the world was coming to an end at the expiration of the first millennial. People were, therefore,

Fig. 357.—Border taken from a Book of the Gospels at the beginning of the Eleventh Century. In the Royal Library, Munich.

otherwise employed than in ornamenting books. Accordingly, this epoch
is one of the most barren in religious or other paintings. Fig. 358
represents the last degree of abasement in this art. Nothing in the world
could be more barbarous, nor farther removed from all sentiment of the
beautiful, and even from the instinctive idea of drawing. Ornamentation,
however, remained sufficiently good, although under very heavy forms, as

Fig. 358.—Miniature taken from a Missal of the Beginning of the Eleventh Century.
(Imperial Library, Paris, No. 821.)

the Sacramentary of Æthelgar, which is preserved in the Library of Rouen,
shows (Fig. 359). The decadency, however, seems to have come to a
stop in France towards the end of the eleventh century, if we judge of
the art from paintings, executed in 1060, and contained in a Latin
manuscript, bearing the number 818, in the Imperial Library.

In the manuscripts of the twelfth century, the influence of the Crusades made itself already felt. At this period, the East regenerated in some sort the West in all that concerned arts, sciences, and literature. Many examples witness that the painting of manuscripts was not the last to undergo this singular transformation. Everything the imagination could invent of the most fantastic was particularly brought into play to give to the Latin letters a peculiar character —imitated, moreover, from the ornaments of Saracenic architecture. This practice was even applied to public acts and documents, as Fig. 360 proves; it represents some of the initial letters in the "Rouleau Mortuaire" of St. Vital Callot, in his "Temptation of St. Anthony," has, we think, imagined nothing stranger than the figure we give; a demon standing on the back of Cerberus forms the vertical line in the letter T; while two other demons, whose feet are in the mouth of the first, form the two lateral branches of the letter.

In the thirteenth century, Saracenic or Gothic art universally prevailed. Everywhere figures assumed gaunt, elongated forms; coats-of-arms invaded the miniatures; but the colouring was of marvellous purity and brightness; burnished gold, applied with the greatest skill, stood out from blue or purple backgrounds which even in our own day have lost nothing of their original freshness.

Fig. 359—Border taken from the Sacramentary of Æthelgar. (Rouen Library.)

Among the most remarkable manuscripts of this century we must mention a Psalter in five colours, containing the French, Hebrew, and Roman versions, with some commentaries (Imperial Library, No. 1,132 *bis*). One should analyse the greater number of subjects depicted in this manuscript to understand all their importance; we will mention only that among

Fig. 360.—Initial Letters extracted from the " Rouleau Mortuaire " of St. Vital, Twelfth Century.
(Imperial Archives of France.)

them are sieges of towns, Gothic fortresses, interiors of Italian banking-houses, various musical instruments, &c. There is, perhaps, no other manuscript which equals this in the richness, the beauty, and multiplicity of its paintings: it contains ninety-nine large miniatures, independently of ninety-

Fig. 361.—Facsimile of a Miniature of a Psalter, of the Thirteenth Century, representing warlike, scientific, commercial, and agricultural Works. (Imperial Library, Paris.)

Fig. 362.—A Border taken from a Gospel in Latin, of the Thirteenth Century.
(Imperial Library, Paris.)

six medallions representing divers episodes suggested by the text of the Psalms (Fig. 361). After this psalter we must place the Breviary of St. Louis, or rather of Queen Blanche, formerly preserved in the Arsenal Library, Paris, and now in the Musée des Souverains; a celebrated manuscript which has, on folio 191, this inscription : "C'est le Psautier monseigneur St. Loys, lequel fu à sa mère." * But the volume is not rich in large miniatures. We observe in it, however, a calendar ornamented with small subjects very delicately executed, representing the labours appropriate to each month, according to the seasons of the year. The character of the paintings exhibits a style anterior to the reign of Louis IX.; and it is supposed, indeed, that this book first belonged to the mother of that king.

We must now mention another Psalter, which was actually used by St. Louis; as is proved not only by an inscription at the beginning of the volume, but still further by the fleurs-de-lis of the king, the arms of Blanche of Castile, his mother, and perhaps also *les pals de gueules* of Margaret of Provence, his wife. Nothing can equal the beautiful preservation of the miniatures in this volume, which contains seventy-eight subjects, with as many explanatory texts in French. The heads of the characters, though almost microscopic, have nevertheless, generally, a fine expression.

The "Livre de Clergie," which bears the date of 1260, merits far less attention: so does the "Roman du Roi Artus," No. 6,963, in the Imperial Library, Paris, executed in 1276. But

* *Translation :* "This is Monseigneur St. Louis' Psalter, which belonged to his mother."

we must point out two of the most beautiful examples of this period, a Book of the Gospels in Latin, No. 665 in the Supplement, Imperial Library, from which we have borrowed an elegant border (Fig. 362), and the "Roman du Saint-Graal," No. 6,769, also in the Imperial Library.

Italy was then at the head of civilisation in everything; it had particularly inherited the grand traditions of painting which had gone to sleep for ever in Greece only to wake up again in Europe.

Here we must introduce a remark, the result of a general examination of the manuscripts bequeathed to us by the thirteenth century; namely, that the miniatures in sacred books are much more beautifully and care-

Fig. 363.—Facsimile of a Miniature of the Thirteenth Century, representing a scene of an old Romance: the beautiful Josiane, disguised as a female juggler, playing a Welsh air on the *Rote* (Fiddle), to make herself known to her friend Bewis. (Imperial Library, Paris.)

fully executed than those of the romances of chivalry and the chronicles of the same period (Figs. 363 and 364). Must we attribute this superiority to the power of religious inspiration? Must we suppose that in the monasteries alone clever artists met with sufficient remuneration? Before answering these questions, or rather as an answer to them, let us remember that in those days religious institutions absorbed nearly all the social intellectual movement, as well as the effective possession of material riches, if not of territorial property. Solely occupied with distant wars or intestine quarrels which impoverished them, the nobles were altogether unable to become protectors of literature and Art. In the abbeys and convents were lay-brethren who sometimes had taken no vow, but whose fervent spirits, burning with poetical imagination, sought in the monastic retreat redemption from their past sins : these men of faith were happy to consecrate their whole existence to the ornamentation of a single sacred book destined for the community which gave them in exchange all the necessaries of life.

This explains the absence of the names of the miniature-painters in ancient manuscripts, particularly in those which are written in Latin. However, when romances and chronicles in the vulgar tongue began to come into fashion, artists of great talent eagerly presented themselves to be

Fig. 364.—The Four Sons of Aymon on their good Steed, Bayart. From a Miniature in the Romance of the "Four Sons of Aymon," a Manuscript of the Thirteenth Century. (Imperial Library, Paris.)

engaged by princes and nobles who wished to have this sort of books ornamented ; but the anonymous which these lay artists generally preserved is explained by the circumstance that in most cases they were considered only as artistic assistants in the lordly houses where they were employed, and in which they fulfilled some other domestic duty; for instance, Colard, de Laon, the favourite painter of Louis of Orleans, was also valet-de-chambre to this prince; Pietro Andrea, another artist, doubtless an Italian, to judge from his Christian name, was gentleman-usher; and

Fig. 365.—Miniature taken from the "Roman de Fauvel" (Fifteenth Century), representing Fauvel, or the Fox, reprimanding a Widow who has married again, and to whom is being given a Serenade of Rough Music. (Imperial Library, Paris.)

we see this same painter "sent from Blois to Tours, to procure certain matters for the accouchement of Madame the Duchess;" or again, "from Blois to Romorantin, to inquire after Madame d'Angoulesme, who was reported to be very unwell."

Certain artists, however, who then took the modest name of illuminators, lived entirely by their profession; working at *tableaux benoîts* (blessed pictures), or popular paintings, which were sold at the church-doors. Others, again, were paid assistants of the recognised painters to princes or nobles; and the anonymous was quite naturally imposed upon them by their subordinate position, if not by the simple modesty which was for a long time the accompaniment of talent. In the fourteenth century the study of miniatures is peculiarly interesting, on account of the scenes of public and private life, of manners and customs, we find reproduced in them. Portraits after life, *d'après le vif*, as they were called in those days, made their appearance; and caricature, at all times so powerful in France, already began to show itself with a daring which, occupying itself with the clergy, women, and chivalry, stopped only before the prestige of royalty.

The miniatures of a French manuscript, dated 1313 (Imperial Library, Paris, No. 8,504, F. L.), deserve to be mentioned, especially on account of the various subjects they represent; for, besides the ceremony of the reception of the King of Navarre into the order of chivalry, we see in it philosophers discussing, judges administering the law, various scenes of conjugal life, singers accompanying themselves on divers instruments of music, villagers engaged in the labours of country life, &c. We must mention also a manuscript of the "Roman de Fauvel," in which is especially prominent the very original scene of a popular concert of rough music, by masked performers, given, according to an old custom, to a widow who had married a second time (Fig. 365).

The period during which Charles V. occupied the throne of France is one of those that produced the finest specimens of manuscript-painting. This monarch, the founder of the Royal Library, was an admirer of illustrated books, and had accumulated, at great cost, a large collection in the great tower of the Louvre. A royal prince, whom we have already mentioned as being excessively devoted to artistic luxuries, was the rival of Charles V. in this respect: this was his brother, the Duke Jean de Berry, who devoted enormous sums to the purchase and production of manuscripts.

Even under Charles VI. this impulse did not abate, and the art of painting manuscripts was never in a more flourishing condition. The border taken from the "Livre d'Heures," or prayer-book, of the Duke d'Anjou, uncle of the king (Fig. 366), is an example of this. We might mention, as specimens of illustrated works of this period, the book of the "Demandes et

Fig. 367.—Miniature taken from "Les Femmes Illustres," translated from Boccacio. (Imperial Library, Paris.)

Réponses," by Peter Salmon, a manuscript executed for the king, and ornamented with exquisite miniatures, in which all the characters are true historical portraits, beautifully finished. Nevertheless, the masterpieces of the French school at this period show themselves in the miniatures of two translations of Boccacio's "De Claris Mulieribus" ("Beautiful Women") (Fig. 367).

Fig. 366.—Border taken from a Prayer-book belonging to Louis of France, Duke of Anjou, King of Naples, of Sicily, and of Jerusalem. (Fourteenth Century.)

nde ven
turus est
indicare
vivos et mortuos.

l est aue
vir iugier
les uis et
les mors.

Fig. 368.—Miniature of the Psalter of John, Duke of Berry, representing the Man of Sorrow, or Christ, showing
the Sign of the Cross.   (Imperial Library, Paris.)

Fig. 369.—Border taken from the Bible called Clement VII.'s. (Fourteenth Century.)

At that time, two new styles appeared in the painting of manuscripts : miniatures *en camaïeu* (in one colour only), and miniatures *en grisaille* (in two colours, viz., a light colour shaded, generally with brown). Of the first kind, we may instance "Les Petites Heures" of John, Duke de Berry (Fig. 368), and "Les Miracles de Notre-Dame."

Germany did not in this respect rise to the height of France ; but miniature-painting in Italy progressed more and more towards perfection. A remarkable specimen of Italian art of this period is the Bible called Clement VII.'s (Fig. 369), which is preserved in the Imperial Library, Paris. But there exists one more admirable still in the same establishment, so rich in curiosities, of the manuscript of "The Institution of the Order of the Holy Ghost," an order of chivalry founded at Naples in 1352, by Louis de Tarento, King of Naples, during a feast on the day of Pentecost ; it is in this superb manuscript, executed by Italian or French artists, may, perhaps, be found the most exquisite miniatures of that day (Fig. 370) ; especially remarkable are the beautiful portraits in *camaïeu* of King Louis and his wife, Jane I., Queen of Naples. A valuable copy of the romance of "Lancelot du Lac," of the same date, recommends itself to the attention of connoisseurs by a rare peculiarity : one can follow in it the successive operations of the painter in miniature ; thus are presented to us consecutively the outline-drawing, then the first tints, generally uniform, executed by the illuminator; next the surface on which the gold is to be applied; then the real work of the miniature-painter in the heads, costumes, &c.

France, in spite of the great troubles which agitated her, and the wars she had to maintain with foreign powers during the fifteenth century, saw, nevertheless, the art of the painter improve very considerably. The fine copy

Fig. 370.—Miniature from a Manuscript of the Fourteenth Century, representing Louis de Tarento, second Husband of Queen Jane of Naples, instituting the Order of the Holy Ghost.
(Imperial Library, Paris.)

of Froissart in the Imperial Library, Paris (Fig. 371), might alone suffice to prove the truth of this assertion. The name of John Foucquet, painter to King Louis XI., deserves to be mentioned with eulogy, as that of one of the artists who contributed most to the progress of painting on manuscripts. Everything thenceforward announced the Renaissance which was to take place in the sixteenth century; and if we wish to follow the onward progress of art from the beginning of the fifteenth century till the time

CORONATION OF CHARLES V., KING OF FRANCE

Miniature from Froissart's Chronicles in the Imperial Library, Paris.

Fig. 371.—Border taken from "Froissart's Chronicles," a French Manuscript of the Fifteenth Century. (Imperial Library, Paris.)

of Raphael, it is in the miniatures of manuscripts we shall find the best evidences of it. Let us observe, by the way, that the Flemish school of the Dukes of Burgundy exercised great influence over this marvellous art for a period of more than a century. Spain was also progressing; but it is to the Italian artists we must, from that time forward, look for the most remarkable works. The Imperial Library of Paris possesses many manuscripts which bear witness to the marked improvement in miniature-painting at this period; among others an "Ovid" of the fifteenth century (Fig. 372); but in order to see the highest expression of the art, we must examine an incomparable copy of Dante's works, preserved in the Vatican, a manuscript proceed-

Fig. 372.—Border taken from an "Ovid." An Italian Manuscript of the Fifteenth Century. (Imperial Library, Paris.)

ing from the hands of Giulio Clovio (Fig. 373), an illustrious painter, pupil and imitator of Raphael : his miniatures are remarkable for beauty.

Fig. 373.—Miniature, painted by Giulio Clovio, of the Sixteenth Century, taken from Dante's " Paradise," representing the Poet and Beatrice transported to the Moon, the abode of Women devoted to Chastity. (Manuscript in the Vatican Library, Rome.)

Lastly, in the reign of Louis XII., the complete regeneration of the Arts

Fig. 374.—Border taken rom the Missal of Pope Paul V. (An Italian Manuscript of the Sixteenth Century.)

was effected. We should, however, mention that at this period there were two very distinct schools: one whose style still showed the influence of ancient Gothic traditions, the other entirely dependent on Italian taste. The Missal of Pope Paul V. emanated from this last school (Fig. 374).

This immense progress, which showed itself simultaneously in France and in Italy by the production of many original works, seems to have attained its climax in the execution of a justly celebrated manuscript, known by the name of "Heures d'Anne de Bretagne" (Fig. 375). Among the numerous pictures which decorate this book of prayers, many would not be unworthy of Raphael's pencil: the expression in the face of the Virgin Mary is, with many others, remarkable for its sweetness; the heads of the angels have something divine in them; and the ornaments which occupy the margin of each page are composed of flowers, fruits, and insects, represented with all the freshness and brilliancy of nature. This inimitable masterpiece was, like a sort of sublime testament, to mark the glorious boundary-line of an art which must necessarily degenerate now that the printing-press was causing the numerous class of scribes and illuminators of the Middle Ages to disappear. It has never revived since, but at intervals; and then more to meet the requirements of fancy than to be of any real use.

A few manuscripts adorned with miniatures of the end of the sixteenth century may still be mentioned, especially two "Livres d'Heures" (prayer-books) painted in *grisaille*, which be-

Fig. 375.—Miniature from the Prayer-book of Anne de Bretagne, representing the Archangel St. Michael.
(Musée des Souverains.)

longed to Henry II., King of France (now in the Musée des Souverains), and the "Livre d'Heures," executed for the Margrave of Baden by a painter of Lorraine or of Metz named Brentel (Fig. 376), who, however, did nothing

Fig. 376.—Miniature in the "Livre d'Heures" belonging to the Margrave of Baden, representing the Portrait of the blessed Bernard of Baden, who died in the odour of Sanctity, on July 15, 1458. (Imperial Library, Paris.)

but put together designs copied from the great masters of Italy and Flanders. There were, nevertheless, good miniature-painters in France up to the seventeenth century, to illustrate the manuscripts executed with so much taste

by the famous Jarry and the caligraphers of his school. The last manifestation of the art shines forth, for example, in the magnificent "Livre
d'Heures" presented to Louis XIV. by the pensioners of the Hôtel des
Invalides, a remarkable work, but yet unworthy to appear by the side of
the "Livre d'Heures d'Anne de Bretagne," which the painter seems to
have adopted as his model.

Fig. 377.—Escutcheon of France, taken from some Ornaments in the Manuscript of the "Institution of the
Order of the Holy Ghost." (Fourteenth Century.)

BOOKBINDING.

S soon as the ancients had made square books, more convenient to read than the rolls, binding—that is to say, the art of reuniting the leaves stitched or stuck (*ligati*) into a movable back, between two square pieces of wood, ivory, metal, or leather—bookbinding was invented. This primitive binding, which had no other object than that of preserving the books, no other merit than that of solidity, was not long ere it became associated with ornament, and thus put itself in relation with the luxury of Greek and Roman civilisation. Not contented with placing on each side of the volume a little tablet of cedar-wood or of oak, on which was written the title of the book (for books were then laid flat on the shelves of the library), a piece of leather was stretched over the edge to preserve it from dust, if the book was valuable, and the volume was tied up with a strap passed round it many times, and which was subsequently replaced by clasps. In certain instances the volume was enveloped in thick cloth, and even enclosed in a case of wood or leather. Such was the state of bookbinding in ancient times.

There were then, as now, good and bad bookbinders. Cicero, in his letters to Atticus, asks for two of his slaves who were very clever *ligatores librorum* (bookbinders). Bookbinding, however, was not an art very generally known, for square books, notwithstanding the convenience of their shape, had not yet superseded rolls; but we see, in the Notices of the Dignities of the Eastern Empire (" Notitia Dignitatum Imperii "), written towards 450, that this accessory art had already made immense progress; since certain officers of the empire used to carry, in the public ceremonies, large square books containing the administrative instructions of the emperor : these books were bound, covered with green, red, blue, or yellow leather, closed by means of leathern straps or by hooks, and ornamented with little golden rods disposed horizontally, or lozengewise, with the portrait of the sovereign painted or gilt on their sides. From the fifth century gold-smiths and lapidaries ornamented binding with great richness. And so we hear St. Jerome exclaiming :—"Your books are covered with precious stones, and Christ died naked before the gate of his temple ! " "The Book of the Gospels," in Greek, given to the basilica of Monza by Theodelinda, queen of the Lombards, about 600, has still one of these costly bindings.

A specimen of Byzantine art, preserved in the Louvre, is a sort of small plate, which is supposed to be one of the sides of the cover of a book; on it we find executed in bas-relief the " Visit of the Holy Women to the Tomb," and several other scenes from the Gospels. In this example the beauty of the figures, the taste which dictated the arrangement of the draperies, and the finish in the execution, furnish us with evidence that, in the industrial arts, the Greeks had maintained till the twelfth century their pre-eminence over all the people of Europe.

In those days the binding of ordinary books was executed without any ornamentation, this being reserved for sacred books. If, in the treasures of churches, abbeys, and palaces, a few manuscripts covered with gold, silver, and precious stones, were kept as relics, books in common use were simply covered in boards or leather; but not without much attention being given to the binding, which was merely intended to preserve the volumes. Many documents bear witness to the great care and precision with which, in certain monasteries, books were bound and preserved. All sorts of skins were employed in covering them when they had been once pressed and joined together between boards of hard wood that would not readily decay : in the North, even the skins of seals and of sharks were employed, but pig-skin seems to have been used in preference to all others.

PANEL OF A BOOK COVER.

Bas-relief in Gold Repoussé.   Ninth Century.   (in the Louvre)

It must be admitted that we, perhaps, owe to their rich bindings, which were well calculated to tempt thieves, the destruction of a number of valuable manuscripts when towns or monasteries were sacked; but, on the other hand, the sumptuous bindings with which kings and nobles covered Bibles, the Gospels, antiphonaries,* and missals, have certainly preserved to us very many curious examples that, without them, would by degrees have deteriorated, or would not have escaped all the chances of destruction to which they were exposed. It is thus, for instance, that the famous manuscript of Sens has descended to us, which contains "La Messe des Fous," set to music in the twelfth century; it is' bound between two pieces of ivory, with bas-relief carvings of the fourth century, representing the festivals of Bacchus. All great public collections show with pride some of these rare and venerable bindings, decorated with gold, silver, or copper, engraved, chased, or inlaid with precious stones or coloured glass, with camoes or antique ivories (Fig. 378). The greater number of rich books of the Gospels mentioned in history date back as far as the period of Charlemagne, and among these we must mention, above all, one given by the emperor himself to the Abbey of St. Riquier, "covered with plates of silver, and ornamented with gold and gems;" that of St. Maximinius of Treves, which came from Ada, daughter of Pepin, sister of Charlemagne, and was ornamented with an engraved agate representing Ada, the emperor, and his sons; and lastly, one that was to be seen as late as 1727 in the convent of Hautvillers, near Epernay, and which was bound in carved ivory.

Sometimes these sumptuous volumes were enclosed in an envelope made of rich stuff; or, in pursuance of an ancient custom, a casket not less gorgeously decorated than the binding, contained it. The Prayer-book of Charlemagne, now preserved in the Library of the Louvre, is known to have been originally enclosed in a small casket of silver gilt, on which were represented in relief the "Mysteries of the Passion."

These books, however, bound with goldsmith's work, were not those that were chained in churches and in certain libraries (Fig. 379), as some volumes still in existence show, with the rings through which passed the chain that fastened them to the desk. These *catenati* (chained books) were generally Bibles and missals, bound in wood and heavily ornamented

---

* *Antiphonaries*—books containing the responses, &c., used in Catholic church-services.—[Ed.]

with metallic corners; which, while placed at the disposition of the faithful and of the public in general, their owners wished to guarantee against being stolen.

We must not forget to mention, among the most beautiful bindings

Fig. 378.—Binding in Gold, adorned with precious Stones, which covered a "Book of the Gospels" of the Eleventh Century, representing Jesus Crucified, with the Virgin and St. John at the Foot of the Cross. (Musée du Louvre.)

of the eleventh and twelfth centuries, the coverings of books in enamelled copper (Fig. 380). The Museum of Cluny possesses two plates of incrusted enamel of Limoges, which must have belonged to one of these bindings: the first has for its subject the "Adoration of the Magi;" the other

IVORY DIPTYCH OF THE LOWER EMPIRE

Serving as a Book Cover, "l'Office des fous." In the Library of Sens.

represents the monk Etienne de Muret, founder of the order of Grandmont (in the twelfth century), conversing with St. Nicholas. The Cathedral of Milan contains in its treasury the covering of a book still more ancient and much richer, about fourteen inches long by twelve inches wide, and profusely covered with incrusted enamel, mounted and ornamented with polished, but uncut, precious stones of various colours.

But all these were only the work of enamellers, goldsmiths, illuminators, and clasp-makers. The binders, or bookbinders properly so called, fastened together the leaves of books, and placed them between two boards, which

Fig. 379.—Library of the University of Leyden, in which all the Books were chained, even in the Seventeenth Century.

they then covered with leather, skin, stuff, or parchment; they added to these coverings sometimes leathern straps, sometimes metal clasps, sometimes hooks, to keep the volume firmly closed, and almost always nails, whose round and projecting heads preserved the flat surface of the binding from being rubbed.

In the year 1299, when the tax was imposed upon the inhabitants of Paris for the exigencies of the king, it was ascertained that the number of bookbinders then actually in the town amounted only to seventeen, who, as well as the scribes and booksellers, were directly dependent on the

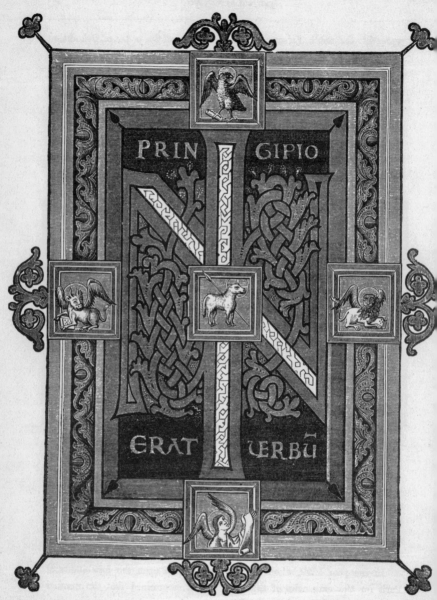

Fig. 380.—Large painted Initial Letter in a Manuscript in the Royal Library, Brussels, showing the arrangement of the Binding, in enamelled Metal, of a book of the Gospels.   (Ninth or Tenth Century.)

University, the authorities of which placed them under the surveillance of four sworn bookbinders, who were considered the *agents* of the University. We must except, however, from this jurisdiction the acknowledged bookbinder to the "Chambre des Comptes," who, before he could be appointed to this office, had to make an affirmation *that he could neither read nor write.*

In the musters, or processions, of the University of Paris, the bookbinders came after the booksellers. To explain the relatively small number of professed bookbinders, we must remember that at this period the majority of scholars bound their own books, as divers passages of ancient authors prove; while the monasteries, which were the principal centres of bookmakers, had one or many members of their community whose special function it was to bind the works written within their walls. Tritheimius, Abbot of Spanheim at the end of the fifteenth century, does not forget the bookbinders in the enumeration he makes of the different employments of his monks:—"Let that one," says he, "fasten the leaves together, and bind the book with boards. You, prepare those boards; you, dress the leather; you, the metal plates, which are to adorn the binding." These bindings are represented on the seal of the University of Oxford (Fig. 381), and on the banners of some French corporation of printers and booksellers (Figs. 382 and 386).

The metal plates, the corners, the nails, the clasps with which these volumes were then laden rendered them so heavy that, in order to enable the reader to turn over the leaves with facility, they were placed on one of those revolving desks having space for many open folios at the same time, and which were capable of accommodating many readers simultaneously. It is said that Petrarch had caused a volume containing the "Epistles of Cicero," transcribed by himself, to be bound so massively, that as he was continually reading it, he often let it fall and injured his leg; so badly once that he was threatened with amputation. This manuscript in Petrarch's handwriting is still to be seen in the Laurentian Library at Florence; it is bound in wood, with edges and clasps of copper.

The Crusades, which introduced into Europe many luxurious customs, must have had great influence on bookbinding, since the Arabs had for a long while known the art of preparing, dyeing, stamping, and gilding the skins they employed to make covers for books: these covers took the name of *alæ* (wings), no doubt from the resemblance between them and

the wings of a bird of rich plumage. The Crusaders having brought back
from their expeditions specimens of Oriental binding, our European workmen did not fail to turn their brilliant models to account.

An entire revolution, moreover, which had taken place in the formation of royal and princely libraries, was to produce a revolution in binding
also. Bibles, missals, reproductions of ancient authors, treatises on theology,
were no longer the only books in common use. The new language had
given rise to histories, romances, and poems, which were the delight of a

Fig. 381.—Seal of the University of Oxford, in which is a Book bound with Corners and Clasps.

society becoming more and more polished every day. For the pleasure
of readers, the gallant of one sex and the fair of the other, books were
required more agreeable to the eye, and less rough to the touch, than those
used for the edification of monks or the instruction of scholars. And
first of all were substituted, for the purpose of manuscripts, sizes more
portable than the grave folio. Then fine and smooth vellum was used for
writing, and books were covered in velvet, silk, or woollen stuffs. Moreover, paper, a recent invention, opened up a new era for libraries; but

two centuries were to elapse before pasteboard had entirely taken the place of wooden covers.

It is in the inventories, in the accounts, and in the archives of kings and princes, we must look for the history of bookbinding in the fourteenth and fifteenth centuries (Fig. 383). We shall limit ourselves to giving a description of some costly bindings, taken from the inventories of the magnificent libraries of the Dukes of Burgundy and of Orleans, now partly destroyed, and partly scattered about among the great public collections of France and other countries.

Belonging to the Dukes of Burgundy, Philip the Bold, Jean sans Peur, and Philip the Good, we see a small Book of the Gospels and of the "Heures de la Croix" (a kind of prayer-book), with "a binding

Fig. 382.—Banner of the Corporation of Printers-Booksellers of Angers.

embellished with gold and fifty-eight large pearls, in a case made of camlet, with one large pearl and a cluster of small pearls;" the romance of the "Moralité des Hommes sur le Ju (jeu) des Eschiers" (the game of chess), "covered in silk, with white and red flowers, and silver-gilt nails, on a green ground;" a Book of Orisons, "covered in red leather, with silver-gilt nails;" a Psalter, "having two silver-gilt clasps, bound in blue, with a golden eagle with two heads and red talons, to which is attached a little silver-gilt instrument for turning over the leaves, with three escutcheons of the same arms, covered with a red velvet *chemise*." *

---

* "Garni de deux fermaulx d'argent, dorez, armoiez d'azur à une aigle d'or à deux testes, onglé de gueulles, auquel a ung tuyau d'argent doré pour tourner les feuilles, à trois escussons desdites armes, couvert d'une chemise de veluyau vermeil."

Fig. 383.—Fragment of an engraved and stamped Binding in an unknown Material (Fifteenth Century),
representing the mystical Chase of the Unicorn, which is taking refuge in the lap of the Virgin.
(Public Library, Rouen.)

The *chemise* was a sort of pocket in which certain valuable books were enveloped. The "Heures de St. Louis" (St. Louis's Prayer-book), now in the Musée des Souverains, is still in its *chemise* of red sandal-wood.

Belonging to the Duke of Orleans, brother of Charles VI., we find Végèce's book, "On Chivalry," "covered in red leather inlaid, which has two little brass clasps;" the book of "Meliadus," "covered in green velvet, with two silver-gilt clasps, enamelled with the arms of his Royal Highness;" the book of Boèce, "On Consolation," "covered in figured silk;" "The Golden Legend," "covered in black velvet, without clasps;" the "Heures de Notre-Dame," "covered in white leather."

The same inventories give an account of the prices paid for some bindings and their accessories. Thus, in 1386, Martin Lhuillier, a bookseller at Paris, received from the Duke of Burgundy 16 francs (equivalent to about 114 francs French money of the present time), "for binding eight books, of which six were covered in grained leather;" on Sept. 19, 1394, the Duke of Orleans paid to Peter Blondel, goldsmith, 12 livres 15 sols, "for having *wrought*, besides the duke's silver seal, two clasps" for the book of Boèce; and on Jan. 15, 1398, to Émelot de Rubert, an embroideress at Paris, 50 *sols tournois*, "for having cut out and worked in gold and silk two covers of green Dampmas cloth, one for the Breviary, the other for the Book of Hours of the aforesaid nobleman, and for having made fifteen markers (*sinets*) and four pair of silk and gold straps for the said books."

The old style of thick, heavy, in some sort armour-plated, binding, could not exist long after the invention of printing, which, while multiplying books, diminished their weight, reduced their size, and, moreover, gave them a less intrinsic value. Wooden boards were replaced by compressed cardboard, nails and clasps were gradually laid aside, and stuffs of different kinds no longer used; only skin, leather, and parchment were employed. This was the beginning of modern binding; but bookbinders were as yet but mechanics working for the booksellers, who, when they had on their premises a bookbinding-room (Fig. 384), assumed, in their editions, the double title of *libraire-relieur* (bookseller-bookbinder) (Fig. 385). In 1578, Nicholas Eve still placed on his books and his sign-board, "Bookseller to the University of Paris and Bookbinder to the King." No volume was sold unbound.

From the end of the fifteenth century, although bookbinding was always considered as an adjunct to the bookseller's shop, certain amateurs who had a taste for art required richer and more *recherché* exteriors for their books. Italy set us the example of beautiful bindings in morocco, stamped and gilt; imitated, however, from those of the Koran and other Arabian manuscripts, which Venetian navigators frequently brought back with them from the East. The expedition of Charles VIII. and the wars of Louis XII. introduced into France not only Italian bindings, but Italian binders also. Without renouncing, however, at least for the *livres d'heures*, the bindings ornamented with goldsmith's work and gems, France had very soon

Fig. 384.—Bookbinders' Work-room, drawn and engraved in the Sixteenth Century, by J. Amman.

binders of her own, surpassing those who had been to them as initiators or masters. Jean Grollier, of Lyons, loved books too much not to wish to give them an exterior ornamentation worthy of the wealth of knowledge they contained. Treasurer of War, and Intendant of the Milanese before the battle of Pavia, he had begun to create a library, which he subsequently transported into France, and did not cease to enlarge and to enrich till his death, which happened in 1565. His books were bound in morocco from the Levant, with such care and taste that, under the supervision of this exacting amateur, bookbinding seemed to have already attained perfection.

Princes and ladies of the court prided themselves on their love of books and the desire to acquire them; they founded libraries, and encouraged the works and inventions of good bookbinders who produced masterpieces of patience and ability in decorating the covers of books, either with enamelled paintings, or with mosaics made of different pieces inlaid, or with plain gildings stamped on the surface with small irons. It would be impossible to enumerate the splendid bindings in all styles that the French bookbinders of the sixteenth century have left us, and which have never been surpassed since. The painter, the engraver, and even the goldsmith, co-operated with the bookbinder in his art, by furnishing him with designs for ornaments.

Fig. 385.—Mark of William Eustace (1512), Bookseller and Binder, Paris.

We now see reappearing some plates obtained from hot or cold dies, representing various subjects, and the designs from which they were taken, reproduced from those that had been in fashion towards the beginning of the sixteenth century, were often drawn by distinguished artists, such as Jean Cousin, Stephen de Laulne, &c.

Nearly all the French kings, especially the Valois, were passionately fond of splending bindings. Catherine de Medicis was such a connoisseur of finely-bound books, that authors and booksellers, who eagerly presented her with copies of their works, tried to distinguish themselves in the choice and beauty of the bindings which they had made expressly for her. Henry III., who appreciated handsomely-bound books no less than his mother, invented a very singular binding, when he had instituted the Order of "Penitents;" this consisted of death's heads and cross bones, tears, crosses, and other instruments of the Passion, gilt or stamped on black morocco leather, and having the following device, "Spes mea Deus" ("God is my hope"), with or without the arms of France.

It is impossible to associate these superb bindings with the usual and common work executed at the booksellers' shops, and under their superintendence. Some booksellers of Paris and of Lyons, the houses of Gryphe and Tournes, of Estienne and Vascosan, paid a little more attention, however, than others of the fraternity, to the binding of books which they sold to the reading public; they adopted patterns of dun-coloured calf, in compartments; or white vellum, with fillets and arabesques in gold, fine specimens of which are now very rare.

At this period Italian bookbinding had reached the most complete state of decadency, while in Germany and other parts of Europe the old massive bindings,—bindings in wood, leather, and parchment, with fastenings of iron or brass,—still held their ground. In France, however, the binders, whom the booksellers kept in a state of obscurity and servitude, had not even been able to form themselves into a guild or fraternity. They might produce masterpieces of their art, but were not allowed to append their names to their works; and we must come down as far as the famous *Gascon* (1641) before we can introduce the name of any illustrious bookbinder.

Fig. 386.—Banner of the Corporation of Printers-Booksellers of Autun.

PRINTING.

IFTEEN towns have laid claim to the honour
of being the birthplace of printing, and writers
who have applied themselves to search out the
origin of this admirable invention, far from coming to
any agreement on the point in their endeavours to clear
up the question, have only confused it. Now, however,
after many centuries of learned and earnest contro-
versy, there only remain three antagonistic propositions, with
three names of towns, four names of inventors, and three different dates. The three places are Haarlem, Strasbourg, and
Mayence; the four inventors, Laurent Coster, Gutenberg, Faust,
and Schoeffer; the three dates which are assigned to the invention of printing are 1420, 1440, 1450. In our opinion these
three propositions, which some try to combat and destroy by opposing each
to the other, ought, on the contrary, to be blended into one, and combined
chronologically in such a manner as to represent the three principal periods
of the discovery of printing.

There is no doubt that printing existed in the germ in ancient times;
that it was known and made use of by the ancients. There were stamps
and seals bearing legends traced the wrong way, from which positive
impressions were obtained on papyrus or parchment, in wax, ink, or colour.
We are shown, in museums, plates of copper or of cedar-wood, covered
with characters carved or cut out in them, which seem to have been

intended for the purpose of printing, and which resemble the block plates
of the fifteenth century.

Something very much like the process of printing in movable type is
described by Cicero in a passage in which he refutes the doctrine of Epicurus
on the creation of the world by atoms : " Why not believe, also, that by

Fig. 387.—Ancient Wood-block Print, cut in Flanders before 1440, representing Jesus Christ after his
Flagellation.   (Delbecq's Collection, Ghent.)

throwing together, indiscriminately, innumerable forms of letters of the
alphabet, either in gold or in any other substance, one can *print* with these
letters, on the ground, the *Annals* of Ennius ?"   The movable letters possessed by the ancients were carved in box-wood or ivory; but they were
only employed for teaching children to read, as Quinctilian testifies in his

" Oratorical Institutions," and St. Jerome in his "Epistles." There was
then only wanting a fortunate chance to cause this carved alphabet to create
the typographic art fifteen centuries earlier than its actual birth.

"The art of taking impressions once discovered," says M. Léon de
Laborde, "and applied to engraving in relief, gave rise to printing,

Fig. 388.—Fac-simile of an Engraving on Wood, by an ancient Flemish Engraver (about 1438); which
was inserted, after the manner of a Miniature, in a Manuscript of the Fifteenth Century, containing
Prayers for the use of the People. (Delbecq's Collection, Ghent.)

which was only the perfection to which a natural and rapid progression
of attempts and efforts would naturally lead." "But it was only," adds
M. Ambroise-Firmin Didot, "when the art of making paper—that art
familiar to the Chinese from the beginning of our era—spread in Europe
and became generally known, that the reproduction, by pressing, of texts,

figures, playing-cards, &c., first by the tabular process, called *xylography* (block-printing), then with movable types, became easy, and was consequently to appear simultaneously in different places."

But, at the end of the fourteenth century, at Haarlem, in Holland, wood-engraving had been discovered, and consequently *tabular impression,* with which the Chinese, it is said, were already acquainted three or four hundred years before the modern era. Perhaps it was some Chinese book or pack of cards brought to Haarlem by a merchant or a navigator, that revealed to the cardmakers and printsellers of the industrious Netherlands a process of impressing more expeditious and more economical. Xylography began on the day when a legend was engraved on a wood-block; this legend, limited at first to a few lines, very soon occupied a whole page; then this page was not long in becoming a volume (Fig. 387 to 389).

Fig. 389.—Wood-block, cut in France, about 1440, representing an Image of St. James the Great, with one of the Commandments as a Text. (Imperial Library, Paris, Collection of Prints.)

Here is an extract from the account given by Adrian Junius, in his Latin work entitled "Batavia," of the discovery of printing at Haarlem, written in 1572:—"More than one hundred and thirty-two years ago there lived at Haarlem, close to the royal palace, one John Laurent, surnamed Coster (or governor), for this honourable post came to him by inheritance, being handed down in his family from father to son. One day, about 1420, as he was walking after dinner in a wood near the town, he set to work and cut the bark of beech-trees into the shape of letters, with which he traced, on paper, by pressing one after the other upon it, a model composed of many lines for the instruction of his children. Encouraged by this success, his genius took a higher flight, and then, in concert with his son-in-law, Thomas Pierre, he invented a species of ink more glutinous and tenacious than that employed in writing, and he thus printed figures (*images*) to which he added his wooden letters. I have myself seen many copies of this first attempt at printing. The text is on one side only of the paper. The book printed was written in the vulgar tongue, by an anonymous author, having as its title 'Speculum nostræ Salutis' ('The Mirror of our Salvation'). Later, Laurent Coster changed his wooden types into leaden, then these into pewter. Laurent's new invention, encouraged by studious men, attracted from all parts an immense concourse of purchasers. The love of the art increased, the labours of his workshop increased also, and Laurent was obliged to add hired workmen to the members of his family, to assist in his operations. Among these workmen there was a certain John, whom I suspect of being none other than Faust, who was treacherous and fatal to his master. Initiated, under the seal of an oath, into all the secrets of printing, and having become very expert in casting type, in setting it up, and in the other processes of his trade, this John took advantage of a Christmas evening, while every one was in church, to rifle his master's workshop and to carry off his typographical implements. He fled with his booty to Amsterdam, thence to Cologne, and afterwards to Mayence, where he established himself; and calculating upon safety here, set up a printing-office. In that very same year, 1422, he printed with the type which Laurent had employed at Haarlem, a grammar then in use, called 'Alexandri Galli Doctrinale,' and a 'Treatise of Peter the Spaniard' ('Petri Hispani Tractatus')."

This account, which came, indeed, rather late, although the author referred to the most respectable authorities in support of it, met at first with nothing but incredulity and contempt. At this period the right of Mayence to be considered the birthplace of printing could only be seriously counterbalanced by the right Strasbourg had to be so considered. The three names of Gutenberg, of Faust, and of Schœffer were already consecrated by universal gratitude. Everywhere, then, except in Holland, this new testimony was rejected; everywhere the new inventor, whose claim had just been made for a share of the honour, was rejected as an apocryphal or legendary being. But very soon, however, criticism, raising itself above the influences of nationality, took up the question, discussed the account given by Junius, examined that famous "Speculum" which no one had yet pointed out, proved the existence of xylographic impressions, sought for those which could be attributed to Coster, and opposed to the Abbé Tritheim (or Trithemius), who had written on the origin of printing from information furnished by Peter Schœffer himself, the more disinterested testimony of the anonymous chronicler of Cologne in 1465, who had learned from Ulric Zell, one of Gutenberg's workmen, and the first printer of Cologne in 1465, this important peculiarity:—"Although the typographic art was invented at Mayence," says he, "nevertheless the first rough sketch of this art was invented in Holland, and it is in imitation of the 'Donatus' (the Latin syntax by Cœlius Donatus, a grammarian of the fourth century, a book then in use in the schools of Europe), which long before that time was printed there; it is in imitation of this, and on account of it, that the said art began under the auspices of Gutenberg."

If Gutenberg imitated the "Donatus," which was printed in Holland before the time he himself printed at Mayence, Gutenberg was not the inventor of printing. It was in 1450 that Gutenberg began to print at Mayence (Fig. 390); but from as early a date as 1436 he had tried to print at Strasbourg; and, before his first attempts, there had been printed in Holland,—at Haarlem, and Dordrecht,—"Specula" and "Donati" on wooden boards; a process known by the name of *xylography* (engraving on wood), while the attempts at *typography* (printing with movable type) made by Gutenberg entirely differed from the other; since the letters, engraved at first on steel points (*poinçons*), and afterwards forced into a copper matrix, reproduced by means of casting in a metal more fusible than copper the impress of the point on shanks (*tiges*) made of pewter or lead, hardened by an alloy (Fig. 391).

Now, a rather singular circumstance comes to corroborate what was said by Adrian Junius. A Latin edition of the "Speculum," an in-folio of sixty-three leaves, with wood engravings in two compartments at the head of each leaf, consists of a mixture of twenty xylographic leaves, and of forty-one leaves printed with movable type, but very imperfect, and cast in moulds which were probably made of baked earth; an edition of a Dutch

"Speculum," in folio, has also two pages in a type smaller and closer than the rest of the text. How are we to explain these anomalies? On the one hand, a mixture of xylography and typography; on the other, a combination of two different kinds of movable type. My hypothesis is, if indeed the details given by Junius, open to suspicion as they are, be correct, that the dishonest workman who, according to his own account, stole the implements

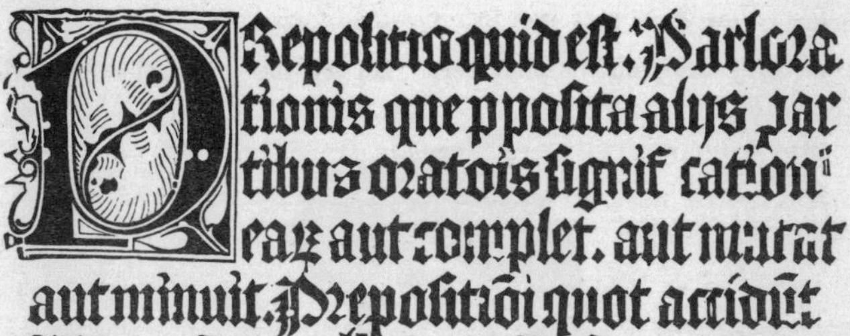

Fig. 390.—Fac-simile of a Page of the most ancient Xylographic " Donatus " (Chapter on Prepositions), printed at Mayence, by Fust and Gutenberg, about 1450.

employed in the workshop of Laurent Coster, and who must have acted with a certain amount of precipitation, contented himself with carrying off some forms of the "Speculum" just ready for the press. The type employed for twenty or twenty-two pages was sufficient to serve as models for a counterfeit edition, and also for a book of small extent, such as the " Alexandri Galli Doctrinale," and the "Petri Hispani Tractatus." It is

probable that the Latin and Dutch editions of the "Speculum" were both
entirely composed, set up, and prepared for the text to be struck off, when
the thief took at hazard the twenty-two forms, which he determined to turn
to account, at any rate as a model for the counterfeit edition he intended to
publish. In cast-iron type, these forms could not have weighed more than
sixty pounds; in wooden type, not half as much; if we add to these the
composing-sticks, the pincers, the galleys, and other indispensable elements
of the trade, we shall find that the booty was not beyond the strength of a
man to carry easily on his shoulders. As for the press, about that there

Fig. 391.—Portrait of Gutenberg, from an Engraving of the Sixteenth Century.
(Imperial Library of Paris, Print Room.)

could be no question, since the impressions produced at Haarlem were made
with a pad and by hand, as is still the case with playing-cards and prints.

It remains now to discover who was this John who appropriated the
secret of printing, and took it from Haarlem to Mayence. Was it John Fust
or Faust, as Adrian Junius suspected? Was it John Gutenberg, as many
Dutch writers have alleged? or was it not rather John Gensfleisch the elder,
a relation of Gutenberg, as, from a very explicit passage of the learned
Joseph Wimpfeling, his contemporary, the latest defenders of the Haarlem
tradition think? The question is still undecided.

The "Speculum," however, is not the only book of the kind which

Fig. 392.—Fac-simile of the Twenty-eighth Xylographic Page of the "Biblia Pauperum;" representing, with Texts taken from the Old Testament, David slaying Goliath, and Christ causing the Souls of the Patriarchs and Prophets to come out of Purgatory.

had appeared in the Low Countries before the period assigned to the discovery of printing in Holland. Some of these were evidently xylographic, others show signs of having been printed with movable type of wood, not of metal. All have engravings of the same character as those of the "Speculum," especially the "Biblia Pauperum" ("Poor Men's Bible") (Fig. 392), the "Ars Moriendi" ("The Art of Dying") (Fig. 393), the "Ars Memorandi" ("The Art of Remembering"), which had a very wide circulation.

However this may be, Laurent Coster, notwithstanding the progress he had made with his invention, was certainly ignorant of its importance. In those days the only libraries were those belonging to convents and to a few nobles of literary acquirements; private individuals, with the exception of some learned men who were richer than their fellows, possessed no books at all. The copyists and illuminators by profession were employed exclusively in reproducing "Livres d'Heures" (prayer-books), and school books : the first were sumptuous volumes, objects of an industry quite exceptional; the second, destined for children, were always simply executed, and composed of a few leaves of strong paper or parchment. The pupils limited themselves to writing passages of their lessons from the dictation of their teachers; to the monks was assigned the task of transcribing, at full length, the sacred and profane authors. Coster could not even have thought of reproducing these works, the sale of which would have seemed to him impossible, and he at first fell back upon the "Specula," religious books which addressed themselves to all the faithful, even to those who could not read, by means of the stories or illustrations (*images*) of which these books were composed; then he occupied himself with the "Donati," which he reprinted many times from xylographic plates, if not with movable type, and for which he must have found a considerable demand. It was one of these "Donati" that, falling under the eyes of Gutenberg, revealed to him, according to the "Chronique de Cologne," the secret of printing.

This secret was kept faithfully for fifteen or twenty years by the workmen employed in his printing-house, who were not initiated into the mysteries of the new art till they had served a certain time of probation and apprenticeship : a terrible oath bound together those whom the master had considered worthy of entering into partnership with him; for on the preservation of the secret depended the prosperity or the ruin of the inventor and his coadjutors, since all printed books were then sold as manuscripts.

Fig. 393.—Fac-simile of the fifth Page of the first Xylographic Edition of the " Ars Moriendi," representing the Sinner on his Death-bed surrounded by his Family. Two Demons are whispering into his ear, "Think of thy treasure," and "Distribute it to thy friends."

But while the secret was so scrupulously maintained by the first Dutch printer and his partners, a lawsuit was brought before the superior court of Strasbourg which, though the motives for it were apparently but of private interest, was nevertheless to give the public the key to the mysterious trade of the typographer. This lawsuit,—the curious documents relating to which were found only in 1760, in an old tower at Strasbourg,—was brought against John Gensfleisch, called Gutenberg (who was born at Mayence, but was exiled from his native town during the political troubles, and had settled at Strasbourg since 1420), by George and Nicholas Dritzehen, who, as heirs of the deceased Andrew Dritzehen, their brother, and formerly Gutenberg's partner, desired to be admitted as his representatives into an association of whose object they were ignorant, but from which they no doubt knew their brother expected to derive some beneficial results. It was, in short, printing itself which was on its trial at Strasbourg towards the end of the year 1439; that is, more than fourteen years before the period at which printing is known to have been first employed in Mayence.

Here is a summary, as we find them in the documents relating to this lawsuit, of the facts stated before the judge. Gutenberg, an ingenious but a poor man, possessed *divers secrets* for becoming rich. Andrew Dritzehen came to him with a request that he would teach him *many arts*. Gutenberg thereupon initiated him into the art of *polishing stones*, and Andrew "derived great profit from this secret." Subsequently, with the object of carrying out *another art* during the pilgrimage of Aix-la-Chapelle,* Gutenberg agreed with Hans Riffen, mayor of Lichtenau, to form a company, which Andrew Dritzehen and a man named Andrew Heilman desired to join. Gutenberg consented to this on condition that they would together purchase of him the right to a third of the profits, for a sum of 160 florins, payable on the day of the contract, and 80 florins payable at a later date. The agreement being made, he taught them the *art* which they were to exercise at the proper period in Aix-la-Chapelle; but the pilgrimage was postponed to the following year, and the partners required of Gutenberg that he should not conceal from them any of the *arts and inventions* of which he was cognisant. New stipulations were entered upon whereby the partners pledged themselves to pay an additional sum, and in which it was stated that

* Probably this "pilgrimage" refers to some one of the great European Councils or Diets held in the city during the Middle Ages, as were Congresses in later times.—[ED].

the *art* should be carried on for the benefit of the four partners during the space of five years; and that, in the event of one of them dying, *all the implements of the art, and all the works already produced*, should belong to the surviving partners; the heirs of the deceased being entitled to receive no more than an indemnity of 100 florins at the expiration of the said five years.

Gutenberg accordingly offered to pay the heirs of his late partner the stipulated sum; but they demanded of him an account of the capital invested by Andrew Dritzehen, which, as they alleged, had been absorbed in the speculation. They mentioned especially a certain account for *lead*, for which their brother had made himself responsible. Without denying this account, Gutenberg refused to satisfy their demands.

Numerous witnesses gave evidence, and their depositions for and against the object of the association show us a faithful picture of what must have been the inner life of four partners exhausting themselves and their money in efforts to realise a scheme the nature of which they were very careful to conceal, but from which they expected to derive the most splendid results.

We find them working by night; we hear them answering those who questioned them on the object of their work, that they were "mirror-makers" (*spiegel-macher*); we find them borrowing money, because they had in hand "something in which they could not invest too much money." Andrew Dritzehen, in whose care the *press* was left, being dead, Gutenberg's first object was to send to the deceased's house a man he could trust, who was commissioned to unscrew the press, so that the pieces (or *forms*), which were fixed closely together by it, might become detached from each other, and then to place these forms in or on the press "in such a manner that no one might be able to understand what they were." Gutenberg regrets that his servant did not bring him back all the forms, many of which "were not to be found." Lastly, we find figuring among the witnesses a turner, a timber-merchant, and a goldsmith who declared that he had worked during three years for Gutenberg, and that he had gained more than 100 florins by preparing for him "the things belonging to printing" (*das zu dem Trucken gehoret*).

Trucken—printing! Thus the grand word was pronounced in the course of the lawsuit, but certainly without producing the least effect on the audience, who wondered what was this occult *art* which Gutenberg and his partners had carried on with so much trouble, and at such great expense. However, it is quite certain that, with the exception of the indiscretion, really very insignificant, of the goldsmith, Gutenberg's secret remained undiscovered, for it was supposed it had to do with the *polishing of stones* and the manufacture of *mirrors*. The judge, being informed as to the good faith of Gutenberg, pronounced the offers he made to the plaintiffs satisfactory, decided against the heirs of Andrew Dritzehen, and the three other partners remained sole proprietors of their process, and continued to carry it out.

If we study with some attention the documents relating to this singular trial at Strasbourg, and if we also notice, that our word *mirror* is the translation of the German word *spiegel* and of the Latin word *speculum*, it is impossible not to recognise all the processes, all the implements made use of in printing, with the names they have not ceased to bear, and which were given to them as soon as they were invented ; the forms, the screw (which is not the *printing*-press, for they printed in those days with the *frotton*, or rubber, but the frame in which the types were *pressed*), the lead, the work, the art, &c. We see Gutenberg accompanied by a turner who made the screw for the press, the timber merchant who had supplied the planks of box or of pear wood, the goldsmith who had engraved or cast the type. Then we ascertain that these "mirrors," in the preparation of which the partners were occupied, and which were to be sold at the pilgrimage of Aix-la-Chapelle, were no other than the future copies of the "Speculum Humanæ Salvationis," an imitation more or less perfect of the famous book of illustrations of which Holland had already published three or four editions, in Latin and in Dutch.

We know, on the other hand, that these "Mirrors" or "Specula" were, in the earliest days of printing, so much in request, that in every place the first printers rivalled each other in executing and publishing different editions of the book with illustrations. Here, there was the reprint of the "Speculum," abridged by L. Coster; there, the "Speculum" of Gutenberg, taken entirely from manuscripts ; now it was the "Speculum Vitæ Humanæ," by Roderick, Bishop of Zamora ; then the "Speculum Consciencæ," of Arnold Gheyloven ; then the "Speculum Sacerdotum," or again, the voluminous "Speculum" of Vincent de Beauvais, &c.

It cannot now any longer be assumed that Gutenberg really made mirrors or looking-glasses at Strasbourg, and that those pieces "laid in a press," those "forms which came to pieces," that lead sold or wrought by a goldsmith, were, as they wished it to be supposed, only intended to be used "for printing ornaments on the frames of looking-glasses!"

Would it not have been surprising that the pilgrims who were to visit Aix-la-Chapelle on the occasion of the grand jubilee of 1440, should be so anxious to buy ornamented mirrors? As to the art "*of polishing stones,*" which Gutenberg had taught at first to Andrew Dritzehen, who

Fig. 394.—Interior of a Printing-office in the Sixteenth Century, by J. Amman

derived from it "*so much profit,*" having anything to do with printing was, no doubt, also questionable; but we have not been able to solve the enigma, and wait to clear up the difficulty till a new *incunable* (*incunabula,* "a cradle," the word is applied to the first editions ever printed) is discovered, the work of some Peter (πέτρος "a stone") or other; as, for example, the Latin sermons of Hermann de Petra on the Lord's Prayer; for Gutenberg, when speaking of *polishing stones,* might have enigmatically designated a book he was printing; just as his partner, in answer to the judge, after having raised his hand on high and sworn to give true evidence, could call himself *a maker of mirrors*, without telling a falsehood, without committing perjury. The secret of printing was to be religiously kept by those who knew it.

In short, it results from all this that Gutenberg, "an ingenious man and a man of invention," having seen a xylographic "Donatus," had endeavoured to imitate it, and had succeeded in doing so, the secret being confided to Andrew Dritzehen; that the other *arts*, which Gutenberg at first kept to himself, but which he subsequently communicated to his partners, consisted in the idea of substituting movable type for tabular printing; a substitution that could only be effected after numerous experiments had been made, and which were just about to be crowned with success when Andrew Dritzehen died. We may then consider it as nearly certain that printing was in some sort discovered twice successively—the first time by Laurent Coster, whose small printed books, or books in letterpress (*en moule*), attracted the attention of Gutenberg; and the second time by Gutenberg, who raised the art to a degree of perfection such as had never been attained by his predecessor.

It was after the Strasbourg lawsuit, between the years 1440 or 1442, as stated by many historians, that Gutenberg went to Holland, and there became a workman in the establishment of Coster; this is asserted in order that they might be able to accuse him of the theft which Junius has laid to the account of a certain man whose name was John. Only—and the coincidence is not, in this case, unworthy of remark—two unedited chronicles of Strasbourg and the Alsatian Wimpfeling relate, almost at the same time, a robbery of type and implements used in printing, but mentioning Strasbourg instead of Haarlem, Gutenberg instead of Laurent Coster, and naming the thief John Gensfleisch. But, according to the Strasbourg tradition, this John Gensfleisch the elder, related to and employed by, Gutenberg, robbed him of his secret and his tools, after having been his rival in the discovery of printing, and established himself at Mayence, where, by a just visitation of Providence, he was soon struck blind. It was then, adds the tradition, that in his repentance he sent for his former master to come to Mayence, and gave up to him the business he had founded. But this last part of the tradition seems to savour too much of the moral deductions of a story; and as it is very improbable, moreover, that two thefts of the same kind were committed at the same period, and under the same circumstances, we are inclined to believe that the John mentioned by Junius was, in fact, Gutenberg's relative, who went to Haarlem to perfect himself in the art of printing, and robbed Coster; for there really existed at Mayence, at the time mentioned, a John Gensfleisch, who might have printed, before Gutenberg went to join him there, the two school books, "Doctrinale Alexandri Galli," and "Petri Hispani Tractatus." This is rendered still more probable from the fact that, after search had been long made for these books, which were absolutely unknown when Junius mentioned them, three fragments of the "Doctrinale," printed on vellum with the type of the Dutch "Speculum," were at length found.

However, Gutenberg had not succeeded with his printing at Strasbourg. When he quitted the town, where he left such pupils as John Mentell and Henry Eggestein, he removed to Mayence, and established himself in the house of *Zum Jungen*. There he again printed, but he exhausted his means in experiments, alternately taking up and laying aside the various processes he had employed—xylography, movable types of wood, lead, and cast iron. He used, for printing, a hand-press which he had made on the same principle as a wine-press; he invented new tools; he began ten works and could finish none. At last, his resources all gone, and himself in a state of despair, he was just going to give up the art altogether, when chance sent him a partner, John Fust or Faust, a rich goldsmith of Mayence.

This partnership took place in 1450. Fust, by a deed properly drawn up by a notary, promised Gutenberg to advance him 800 gold florins for the manufacture of implements and tools, and 300 for other expenses— servants' wages, rent, firing, parchment, paper, ink, &c. Besides the "Specula" and "Donati" already in circulation, which Gutenberg probably continued to print, the object of the partnership was the printing of a Bible in folio of two columns, in large type, with initial letters engraved on wood; an important work requiring a great outlay.

A caligrapher was attached to Gutenberg's printing-establishment, either to trace on wood the characters to be engraved, or to *rubricate* the printed pages; in other words, to write in red ink, to paint with a brush or to illuminate (*au frotton*) the initials, the capital letters, and the headings of chapters. This caligrapher was probably Peter Schœffer or

Schoiffer, of Gernsheim, a small town in the diocese of Darmstadt, a clerk of the diocese of Mayence, as he styles himself, and perhaps a German student in the University of Paris ; since a manuscript copied by him, and preserved at Strasbourg, is terminated by an inscription in which he testifies that he himself wrote it in the year 1449, in "the very glorious University of Paris." Schœffer was not only a literary man, but was also a man of ingenuity and prudence (*ingeniosus et prudens*). Having entered Gutenberg's establishment, on whom Fust had forced him, in 1452, to take part in the new association they were then forming, Schœffer invented an improved mould with which he could cast separately all the letters of the alphabet in metal, whereas up to this time they had been obliged to engrave the type with a *burin*. He concealed his discovery from Gutenberg, who would naturally have availed himself of it ; but he confided the secret to Fust, who, being very experienced in casting metals, carried out his idea. It was evidently with this cast type, which resisted the action of the press, that Schœffer composed and executed a "Donatus," of which four leaves, in parchment, were found at Treves in 1803, in the interior of an old book-cover, and were deposited in the Imperial Library of Paris. An inscription in this edition, printed in red, announces formally that Peter Schœffer alone had executed it, with its type and its initial letters, according to the "new art of the printer, without the help of the pen."

That was certainly the first public disclosure of the existence of printing, which up to this time had passed off its productions as the work of caligraphers. It seems that Schœffer thus desired to mark the date, and to appropriate to himself the invention of Gutenberg. It is certain that Fust, allured by the results Schœffer had obtained, secretly entered into partnership with him, and, in order to get rid of Gutenberg, profited by the power which his bond gave him over that unfortunate individual. Gutenberg, summoned to dissolve the partnership and to return the sums he had received, which he was quite incapable of paying, was obliged, in order to satisfy the demands of his pitiless creditor, to give up to him his printing establishment with all the materials it contained ; among them was included this same Bible, the last leaves of which were, perhaps, in the press at the moment when they robbed him of the fruits of his long-protracted labours.

Gutenberg evicted, Peter Schœffer, and Fust, who had given Schœffer his daughter in marriage, completed the great Bible, which was ready for sale in the early months of 1456. This Bible, being passed off as a manuscript, must have commanded a very high price. This accounts for the non-appearance on it of any inscription to show by what means this immense work had been executed; let us add that in any case we may well suppose Schœffer and Fust were not willing to give to Gutenberg a share of the glory which they dared not yet appropriate to themselves.

The Latin Bible, without date, which all bibliographers agree in con-

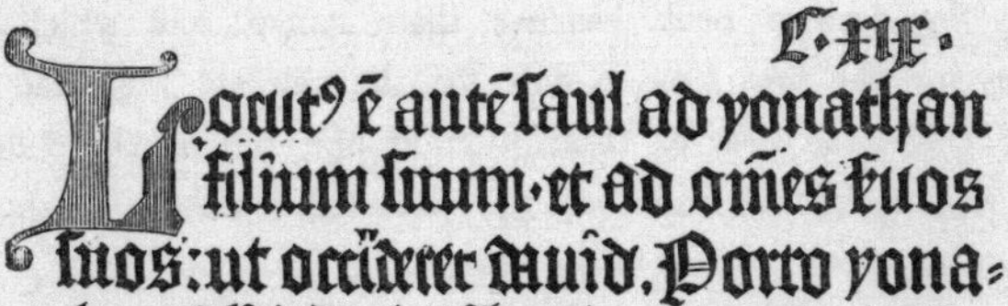
C. XIX.
Locut9 ē autē saul ad yonathan
filium suum. et ad omēs servos
suos: ut occideret dauid. Porro yonathas fili9 saul. diligebat dauid valde.
Et indicauit yonathas dauid dicens
Querit saul pr̄ meus occidere te. Qua-
propt̄ observa te q̄so mane: & manebis
clam et abscōderis Ego autē egrediēs
stabo iuxta patrē meū i agro vbicūq;
fuerit: et ego loquar de te ad patrē meū:
& q̄dcūq; videro nūciabo tibi. Locut9
est ergo yonathas de dauid bona: ad
saul patrem suum. Dixitq; ad eū. Ne

Fig. 395.—Fac-simile of the Bible of 1456 (1 Samuel xix. 1—5), printed at Mayence by Gutenberg.

sidering as that of Gutenberg, is a large in-folio of six hundred and forty-one leaves, divided into two, or three, or even four volumes. It is printed in double columns, of forty-two lines each in the full pages, with the exception of the first ten, which consisted of only forty or forty-one lines (Fig. 395). The characters are Gothic; the leaves are all numbered, and have neither *signatures* nor *catchwords*. Some copies of it are on vellum, others on paper. The number of copies which were printed of this Bible may be estimated at one hundred and fifty—a considerable number for that period. The simultaneous publication of so many Bibles, exactly alike, did not contribute less than the lawsuit of Gutenberg and Fust to make known the discovery of printing. Besides which, Fust and his new partner, although they had mutually agreed to keep the secret as long as possible, were the first to reveal it, in order to get all the credit of the invention for themselves, when public rumour allowed them no longer to conceal it within their printing-office.

It was then they printed the "Psalmorum Codex" (Collection of Psalms), the earliest book bearing their names, and which fixed, in a manner, for the first time, a date for the new art they had so much improved. The *colophon*, or inscription at the end of the "Psalmorum Codex," announces that the book was executed "without the help of the pen, by an ingenious process, in the year of our Lord, 1457."

This magnificent Psalter, which went through three editions without any considerable alterations being made in it in the space of thirty-three years, is a large in-folio volume of one-hundred and seventy-five leaves, printed in red and black characters, imitated from those used in the liturgical manuscripts of the fifteenth century. There exists, however, of the rarest edition of this book but six or seven copies on vellum (Fig. 396).

From this period printing, instead of concealing itself, endeavoured, on the contrary, to make itself generally known. But it does not as yet seem to have occurred to any one that it could be applied to the reproduction of other books than Bibles, psalters, and missals, because these were the only books that commanded a quick and extensive sale. Fust and Schffœer then undertook the printing of a voluminous work, which served as a liturgical manual to the whole of Christendom, the celebrated "Rationale Divinorum Officiorum" ("Manual of Divine Offices"), by William Durand, Bishop of Mende, in the thirteenth century. It suffices to glance over this "Rationale," and to compare it with the coarse "Specula" printed in Holland, to be convinced that in the year 1459 printing had reached the highest degree of perfection. This edition, dated from Mayence (*Moguntiæ*), was no longer intended for a small number of buyers; it was addressed to the entire Catholic world, and copies of it on vellum and on paper were disseminated so rapidly over the whole of Europe as to cause the belief, thenceforward, that printing was invented at Mayence.

Uenite exultemus domino,
Eterne recu̅-In p̅mo Noctur̅
Exultate iu=
sti in dn̅o:re
Cōfitemi̅ d
psalterio decē
Cantate ei cāticu̅ nouū:
feracōe Quia rectū e̅ ūbū
in fide Diligit misedia̅m
dn̅i plena est tra, Uerbo
et spiritu oris eius oñis

Fig. 396.—Fac-simile of a page of the Psalter of 1459, second edition, or the second copy that was struck off. Printed at Mayence, by J. Fust and P. Schœffer.

The fourth work printed by Fust and Schœffer, and dated 1460, is the collection of the Constitutions of Pope Clement V., known by the name of "Clementines"—a large in-folio in double columns, having superb initial letters painted in gold and colours in the small number of copies still extant.

But Gutenberg, though deprived of his typographic apparatus, had not renounced the art of which he considered himself, and with reason, the principal inventor. He was, above all, anxious to prove himself as capable as his former partners of producing books "without the help of the pen." He formed a new association, and fitted up a printing-office which, we know by tradition, was actively at work till 1460, the year wherein appeared the "Catholicon" (a kind of encyclopædia of the thirteenth century), by John

Fig. 397.—Fac-simile of the "Catholicon" of 1460, printed at Mayence by Gutenberg.

Balbi, of Genoa, the only important work the printing of which can be attributed to Gutenberg (Fig. 397), and which can bear comparison with the editions of Fust and Schœffer. Gutenberg, who had imitated the Dutch "Donati" and "Specula," doubtless felt a repugnance at appropriating to himself the credit of an invention he had only improved; accordingly, in the long and explicit anonymous inscription placed at the end of the volume, he attributed to God alone the glory of this divine invention, declaring that the "Catholicon" had been printed without the assistance of reed, *stylus,* or pen, but by a marvellous combination of points, matrices, and letters.

This undertaking brought to a happy termination, Gutenberg, no doubt weary of the annoyances incident to business, transferred his printing-office to his workmen, Henry and Nicholas Bechtermuncze, Weigand Spyes, and Ulric Zell. Then, having retired near to Adolphus II., elector and archbishop of Mayence, where he occupied the post of gentleman of the ecclesiastical court of that prince, he contented himself with the modest stipend attached to that office, and died at a date not authentically determined, but which cannot be later than February 24, 1468. His friend, Adam Gelth, erected in the Church of the Récollets at Mayence, a monument to his memory, with an epitaph styling him formally " the inventor of the typographic art."

Fust and Schœffer did not the less continue to print books with indefatigable ardour. In 1462 they completed a new edition of the Bible, much more perfect than that of 1456, and of which copies were probably sold, as were those of the first edition, as manuscripts, especially in countries where, as in France, printing did not already exist. It seems that the appearance in Paris of this Bible, (called the Mayence Bible), greatly excited the community of scribes and booksellers, who saw in the new method of producing books, *without the aid of the pen*, " the destruction of their trade." They charged, it is said, the sellers of these books with magic ; but it is more probable the latter were proceeded against, and condemned to fine and imprisonment, for having omitted to procure from the University authority for the sale of their Bible ; such permission being then indispensable for the sale of every kind of book.

In the meantime the town of Mayence had been taken by assault and given up to pillage (October 27, 1462). This event, in consequence of which the printing-office of Fust and Schœffer remained shut up for two years, resulted in the dissemination over the whole of Europe of printers and the art of printing. Cologne, Hamburg, and Strasbourg appear to have been the first towns in which the emigrants established themselves.

When these printers left Mayence, and carried their art elsewhere, it had never produced any book of classic literature ; but it had proved by important publications, such as the Bible and the " Catholicon," that it could create entire libraries, and thus propagate, *ad infinitum*, the masterpieces of human genius. It was reserved for the printing-office of Fust and Schœffer to set the example in that direction, and of printing the first classical work. In 1465, Cicero's treatise " De Officiis," issued from the press of these two faithful associates, and marked, as we may say, the commencement of the printing of books for libraries, and with so great success that in the following year a new edition of the treatise was published, in quarto.

At this period, Fust himself came to Paris, where he established a dépôt of printed books, but left the management of the concern to one of his own fellow-countrymen. This person dying soon afterwards, the books found in his house, being the property of a foreigner, were sold by right of forfeiture, for the king's benefit. But upon the petition of Peter Schœffer, backed up by the Elector of Mayence, the King, Louis XI., granted to the petitioners a sum of 2,425 golden dollars, " in consideration of the trouble and labour which the said petitioners had taken for the said art and trade of printing, and of the benefit and utility which resulted and may result from this art to the whole world, as well by increasing knowledge as in other ways." This memorable decree of the King of France bears date April 21, 1475.

We must mention, however, that about the year 1462, Louis XI., inquisitive and uneasy at what he had heard of the invention of Gutenberg, sent to Mayence Nicholas Jenson, a clever engraver, attached to the mint at Tours, " to obtain secret information of the cutting of the points and type, by means of which the rarest manuscripts could be multiplied, and to carry off surreptitiously the invention and introduce it into France." Nicholas Jenson, after having succeeded in his mission, did not return to France (it was never known why), but went to Venice and established himself there as a printer. It would seem, however, that Louis XI., not discouraged at the ill success of his attempt, despatched, it is said, another envoy, less enterprising but more conscientious than the first, to discover the secrets of printing. In 1469, three German printers, Ulric Gering, Martin Crantz, and Michael Friburger, began to print in Paris, in a room of the Sorbonne, of which their fellow-countryman, John Heylin, named De la Pierre, was then the prior; in the following year they dedicated to the king, "their protector," one of their editions, revised by the learned William Fichet; and in the space of four years they published about fifteen works, quartos and folios, the majority being printed for the first time. Then, when they were forced to leave the Sorbonne, because John de la Pierre, who had returned to Germany, had no longer authority over the institution, they set up in the Rue Saint-Jacques a new printing establishment, whose sign-board was the "Soleil d'Or," from which, during the next five years, were issued twelve other important works.

The Sorbonne then, like the University, was the cradle and the foster-mother in Paris of the art of printing, which soon attained to a flourishing condition, and produced, during the last twenty years of the fourteenth * century, numerous fine books of history, poetry, literature, and devotion, under the direction of the able and learned Pierre Caron, Pasquier Bonhomme, Anthony Vérard, Simon Vostre (Fig. 398), &c.

After the capture of Mayence, two workmen who had been dismissed from the establishment of Fust and Schœffer, Conrad Sweynheim and Arnold Pannartz, carried beyond the Alps the secret that had been confided to them under the guarantee of an oath. They remained for a time in the Convent of Subiaco, near Rome, in which were some German monks, and there they organised a printing apparatus, and printed many fine editions of Lactantius, Cicero, St. Augustine, &c. They were soon invited to Rome, and met with an asylum in the house of the illustrious family of Massimi; but they found an opponent in the city in one of their own workmen from the convent, who had come to Rome and engaged himself as printer to the cardinal John of Torquemada. Henceforward sprang up between the two printing establishments a rivalry which showed itself in unparallelled zeal and activity on both sides. In ten years the greater number of the writings of the ancient Latin authors, which had been preserved in manuscripts more or less rare, passed through the press. In 1476 there were in Rome more than twenty printers, who employed about a hundred presses, and whose great object was to surpass each other in the rapidity with which they produced their publications; so that the day soon arrived when the most precious manuscripts retained any value only because they contained what had not been already made public by printing. Those of which printed editions already existed were so universally disregarded, that we must refer to this period the destruction of a large number. They were used, when written on parchment, for binding the new books; and to this circumstance may be attributed the loss of certain celebrated works which printing in nowise tended to preserve from the knife of the binder.

While printing was displaying such prodigious activity in Rome, it was

---

* *Sic;* but it should evidently be the fifteenth century.—[ED.]

Fig. 398.—Fac-simile of a page of a "Livre d'Heures" printed in Paris, in 1512, by Simon Vostre.

not less active in Venice, where it seems to have been imported by that
Nicholas Jenson whom Louis XI. had sent to Gutenberg, and whom for a
long time even the Venetians looked on as the inventor of the art with
which he had clandestinely become acquainted at Mayence. From the

Fig. 399.—The Mark of Gérard Leeu, Printer at
Gouwe (1482).

Fig. 400.—The Mark of Fust and Schœffer,
Printers. (Fifteenth Century.)

year 1469, however, Jenson had no longer the monopoly of printing in
Venice, where John de Spire had arrived, bringing also from Mayence
all the improvements Gutenberg and Schœffer had obtained. This
art having ceased to be a secret in the city of the Doges, great

Fig. 401.—Mark of Arnold de Keyser, Printer at Ghent.
(1480.)

competition arose among printers, who flocked to Venice, where they
found a market for their volumes which a thousand ships carried to all
parts of the world. At this period important and admirable publications
issued from the numerous rival printing establishments in Venice.

Christopher Waltdorfer, of Ratisbon, published in 1471 the first edition
of the "Decameron" of Boccacio, of which a copy was sold for £2,080
at the Roxburgh sale; John of Cologne published, in the same year,
the first dated edition of "Terence;" Adam of Amberg reprinted,
from the Roman editions, "Lactantius" and "Virgil," &c. Finally,
Venice already possessed more than two hundred printers, when in
1494 the great Aldo Manuzio made his appearance, the precursor of
the Estiennes,* who were the glory of French printing. From every
part of Europe printing spread itself and flourished (Figs. 399 to 411); the
printers, however, often neglected, perhaps intentionally, to date their

Fig. 402.—Mark of Colard
Mansion, Printer at Bruges.
(1477.)

Fig. 403.—Mark of Trechsel,
Printer at Lyons.
(1489.)

productions. In the course of 1469 there were only two towns, Venice
and Milan, that revealed, by their dated editions, the time at which
printing was first established within their walls; in 1470, five towns—
Nuremberg, Paris, Foligno, Treviso, and Verona; in 1471, eight towns—
Strasbourg, Spires, Treviso, Bologna, Ferrara, Naples, Pavia, and Florence;
in 1472, eight others—Cremona, Felizzano, Padua, Mantua, Montreuil,
Jesi, Munster, and Parma; in 1473, ten—Brescia, Messina, Ulm, Bude,

* *Anglicè*, Stephens, by which name this illustrious family of scholars and printers is most
popularly known in England. They were ten in number, who flourished between 1512 and about
1660. Anthony, the last distinguished representative of the family, died in poverty at the Hôtel
Dieu, Paris, in 1674, at the age of eighty-two.—[ED.]

Lauingen, Mersebourg, Alost, Utrecht, Lyons, and St. Ursio, near Vicenza ; in 1474, thirteen towns, among which are Valentia (in Spain) and London ; in 1475, twelve towns, &c. Each year we find the art gaining ground, and each year an increase in the number of books newly edited, rendering science and literature popular by considerably diminishing the price of books. Thus, for example, at the beginning of the fifteenth century, the illustrious Poggio sold his fine manuscript of "Livy," to raise money enough to buy himself a villa near Florence ; Anthony of Palermo mortgaged his

Fig. 404.—Mark of Simon Vostre, Printer at Paris, in 1531, living in the Rue Neuve Nostre-Dame, at the Sign of St. John the Evangelist.

Fig. 405.—Mark of Galliot du Pré, Bookseller at Paris. (1531.)

estate in order to be able to purchase a manuscript of the same historical writer, valued at a hundred and twenty-five dollars; yet a few years later the "Livy," printed at Rome by Sweynheim and Pannartz, in one folio volume on vellum, was worth only five golden dollars.

The largest number of the early editions resembled each other, for they were generally printed in Gothic characters, or *lettres de somme*—letters which bristled with points and angular appendices. These characters, when printing was only just invented, had preserved in Holland and in Germany their original form; and the celebrated printer of Bruges, Colard Mansion, only improved on them in his valuable publications, which were almost contemporaneous with Gutenberg's "Catholicon;" but they had already undergone in France a semi-metamorphosis in getting rid of their angularities and their most extravagant features. These *lettres de somme* were then adopted under the name of *bâtarde* (bastard) or *ronde* (round), in the first books printed in France, and when Nicholas Jenson established himself in Venice he used the *Roman*, which were only an elegant variety of the *lettres de*

Fig. 406.—Mark of Philippe le Noir, Printer, Bookseller, and Bookbinder, at Paris, 1536, living in the Rue St. Jacques, at the sign of the "Rose Couronnée."

Fig. 407.—Mark of Temporal, Printer at Lyons, 1550 —1559, with two devices; one in Latin, "And in the meanwhile time flieth, flieth irreparably;" the other in Greek, "Mark, or know, Time." (Observe the play upon the words *tempus*, καιρός, and Temporal.)

somme of France (Gothic characters). Aldo Manuzio, with the sole object of insuring that Venice should not owe its national type to a Frenchman, adopted the *Italic* character, renewed from the writing called cursive or *de chancellerie* (of the chancellor's office), which was never generally used in printing, notwithstanding the fine editions of Aldo. Hereafter the Ciceronean character was to come into use, so called because it had been employed at Rome in the first edition of the "Epistolæ Familiares" (Familiar Letters) of Cicero, in 1467. The character called "St. Augustinian," which appeared later, likewise owes its name to the large edition of the works of St. Augustine, published at Basle in 1506. Moreover, during this first period in which each printer engraved, or caused to be engraved under his own direc-

Fig. 408.—Mark of Robert Estienne,
Printer at Paris, 1536.
"Do not aspire to know high things."

Fig. 409.—Mark of Gryphe, Printer
at Lyons, 1529.
"Virtue my Leader, Fortune my Companion."

tions, the characters he made use of, there was an infinite number of different types. The *register*, a table indicative of the quires which composed the book, was necessary to point out in what order these were to be arranged

Fig. 410.—Mark of Plantin, Printer,
at Antwerp, 1557.
"Christ the true Vine."

Fig. 411.—Mark of J. Le Noble, Printer
at Troyes. (1595.)

and bound together. After the *register* came *the catchwords*, which, at the end of each quire or of each leaf, were destined to serve an analogous purpose; and the *signatures*, indicating the place of quires or of leaves by letters or figures; but signatures and catchwords existed already in the manuscripts,

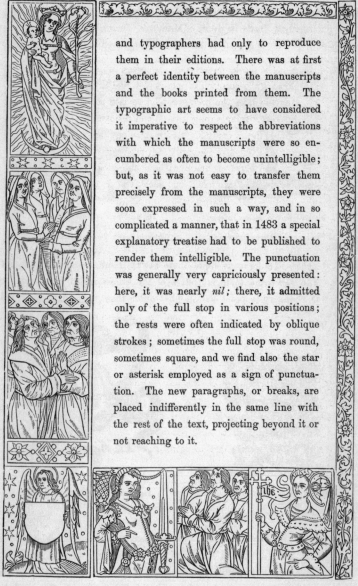

and typographers had only to reproduce them in their editions. There was at first a perfect identity between the manuscripts and the books printed from them. The typographic art seems to have considered it imperative to respect the abbreviations with which the manuscripts were so encumbered as often to become unintelligible; but, as it was not easy to transfer them precisely from the manuscripts, they were soon expressed in such a way, and in so complicated a manner, that in 1483 a special explanatory treatise had to be published to render them intelligible. The punctuation was generally very capriciously presented: here, it was nearly *nil;* there, it admitted only of the full stop in various positions; the rests were often indicated by oblique strokes; sometimes the full stop was round, sometimes square, and we find also the star or asterisk employed as a sign of punctuation. The new paragraphs, or breaks, are placed indifferently in the same line with the rest of the text, projecting beyond it or not reaching to it.

Fig. 412.—Border from the "Livre d'Heures" of Anthony Vérard (1488), representing the Assumption of the Virgin in the presence of the Apostles and Holy Women, and at the bottom of the page two Mystical Figures.

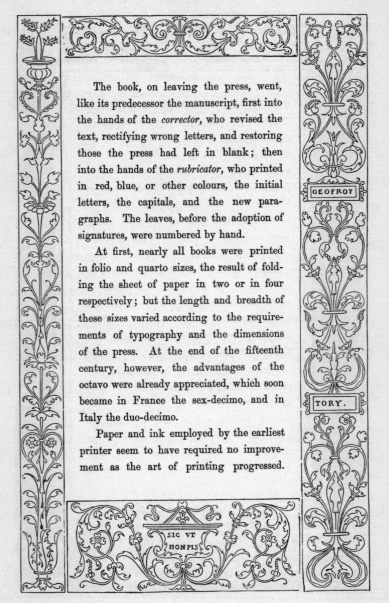

The book, on leaving the press, went, like its predecessor the manuscript, first into the hands of the *corrector*, who revised the text, rectifying wrong letters, and restoring those the press had left in blank; then into the hands of the *rubricator*, who printed in red, blue, or other colours, the initial letters, the capitals, and the new paragraphs. The leaves, before the adoption of signatures, were numbered by hand.

At first, nearly all books were printed in folio and quarto sizes, the result of folding the sheet of paper in two or in four respectively; but the length and breadth of these sizes varied according to the requirements of typography and the dimensions of the press. At the end of the fifteenth century, however, the advantages of the octavo were already appreciated, which soon became in France the sex-decimo, and in Italy the duo-decimo.

Paper and ink employed by the earliest printer seem to have required no improvement as the art of printing progressed.

Fig. 413.—Border taken from the "Livre d'Heures" of Geoffroi Tory (1525).

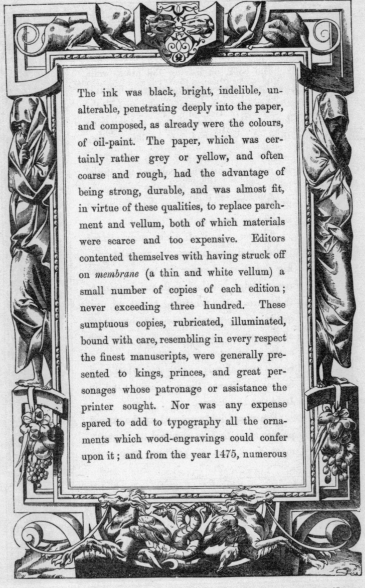

The ink was black, bright, indelible, unalterable, penetrating deeply into the paper, and composed, as already were the colours, of oil-paint. The paper, which was certainly rather grey or yellow, and often coarse and rough, had the advantage of being strong, durable, and was almost fit, in virtue of these qualities, to replace parchment and vellum, both of which materials were scarce and too expensive. Editors contented themselves with having struck off on *membrane* (a thin and white vellum) a small number of copies of each edition; never exceeding three hundred. These sumptuous copies, rubricated, illuminated, bound with care, resembling in every respect the finest manuscripts, were generally presented to kings, princes, and great personages whose patronage or assistance the printer sought. Nor was any expense spared to add to typography all the ornaments which wood-engravings could confer upon it; and from the year 1475, numerous

Fig. 414.—" Livre d'Heures," by Guillaume Roville (1551), a composition in the style of the school of Lyons, with Caryatides representing female Saints semi-veiled.

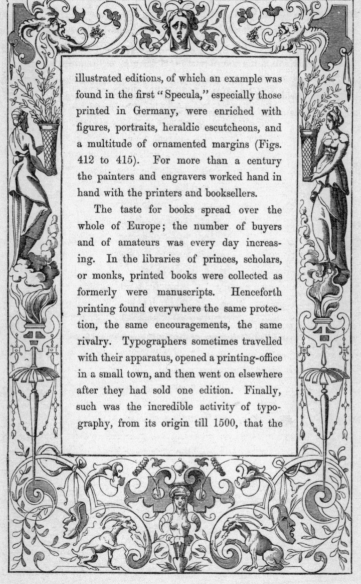

illustrated editions, of which an example was found in the first "Specula," especially those printed in Germany, were enriched with figures, portraits, heraldic escutcheons, and a multitude of ornamented margins (Figs. 412 to 415). For more than a century the painters and engravers worked hand in hand with the printers and booksellers.

The taste for books spread over the whole of Europe; the number of buyers and of amateurs was every day increasing. In the libraries of princes, scholars, or monks, printed books were collected as formerly were manuscripts. Henceforth printing found everywhere the same protection, the same encouragements, the same rivalry. Typographers sometimes travelled with their apparatus, opened a printing-office in a small town, and then went on elsewhere after they had sold one edition. Finally, such was the incredible activity of typography, from its origin till 1500, that the

Fig. 415.—Border employed by John of Tournes, in 1557, ornamented with Antique Masks and Allegorical Personages bearing Baskets containing Laurel Branches.

number of editions published in Europe in the space of half a century amounted to *sixteen thousand.* But the most remarkable result of printing was the important part it played in the movement of the sixteenth century, from which resulted the transformation of the arts, of literature, and science; the discoveries of Laurent Coster and of Gutenberg had cast a new light over the world, and the press made its appearance to modify profoundly the conditions of the intellectual life of peoples.

Fig. 416.—Mark of Bonaventure and Abraham Elsevier, Printers at Leyden, 1620.